WEST'S LAW SCHOOL ADVISORY BOARD

THE LAW OF CORPORATIONS

IN A NUTSHELL

Third Edition

By

ROBERT W. HAMILTON

Minerva House Drysdale Regents Chair in Law
The University of Texas at Austin

ST. PAUL, MINN.
WEST PUBLISHING CO.
1991

Nutshell Series, In a Nutshell, the Nutshell Logo and the WP symbol are registered trademarks of West Publishing Co. Registered in U.S. Patent and Trademark Office.

COPYRIGHT © 1980, 1987 WEST PUBLISHING CO.
COPYRIGHT © 1991 By WEST PUBLISHING CO.
610 Opperman Drive
P.O. Box 64526
St. Paul, MN 55164–0526

Printed in the United States of America

Library of Congress Cataloging-in-Publication Data

Hamilton, Robert W., 1931–
    The law of corporations in a nutshell / by Robert W. Hamilton. —
3rd ed.
        p.   cm. — (Nutshell series)
    Includes index.
    ISBN 0–314–82446–4
    1. Corporation law—United States. I. Title. II. Series.
KF1414.3.H35 1991
346.73'066—dc20
[347.30666]   90–26207
                                                                CIP

ISBN 0–314–82446–4

Hamilton, Corps. 3rd NS
2nd Reprint—1995

OUTLINE

III

TABLE OF CASES

References are to Pages

*

THE LAW OF CORPORATIONS
IN A NUTSHELL

Third Edition

*

CHAPTER ONE

THE CORPORATION IN PERSPECTIVE

§ 1.1 What Is a Corporation? The Concept of an Artificial Entity

A corporation may be formed simply by filing an appropriate document with a state official, usually the secretary of state, and paying the appropriate fee. (Some states, however, require additional steps; see § 3.3 of this Nutshell.) Assuming that the necessary steps have been followed, what has been created?

The simplest and usually the most useful way of viewing a corporation is to consider it a *fictitious being* or *artificial entity* independent of the owners or investors. This artificial entity may conduct a business or businesses in its own name much in the same way that a "real" person could. Business is done, assets acquired, contracts entered into, and liabilities incurred, all in the name of the corporation rather than in the name of any individual. Also, the artificial entity may sue or be sued as though it were a person, it pays taxes, it may apply for business licenses in its own name, it may have its own bank account, it may have its own seal, and so forth.

Conducting a business in this way often has several advantages over conducting business in the name of one or more individuals. For example:

(a) The corporation is unlimitedly liable for the debts and obligations of the business but the shareholders are not, since in theory all debts are the artificial entity's obligations, not the shareholders'. In effect, the shareholders risk what they have invested but no more; in legal language the shareholders enjoy "limited liability."

1

(b) The existence of the corporation is not dependent on who the owners or investors are at any one time. If shareholders die, or decide to sell out, or what have you, the corporation continues to exist as a separate entity. If it is necessary to raise additional capital, new shareholders or investors may be brought in without changing or disturbing the corporate form.

There are other advantages of the corporate form (and some disadvantages as well) which are discussed below when the corporation is contrasted with a partnership (see § 2.1 of this Nutshell). The basic point is that the concept of a corporation greatly simplifies things by permitting a business to have a separate legal identity independent of the flesh-and-blood persons who own and operate it.

The artificial entity approach has come under some criticism from legal writers and thinkers who view themselves as "legal realists." The starting point for this criticism is a fundamental truth about corporations: flesh-and-blood people underlie every corporation, and are essential to everything a corporation does. Some individual must decide what the corporation is to do; some individual must actually do the required act on behalf of the corporation, because manifestly an artificial entity has no arms, legs, mouth, or eyes. Some individual will ultimately reap the profits earned by the corporation, and some person must ultimately bear any loss. Realistically, a corporation is simply a device by which some individuals conduct a business and the same or different individuals share in the profit or loss. Professor Hohfeld represented one modern view of the corporation when he said, "Strangely enough, it has not always been perceived with perfect clearness that transacting business under the forms, methods, and procedure pertaining to so-called corporations is simply another mode by which individuals or natural persons can enjoy their property and engage in business. Just as several individuals may transact business collectively as partners, so they may as members of a corporation—the corporation being nothing more than an association of such individuals * * * ." He added, when "we speak of the corporation * * * contracting in the corporate name, * * * we are merely employing a short and convenient mode of describing the complex and peculiar process by which the benefits and burdens of the corporate members are worked out * * *." Hohfeld, Fundamental Legal Conceptions 197 (1923). Hohfeld's analysis illustrates the fallacy of accepting too literally the "artificial entity" theory. A corporation is treated as an entity for most purposes but it need not be treated as an entity for all purposes. At some point the reality which Hohfeld describes may control over the fiction being relied on. For this reason, arguments grounded solely on the artificial entity thesis and not supported by considerations of fairness, justice, or policy have sometimes not prevailed.

Most provisions of modern corporation statutes are consistent with the theory that a corporation is a separate legal entity. As a "short and convenient mode" of describing most of the powers of a corporation and the legal relationships surrounding it, therefore, the artificial entity concept is extremely useful. It should be emphasized, however, that a corporation possesses these statutory attributes not because it is an artificial entity but because the statute so provides. And it does not follow that because a corporation possesses many entity attributes under the statutes, it necessarily possesses other entity attributes as well.

§ 1.2 What Is a Corporation? Other Theories

The artificial entity theory is the most useful one in the context of most modern problems. However, there have been other attempts to describe the theoretical concept of a corporation. These other formulations usually arise in situations involving the power of states to regulate corporations or the rights or duties of participants in a corporation among themselves. They include:

(a) The corporation may be viewed as a "privilege," "concession," or "grant" from the state which allows the owners and investors to conduct business as a corporation. Conceptually, when documents are filed with the secretary of state, that officer's issuance of a "charter" or "certificate of incorporation" can be viewed as a grant by the state of the privilege to conduct business in corporate form. This conception had greater importance in an earlier day when significant limitations or conditions were imposed on the privilege of incorporating. Indeed, in an earlier age, individual charters were granted individually by the state legislature; when a charter was obtained through the legislative process, the concept of privilege or grant had considerable meaning. Today, incorporation involves only routine or ministerial acts. However, the concession theory is still sometimes referred to usually in connection with the social policy debate about the appropriate role of corporations in modern society (see § 1.4 of this Nutshell).

(b) The corporate charter may also be viewed as a "compact" or "contract." Depending on the circumstances, the parties to this contract may be:

(i) The shareholders themselves; or

(ii) The shareholders and the corporation; or

(iii) The corporation and the state.

For example, the contract theory often appears in situations where disputes have arisen between classes or members. In a dispute between preferred and common shareholders, for example, it is not uncommon to refer to the provisions of the charter that describes the rights of preferred shareholders as "the preferred shareholders' contract" which, many cases state, constitutes the full and exclusive description of the rights of that class of shareholders as against the common shareholders.

In the famous decision in Dartmouth College v. Woodward [4 Wheat. (17 U.S.) 518 (1819)], the Court considered the charter of Dartmouth College to be a contract between the corporation and the state which was protected against unilateral impairment by the state under the contracts clause of the United States Constitution. This case is of historic interest today since all states have adopted constitutional provisions or incorporation statutes that specifically require every charter granted by that state to be subject to later amendments by the state. An example of such a statute is section 1.02 of the Revised Model Business Corporation Act.

The economist has developed another theory of the corporation that permits the creation of an economic model to study corporate issues. This theory is usually called the "nexus of contracts" theory. It views the corporation as a legal fiction that embodies a web (or "nexus") of contractual relationships among individuals. These individuals include "owners" of labor, material, and capital inputs as well as consumers of the firm's output and others. In this theory the managers of the firm are the principal actors, blending the mix of resources being supplied in order to reach optimal (i.e. most profitable) performance. Shareholders are not viewed as "owners" of the enterprise but rather as providers of capital along with bondholders and other creditors in anticipation of receiving a return from the investment. In many circumstances, of course, shareholders may also independently provide management services to the corporation.

The theories of corporateness discussed in these first two sections—the "artificial entity" theory, the "realistic" theory, the "concession" theory, the "contract" theory, and the "nexus of contracts" theory—all help to explain the modern concept of a corporation. None is totally correct, none is totally wrong, and each has its place in defining the concept of corporateness.

§ 1.3   The Development of Corporation Law in the United States

While the concept of a corporation was clearly developed by the time of Blackstone and can be traced much earlier, the modern law of corporations is largely a product of developments in the latter part of the nineteenth and, particularly, the twentieth centuries. Prior to that time, business in the United States tended to be local in nature and of primary concern to individual states (though there were some exceptions such as the national bank). Corporations during this period were often created for public or near public purposes—e.g. to build canals, bridges, or toll roads—and often enjoyed some monopoly privileges. However, about 1825 intensive industrial development began. The corporation proved to be an ideal instrument for this development since it could raise large amounts of capital from numerous investors and yet provide centralized direction of large industrial concerns. Even though many corporations rapidly became national in scope during this period, they were and remained the descendants of local state-related enterprises, and received their charters from states rather than from the Federal Government.

In the early nineteenth century, several states enacted general incorporation statutes permitting all lawful businesses to incorporate without specific legislative approval, though restrictions were often imposed in terms of size, capital invested, and purposes or powers of the corporation. Beginning roughly in the early twentieth century, a number of states systematically eliminated restrictions in their statutes to attract the incorporation business that otherwise might gravitate to other states. This rather unseemly competition among states is vividly described in Mr. Justice Brandeis's dissent in Liggett Co. v. Lee (1933). The incorporation business provided tax revenues for the state, fees for members of the local bar, revenues for local newspapers, and the like. Other states, in an effort to preserve whatever incorporation business they already had, found themselves forced to follow suit. The result was a race "not of diligence but of laxity," to use Mr. Justice Brandeis's phrase, or a "race for the bottom," to quote a modern commentator.

The uncrowned winner of this "race" in the latter part of the twentieth century unquestionably has been the small state of Delaware. Over one-third of all the corporations listed on the New York Stock Exchange are incorporated in that single state. As a result, the Delaware Legislature and the Delaware Supreme Court are the principal sources of modern corporation law today. The reason for the popularity and primacy of the state of Delaware has been the subject of considerable academic discussion and commentary; it is explained partially on the basis of history, partially on the continued efforts by the bar of that state to provide an effective, flexible, and modern body of corporate law, and partially on the relative certainty and easy availability of Delaware law. Recent studies indicate that Delaware law is not significantly more flexible or permissive than the statutes of many other states, and some recent decisions by the Delaware Supreme Court have imposed significant liabilities and duties on corporate management. The continued attractiveness of Delaware law today must be explained on grounds other than the simplistic explanation that Delaware has won the "race to the bottom" and has a significantly more permissive law than that which exists in other states. More plausible explanations are the certainty and ready availability of the Delaware statutory and case law, the familiarity of corporate lawyers throughout the country with this law, the sophistication of the judiciary and bar on corporate matters in Delaware, and the knowledge and experience of the individuals in the office of the Delaware Secretary of State.

In addition to Delaware, a second major influence on modern corporation law has been the Model Business Corporation Act, developed and maintained by a committee of the American Bar Association. The original MBCA, as it was usually referred to, was first published in 1950 and was influential in the development of state incorporation statutes in some thirty states. In 1984, a new version of the Model Act, usually referred to as the Revised Model Business Corporation Act or RMBCA, was published and has received a favorable reception in numerous states in the relatively brief period since its introduction. The RMBCA largely builds on the provisions of the older MBCA, but adopts innovative provisions in a number of areas and effects a considerable simplification of language in many provisions. All references in this book are to the RMBCA rather than to the older MBCA. (Candor also requires disclosure that the author of this book served as the reporter for the RMBCA.)

The RMBCA is in the tradition of most modern corporation statutes: it is primarily an enabling statute rather than a regulatory statute. Whether or not it (or the Delaware statute, for that matter) is too flexible or too permissive depends to a large extent on the social views of the observer. Not all states, however, have followed the trend toward increasingly permissive or flexible statutes. California is the principal state that has retained significant substantive regulation on corporations subject to its jurisdiction. Other states may be tempted to follow the same approach in the future.

Finally, mention should be made of developments at the federal level. In the early 1930s, Congress enacted two statutes relating to corporate matters. The Securities Act of 1933 and the Securities Exchange Act of 1934 have formed the springboard for considerable federal regulation of the internal affairs of publicly held corporations; at one stage a trend appeared to be developing toward an inclusive "federal law of corporations" based on these two statutes. While this development has been stopped in its tracks by the modern trend toward deregulation and by a series of narrow and restrictive holdings by the federal courts, federal regulation is still of great importance in corporation law. And, new federal legislation, shifting the current balance between state and federal jurisdiction, is always possible.

§ 1.4 The Debate Over Social Responsibility and the Publicly Held Corporation

The discussion in the last section leads naturally to a brief exploration of the debate over the social responsibility of large publicly held corporations in modern society. Such corporations wield immense economic power when they make decisions. A decision where to locate a plant, what environmental equipment to install, what products to manufacture, what to charge for them, what safety devices to build into them, and so forth, are all decisions that may fairly be described as "social" as well as "economic" since they have dramatic consequences for individuals, communities, and entire states. These decisions, furthermore, are usually made by corporate management without public input or the approval of voters, investors, shareholders, or anyone else. The concentration of power in such corporations has been decried by some commentators and defended by others. The debate goes back to before the New Deal era and shows no sign of abating today.

The social responsibility debate has several different levels. At the most basic level the issue can be phrased in terms of whether corporate management should take social considerations expressly into account when they make important decisions or whether they should make the decision on the basis of the "bottom line" of what produces the best profit for investors. While these two positions may at first seem polar opposites, in fact they are not. Profit-maximizing decisions are not made in the abstract but in the broader societal context of possible governmental intervention, and the like. Further, since the accepted aim of corporate governance is to maximize long run rather than short run profits, these social factors may quite legitimately be taken into account in the overall profit calculation. A decision to raise prices to monopoly levels (assuming that that is feasible), for example, may maximize short run profits but have devastating long run consequences in terms of adverse publicity, the entry of new competitors in the industry, and governmental intervention. Rational profit maximizers take these long run consequences into account.

Another branch of the social responsibility debate considers whether the interests represented in the governing body of large publicly held corporations—the board of directors—should be broadened. Suggestions typically include adding one or more representatives of government, labor, suppliers, consumers, creditors, etc. to the board. While there has been limited experimentation with this idea, it has never really caught on, and, where it has been tried, it is difficult to find tangible evidence that the representational directors have made any significant difference.

In the middle nineteen-seventies the debate over social responsibility received new impetus from the disclosure by hundreds of publicly held corporations that they had paid domestic or foreign bribes, made illegal payments overseas to obtain business, or had made illegal campaign contributions in the United States. These disclosures led not only to new calls for greater social responsibility of corporations but also focused on the role of the board of directors and the need for better control mechanisms to insure that corporate management conform with legal and moral principles of conduct. The takeover movement of the 1980s also focussed attention on the decisions by boards of directors faced with unwanted bids from outside interests to purchase a majority or more of the outstanding shares. Many public corporations made important changes in their methods of internal governance as a result of these pressures. See

Chapter 13. Also, in the early 1980s the American Law Institute began an intensive and highly controversial study of the principles of corporate governance as a result of these developments, a study that will probably be completed in the early 1990s.

One proposal that dates back to the early years of this century has resurfaced from time to time: the proposal to have a federal incorporation act for very large publicly held corporations. "Federal chartering," it has been argued, will improve the social accountability of corporations and guarantee better democratic procedures. Present trends, however, appear to be in the direction of continued reliance on state law rather than in a federalization of this sensitive area. This trend was solidified by Justice Powell's majority opinion in CTS Corporation v. Dynamics Corp. of America, 481 U.S. 69 (1987), which restated the traditional role and interest of states in the regulation of state-created corporations in near constitutional terms.

§ 1.5   Alternative Constituency Statutes

During the 1980s more than twenty states enacted statutes that permit boards of directors to take into account the concerns of employees, creditors, localities, customers, and similar non-profitmaking interests along with the interests of shareholders when making decisions. At first blush these statutes appear to make a revolutionary change in corporation law which assumes that profit maximization for shareholders is the ultimate goal of the corporation. These statutes were hastily enacted (in most states) in order to provide management with a justification to defeat takeover bids from outsiders even though they provided shareholders a much greater profit on their shares than would be available if the bid were defeated. They may be construed narrowly as being applicable only in the unwanted takeover bid context, or as permitting the consideration of non-shareholder interests only when those interests are not directly and significantly in conflict with the interests of shareholders. Both the American Law Institute and an important committee of the American Bar Association have suggested that these statutes should be construed in this manner so that they are consistent with the generally accepted goals of the modern business corporation.

§ 1.6 The Corporate Population: Closely Held and Publicly Held Corporations

Throughout the cases and literature dealing with the law of corporations appear references to "publicly held" corporations and "closely held" corporations. There are many similar references scattered throughout this book. This section explores what is meant by these terms.

A "publicly held" corporation is one that has outstanding shares held by a large number of people. While there is no minimum number that defines when a corporation is "publicly held," corporations with shares traded on the securities exchanges, or shares for which there are regular published price quotations, are clearly "publicly held" corporations. Corporations with more than $5,000,000 of assets and an outstanding class of securities held by more than 500 shareholders of record are subject to special regulation under the Federal Securities and Exchange Act of 1934, including requirements that the corporation register that class with the SEC and submit periodic financial information. Corporations with securities registered with the SEC (often called, not surprisingly, "registered corporations"), are also publicly held corporations. However, there may be corporations that are considered publicly held that are not large enough or whose securities are not widely enough held to require registration of them with the SEC.

Publicly held corporations may also be defined in terms of whether they have ever made a registered public distribu-

tion of securities. The Federal Securities Act of 1933 and
state statutes colloquially called "blue sky laws" provide that
corporations may not make public distributions of securities
unless a registration statement filed with the SEC or state
security commissions is effective. Before 1982, registration
of an issue of securities under the Securities Act of 1933 was
entirely independent of the registration of classes of securities under the size and number of shareholder requirements
of the Federal Securities and Exchange Act of 1934 described in the previous paragraph; in 1982 the SEC adopted
its "integrated disclosure" program that allows many corporations to incorporate information taken from their 1934
Act filings into 1933 Act registration statements. (If you
think it peculiar first, that the federal government requires
two different registration procedures often for the same
corporation, and second, that it took the SEC nearly fifty
years to decide that it should permit an issuer to integrate
the two sets of filings, do not be surprised; you are not the
first.) In any event, a "publicly held corporation" may also
be defined as a corporation that has registered a public
distribution of securities in the past.

The "closely held" corporation is one with relatively few
shareholders. Again there is no definite maximum number,
but everyone agrees that a corporation with less than fifteen
shareholders is a closely held corporation, and one may
argue that a corporation is still closely held if the number of
shareholders is as large as, say thirty-five or fifty. Typically
a "closely held" corporation is characterized by the following: (1) there is no outside market for shares if a person
wants to sell, (2) all or most of the shareholders participate
in management, and (3) the free transferability of shares is
restricted. The presence of restrictions on transfer and the
absence of a ready market for shares are usually considered
the essential characteristics of a closely held corporation,
more important than the number of shareholders or the
participation in management by shareholders. Almost by

definition a closely held corporation is one that never had a registered public distribution of securities and certainly is not registered with the SEC under the 1934 Act. Obviously, most closely held corporations are small and most publicly held corporations are large, but that is not universally true since there are some very large closely held corporations and some publicly held corporations with virtually no assets.

The corporate model that appears in state incorporation statutes and the RMBCA is an idealized model that is not tailored specifically either for the close corporation or for the publicly held corporation. It is a model that is sufficiently broad and generalized that large portions of it are appropriate for both the very large and the very small. About a dozen states have supplemented their general corporation statutes by adopting special statutes to provide relaxed rules for closely held corporations that elect to take advantage of their provisions. See § 12.8 of this Nutshell. A "close corporation supplement" was approved in 1983 to accompany the RMBCA; this supplement is not part of the Revised Model Business Corporation Act and the decision whether or not to adopt such a statute is entirely independent of the decision whether or not to adopt the RMBCA.

In one sense the distinction between publicly held and closely held corporations is unsatisfactory because there are many corporations that do not precisely fit either definition. A study by Professor Melvin Eisenberg using a variety of different sources approximates the actual population of corporations as follows:

No. of Shareholders	Approximate No. of Corporations
1–10	1,630,000
11–99	70,000
100–499	26,500
500–1499	5,000
1500–2999	1,700
3000–10,000	1,200
Over 10,000	600

Source: M. Eisenberg, The Structure of the Corporation (1976) at 42.

The table reveals that the closely held corporation is by far the most numerous, that publicly held corporations probably number under 10,000, and that "in-between corporations" are probably ten times as numerous as publicly held corporations. Because the asset holdings of publicly held corporations are immense, however, they have tremendous economic importance. In 1984 the 100 largest industrial publicly held corporations owned nearly 49 per cent of all manufacturing company assets; the 200 largest owned over 60 per cent!

[For unfamiliar terms see the Glossary]

CHAPTER TWO

SELECTION OF THE MOST APPROPRIATE BUSINESS FORM FOR A VENTURE

§ 2.1 The Corporation Compared to a Partnership and Limited Partnership

A new venture must select the business form in which it is to operate. In most instances, the basic choices are (a) a partnership (or proprietorship if there is only one owner), (b) a limited partnership, or (c) a corporation. Where a business cannot be incorporated under the general business corporation act because of professional or ethical considerations, e.g., a law firm, the choice is between a traditional partnership and a professional corporation. If a conscious selection is not made but a new venture is simply launched, the partnership or proprietorship form has been chosen, for better or for worse.

A partnership is the simplest form of organization involving more than one person. It is formed merely by agreement of the partners, who share the right to manage and the right to participate in the profits. Each also shares the unlimited obligation to answer personally for all the liabilities of the business. A proprietorship is a business owned by a single person who has the sole right to manage, is solely entitled to the profits, and is unlimitedly liable for the debts of the business. A proprietorship is essentially a one person partnership.

A limited partnership is a partnership of two or more persons in which there are one or more general partners unlimitedly liable for the debts of the business with general powers of management and one or more limited partners who have no personal liability for the debts of the business (except to the extent of their capital contributions) and virtually no powers of management. In order to create a limited partnership a certificate must be filed with an appropriate state or county official and a fee paid. In most states the limited partnership certificate bears little resemblance to corporate articles of incorporation (though in some states the two filings are roughly comparable) and the state official authorized to accept limited partnership certificates may or may not be the official who is authorized to accept articles of incorporation. Partnership agreements that state that certain people are "limited partners" or that specified persons "are not personally liable for the debts of the business" without a certificate being filed are not effective of themselves to limit the personal liability of partners. To ensure limited liability, a certificate of limited partnership must be filed.

The fundamental differences between partnerships, limited partnerships, and corporations may be summarized as follows:

(1) *Limited Liability.* A corporation possesses the attribute of limited liability: usually the shareholders are not personally liable for the business debts of the corporation. A shareholder risks what he or she has agreed to invest in the corporation and nothing more. As described above, a partnership involves unlimited liability, while a limited partnership has two classes of partners: general partners who are jointly and severally liable for business obligations, and limited partners who, like shareholders, risk only what they have agreed to invest in the venture.

(2) *Federal Income Taxation.* A corporation is typically a separate tax paying entity. Corporations have their own tax rates, and distributions by a corporation to its shareholders are usually taxable to the shareholders even though made from income previously taxed to the corporation. A partnership on the other hand is treated as an extension of the

partners themselves. A separate partnership return is required to reflect the receipts and expenditures of the business. However, no tax is paid with this return; rather, the net income or loss is allocated among the partners and then carried directly over to each partner's individual return. Since the income is taxable to each partner whether or not actually distributed, distributions from the partnership to a partner are normally not themselves taxable. A limited partnership is usually treated as a partnership for tax purposes.

The S corporation tax election permits corporations with less than 35 shareholders to elect a "pass through" tax treatment similar to a partnership's. Corporations that are taxed as separate taxable entities in the traditional fashion are called C corporations.

(3) *Centralized Management.* A corporation has the attribute of centralized management: the management of corporate affairs is vested in the directors and officers who may consist of all or some of the shareholders or of persons having no ownership interest in the corporation. A partnership on the other hand is managed by the partners. Each partner possesses authority to bind the partnership and a right to participate in management. In a limited partnership the general partners are vested with the power to manage the partnership affairs. As between the general partners, power to manage the affairs of a limited partnership is diffused as in a general partnership. Limited partners do not participate in management; if they do, they may lose the shield of limited liability and assume the obligations of a general partner. The Revised Uniform Limited Partnership Act permits limited partners to participate in many management decisions without losing their shield of limited liability. Modern limited partnership agreements may grant limited partners the right to vote on certain fundamental changes but exclude them from participating in management of the venture in any additional way.

(4) *Continuity of Life.* Corporations are usually formed with perpetual existence. This simply means that the corporation continues indefinitely, that the death or withdrawal of a shareholder does not terminate the corporate existence, and that a shareholder does not have the power to compel or force a dissolution. A partnership's existence is more flimsy. Numerous events automatically cause the dissolution of a partnership, and each partner has the inherent power to dissolve the partnership at any time, though in some circumstances such a dissolution may constitute a breach of contract. In a limited partnership, the general partners have the dissolution powers of a partner in a general partnership, while the limited partners usually have power only to obtain dissolution by decree of court.

(5) *Free Transferability of Interest.* In the absence of contractual restriction, shares of stock of a corporation may be freely sold, assigned, or otherwise disposed of by the owner. A purchaser of a share of stock becomes a shareholder in the corporation with whatever rights pertain to that status. In contrast, the holder of a partnership interest can only convey limited rights to an assignee or purchaser of the partnership interest unless the other partners agree to accept the assignee or purchaser as a partner. General partners in a limited partnership have no more power to dispose of their interest than do partners in a general partnership, while a limited partner's interest usually is made assignable by appropriate provision in the limited partnership agreement.

(6) *Simplicity of Operation.* A corporation involves a considerable degree of formality and paperwork. In even the smallest one-man corporation, the statute assumes that there will be a board of directors and one or more corporate officers, usually a corporate president, a vice-president, a secretary, and a treasurer (though some of these offices may be held simultaneously by a single person). Minutes should be kept; annual reports and separate franchise tax returns filed. A registered office and registered agent must be

maintained. If the corporation desires to do business in another state, it may have to qualify to transact business in that state. In contrast, partnerships and limited partnerships are permitted relatively great freedom in their form of operation and are subject to relatively few formal legal requirements, though there is a modern trend in many states to impose at least some corporate requirements on large limited partnerships.

(7) *Costs of Creation and Operation.* Both corporations and limited partnerships involve filing fees; a general partnership does not. A corporation may also be required to pay franchise taxes, share transfer taxes, and other miscellaneous taxes to the incorporating state. Partnerships and limited partnerships generally are not subject to such taxes, though some states impose taxes on large limited partnerships that are analogous to those imposed on corporations.

So far as the costs of creation are concerned, legal fees are apt to be the single most important item. The cost of preparing formation documents for either a corporation or a partnership is likely to be more dependent on the complexity of the venture than on the form it takes, and, of course, creation costs are only paid once.

§ 2.2 Principal Factors in the Selection of the Business Form

In the real world lawyers often must give advice as to which form of business enterprise is most suitable for a specific venture. The choice usually comes down to weighing three basic variables: (1) the advantages of limited liability for shareholders in corporations and limited partners in limited partnerships, (2) the differences in federal income tax treatment of corporations and partnerships, and (3) the various costs and complexities of creating and operating corporations and limited partnerships. In some instances, the restrictions on the power of a limited partner to participate in the control of the business and yet retain a shield against liability may rule out that form of business organization. It is not generally possible to evaluate all these variables in the abstract; as described below each must be weighed in the context of the particular business under discussion.

§ 2.3   Federal Income Taxation

For many students, the role of federal income taxation in the selection of the business form is the most difficult to understand. Often, they are not familiar with the broad structure of the federal income tax which, of course, is the subject of a separate law school course. Indeed, in many corporations courses, the role of federal income taxes is not covered for just this reason. However, it is covered briefly in many courses and this section is included for the benefit of students in those courses.

(a) *In General.* The fundamental difference in the tax treatment of partnerships and corporations is that the corporation is taxed as a separate entity with its own tax rate whereas the partnership is taxed as an extension of the individual. There is an element of double taxation in the corporate form if the corporation pays dividends. The corporate earnings are taxed to the corporation, and when the diminished earnings are distributed as dividends, they are treated as income in the hands of the shareholders, and taxed again. In contrast, in a partnership, the total income is taxed only once, directly to the partners. It is generally disadvantageous to subject a business to this double taxation; in many situations devices are available to avoid or minimize this double taxation.

A corporation that is subject to general corporate taxation is called a C corporation, since it is taxed pursuant to subchapter C of the Internal Revenue Code. In many small corporations, general corporate taxation under subchapter C can be avoided by the election of subchapter S. A corporation making this election (such a corporation is called an S corporation) is subject to a special tax treatment that is sometimes loosely referred to as a corporation being "taxed as a partnership" or "electing partnership taxation." However, there are differences in detail between the tax treatment of a partnership and an S corporation (which may be significant in individual situations) though in broad outline they are similar: under subchapter S, only a single tax on corporate income is imposed at individual income tax rates at the shareholder level. The income is taxable to the shareholder whether or not the income is actually distributed.

To be eligible for subchapter S, a corporation must meet the following conditions on the date of election:

(a) It must be a domestic corporation;

(b) It must not be part of an affiliated group of corporations;

(c) It must have no more than 35 shareholders;

(d) Each shareholder must be an individual, a decedent's estate, or certain types of trusts; no shareholder may be a nonresident alien; and

(e) It may have only one class of stock outstanding, except that classes of common stock differing only in voting rights do not result in the loss of the election.

An S corporation is a true corporation with all attributes of a corporation other than the peculiar tax treatment. Thus, an S corporation has the corporate characteristics of limited liability and centralization of management.

Where the S corporation election is not available because of the number of shareholders, the types of shareholders, or the existence of multiple classes of stock, the disadvantage of subchapter C taxation can often be minimized by appropriate planning. For example, it is usually possible to reduce substantially the tax at the corporate level through the payment of salaries, rent, or interest to the shareholders. If reasonable in amount, such payments are deductible by the corporation as ordinary and necessary business expenses. Of course, the payments received by the shareholders are taxable income, but if the same money were distributed as dividends, it would also be taxable income. Ideally, if all the corporate income can be paid out in the form of salaries (and the reasonableness of the salaries is accepted by the Internal Revenue Service), the venture ends up paying no tax and the entire income is taxed to the shareholders. However, it usually is not feasible to distribute earnings in the form of salaries, etc. in the same proportion as shares are held, so that from the standpoint of individual shareholders some may be better off and some worse off than if the subchapter S election were available.

If earnings are accumulated in the corporation they are subject to corporate tax but not immediately to the individual tax; the value of the shares of stock will presumably increase as earnings are retained. The tax cost of ultimately selling or disposing of the stock must also be considered. Under the tax rates in effect under the 1986 amendments, it appears to be marginally more attractive at the maximum tax rates to pay out the accumulated earnings in the form of dividends rather than engaging in an accumulation strategy.

Where it is expected that tax losses will be generated, partnership or S corporation treatment may be desirable, since the losses may be used to "shelter" other income from tax. The 1986 amendments, however, sharply restricted the right of taxpayers to deduct so-called passive losses as part of the general attack against tax shelters.

An additional factor favoring corporate tax treatment is the availability of tax-free employee fringe benefits for shareholders who are also employees of the corporation. Such benefits include group life insurance, medical insurance, and so forth. In the aggregate, these benefits may be substantial in amount, though not as great as in the past, when corporate pension and profit sharing plans received particularly favorable tax treatment. A partnership cannot provide these benefits for partners because for tax purposes a partner is generally considered to be an owner, not an employee, of the partnership. The desire of persons such as lawyers or doctors, who are prohibited by law from incorporating, to obtain these tax benefits is an important reason why the professional corporation continues to be popular.

§ 2.4 Uses of Multiple Business Forms for Tax and Other Benefits

Imaginative uses of multiple business forms are possible. Assume that X and Y desire to form a business the income of which is taxed to them individually; they desire to take part in the operation of the business, and yet have limited liability. Subchapter S is not available perhaps because X's grandmother is providing much of the financing in exchange for preferred stock or because Y is in fact a trust for X's children. X and Y might conduct their business as follows: A limited partnership is formed with X and Y as limited partners; the general partner is a newly formed corporation (owned by X and Y) with more than nominal assets. Under the limited partnership agreement the limited partners will be entitled to all but a nominal amount of the income. There is a good possibility that X and Y may function as corporate officers, operate the business, and receive the various attributes that are desired, including limited liability.

Of course, such a combination of forms contains some elements of risk. It is possible (but very unlikely under modern limited partnership statutes) that X and Y might be held to have participated in the business (since they are corporate officers) and thus be liable as general partners. Also, it is possible that they might be held personally liable on the theory that the corporate veil of the general partner should be pierced. (See § 6.4 of this Nutshell). However, there is a good chance that neither of these arguments would be accepted, and there is no other way of obtaining all the desired characteristics in the absence of subchapter S.

Other imaginative uses of multiple business forms may doubtless be found.

§ 2.5   The Importance of Limited Liability

The protection against unlimited liability for business obligations provided by the corporate form is often stressed as a significant reason for incorporating a business. If all other things are equal (which they often are not), this advantage of the corporate form should usually tip the scales toward incorporating. In practice, however, limited liability is not as important as often thought.

Both corporations and partnerships buy liability insurance against claims based on tort. Both buy fire, theft, and extended coverage insurance to protect their property. Employees with access to large amounts of money are bonded whether the business is a partnership or a corporation. Thus the existence of such risks does not materially affect the question whether or not to incorporate, since the great bulk of such risks are in fact borne by others. One can obviously envision tort claims that exceed the amount of insurance, but the likelihood of that occurring is small.

So far as contract obligations are concerned, banks and extenders of substantial credit are aware of the limited liability of a corporation, and, if in their view the assets of the corporation are insufficient to provide reasonable security, they routinely insist that the persons behind the corporation give their personal guarantees. Such guarantees may also be required on leases and other long term corporate commitments. Of course, some creditors may not require personal guarantees, and it is here that limited liability may be advantageous. Small creditors—sellers of office supplies, minor parts, and the like—usually rely on corporate credit exclusively; when added together such obligations may be substantial. Federal, state, and local tax claims and employee wage claims are also typically unguaranteed and substantial in amount. Finally, some creditors may be careless, or may make a mistake, and not require a guarantee.

On balance, it is fair to say that limited liability is a distinct plus for the corporate form of business from the investors' standpoint but is usually not the determinative factor in deciding whether to incorporate a small business.

§ 2.6 The Importance of Continuity of Life

A partnership lacks the attribute of continuity of life in the sense that the death or resignation of a partner dissolves the partnership; the existence of a corporation is unaffected by such an event. This legal difference, however, is seldom of practical importance.

At the outset, a distinction should be made between economic continuity and legal continuity. In many businesses, the death or retirement of the key person may render the continuation of the business impractical as an economic matter. In such situations the business will (or should) in fact end upon the death or retirement of the key person whether the business is conducted in partnership or corporate form. The death or retirement of a person whose principal function was providing capital, on the other hand, rarely renders the continuation of the business impractical; if worst comes to worst a substitute source of capital can usually be found. The legal differences in continuity of life between a corporation and partnership usually become significant only where the economic viability of the business is not seriously affected by the death or retirement. However, even here the difference between a partnership and a corporation is usually not important if there has been advance planning: appropriate provisions in a partnership agreement can guarantee virtually as much continuity of life as exists in a corporation.

§ 2.7 The Importance of Centralized Management

Sometimes it is desired to vest the power to manage the affairs of the enterprise in the hands of less than all the participants, or in the hands of a nonparticipant. In such circumstances, a corporation rather than a general partnership is generally the preferred form of organization. In a corporation, management is vested in the directors and officers who may but need not be the shareholders. In most states, all management power may effectively be vested in a single individual through the device of a board consisting of a single director. In a general partnership, on the other hand, the power to exclude specific partners from participating in management is limited. With respect to third parties, each partner has power to participate in management. Even if the agreement excludes certain partners from management, the excluded partners may negotiate on behalf of the partnership with third persons who are unaware of the restriction on their authority.

§ 2.8 The Importance of Transferability of Interest and Access to Capital

Shares of corporate stock are usually freely transferable while the assignability of partnership interests is sharply restricted. However, free transferability of interests can largely be provided by agreement in the case of partnerships or avoided by appropriate provision in the bylaws or articles of incorporation of a corporation. Since shares in a closely held corporation have no market, only the other participants in the corporation may be interested in buying them; such purchasers may not be disposed to pay very much for the shares. Closely held shares sometimes may also be sold to third persons at greatly discounted prices. Hence this attribute is not usually a major factor in the decision whether or not to incorporate a small, closely held venture.

In a small business, the participants often desire to retain a veto power over who is admitted to the enterprise. This veto power is usually automatically present in the partnership, and can be provided in the corporation by appropriate share transfer restrictions. However, in the latter case, it may be necessary for the corporation or other shareholders to raise capital to purchase the shares of a person desiring to withdraw from the venture. Absolute prohibitions on transfer are against public policy in many states.

In a small business, there is often a need to raise capital by borrowing. There is little difference in borrowing ability between a partnership and a corporation; the unlimited liability of partners is relatively unimportant since shareholder guarantees of payment provide the same protection to creditors of a corporation. If it is contemplated that additional capital will be raised by selling new equity interests in the venture, the corporate form is generally preferred, though some large limited partnerships have in the past demonstrated that capital can also be raised by the sale of limited partnership interests. A business that is planning to sell interests publicly in the near future will almost always choose the corporate form absent overwhelming reasons to use the limited partnership form. General partnership interests are rarely sold publicly since they carry with them unlimited liability, and may be unattractive to general investors.

§ 2.9 The Importance of Informality, Privacy, Cost, and Ease of Interstate Operation

In a small business particularly, costs of organization and operation should obviously be kept to a minimum, as should formal requirements without substantive impact. The usually sound advice, "when in doubt, don't incorporate," is based primarily on the fact that partnerships have advantages over other forms of organizations in informality, privacy, cost, and ease of interstate operation. Other things being equal, the simpler and cheaper form should be preferred over the more expensive and more complex. These factors favoring the partnership form must be weighed against the disadvantage of unlimited liability, or in the case of a limited partnership, the restrictions on the right of a limited partner to participate freely in control of the business.

[For unfamiliar terms see the Glossary]

CHAPTER THREE

FORMATION OF CORPORATIONS

§ 3.1 In General

The process of corporate formation is essentially a very simple one, and much (though not all) of it may be performed by a competent legal secretary. Indeed, one of the great modern innovations in corporate formation is the microcomputer word processor which permits the mass production of corporate documents with only special name and other minor changes. Many readers have doubtless seen advertisements in legal journals for "kits" for the creation of corporations; they are also based on mass produced, standard-form incorporation documents. There are two significant pitfalls in the routine use of such forms. The first is the danger that no one with a broad perspective on the law of corporations will bring that perspective to bear on the potentially unique problems of the particular venture. The second is the universal danger in the use of "boiler-plate" forms: they may contain some provision that was suitable for the last corporation but is egregiously inappropriate for the next one. Overall, however, the process by which a corporation is formed is simple and routine and not in any way mysterious.

§ 3.2 Selection of the State of Incorporation

A large, publicly held corporation that transacts business in every state may theoretically choose its state of incorporation from among any of the fifty states. As a practical matter, however, most such corporations have selected Delaware as their state of incorporation. The small corporation doing business in only a single state or locality has the same theoretical freedom as the publicly held corporation in this regard, since it is possible to incorporate in any state and qualify to transact business as a foreign corporation in any other state. However, practical considerations usually dictate that the small corporation be formed in the jurisdiction in which it is solely or principally doing business. There are real costs if any foreign state is selected: the corporation will have to qualify as a foreign corporation in its "home state;" it will be subject to two taxing authorities; and it may be subject to suit in a distant state. If there is some reason not to incorporate in the local jurisdiction despite these costs, the alternative usually is Delaware, with its popular statute. As other states have modernized their corporation statutes, the advantages of Delaware as a state of incorporation for small businesses active in other jurisdictions have lessened, and most local businesses today are incorporated in the state in which they primarily conduct business.

§ 3.3 Mechanics of Creating a Corporation

The mechanics of creating a corporation vary from state to state, and the specific statute must be consulted for details.

Every state requires the filing of a document with a state official, usually the secretary of state, together with the payment of a filing fee. Depending on the state, the document may be called the "articles of incorporation," the "certificate of incorporation," the "charter" or some other name. In every state, the filing is reviewed by the state officer, which commonly means by a professional staff within his or her office. If the document is approved, the corporate existence is usually deemed to begin as of the date and time the document was originally filed. The filing authority reflects its approval of the document by some step, traditionally the issuance of a formal "charter" or "certificate of incorporation" and attaching to it a duplicate original or copy of the original document that was filed, or increasingly, by the mere issuance of a receipt for the filing fee. The original document is retained by the secretary of state in most states, and the same information may also be kept in computer-readable form. Some states have additional filing requirements. Delaware, for example, requires local filing in the county in which the corporation's registered office is located (as well as filing in a state office) [Del.Code Ann. Tit. 8, § 103(c)(5)]. Arizona requires that the articles be published in a newspaper of general circulation in the county in which the corporation's known place of business is located three consecutive times within 60 days after the articles are filed [Ariz.Rev.Stat.Ann. § 10–055]. A handful of states still require recording in every county in which the corporation transacts business. It is generally believed that these additional requirements serve little or no practical benefit; they are retained usually because of the political power of county clerks or newspaper publishers who have come to rely on the fees or charges generated by those requirements.

Local filing or advertising requirements may also create legal problems as to when the corporate existence begins if some, but not all of them, are complied with. A few states have statutes that deal with this question. Delaware, for example, provides that corporate existence begins with the acceptance of the filing by the secretary of state, and the failure to file locally within the specified period increases the filing fee but does not affect the existence of the corporation [Del.Code Ann. Tit. 8, § 103(d)]. Some states, however, condition the existence of the corporation on the completion of all filing and advertising requirements.

§ 3.4 Incorporators

The person or persons who execute the articles of incorporation are called "incorporators." The number required varies from state to state, with three being the traditional number; all but a handful of states today require only a single incorporator. A few states still have residency or age requirements for incorporators, but most states now permit an incorporator to be anyone of legal age without regard to residency. Traditionally, only natural persons could act as incorporators, but many states now permit artificial entities such as corporations also to serve as incorporators.

The relaxation of the requirements relating to incorporators reflects the minor role they play in the formation of a modern corporation. Depending on the state, incorporators may serve one or more of the following roles:

(1) They execute and deliver the articles or certificate of incorporation to the secretary of state;

(2) They, or their representatives, receive the charter or certificate of incorporation back from the secretary of state;

(3) They either (i) meet to complete the organization of the corporation or (ii) call the first meeting of the initial board of directors (named in the articles of incorporation) at which the organization of the corporation is completed;

(4) They may voluntarily dissolve the corporation if the corporation has not commenced business and has not issued any shares; and

(5) They may amend the articles of incorporation by unanimous consent if the corporation has not commenced business and has not issued any shares.

Traditionally the incorporators met to complete the organization of the corporation. The original Model Business Corporation Act changed this pattern by providing that initial directors should be named in the articles of incorporation, and the initial directors meet to complete the organization of the corporation. Many states today follow this pattern. In these states, the role of incorporators is basically limited to the ceremonial function of signing the articles of incorporation. Sections 2.02(b)(1) and 2.05(a) of the Revised Model Business Corporation Act give each new corporation the option either of having the incorporators complete the formation of the corporation or of naming initial directors in the articles of incorporation and having them complete the organization of the corporation. As discussed below, (see section 3.15 of this Nutshell) this flexibility was added to permit corporations in diverse situations to complete their formation with a minimum number of meetings and a minimum of expense.

It is generally believed that there is no risk of liability for actions taken while acting as incorporator of a corporation. Indeed, many attorneys or their secretaries or other law office employees routinely serve as incorporators. The same may not always be true of acting as a director or an initial director. Many attorneys decline to serve as a director of small corporations they form, or do so only reluctantly.

An "incorporator" must be sharply distinguished from a "subscriber." The latter agrees to buy shares in the corporation; in other words, a subscriber is an investor and participant in the venture. An "incorporator" on the other hand serves the largely ceremonial or ministerial functions described in this section. At one time many states required that an incorporator also be a subscriber of shares; however, such requirements appear to have disappeared in all states.

§ 3.5   Articles of Incorporation: In General

The document filed with the secretary of state must contain certain mandatory information. While the requirements vary from state to state, the following modest list (drawn from § 54 of the old Model Business Corporation Act) is typical:

(a) The name of the corporation;

(b) The period of duration which may be perpetual;

(c) The purpose or purposes of the corporation, which may be generally described as "for any lawful business purpose;"

(d) The number of shares authorized to be issued, including information about the rights and preferences of such shares;

(e) The address of its registered office and the name of its registered agent at that office;

(f) The number of directors and the names and addresses of the members of the initial board of directors; and

(g) The names and addresses of each incorporator.

When the committee drafting the new Revised Model Business Corporation Act considered the analogous section, RMBCA § 2.02, it was recognized that virtually all modern corporations elected perpetual duration and a purpose of engaging in any lawful business. In order to simplify the articles of incorporation even further, the RMBCA simply provides that every corporation has these attributes unless a shorter duration or narrower purpose is set forth in the articles of incorporation. Further, if the corporation has only a single class of shares and elects to be created and organized by a single incorporator rather than by initial directors, item (f) is eliminated and item (d) is responded to in a single sentence; the resulting minimum form of articles of incorporation fits conveniently on a post card!

In addition, state statutes provide that a corporation may elect to be governed by certain statutory provisions, the election of which must be reflected by an appropriate provision in the articles of incorporation. For example, many statutes provide that a majority in interest of the shareholders shall constitute a quorum of shareholders except that the quorum may be reduced by specific provision in the articles of incorporation to a number smaller than a majority (RMBCA § 7.25). Many statutes provide that shareholders shall have a preemptive right to acquire new shares (see § 7.17 of this Nutshell) or to vote shares cumulatively (see § 9.4 of this Nutshell) unless these rights are specifically negated by appropriate provisions in the articles of incorporation. The Revised Model Business Corporation Act (§§ 6.30, 7.28(b)) and the statutes of some states instead provide "opt in" provisions for these rights—i.e., a corporation's shareholders do not have preemptive rights or the right to vote cumulatively unless the articles of incorporation specifically provide for them. The statute of each specific state must be consulted to determine the pattern adopted by that state in connection with these rights.

Finally, corporations may elect to place optional provisions relating to internal governance in the articles of incorporation in order to make them more permanent, more difficult to amend, and, hopefully, binding on persons who may not have actual knowledge of them. Such provisions usually may also be placed in the corporation's bylaws. However, many lawyers and judges expect important provisions, or unusual provisions denying customary rights to shareholders or others, to appear in the articles of incorporation. Such provisions are often repeated in the bylaws.

§ 3.6   Articles of Incorporation: The Corporate Name

Most statutes set up minimum requirements with respect to the corporate name. Typical provisions include:

(1) The name must contain a word indicating corporateness, such as "corporation," "company," or "incorporated," or an abbreviation of one or more such words.

(2) The name may not contain any word or phrase which indicates that it is organized for a purpose that it is not

permitted to engage in. As a practical matter, with the development of very general purposes clauses, the principal impact of this restriction is to preclude the use of names which suggest a purpose for which corporations may not be organized under the state business corporation act. Thus, in many states, "bank," "bank and trust," "certificate of deposit," "title guaranty," and "insurance" may not appear in corporate names since there are special regulatory requirements in statutes relating to formation of corporations for such purposes.

(3) The name may not resemble too closely the name of any other corporation formed or qualified to transact business in the state. The precise statutory test varies. The old Model Business Corporation Act prohibited a name that was the "same or deceptively similar" to any other corporate name, and most state statutes embody this test. The Revised Model Business Corporation Act, § 4.01, substitutes the test that the name be "distinguishable upon the records of the secretary of state" from any other corporate name. This language was basically taken from the Delaware statute. The primary purpose of this requirement, however it is phrased, is to make sure that each corporation has a unique name. States that adopt the "same or deceptively similar" standard may also be seeking to enforce a policy of preventing unfair competition.

(4) Some states add another layer to the name availability rules. Texas, for example, provides that if the name is "similar" (as contrasted with the "same or deceptively similar") to any other corporate name, it may be used only if a "letter of consent" is obtained from the owner of the similar name which expressly permits the name to be used. The purpose of this requirement appears to be solely to prevent unfair competition.

Secretaries of state usually maintain lists of corporate names that are in use and therefore not currently available, and check proposed new names against that list. This list is usually stored on a computer to provide instant access. This list is usually the sole standard applied by the secretary of state who typically has neither the staff nor the resources to make an independent investigation of whether the use of the proposed name may constitute unfair competition. It was for this reason that the Revised Model Business Corporation Act rephrases the test of name availability as "distinguishable upon the records of the secretary of state." However, it is important to recognize that the decision as to name availability (whether the test is that the name is "the same," "distinguishable," or "deceptively similar") involves questions of judgment; some secretaries of state have developed "rules of thumb" or "house rules" to guide their discretion on judgments as to name availability. As a practical matter, the issue whether or not a specific name is available is seldom litigated. Even if an attorney strongly disagrees with the secretary of state as to the availability of a name, it is much simpler and cheaper to select another name than to litigate over name availability. However, when two corporations or businesses have used similar names in the past, the right to the continued use of such name may be so valuable as to lead to bitter litigation over whether the use of the name constitutes unfair competition. Secretaries of state are usually directed by statute to accept the results of such litigation in establishing name availability.

The discussion so far deals only with "official names," that is the name of the corporation that appears in its articles of incorporation and in the records of the secretary of state. A corporation, like an individual, may do business under an assumed name so long as the purpose is not fraudulent and does not constitute unfair competition. Many states have assumed name statutes that require a person, whether an individual or a corporation, that is conducting a business under an assumed name to file a statement (usually at the county level) disclosing who is conducting business under that assumed name. The possible use of an assumed name by a corporation reduces significantly the importance of the name availability determination by the secretary of state. A corporation named ABC Corporation, for example, may do business under the name XYZ Corporation upon complying with the assumed name statute, if the state has one. If there happens to be another corporation that has the official name XYZ Corporation, it can enjoin ABC Corporation from using that name as an assumed name only if there is unfair competition, typically name confusion. If the two corporations are not competing against each other because they are in different geographic locations or in totally different businesses, there is probably nothing that the "real" XYZ Corporation can do about it. The secretary of state typically does not know what assumed name a corporation is using or plans to use or in what area of the state the corporation is operating, or even what the nature of the business of the corporation is; as a result the secretary of state is usually not in a position to make reliable judgments about questions of unfair competition.

Because official corporate names are handled on a first-come first-serve basis, many state statutes permit the reservation of a proposed corporate name for a limited time for a nominal fee while corporate papers are prepared. See RMBCA § 4.02. This reservation of a corporate name should be contrasted with the registration of a name by a foreign corporation permitted in some states. See RMBCA § 4.03. A registration of a corporate name allows a foreign corporation with long-term plans to expand into the state to reserve the exclusive use of its name and prevent a local corporation from using the same name as an "official name." A reservation of a name is for a brief period, usually three months, and in most states is not renewable (though once a reservation period has expired, anyone, including the holder of the original reserved name, may thereafter reserve the name again); a registration is for a year or more and may be renewed indefinitely without any break in continuity of protection. It is unclear what effect, if any, should be given to a registered name in a suit for unfair competition.

§ 3.7 Articles of Incorporation: Period of Duration

All business corporation acts now permit a corporation to have perpetual existence. In the past some statutes limited corporations to a fifty year or some other specified life span. These provisions are now obsolete. As noted earlier, the old Model Act requires a statement of the duration of the corporation; the practice of stating the duration to be perpetual was so common that the Revised Model Business Corporation Act omitted this requirement unless a limited period of duration is desired. It is probably unwise ever to take advantage of this option and designate a term less than perpetual even if it is contemplated that the corporation will exist only for a limited period: such provisions are apt to create more problems than benefits in the long run since expiration of the term before the business of the corporation is completed may result in the corporation having uncertain status. If this occurs, it is always possible to amend the articles to extend the term (or make the term perpetual), but why create a corporate structure that requires someone to remember to do this?

§ 3.8 Articles of Incorporation: The Purposes Clause

All state statutes now provide that a corporation may be formed for any lawful purpose. Many state statutes still require that the articles of incorporation specify what the corporation's purpose or purposes are, but permit a general statement such as the corporation is formed "for general business purposes" or "to engage in any lawful business." The use of such clauses has become so common that the Revised Model Business Corporation Act, § 3.01, provides that all corporations have the "purpose of engaging in any lawful business unless a more limited purpose is set forth in the articles of incorporation."

The historical development of purposes clauses is interesting and is typical of basic trends in state corporation law. In the nineteenth century, corporations could only be formed for specific purposes, and under many statutes could only list a single purpose. Statutes also usually required that the purposes of a corporation be "fully stated." These provisions were viewed as providing a significant regulatory component: corporations were viewed with mistrust and permission to do business in corporate form was given only grudgingly. Application of these limiting principles often raised problems of ultra vires (discussed in § 4.2 of this Nutshell; literally, beyond the purposes or powers of the corporation) and led to a large amount of litigation construing purposes clauses. The first major innovation was a superficially simple one: it permitted a corporation to state multiple purposes while preserving the rules that the purposes must be "fully stated" and that the corporation was organized only for the limited purposes set forth in the articles of incorporation. This, however, opened the proverbial flood gates since there was no limitation on the number of purposes for which a single corporation may be formed. It was theoretically possible for a corporation's purposes clause to list every conceivable business in which a corporation may engage, including mining diamonds on the moon. Purposes clauses therefore had a tendency to become increasingly prolix, increasingly unreadable, and often completely uninformative as to what business the corporation actually planned to engage in. The next step, permitting a corporation to use a very simple and general clause, e.g., "this corporation may engage in any lawful business," was a natural and sensible innovation. Since practically all corporations elected to take advantage of this innovation, the requirement of a purposes clause has been reduced to a formality, and the final step taken in the RMBCA also seems to be natural and sensible.

Despite the modern freedom to use "any lawful business" clauses (or to omit the purpose clause entirely), articles of incorporation are sometimes filed with a narrow purposes clause as part of internal corporate planning. Like the limited duration clause, such a provision is apt to create more problems than benefits since, as discussed in the section on ultra vires (§ 4.2 of this Nutshell), a limited purposes clause does not effectively limit the scope of the corporation's activities.

Some attorneys use purposes clauses that specify the principal business or activity of the corporation, but couple it with language such as, "and to engage in any other lawful business." This provides the reader of the articles of incorporation some information as to the nature of the corporation's business without restricting the freedom of the corporation to engage in new businesses. It also may be important to use narrow purposes clauses in corporations that are to engage in businesses subject to specific state or federal regulation that require regulated corporations to have specified purposes.

Corporate "purposes" should be distinguished from corporate "powers." Every state business corporation act contains a list of corporate powers that every corporation organized under that act automatically possesses. In most states this list is broad and not exclusive. Section 3.02 of the Revised Model Business Corporation Act is based on the long tradition of powers clauses in state statutes, but it contains additional language in the introductory clause, "and has the same powers as an individual to do all things necessary or convenient to carry out its business and affairs," that is designed to eliminate any historical remnant of doctrines of limited or enumerated powers. Section 3.02 is also broader than many state statutes in specific areas, such as section 3.02(15), authorizing the making of payments or donations or doing of other acts "not inconsistent with law, that furthers the business and affairs of the corporation." This language is independent of the power to make charitable donations [section 3.02(13)], and includes payments for political purposes or to influence elections.

A corporation with a narrow purposes clause may nevertheless possess broad powers under section 3.02 of the RMBCA or similar state statutes, the broad powers to be exercised in furtherance of the narrow purpose.

Where a state statute contains a modern and broad list of powers, it is generally undesirable to include powers clauses in articles of incorporation since the inclusion of certain powers may be construed as negating the existence of non-enumerated ones. Because of peculiar historical problems in some states, however, it may be desirable to refer to certain specific powers in the articles. Where this is felt necessary, the drafting should make clear that the clause relates to powers rather than purposes. A clause that permits a corporation, for example, "to enter into partnerships or joint ventures" states a "power" and not a "purpose." The corporation is utilizing the "power" of entering into a partnership to achieve a "purpose," e.g., a purpose of buying, selling, and trading in real estate. The partnership power clause in this example, incidentally, changes the common law rule that a corporation could not be a general partner in a partnership, and therefore may be appropriate in states which do not recognize expressly in their business corporation acts that a corporation may act as a general partner in a partnership.

§ 3.9 Articles of Incorporation: Capitalization

Articles of incorporation must include information about the types or kinds of securities the corporation is authorized to issue. A separate chapter of this Nutshell is devoted to corporate securities, and the disclosure requirements applicable to articles of incorporation are discussed there. (See Chapter Seven, particularly § 7.2.)

The required information about types or kinds of securities in articles of incorporation relates to securities the corporation is authorized to issue rather than the securities the corporation actually plans to issue. However, the statutes of several states require disclosure of what securities will actually be issued, either as a part of a tax return or a general information filing available to the public generally.

Minimum capital requirements in state statutes were practically universal twenty-five years ago. These statutes prohibited the corporation from commencing business unless it had received a specified minimum amount of capital and usually imposed personal liability on the directors if they permitted a corporation to commence business without the minimum capital. The most popular amount was $1,000, but some statutes required $500 or some other amount, and some required some specified percentage of authorized capital. Today all but ten states have eliminated such requirements on the theory that any minimum amount of capitalization is arbitrary and does not provide meaningful protection to creditors. The major problem with these minimum capital provisions was that they took no account of the specific capital needs of the particular business. It made no difference whether a corporation needed $1,000,000 or $100 to start up the contemplated business; both needed an initial capitalization of $1,000 under these minimum capital requirements. Also, the requirement of $1,000, while perhaps meaningful in the 1950's and 1960's, had become the victim of inflation and was much less significant by the 1980's. The old Model Business Corporation Act eliminated its minimum capitalization requirement in 1969, and the trend is definitely in the direction of eliminating all such requirements. Thus, in most states today it is theoretically possible (as it is under the Revised Model Business Corporation Act) to form a corporation with a capitalization of one cent.

In states with a minimum capital requirement, the principal enforcement mechanism was to make directors who assent to the corporation commencing business before it had received the required capital liable jointly and severally for such part of the capital as had not been received. Usually this liability terminated when the required consideration was received. A few states had *in terrorem* statutes that made the directors personally liable for all corporate obligations incurred before the minimum capital was paid in, even if the shortfall of capital was small and the liabilities incurred were large. None of the remaining states with minimum capital requirements appear to fall within this category.

§ 3.10   Articles of Incorporation: Registered Office and Registered Agent

Every corporation must maintain a registered office and a registered agent at that office. The registered office may but need not be the corporation's business office. The primary purpose of a registered office and registered agent is to provide an agent for service of process. The underlying idea is that it should be possible at all times to find a corporation and to have a person upon whom, and a place at which, any notice or process required or permitted by law may be served. A second purpose is to have an office to which tax notices and other official communications from the state may be sent. The original registered office and registered agent must usually be specified in the articles of incorporation; if either is changed thereafter a statement describing the change must be filed with the Secretary of State.

Often a corporation designates its principal business office to be its registered office. In such a case, the registered agent usually is a corporate officer or employee. The principal disadvantage of this is the possibility that summons, legal documents, or other communications may be mixed in with routine business mail and not receive the attention they deserve. For this reason, many attorneys suggest that they be designated as the registered agent and their office be designated as the registered office.

§ 3.11 Articles of Incorporation: Initial Board of Directors

In states where the incorporators meet to complete the formation of the corporation, there is usually no requirement that the initial board of directors be named in the articles of incorporation. The purpose of this requirement, in other words, is to designate who will complete the organization of the corporation. Many states today provide that the organization of the corporation is to be completed by the initial directors who are named in the articles.

In general, there is no requirement that changes in the board of directors be reflected by amendments to the articles of incorporation or in later filings with the secretary of state. Unlike the registered office and registered agent, the records maintained by the secretary of state do not indicate who the current directors or officers of a corporation are.

Where the initial board of directors is named in the articles, it serves as the board only until the first annual meeting of shareholders or until the directors' successors are elected and qualify. The first annual meeting of shareholders may be set immediately after the organizational meeting of the initial board of directors so that elected directors take office almost immediately. It is therefore possible in these states to name in the articles of incorporation persons who are nominal directors (that is, directors who have no continuing interest in the business and cease to serve as directors immediately after the organizational meeting). In this way all disclosure of the identity of the permanent board of directors in the articles of incorporation may be avoided. Whether or not this is desirable depends on the wishes of the clients.

Unlike incorporators, directors may sometimes incur liabilities by virtue of their office. Hence, it may be unwise for an attorney or his or her employees to serve as directors, nominal or otherwise, though the risk may be slight as a practical matter if the directorship is for a short period.

§ 3.12 Completion of the Organization of the Corporation: In General

In addition to preparing and filing the articles of incorporation, attorneys usually handle a number of other routine details in connection with the formation of a corporation. They may:

(1) Prepare the corporate bylaws;

(2) Prepare the call of meeting of the initial board of directors or the incorporators, minutes of this meeting, and waivers of notice or consents if necessary;

(3) Obtain a corporate seal and minute book for the corporation;

(4) Obtain blank certificates for the shares of stock, arrange for their printing or typing, and ensure that they are properly issued;

(5) Arrange for the opening of the corporate bank account;

(6) Prepare the call of meeting of the shareholders, minutes of this meeting and waivers of notice, if necessary;

(7) Prepare employment contracts, voting trusts, pooling agreements, share transfer restrictions, and other special arrangements which are to be entered into with respect to the corporation and its shares; and

(8) Obtain taxpayer and employer identification numbers from the Internal Revenue Service and from appropriate state agencies.

§ 3.13 Nature and Purpose of Bylaws

The bylaws of a corporation are a set of rules for governing the internal affairs of the corporation. They are adopted by the corporation and technically are binding only on intra-corporate matters. They are often viewed as a contract between the corporation and its members, and among the members themselves.

Bylaws are generally not filed with the secretary of state, and are not a matter of public record. They usually may be amended with considerable more facility than the articles of incorporation. In case of conflict between the articles of incorporation and the bylaws, the former, of course, control.

As indicated earlier, it is often optional whether a specific provision is included in the articles of incorporation or in the bylaws. If the provision is unusual or important, maximum legal efficacy is obtained by placing the provision on public record in the articles. On the other hand, corporate officers are much more likely to be conversant with the provisions of the bylaws. For this reason, procedural matters and mandatory provisions that appear in the articles of incorporation and even in the statute should be repeated in the bylaws. In short, the bylaws should set out what amounts to an operating manual of basic rules for ordinary transactions, sufficiently complete to be relied upon by the officers of the corporation as a checklist in administering the affairs of the corporation.

See § 8.9 of this Nutshell for a discussion of the power to amend bylaws.

§ 3.14   The Corporate Seal

In most states a formal corporate seal is no longer necessary. A handwritten facsimile seal has the same legal effect as a metal die, and some states have attempted to dispense entirely with the requirement of a seal. See RMBCA § 3.02(2). Nevertheless, a seal is probably desirable since it helps to delineate corporate transactions from individual transactions. Also, title and abstract companies and attorneys in real estate work are accustomed to corporate conveyances being under seal, and it may be easier to satisfy them if a formal seal is available. No one need fight city hall unnecessarily.

The corporate seal is usually affixed to share certificates, bonds, debentures, evidences of indebtedness, corporate conveyances of land, certified excerpts from minutes of meetings, and important corporate contracts.

§ 3.15   Organizational Meetings

Most of the miscellaneous matters relating to the launching of a new corporation are accomplished at a meeting of the initial directors, or in some states, the incorporators. Typical actions include the acceptance of share subscriptions or contracts; the issuance of shares and the establishment of the consideration for them (see Chapter Seven of this Nutshell); the selection and election of officers; the approval of contracts, loans, leases and other business-related matters; approval of the bylaws and the seal; the approval of the payment of the expenses of incorporation (see § 5.7 of this Nutshell); the adoption of a resolution opening a bank account and the designation of the officers authorized to sign checks; and numerous other possible business-related matters. As a practical matter, the attorney normally drafts the minutes of this meeting before the meeting takes place. Also, in some circumstances it may be necessary to have a meeting of the shareholders to elect permanent directors; the attorney normally also drafts the minutes of this meeting before the meeting takes place. If meetings are held pursuant to waivers of notice, the attorney also prepares the waiver to be executed before or at the meeting.

Experience with organizing corporations reveals that no single pattern of organizational meetings is suitable for all corporations. In states that require the organizational meeting to be held by initial directors named in the articles of incorporation, attorneys sometimes found it necessary, where the permanent parties in interest did not want their names to appear in the records of the secretary of state, to hold a meeting of the initial directors to organize the corporation and issue stock, followed immediately by a meeting of shareholders to elect permanent directors, followed immediately by a meeting of the permanent directors to conduct other necessary business transactions. It would be somewhat more efficient in this scenario to have incorporators organize the corporation since they could issue stock and name the permanent board of directors at a single meeting: two meetings rather than three would therefore complete the organization of the corporation. On the other hand, if the permanent directors are willing to serve as the initial directors and be named as such in the articles of incorporation, it would be more efficient for the permanent directors to be named as initial directors, since there would normally be no need for a shareholders meeting or a second directors meeting in connection with the organization of the corporation. Only a single meeting would suffice, whereas if the corporation were organized by incorporators, a meeting of the directors to conduct necessary business transactions, might have to be held immediately after the meeting of incorporators. It was because of scenarios such as these that the draftsmen of the Revised Model Business Corporation Act decided to give each new corporation an option whether to have organizational meetings conducted by incorporators or by initial directors named in the articles of incorporation. As a practical matter, of course, this is made by the attorney forming the corporation as he or she contemplated the desires of the client and the steps needed to complete the formation of the corporation.

The question often arises as to whether it is necessary to actually hold meetings to reflect what the minutes describe. If the corporation is closely held and there is no disagreement about what is to be done, it seems to be a waste of time and silly play-acting to assemble several persons in a single room and actually hold a meeting at which the already-prepared minutes serve as a script. Generally, a written consent signed by all the directors or shareholders is as effective as a meeting. If the consent procedure is not available under applicable state law, or cannot be utilized (as may be the case, for example, where one director is absent), it is generally desirable to actually hold an informal meeting at which the actions referred to in the minutes are quickly approved. Such meetings do have a play-acting atmosphere but the validity of actions taken without a meeting may be questioned otherwise.

[For unfamiliar terms see the Glossary]

CHAPTER FOUR

THE LIMITED ROLE OF ULTRA VIRES

§ 4.1 The Common Law Doctrine of Ultra Vires

The doctrine of ultra vires (literally beyond the scope of the purposes or powers of a corporation) is now largely obsolete in modern corporation law. In an earlier day, however, the doctrine had considerable practical importance and was given major attention. Before turning to the vestigial remnants of the doctrine in modern law, a brief description of the scope of the doctrine at common law should be given.

An ultra vires act was one beyond the purposes or powers of a corporation. The earliest view of the matter was that such acts were totally void. A corporation was formed only for limited purposes, the argument ran, and it could do nothing more than it was authorized to do. This early view, however, was unworkable and unrealistic. Carried to its logical conclusion it would permit a corporation to accept the benefits of a contract and then refuse to perform its obligations on the ground that the contract was ultra vires. (Indeed that may have been the view taken early by the English courts.) It would also impair the security of title to property in fully executed transactions in which a corporation participated. As a result, even though dicta supporting the view that ultra vires acts were totally void appeared in many cases, most courts actually adopted the view that such acts were voidable rather than void. The doctrine continued to be firmly grounded on the notion that a corporation possessed only limited power, but a rather elaborate body of principles developed defining when the defense of ultra vires might be asserted. Basic principles included the following:

(a) An ultra vires transaction might be ratified by all the shareholders. Ratification could be express or implied, e.g., by the receipt of benefits without objection. Ratification, however, had to be by unanimous consent.

(b) The doctrine of estoppel usually precluded reliance on the defense of ultra vires where the transaction was fully performed by one party. In some cases, however, the corporation was held not to be estopped even where the other party had performed fully because the corporation had not received a "direct" benefit from the transaction. When benefits were classed as "direct" or "indirect" appeared to be erratic.

(c) A fortiori, a transaction which was fully performed by both parties could not be attacked. This principle was generally applied to assure security of land titles in transactions that had been closed.

(d) If the contract was fully executory, the defense of ultra vires might be raised by either party.

(e) If the contract was partially performed, and the performance was held to be insufficient to bring the doctrine of estoppel into play, a suit in quasi-contract for recovery of benefits conferred was available.

(f) If an agent of the corporation committed a tort within the scope of his or her employment, the corporation could not defend on the ground the act was ultra vires. This conclusion was reached because of the overriding necessity of protecting innocent third parties from corporate abuses over which they had no means of control.

These principles somewhat tamed the doctrine of ultra vires. That doctrine, however, continued to defeat legitimate expectations where the contract was still executory and possessed an unfortunate capacity to be applied in an erratic fashion in other situations as well. As a result, the modern trend has been to eliminate this doctrine from the law of corporations, or at least to sharply restrict its availability.

§ 4.2   The Modern Role of Ultra Vires

Several modern developments relating to corporate formation have limited the probability that ultra vires acts will occur. Thus, the development of multiple purposes clauses and general clauses permitting corporations to "engage in any lawful business" indirectly limits the role of the doctrine. Further, it is now very simple to amend purposes clauses to broaden them to cover new activities if an ultra vires issue is presented. However, despite these factors, cases involving narrowly drawn purposes clauses still occasionally arise. In order to eliminate the complicated and arbitrary ultra vires rules in these cases, virtually all states have adopted statutes patterned on the following 1950 Model Act provision:

> No act of a corporation and no conveyance or transfer of real or personal property to or by a corporation shall be invalid by reason of the fact that the corporation was without capacity or power to do such act or to make or receive such conveyance or transfer. (MBCA § 7.)

The Revised Model Business Corporation Act says exactly the same thing in somewhat more elegant language: "The validity of corporate action may not be challenged on the ground that the corporation lacks or lacked power to act." [RMBCA § 3.04(a)] However, both statutes permit the lack of capacity or power to be asserted in the following types of proceedings:

(1) In a proceeding by the corporation (or by a shareholder in a representative capacity) against the incumbent or former officers or directors of the corporation for exceeding their authority;

(2) In a proceeding by the Attorney General to dissolve the corporation, or to enjoin it from the transaction of unauthorized business; or

(3) In a proceeding by the shareholder against the corporation to enjoin the commission of an ultra vires act or the ultra vires transfer of real or personal property if all parties are before the court and circumstances make such an action equitable.

A limited purposes clause may be included because one or more of the participants desire to restrict the freedom of a corporation to go into new or different ventures (see § 3.8 of this Nutshell). The possibility of enjoining a corporation from violating such a limited clause is recognized in clause (3) "if the circumstances make such an action equitable." However, the Official Comment to section 3.04 points out that rights of third persons who may be unaware of the restrictions must be taken into account in assessing equity; in view of the routine and pro forma nature of the modern incorporation process it is unlikely that a third person would be held subject to a limited purposes clause unless he or she was actually aware of it. The notion that a filing in a public office creates "constructive notice," whatever its merits in other contexts, probably should not extend to unusual provisions in articles of incorporation and, given the modern practice of virtual universal use of general purposes clauses, certainly should not extend to limited purposes clauses.

§ 4.3 Ultra Vires Problems in Connection With Corporate Powers

The concept of ultra vires may arise in one other modern context. As described earlier, modern corporation statutes contain a list of powers that every corporation formed under the statute automatically possesses. A corporation may do some act that is beyond its powers as set forth in this list. The language of the Revised Model Business Corporation

Act is so broad that it is unlikely that any action of a corporation might be beyond its powers, and therefore ultra vires. However, the language of powers clauses vary and in some states corporations may not be specifically authorized to engage in certain actions even though they appear to be in furtherance of the stated purposes of the corporation. This problem is also declining in importance as the language of statutes are modernized, but the following kinds of activities may create ultra vires problems in some states.

(1) *Charitable or Political Contributions.* Under early decisions corporations did not have implied power to make donations to charitable, religious, or civic organizations. Most states now generally authorize such contributions though doubt may exist whether power exists to make gifts that are large in comparison to the income or assets of the corporation. A leading Delaware case, Theodora Holding Corp. v. Henderson (1969), upholds such gifts so long as they are reasonable in amount given the corporate assets and do not exceed the maximum deduction allowed under the federal income tax law. Also a distinction may be drawn between gifts to established charities such as universities, hospitals, or the Red Cross and gifts to organizations or foundations chartered by a controlling shareholder or director. Arguments may also be made that many charitable gifts directly further the corporation's purpose and should be viewed as business rather than eleemosynary transactions.

Direct political contributions by corporations are unlawful and subject to severe civil and criminal sanctions in many states. In First National Bank v. Bellotti (1978), however, the United States Supreme Court held unconstitutional a Massachusetts criminal statute that prohibited corporations from making contributions or expenditures to influence a state referendum. In establishing First Amendment rights for corporations, the Supreme Court appeared to be concerned with the rights of the hearer of the speech rather than its source.

Sections 3.02(13) and 3.02(15) of the Revised Model Business Corporation Act codify the power of corporations to make charitable contributions and other payments or donations in furtherance of the corporation's business and affairs.

(2) *Pensions, Bonuses, Stock Option Plans, Job Severance Payments, and Other Fringe Benefits.* Such arrangements obviously serve legitimate business purposes, and it is clear that a corporation in an appropriate case may award such benefits without express statutory authority.

Most doubts about the propriety of such arrangements arise in either of two contexts: where the compensation appears to be excessive or based on self-dealing (discussed in § 14.7 of this Nutshell), or where arguably there is an absence of consideration. For example, consideration may be lacking where, as a humanitarian gesture, a corporation supplements the modest pension of a retired employee. Or a bonus may be paid to an employee at the end of the year without a prior agreement that a bonus would be paid. Or a voluntary payment may be made to the spouse of a deceased employee. Technically, the argument about lack of consideration is not based on lack of corporate power but on substantive contract law. In most cases consideration may be found if the court is willing to look for it. For example, a bonus in one year may lead to an inference that a bonus will be paid the following year; a promise to remain in the corporation's employment may be implied; or the payment of an apparently gratuitous pension may yield contemplated benefits to the corporation in the form of improved employee morale and a happier labor force. In the absence of excessive compensation or blatant self-dealing, courts generally strive to uphold rather than strike down compensation arrangements.

Section 3.02(12) of the Revised Model Business Corporation Act expressly addresses the power of corporations to provide pension and similar benefits to present or former employees.

(3) *The Power to Enter Into a Partnership.* The statement that it is ultra vires for corporations to enter into partnerships appears in numerous cases. The concern is that the fiduciary duties owed to other partners may conflict with the directors' duties to the shareholders. Because of the prominence of these statements the Revised Model Business Corporation Act specifically authorizes every corporation "to be a promoter, partner, member, associate, or manager of any partnership, joint venture, trust or other enterprise." [RMBCA § 3.02(9)] The same language appears in the 1969 Model Act. Under such a statute there seems to be no doubt that a corporation has the power to become a partner. All but a handful of states have adopted such a provision.

(4) *The Power to Acquire Shares of Other Corporations.* The power of corporations at common law to acquire shares of other corporations was sharply restricted on the theory that a general power to invest in shares of another corporation constituted an indirect way for corporations to avoid limitations in their own purposes clauses. These restrictions are obsolete; corporations today generally have power to purchase, sell, and hold shares or other interests in, or obligations of, other domestic or foreign corporations. This power is now codified in section 3.02(6) of the Revised Model Business Corporation Act; virtually identical language appeared in earlier versions of the Model Act.

(5) *Guaranty of Indebtedness of Another.* At common law, it was ultra vires for a general business corporation to guarantee the indebtedness of another person, e.g., a potential customer (an exception was made for corporations who were formed for the specific purpose of writing surety bonds for a fee). This principle, which has little to commend it as an abstract matter, gave rise to a considerable amount of injustice since third persons might readily rely on a corporate guarantee. Fortunately, it has been reversed by statutory provision or judicial decision; section 3.02(7) of

the Revised Model Business Corporation Act, for example, authorizes corporations "to make contracts and guarantees [and] incur liabilities;" virtually identical language appeared in earlier versions of the Model Act.

(6) *Loans to Officers or Directors.* Section 3.02(11) of the Revised Model Business Corporation Act provides that a corporation may elect directors, appoint officers, employees, and agents "and lend them money and credit." The RMBCA recognizes that loans to officers or directors may be beneficial to the corporation, and imposes no special restraints or limitations on them. It was not always so, and it is not so in most states today.

The 1969 and earlier versions of the Model Business Corporation Act contained an unqualified prohibition against such loans: it simply stated that "no loans shall be made by a corporation to its officers or directors." In one form or another, restrictions on loans to officers or directors appear in the statutes of many states; most of these restrictions are not total prohibitions (as in the 1969 Model Act) but permit loans, for example, that are approved by the shareholders or loans that are for the express purpose of permitting the individual to purchase shares of the corporation. Generally these restrictions have been construed as a "limitation on a specific power granted, not a positive prohibition." In other words, loans that violate these restrictions are ultra vires but not illegal. The 1969 version of the Model Act and the statutes of many states also provide that directors who vote for or assent to the making of an improper loan to an officer or director are jointly and severally liable for the amount of the loan until it is repaid. It may be argued that this specific provision constitutes the sole remedy for a violation of this restriction on the general powers of a corporation.

As originally approved in 1984, section 8.32 of the RMBCA dealt specifically with loans by a corporation to a director. This section built off the more liberal state statutes, and permitted loans to directors that were (1) approved by a majority of the voting shareholders, (2) approved by the board of directors after a finding that the loan benefits the corporation, or (3) made pursuant to a general plan authorizing loans that was approved by the board of directors after a finding that the plan benefits the corporation. In 1988, however, the Committee on Corporate Laws adopted a new Model Act provision that dealt systematically with conflict of interest transactions between directors and their corporations. Viewing loans to directors as only a special case of conflict of interest transactions that did not require special treatment, the Committee repealed section 8.32. There is therefore now no special provision in the RMBCA dealing with loans to directors.

Restrictions on loans to officers and directors are based on fear that loans to corporate decision-makers are peculiarly subject to abuse; in effect statutes like the 1969 Model Act address this fear by making ultra vires all loans to officers or directors whether or not they are in fact abusive. The RMBCA rejects this per se rule and treats such loans as merely one type of conflict of interest transaction. (See § 14.7 of this Nutshell for a discussion of the new RMBCA provisions dealing with conflict of interest transactions.)

The early statutes prohibiting loans to officers or directors sometimes also included a general prohibition (which appears in the 1969 version of the Model Act) against loans "secured by shares of stock of a corporation." Apparently this provision was included to emphasize that from the standpoint of the corporation such a loan was in fact unsecured. (See § 7.8 of this Nutshell, discussing the role of treasury shares.) However, the desirability of including such a limitation on powers seems questionable and the clause was eliminated from the Model Act in 1969; it also has been eliminated from the statutes of all but a handful of states.

[For unfamiliar terms see the Glossary]

CHAPTER FIVE

PREINCORPORATION TRANSACTIONS

§ 5.1 Introduction

The formation of a new corporation is often not a clean birth. Transactions on behalf of the corporation, or in the corporate name, may occur before the articles of incorporation are filed and the corporate existence begins. Such transactions may be entered into with full knowledge that the corporation is not yet formed (such as subscription agreements or contracts by promoters to ensure that the necessary business assets are available), or inadvertently, resulting from unexpected delays in the formation of the corporation. Preliminary transactions are usually classified under several different headings: promoters' transactions, de facto corporations, and so forth. They are, however, all closely related and often factual situations may be classified under more than one of these headings.

§ 5.2 Subscriptions for Shares

A "subscription" is simply an offer to purchase and pay for a specified number of theretofore unissued shares of a corporation. Subscriptions may be divided into "preincorporation subscriptions," that is, subscriptions for shares of a corporation that has not yet been formed, and "postincorporation subscriptions," that is, subscriptions for unissued shares of an already existing corporation. Older texts devote a great deal of attention to preincorporation subscriptions as a device by which a new venture may be assured of adequate capitalization before it is launched. At common law, uncertainty existed whether a subscriber might withdraw from such subscriptions before the corporation came into existence and accepted them. The reason for this uncertainty was that preincorporation subscriptions which were obtained individually were usually viewed as independent offers running from each subscriber to the corporation rather than as a contract among subscribers with the promise of each subscriber supporting the promises of other subscribers. There was no contract in this situation since one "party"—the corporation—was not in existence and could not be bound so that the other party—the subscriber—was not bound either.

This problem has largely faded away. Corporation statutes make preincorporation subscriptions irrevocable for a limited period (six months in section 6.20(a) of the Revised Model Business Corporation Act) during which the formation of the corporation may be completed and the subscriptions accepted without regard to technical questions of consideration; until that period has expired, the statute makes the preincorporation subscription irrevocable by the subscriber. This six month period is itself a matter of negotiation between promoter and subscriber, and a longer or shorter period of irrevocability may be agreed upon. Also, without regard to the period of irrevocability, all the subscribers to shares of a putative corporation may agree to revocation of a subscription by one or more specific subscribers.

A subscription may be conditioned on the occurrence of certain events, such as obtaining a specified amount of capital, or a specified loan, or a specified lease. The fulfillment of such conditions is a condition precedent to the obligation of the subscribers. The common law developed a rather confusing distinction between such conditions and "subscriptions on special terms" which constituted a type of condition subsequent. There was little practical difference, however, because failure of the corporation to comply with a "special term", also permitted the subscriber to rescind his or her subscription. A subscription induced by fraud may be rescinded as any other contract. The fraud may be committed by an agent of the corporation or a promoter of the corporation.

Modern distribution techniques for securities permit the meeting of all capital needs of publicly held corporations without resort to subscriptions. Indeed, the use of subscriptions by such a corporation is unattractive as a practical matter under the Federal Securities Act of 1933 and state "blue sky laws," because the subscriptions themselves constitute securities and must be registered as provided by those acts. Since the underlying securities themselves also must be registered, the use of subscriptions results in two expensive registrations.

In closely held corporations where there are only a few shareholders, a contractual agreement among the shareholders to form a corporation and purchase specified shares is a binding agreement whether or not it is described as a "subscription agreement." Such agreements have largely supplanted the common law subscription, though the wording in such agreements is usually that each investor "agrees to purchase *and subscribe* for * * *" the securities he or she agreed to purchase. Such agreements are enforceable as multilateral contracts among the subscribers without reference to the special statutory provision relating to preincorporation subscriptions described above (which applies when each subscriber commits to a subscription individually and not in consideration of other subscribers' similar commitments).

A person who subscribes or agrees to purchase shares does not become a shareholder until the subscription price has been fully paid, though some states permit shares to be issued for promissory notes for the unpaid portion of the purchase price.

§ 5.3   Promoters in General

A promoter is a person who takes the initiative in developing and organizing a new business venture. A promoter may act either alone or with co-promoters. The term "promoter" is not one of opprobrium; indeed, the promoter is often an aggressive, imaginative entrepreneur who fulfills the essential economic function of taking an idea and creating a profitable business to capitalize on the idea.

The activities of promoters fall into three principal areas. (1) The promoter must arrange for the necessary capital for the corporation. He or she may invest only personal funds, or use personal funds plus loans from banks to obtain the necessary capital. Outside capital may be obtained from a small number of investors, who may be friends or neighbors. If so, the promoter must negotiate with the outside investors to determine their share in the forthcoming enterprise, and arrange either by contract or subscription to ensure that the capital will be forthcoming when needed. If a public offering is to be made (which is rare for a newly-commenced business) the promoter must secure compliance with the Federal Securities Act of 1933 and state "blue sky" laws as well as arranging for the distribution and sale of the securities, often through an underwriter. (2) The promoter must obtain the necessary assets and personnel so that the corporation may function. He or she may obtain a lease or an option to purchase needed land, or may enter into a contract to purchase with a view of assigning the contract to the corporation. He or she may negotiate construction contracts to build or remodel the necessary buildings. Arrangements must be made to secure the necessary employees which usually will include the promoter as an officer of the new enterprise. The necessary machinery, equipment, or fixtures must be secured; customers must be contacted; arrangements made for advertising; and so forth. Obviously, in this area, the kinds of activities promoters engage in are numerous and varied, depending on the nature of the business being promoted. (3) The promoter must arrange for the formation of the corporation itself. He or she must arrange for the filing of the articles of incorporation, the preparation of the necessary papers, the issuance of shares, and the like. If the promoter first forms the corporation, subsequent contractual problems are usually minimized since all the necessary steps may thereafter be conducted in the name of the corporation, and there is little chance of confusion between the promoter's individual liability and the corporate liability on the arrangements being negotiated. Thus, actions may be taken in the corporate name, and only if a third person requests the personal liability of the promoter as well as the corporation, as may be the case with banks, will the promoter execute an obligation individually or separately guaranteeing its performance.

Often, however, the formation of the corporation turns out to be one of the last steps in the promotional process. The promoter may begin investigation of the profitability of the proposed business, determine that the prospects of success are good, and proceed at once with business negotiations in the areas of capital formation and obtaining business assets and contracts without actually forming the corporation. In this situation there is great likelihood of confusion and uncertainty, and most of the contractual litigation involving promoters arises in this way.

§ 5.4   Promoters' Contracts

Let us assume that a promoter enters into a contract to purchase machinery for the new business being promoted, and consider whether the promoter is personally liable on that contract. No single, simple answer is possible. In some circumstances personal liability will exist, in other circumstances it will not. If the corporation has been duly formed and the contract is entered into and executed by the promoter in the corporate name, the promoter would normally not be personally liable since he or she executed the contract merely as an agent and not as a principal. On the other hand, if the corporation has not been formed, and the promoter enters into the contract in his or her own name without referring to the corporation with the thought of subsequently assigning the contract to the corporation, personal liability clearly exists. These are the easy cases. The more difficult cases fall into two major categories:

(1) *Contracts Entered in the Name of the Corporation.* In this class of case the promoter executes a contract in the corporate name in a way that makes it appear that the corporation has been formed when it actually has not been. Many cases say that such a promoter is personally liable on the theory that a person acting as agent represents that a principal exists, and the promoter is liable because of a misrepresentation. Other cases merely state that a person who purports to act as agent for a nonexistent principal thereby automatically becomes a principal. The latter theory is based on contract and the former on tort, though in most cases they should lead to the same result.

These cases holding the promoter personally liable when the corporation has not been formed often give the third person a windfall because that person is usually not relying on the promoter's credit when entering into the contract; rather he or she is relying on the corporation's credit or, more likely, on the possibility that the corporation will do well and be able to pay off the obligations. (A third person relying on the promoter's credit would usually require the promoter to guarantee the "corporation's" obligation.) However, virtually all courts in this situation hold the promoter personally liable despite the potential windfall.

If the corporation is thereafter formed and adopts the contract, the promoter may then seek to avoid liability on the basis of several possible arguments. One argument is that the subsequent formation of the corporation corrected any misrepresentation or deception that may have occurred.

Another argument is that the manner of execution of the agreement indicates that the third person was content to accept the liability of the corporation, and that therefore the adoption of the contract by the corporation should release the promoter—in other words, that the transaction should be construed as a novation. Also, depending to some extent on the wording of the agreement, the promoter may be able to argue that he or she should not be held liable on the basis of the parol evidence rule (since only the corporation was referred to in the contract). Finally, the promoter may also seek to defend on the ground that the corporation was sufficiently formed so that it was a "corporation de facto," or a "corporation by estoppel" (concepts that are discussed in §§ 5.8 and 5.9), and therefore it was "in existence" when the contract was entered into. Even though these arguments are superficially plausible, the chances of success are problematic.

To summarize: if the promoter enters into a contract with a third person in the name of the corporation without disclosing that it is not in existence, the promoter is personally liable on the contract. If the corporation is thereafter created and takes over the contract, the promoter has a better chance of being relieved of liability but there is a substantial chance that a court will conclude that no novation was intended and the promoter remains liable.

(2) *Contracts Referring to the Fact the Corporation Is Not Yet Formed.* In this class of case the contract is executed by the promoter and the third party when both are aware that the corporation has not been formed. The contract itself usually reveals this fact, as for example when it is executed in a name such as "ABC Corporation, a corporation to be formed." Or the promoter may advise the third person that the corporation has not yet been formed when the contract is executed in the corporate name. It will be noted that this situation differs from situation (1) in that both parties are

aware that the corporation is not yet in existence and there is no possible misrepresentation as to that fact.

This pattern may be analyzed in several different ways with widely divergent consequences. For example, it may be analyzed as an offer to the corporation which is revocable by either party and will result in a contract only if the corporation is thereafter formed and accepts the offer before it is withdrawn. Or it may be analyzed as an irrevocable option running to the corporation, with the consideration being a promise, express or implied, by the promoter to form the corporation and use best efforts to cause the corporation to adopt the contract. Or, it may be analyzed as a present contract between the third person and the promoter by which the promoter is bound, with the understanding that if the contract is adopted by the corporation the promoter will nevertheless remain secondarily liable in the contract.

Which of these various alternatives is the proper one in any specific situation depends on the elusive "intention of the parties." If an attorney is called upon to draft a preincorporation agreement it is relatively simple to ascertain the parties' intention and describe it in a written agreement in terms so precise that there can be no cause for misunderstanding. If the promoter is to be bound until the corporation adopts the contract, and then is to be released from liability, the contract that specifically so provides should avoid later disputes.

Litigation in this area generally involves agreements in which the intention is not clearly spelled out. The contract may have been negotiated by the parties without legal assistance, or the language chosen may not illuminate the specific problem one way or the other. Or the parties may have been unable to agree on their respective rights in the event of some remote contingency. Rather than forego a lucrative transaction, the parties use language such as "ABC Corporation, a corporation to be formed," hoping that the question of the liability of the promoter will not arise. In such situations, the search for intent is truly hopeless, though the courts must resolve the dispute one way or another.

Generalizations about tests which courts use to find "intention" are hazardous. Probably most courts feel that it is likely that the third person intended for *someone* to be liable. Hence, there is a distinct tendency to hold the promoter at least initially liable, especially where the corporation is never formed. Indeed, some cases state that the promoter is personally liable in this situation unless there is specific agreement to the contrary. This view is strengthened where the third person is to receive payments or partial performance before the corporation is formed; presumably the promoter intends to make those payments or render the performance personally until the corporation is formed.

Professor Williston suggested that most persons assume that even if the promoter is initially liable, he or she is nevertheless to be released if the corporation is later formed and adopts the contract. In other words, there is to be a novation. The testimony of the plaintiff in Bradshaw v. Jones (1912) is representative of this understanding: "I understood that I was working for [Mr. Jones] personally until the railroad was organized; and after the railroad was organized, I was working for the railroad, of course." Not surprisingly, the court concluded that a novation was intended. There are, however, some holdings and a considerable amount of dicta to the contrary. One problem with the Williston approach is that it may encourage promoters to create "straw" corporations to take over contracts even after it is clear that the venture should be abandoned.

If the promoters are held liable, they are considered to be partners, and liable for all promotional contracts on a joint and several basis.

Where both parties are aware that the corporation has not yet been formed, several cases have held the promoter not personally liable on the contract.   In Quaker Hill, Inc. v. Parr (1961), for example, the court concluded that on the facts the third party never intended to rely on the promoters' performance of the contract and therefore should not be able to hold the promoters personally liable.   Later cases, however, have held that the burden of proving intention rests on the promoter, and that inferences about intention cannot be based merely on knowledge that formation of a corporation was contemplated.   These recent cases demonstrate again the difficulty of prediction of result in this shadowy area, though it is probable in many cases that the third person in fact intended to look only to the corporation for performance of the contract.

§ 5.5 Liability of Corporations for Promoters' Contracts

A corporation, after it is formed, is not automatically liable on obligations incurred by its promoters on its behalf. The reason usually given is that the promoter cannot be the corporation's agent since the corporation is not in existence. This conceptualistic argument can be partially justified on the practical ground that the rule permits investors in a corporation an opportunity to consider and reject undesirable arrangements agreed to by the promoter.   Of particular importance, it permits review by subsequent investors of contracts entered into between the promoters personally and the corporation (see § 5.6).   This practical justification is not particularly persuasive since it does not provide a systematic review of all promoters' contracts by subsequent investors.

The theory on which corporations voluntarily become liable on contracts negotiated by their promoters has been the subject of a great deal of confusing discussion. Assuming that the arrangement constitutes a contract between the promoter and third person in which it is understood that a corporation will be formed, the corporation "adopts" the contract. Technically, "ratification" is not the proper word to describe this situation because "ratification" assumes that the corporation was in existence at the time the contract was entered into. Courts nevertheless sometimes use the words "ratification" and "adoption" interchangeably. If the promoter is then relieved from liability, the "adoption" or "ratification" becomes a "novation."

In the last analysis, the legal words used are not particularly important. What is necessary is some form of assent by the corporation to the contract after it has been formed. The necessary assent may be express, or it may be implied from the circumstances. If a corporation takes the benefits of a contract made by its promoter, it will usually be concluded that it has assented to the burdens of the contract. For example, if a promoter negotiates a contract by which a third person agrees to become an employee of the corporation for a specified period, the corporation "adopts" the contract if it permits the employee to render services for the corporation, and thereafter cannot fire the employee without cause during the contract period.

Since the corporation becomes liable on the contract only when it assents, it has been held that the contract term begins when the assent occurs. This may be of importance for purposes of the statute of limitations or the one year statute of frauds provision.

§ 5.6 Promoter's Fiduciary Duties

Co-promoters of a venture owe fiduciary duties to each other. In effect they are treated as partners in a venture to organize the business.

Difficult questions may be raised where a promoter enters into transactions with the corporation before outside creditors, investors, or shareholders are brought into the venture. The transaction may involve the receipt of shares of the corporation by the promoter, or the creation of corporate indebtedness in favor of the promoter for services or property. The transaction may be entered into when the promoter is the sole shareholder, or with the approval of the then-shareholders. Later or subsequent creditors, investors, or shareholders may object to the transaction on the ground that the services or property were overvalued or the amount awarded to the promoter was excessive. In many cases of this kind the courts have used language of fiduciary duty in reviewing and setting aside such transactions to the extent they are believed to be unfair. The leading case finding a fiduciary duty is Old Dominion Copper Mining & Smelting Co. v. Bigelow (1909), announcing the so-called "Massachusetts rule." Not all courts have agreed, however; see particularly Old Dominion Copper Mining & Smelting Co. v. Lewisohn (1908), involving the same transaction and announcing the "federal rule" that subsequent shareholders or investors may not set aside previously approved promoters' transactions.

As a practical matter, the issue in these cases is not so much whether or not a fiduciary duty exists as whether or not there has been full disclosure of the transaction to the subsequent interests. If there has been full disclosure, subsequent creditors, investors, or shareholders may readily protect themselves by refusing to deal with the corporation or by reducing the price at which they acquire shares to reflect the reduction in value caused by the promoter's transaction. Indeed, the fiduciary duty described above is basically a duty of full disclosure rather than a duty of fair dealing. Cases continue to arise, however, in which subsequent investors attack promoter's transactions, and some courts have set them aside on the basis of vague discussion of "fiduciary" duties.

Since failure to disclose may constitute a violation of federal or state securities acts, many cases that fifty years ago would have been analyzed as "promoter's fraud" cases are now analyzed as securities act cases.

§ 5.7   Organizational Expenses Incurred by Promoters

Logically, expenses incurred in connection with the organization of a corporation should be treated no differently than other contracts entered into by promoters. For example, if an attorney is employed by promoters to draw up the articles of incorporation, the promoter should be liable for the attorney's fee unless the attorney agrees to look only to the corporation. If the corporation is formed and adopts the contract, it becomes liable for the fee, and whether or not the promoter is released from his or her obligation depends on whether the transaction is deemed a novation.

There are complications, however. Organizational expenses such as attorneys' fees are peculiar in that the mere corporate existence is in effect a use of the benefits of the contract by the corporation. Arguably, therefore, by its mere existence the corporation has agreed to pay whatever fee was negotiated by the promoter. The majority view, however, is that the corporation is not automatically bound. Rather the corporation—since it cannot refuse the services—can only be compelled to pay a reasonable fee under the circumstances.

Many states have statutes that permit the payment of reasonable charges and expenses of organization of a corporation out of the capital received by it in payment for its shares without impairing capital or rendering such shares not fully paid and non-assessable. See RMBCA § 6.28. It is not clear whether such a provision is necessary in modern corporation statutes; it was retained by the draftsmen of the Revised Model Business Corporation Act essentially because it could do no harm and might do some good.

The promoter or the attorney may suggest that the attorney take shares in the corporation for organizational expenses and services. There is nothing inherently wrong with this practice: indeed, it somewhat resembles a contingent fee which is based on the success of the business rather than on the outcome of litigation. The value of shares received by an attorney or promoter for services is, of course, taxable income to him or her and may be deducted by the corporation as an expense over a 60 month period.

Promoters naturally expect to be compensated for their efforts, and in view of the nature of their innovative efforts, they may legitimately expect compensation which would be considered generous by a salaried person. Typically, a promoter will form a corporation with nominal capital, and then seek outside financial support to make the promotion a success. The subsequent investors will usually purchase shares in the corporation at a higher price than the shares previously issued to the promoter. The investors' interest is thereby diluted and the promoters' interest increased in value. In a sense this increase in value represents partial compensation to the promoter; it is often a subject of negotiation between promoters and investors. However, both hope that the major portion of the promoter's compensation will result from the fact that the business does well so that the value of everyone's shares will be enhanced.

§ 5.8 Premature Commencement of Business and the De Facto Doctrine

The procedure to form a corporation under most corporation statutes is basically a very simple one. As a matter of fact, it is so simple and routine that attorneys may become careless and fail to comply with all the requirements that do exist. Mistakes may range from the trivial, such as using an incorrect address, to the more serious, where the attorney becomes so careless that he or she prepares but fails to file the articles of incorporation at all (this has actually happened). Delays in filing are not uncommon. Perhaps the secretary of state declines to accept the first filing because of some minor defect which the attorney subsequently corrects. In the mean time, the "corporation" has commenced business. What is the liability of shareholders for the interim debts in such situations?

At common law, these problems were usually handled under the "de facto corporation" doctrine, though occasionally they appeared as promoters contracts; today many courts still apply this common law concept though it has been largely superseded by a statutory analysis. A "de facto corporation" according to the common law was not a fully formed corporation (a "de jure corporation"), but was nearly as good since it was sufficiently formed to be immune from attack by everyone but the state. The usual test for de facto existence was threefold: there must be a statute under which incorporation was permitted, there must have been a "good faith" or "colorable" attempt to comply with the statute, and there must have been actual user of the corporate privilege. However, the cases arising under this doctrine were confusing, particularly with regard to the second requirement and legal commentators convincingly proved that the traditional tests provide little guidance for the decisions of concrete cases. After examining more than 200 de facto corporation cases arising prior to 1950, for example, the late Professor Frey concluded that the de facto doctrine was "legal conceptualism at its worst."

At common law a "de jure corporation" might exist even though there were some minor defects in its formation. The common law drew a distinction between "mandatory" and "directory" requirements; failure to comply with the latter did not prevent the creation of a de jure corporation. An example of a "directory" requirement was the listing of addresses of directors or incorporators.

These problems today are usually resolved by reference to the specific language of the state's incorporation statute. Every state has a statute that provides in substance that the corporate existence begins either upon the filing of the articles of incorporation or the issuance of the certificate of incorporation. See RMBCA § 2.03(a). Most statutes add that acceptance of the articles (or the issuance of the certificate of incorporation) is "conclusive proof" that all conditions precedent to incorporation have been complied with except in suits brought by the State. See RMBCA § 2.03(b). Thus, if the Secretary of State accepts a filing (or issues a certificate of incorporation), a de jure corporation is in existence despite mistakes or omissions in the articles of incorporation. Despite this unequivocal statutory command, at least one court has decided to rely on general common law principles of de facto corporation in a case involving a corporation that was de jure under this statute. Matter of Whatley (1989).

The problem that usually arises under section 2.03(b) and similar statutes is whether a negative inference should be drawn that the corporate existence has *not* begun before the articles are filed or the certificate is issued, so that personal liability exists for all prefiling transactions. A few states have addressed this issue by adopting an additional statute that deals specifically with prefiling transactions. Many of these statutes are based on section 146 of the 1969 Model Act, which states that "all persons who assume to act as a corporation without authority so to do shall be jointly and severally liable" for all debts and liabilities. However, even in states in which this statute is in effect, some courts have refused to hold participants personally liable on preincorporation transactions. One court has construed the phrase "all persons who assume to act" as referring only to active participants in the venture, thereby immunizing inactive participants from liability. Timberline Equipment Co., Inc. v. Davenport (1973). All in all, the predictability of result under this statute was not much greater than under the de facto-de jure tests of common law.

The committee creating the Revised Model Business Corporation Act took a fresh look at the standard to be applied to shareholder liability for pre-formation transactions, and came up with a somewhat different standard in section 2.04: "all persons purporting to act as or on behalf of a corporation, knowing there was no incorporation under this Act, are jointly and severally liable for all liabilities created while so acting." This test is explained at some length in the Official Comment that considers several different factual patterns.

The basic problem with the simple rule conditioning the existence or nonexistence of a corporation on the acceptance of a filing (or the issuance of a certificate by the secretary of state) is that it has a substantial capacity for unfairness. Under such a rule, if the secretary of state has not accepted the articles (or issued the certificate), the shareholders and promoters are all presumably liable as partners for the preincorporation debts of the business. The result is that negligence in filing on the part of A may cause crushing liabilities to be imposed on B who may have bought "shares" in the honest belief that the corporation's articles had been properly filed. Of course, B might first check with the secretary of state's office, but most investors would not normally think to do so. The standard of section 2.04 of the RMBCA, "knowing there was no incorporation under this Act," provides protection to B in this situation.

§ 5.9   Corporations by Estoppel

Problems of the type discussed in the last section have sometimes been handled in the absence of statute under the phrase "corporation by estoppel." This phrase is not meaningful in and of itself. It is necessary to ask who is "estopped," under what circumstances, and for what reason.

The classic requirements for equitable estoppel (or "estoppel in pais") are that there be a false representation or concealment of a fact to a person ignorant of the truth with the intention by the person making the representation of causing reliance, and actual reliance on the basis of the misrepresentation. "Corporations by estoppel" do not involve these principles. For example, consider the situation where a third person deals with a "corporation" as such relying only on its credit, and then, finding that a certificate of incorporation was never obtained, seeks to hold the promoters and shareholders liable as partners. The defendants in turn may well argue successfully that the plaintiff is "estopped" by his or her prior dealings from holding the promoters or shareholders personally liable. This is certainly not equitable estoppel in the classic sense, since the third person who is being "estopped" never made any representation of any kind which was relied on by any other party. In effect, courts are applying the label "corporation by estoppel" to reach a desirable result: used in this way "estoppel" is a conclusion-oriented term, not an explanation. Nevertheless, there may be strong equitable grounds for limiting the third person's claim to the business assets. The third person receives a windfall if, after dealing and relying solely on the "corporation," he or she is permitted to hold the promoters or shareholders personally liable. Further, for the reasons set forth in the previous section, it may be harsh to hold investors personally liable because of the negligence or neglect of some other person, particularly where the investors honestly and reasonably believed that the articles of incorporation had been filed. For these various reasons, a number of courts have held that the third person is "estopped" from suing the promoters or shareholders, or that there is a "corporation by estoppel."

It should be noted that this reasoning apparently results in the recognition of limited liability despite the fact that the promoters may have failed to comply with the most important statutory requirement for obtaining this privilege. Indeed, if this principle were universally recognized one could save the filing fee by not filing anything and simply conducting business in the corporate name. As a result, not all courts agree that "estoppel" should be applied in this type of situation (though the variations in decisions possibly may be explained by factual variations and variations in statutory wording). There is much to be said for the proposition that a "shareholder" should not be personally liable where (a) the plaintiff dealt with the "corporation" as such, and (b) the defendant believed that the articles of incorporation had been properly filed and was not personally negligent in failing to make sure that the filing actually occurred. This position—which of course should also be reached under § 2.04 of the Revised Model Business Corporation Act— appears to do justice to all parties and not seriously undermine the statutory policy requiring filing of articles of incorporation, since persons knowing that the articles have not been filed would not receive the benefits of limited liability under any circumstances. It is believed that the results of the pre-statutory case law are basically consistent with this view, which is incorporated in the Revised Model Business Corporation Act.

§ 5.10 Agreements to Form Corporation

A so-called preincorporation agreement is a contract between proposed shareholders to develop a business to be conducted in the form of a corporation. It may be a summary memorandum outlining the main points of an oral agreement, or a complete formal document describing all the details of the understanding. In a formal document, all aspects of the agreement between shareholders may be stated, as may understandings as to employment, capitalization, or any other matter which is the subject of preliminary agreement. Copies of proposed articles of incorporation, bylaws, and even minutes of meetings may be attached as exhibits.

The major problem with a preincorporation contract is whether it will be fully executed by the formation of a corporation as provided in the agreement or whether specific provisions will survive the creation of the corporation. If it is desired to have certain provisions of the agreement survive and continue to bind the parties, the agreement should specifically so state, since otherwise a court may easily infer that only the provisions actually included in the articles of incorporation, bylaws, and minutes were intended to survive. If the agreement is to survive it should usually be specifically assumed by the corporation after its formation.

An agreement to form a corporation usually places the parties to the agreement in the relationship of joint venturers, the object of the venture being the formation of the corporation and the establishment of its business. If the agreement survives, there is a conceptual difficulty since after the corporation is formed the parties are simultaneously being treated as having the rights of shareholders in the corporation and the rights of joint venturers in an underlying arrangement to form the corporation. To avoid possible conflicts, some courts have taken the position that when the parties adopt the corporate form, with the corporate shield to protect them, they necessarily "cease to be partners and have only the rights, duties and obligations of stockholders." Other courts however, have taken the more sensible position that the joint venture may continue after the formation of the corporation, at least where the parties' intention to this effect is clear. The question appears to be one of "intention" since there appears to be no reason why both relationships cannot exist simultaneously if that is what the parties desire.

[For unfamiliar terms see the Glossary]

CHAPTER SIX

"PIERCING THE CORPORATE VEIL" AND RELATED PROBLEMS

§ 6.1 "Piercing the Corporate Veil" In Context

Assume for a moment that a corporation has been properly and fully created in accordance with state law so that a "de jure corporation" has been created in the fullest sense of that phrase. The basic question discussed in this Chapter is whether and to what extent the separate existence of such a corporation should be ignored in order to do basic justice or avoid the frustration of some clearly articulated public policy. At first blush, the basic concept that a corporation is a fictitious person or separate legal entity seems to dictate the answer that the separate existence of such a duly formed corporation should never be ignored. The law has not taken this extreme position, however, and the courts in a large number of cases have refused to recognize the separate existence of a duly formed corporation. To put the matter into perspective, it should be added that in an even larger number of cases courts have respected the separate existence of corporations despite arguments that they should not do so. The corporate fiction is a basic assumption that underlies commercial transactions; there must be compelling reasons before a court will ignore such a basic assumption.

When the separate existence of the corporation is ignored, courts often use the colorful metaphor of "piercing the corporate veil."

§ 6.2   Shareholder Responsibility for Corporate Indebtedness: Introduction

The question of the status of a corporation usually arises when a liability has been incurred in the name of a corporation, but the corporation has become insolvent. The creditor, seeking to find a solvent defendant, may sue some or all of the shareholders, arguing that for some reason they should be called upon to pay the corporation's debts. [Indeed, such a creditor may also sue directors, officers, and anyone else in any way connected with the corporation. The possible liabilities of directors, officers, or employees are discussed in later chapters (see particularly Chapters 11 and 14 of this Nutshell); this Chapter is limited to the possible liability of shareholders.] When the corporation is insolvent and recovery is sought from shareholders, the court is faced with deciding whether a loss should be imposed on third persons or on shareholders; there is a loss and someone must pay. A blind application of the "artificial entity" approach would mean that the creditor always suffers the loss; certainly that result is often reasonable but it is not inevitable.

Most opinions by courts shed little light on the considerations governing when corporate obligations should be imposed on the shareholders. The traditional statement of this doctrine, taken from the leading case of Bartle v. Home Owners Cooperative (1955), is that:

> The law permits the incorporation of a business for the very purpose of escaping personal liability. Generally speaking, the doctrine of "piercing the corporate veil" is invoked "to prevent fraud or to achieve equity." But in the instant case there has been neither fraud, misrepresentation nor illegality.

Such statements essentially restate the issue in different terms—fraud, equity, misrepresentation, or illegality. Other cases suggest that the test should be whether the corporation is the "instrumentality" of the shareholder [i.e. the shareholder has exercised excessive control and there is wrongful or inequitable conduct]; or whether the corporation is the "alter ego" of the shareholder [i.e. such unity of ownership and interest exists that the separate existence of the corporation has ceased and recognition of the separate entity would lead to fraud or an inequitable result]. Still other cases utilize a variety of metaphors [e.g., "shell," "dummy," or "fiction"] rather than analysis; all such name-calling obviously asserts the conclusion without giving any clue as to the reasons underlying it. As early as 1926, Justice Cardozo commented that the whole problem "is still enveloped in the mists of metaphor" and that the appropriate tests are "honesty and justice." Berkey v. Third Avenue R. Co. (1926).

§ 6.3 Shareholder Responsibility for Corporate Indebtedness: Contract and Tort Claims

In considering cases involving shareholder responsibility for corporate indebtedness, there should first be put to one side cases where liability is imposed upon shareholders under conventional theories of agency or tort law. To argue that the corporate veil is "pierced" in such cases is both unnecessary and confusing. Where the shareholder is actually acting as a principal in his or her own name, there is clearly liability on the obligation. Moreover, if the corporation is the shareholder's agent under accepted principles of agency law, the shareholder-principal is liable on a contract made by an agent on behalf of a principal, and it is unnecessary to consider whether the "veil" of the corporation should be "pierced." Similarly, if the shareholder personally commits a tort while acting as an agent for his or her corporation, he or she is personally liable for the tort because of the general rule that tortfeasors are personally liable even though they are acting as agents.

In the great bulk of the remaining cases, a major consideration in determining whether the shareholder or the third party should bear the loss is whether the third party dealt voluntarily with the corporation or whether he or she is an involuntary creditor, typically a tort claimant. In a contract case, the third party has usually dealt in some way with the corporation and should be aware that the corporation lacks substance. In the absence of some sort of deception, the creditor thus more or less assumed the risk of loss; if the creditor was concerned that the corporation might not be able to pay the obligation, a simple solution is to insist that some solvent third person guarantee the performance by the corporation. Hence in the absence of deception the loss should be placed on the third person in contract cases—a result actually reached in the great bulk of the contract cases by not "piercing the corporate veil." In tort cases, on the other hand, there is usually no element of voluntary dealing, and the question is whether it is reasonable for owners of businesses to transfer a risk of loss or injury to members of the general public through the device of conducting business in the name of a corporation that is marginally financed. The issues of public policy raised by tort claims thus bear little relationship to the issues raised by contract claims and one would expect that the "corporate veil" is more likely to be "pierced" in a tort case than in a contract case. This fundamental distinction, however, has not always been perceived by courts, which sometimes indiscriminately cite, and purport to apply, tort precedents in contract cases and vice versa.

The distinction between contract and tort claims is particularly important in considering whether "inadequate capitalization" should be a factor in "piercing the corporate veil." Opinions in many cases rely on this factor in holding shareholders liable for corporate obligations; other cases expressly disavow the relevance of the amount of capitalization in determining whether or not to pierce the corporate veil, since, under modern corporation statutes it is theoretically possible to form a corporation with only one cent of capitalization. Unfortunately, the phrase "inadequate capitalization" has more than one possible meaning. Some corporation acts require every corporation, before commencing business, to have received some minimum amount of capital, usually $1,000, for the issuance of shares. In a sense, a corporation in such a state that begins business with less than $1,000 is inadequately capitalized, but that is not the meaning used here. In the "piercing" area, "inadequate capitalization" usually means a capitalization that is very small in relation to the nature of the business of the corporation and the risks the business necessarily entails; in other words it is based on likely economic needs rather than legal requirements. Inadequate capitalization is measured at the time of formation of the corporation or at the time an existing corporation goes into a new line of business; a corporation in a continuing business that was originally adequately capitalized but has suffered unavoidable losses is not normally considered under capitalized. Whether a corporation is under capitalized in the sense used here obviously presents a question of fact that turns on the nature of the business of the particular corporation.

Judicial statements that inadequate capitalization is irrelevant to the "piercing" issue appear most commonly in contract cases. In those cases the separate existence of an inadequately capitalized corporation (often called a "shell" corporation) is usually recognized, since a person who knowingly deals with an under capitalized corporation is, in effect, assuming the risk of loss if the transaction does not work out. Indeed, shell corporations are often created to enter into transactions precisely because the shareholders do not wish to assume personal liability. A refusal by a shareholder to assume personal liability when requested to do so presents the strongest case against judicial imposition of that liability, since when the parties themselves are apportioning the risk of loss through their relative bargaining power, there is no reason for a court to disturb that allocation. There are some contract cases, however, in which inadequate capitalization should result in the shareholders being held personally responsible. If the shareholder misleads a third person regarding the financial status of the corporations so that the third person believes the corporation has more capital than it actually has, then the element of voluntary risk allocation disappears, and shareholder liability should be imposed. Depending on the nature of the misrepresentation, the person making the representation may also be independently liable for fraud or deceit, though many cases exist in which the shell corporation was substituted—without overt misrepresentation—at the last minute. Mere silence or an oral promise by a shareholder to guarantee the payment of the corporation's debt, which itself is unenforceable under the statute of frauds, should not normally be grounds for piercing the corporate veil.

There may also be other contract situations in which inadequate capitalization may lead to the separate existence of a corporation being ignored. Perhaps a person might be tricked into dealing with the corporation. Situations involving manifest unfairness arising from unequal bargaining power not reaching the level of unconscionability may also be envisioned. These situations gradually shade over into those involving duress, coercion, or other independent grounds for setting aside a contract.

There is also the possibility in contract cases that the subsequent operation of the corporation may be unfair to creditors. The controlling shareholder, for example, may engage in a series of self-dealing transactions that result in most of the assets of the corporation being transferred to his or her personal accounts and the balance being insufficient to pay trade creditors. Such transactions may in fact involve fraud on creditors, but in close cases courts may prefer to analyze the situation in terms of piercing the corporate veil rather than fraudulent transfers or fraud on creditors. Since these cases involve shareholder enrichment at the expense of creditors, it is not surprising that judicial rhetoric in such cases is strong.

In tort cases there is usually no element of prior dealing between the corporation and the plaintiff. As a result, inadequate capitalization is usually given considerable importance in determining whether shareholders should be held liable for the tort liabilities of the corporation, though not all cases are in agreement. The underlying policy argument was stated earlier: an inadequately capitalized corporation in a risky business in effect transfers the risk of loss to innocent members of the general public. While the corporation need not be capitalized to ensure that all conceivable liabilities will be discharged, a corporation should be reasonably capitalized in light of the nature and risks of the business. This argument was accepted in the leading California case of Minton v. Cavaney (1961), and traces of it appear in opinions in several other jurisdictions. Minton v. Cavaney, like many other cases in this area, also involved another factor: a failure to complete the formation of the corporation, and the court may have been partially influenced by that factor as well.

A further powerful policy argument may be made in tort cases if the corporate affairs are not conducted in a reasonable manner in the light of business risks. If assets that might be used for the purchase of insurance or retained in the business to increase the creditor's cushion are siphoned off through dividends, salaries or similar payments, the risk of shareholder liability is increased. Corporate affairs should not be conducted so as to minimize the assets available for tort claimants. The bounds of this rather appealing policy argument are totally undefined, and as a result it seldom appears in court opinions. Indeed, it was apparently rejected in the majority opinion in another leading New York case, Walkovszky v. Carlton (1966). Its influence, however, should not be underestimated: courts are much more likely to "pierce the corporate veil" and hold shareholders liable in tort cases when the elements of marginal capitalization and systematic dispersal of assets are combined. Conversely adequate capitalization and clear evidence that the corporation "did the best it could" are likely to protect shareholders against tort claims based on the corporation's acts.

The taxicab industry has been an important source of new cases concerning shareholder responsibility for tort liabilities of the corporation. Particularly in New York City the practice has developed of separately incorporating one or two taxicabs in a large fleet and establishing a separate corporation to operate the central garage, and perhaps yet another corporation to run the dispatching service. Each operating taxicab company has the minimum required capitalization (usually invested in the taxicab itself) and carries the minimum insurance required by state law. The drivers themselves are usually judgment proof, so that seriously injured victims of taxicab accidents go largely uncompensated unless they can look to the assets of the shareholders. The theory of "enterprise entity" discussed in section 6.6 of this Nutshell dictates that the separate existence of each minimally capitalized taxicab corporation should be ignored and the entire fleet of taxicabs treated as a single entity; the more difficult question is whether a claim may also be made against the shareholders individually. In Walkovszky v. Carlton, the New York Court refused to hold the shareholder liable in the absence of allegations that he or she was conducting business in his or her individual capacity, and "shuttling * * * personal funds in and out of the corporations 'without regard to formality and to suit their immediate convenience.'" However, after the complaint was amended to make this specific allegation, it was upheld on a motion to dismiss; the case was thereafter settled. The reluctance of the defendants to go to a jury in cases of this character is understandable; most of the litigation arises on a motion to dismiss, and the cases are settled if the complaint survives that motion.

§ 6.4   Shareholder Responsibility for Corporate Indebtedness: Failure to Follow Corporate Formalities

Anyone reading cases dealing with shareholder liability for corporate obligations is struck by the emphasis placed by the courts on the failure to follow the requisite corporate formalities as a ground for imposing shareholder liability in both contract and tort cases. In many opinions, the court describes the failure to follow normal corporate routine and then concludes that the corporation is the "alter ego" or "instrumentality" of the shareholder or that the "corporate veil should be pierced." While a complete catalogue of dangerous acts is probably impossible to prepare, there appears to be a substantial risk that the separate corporate existence will be ignored when business is commenced without completing the organization of the corporation or without issuing shares and receiving the consideration therefor, when shareholders' meetings or directors' meetings are not held (or consents are not signed), when decisions are made by shareholders as though they were partners, when shareholders do not sharply distinguish between corporate property and personal property, when corporate funds are used to pay personal expenses, when personal funds are used for corporate expenses without proper accounting, or when complete corporate and financial records are not maintained.

It is difficult to see, as a matter of logic, why corporate confusion and informality have been given the importance that they have. In most case, the confusion and informality are not related to the claim advanced by either tort or contract plaintiffs. As a matter of fact, evidence of informality or commingling of affairs is first found long after the transaction giving rise to the particular litigation took place. To hold shareholders personally liable because of activities which are almost always unrelated to the plaintiff's claim, creates a windfall. For this reason, some courts have refused to "pierce the corporate veil" despite considerable evidence of confusion. One possible explanation for "piercing the corporate veil" in these cases is that the shareholder should not be permitted first to ignore the rules of corporate behavior and then later to claim the advantage of the corporate shield. In the absence of harm to anyone or to the state, however, it is difficult to see why the premise should lead to the conclusion.

The importance given to corporate formalities as the test for determining whether the corporation's separate existence will be recognized tends to create a trap for unwary shareholders in closely held corporations. Shareholders in a small corporation often find managing the business a full-time occupation; formal corporate affairs such as meetings and the like are put off or ignored because there is full agreement in fact by all interested parties regarding what should be done and who should do it. The play-acting aspects of corporate meetings, elections, and the like in a closely held corporation may also strike businessmen as rather silly. Insistence by an attorney that formal corporate procedures be followed may be dismissed as a subtle attempt at an additional fee. This attitude invites disaster.

When failure to follow appropriate corporate procedures tends to injure third persons, there is little objection to holding the shareholder liable. Procedures within the corporation may be so undifferentiated that a person may believe he or she is dealing with a shareholder individually rather than with the corporation. Similarly, intermingled personal and corporate assets may disappear into the personal coffers of the shareholder to the detriment of corporate creditors. These factors, however, are present in only a small minority of the confusion cases.

§ 6.5   Shareholder Responsibility for Corporate Indebtedness: Parent–Subsidiary Cases

Many cases in which shareholder liability has been found concern shareholders that are themselves corporations. In these cases, a parent corporation is being held liable for the debts of a subsidiary. They have a different flavor than cases in which the shareholder defendant is an individual, and some cases even suggest that different tests are being applied depending on whether the shareholder-defendant is an individual or a corporation. When a corporation is the defendant, only a larger corporate entity is being held responsible for the debt; when an individual is the defendant, however, personal liability extending to non-business assets is being imposed. On the other hand, many corporations create subsidiary corporations for the specific purpose of limiting their liability in connection with risky new businesses; if the judicial system is too generous in piercing the corporate veil in parent-subsidiary cases, desirable entrepreneurial conduct may be discouraged, or may not occur at all. Whatever the merits of these policy arguments, courts are likely to find the parent business entity liable under the following circumstances:

(a) When the subsidiary is being operated in an "unfair manner," e.g., the terms of transactions between parent and subsidiary are set so that profits accumulate in the parent and losses in the subsidiary;

(b) When the subsidiary is consistently represented as being a part of the parent, e.g., as a "division" or "local office" rather than as a subsidiary;

(c) When the separate corporate formalities of the subsidiary are not followed;

(d) When the subsidiary and parent are operating essentially parts of the same business, and the subsidiary is under capitalized; or

(e) When there is no consistent clear delineation of which transactions are the parent's and which are the subsidiary's.

The lack of a consistent clear delineation between the parent's affairs and the subsidiary's affairs is often virtually determinative of liability. These cases may phrase the test in terms of agency. Often the individual acting for the subsidiary is also an agent of the parent; unless the "hat" he or she is wearing is clear, the argument may be made that he or she was actually acting on behalf of the parent rather than the subsidiary or on behalf of both. Thus the probability of parental liability increases significantly when there are close relationships, informality of operation, and overlapping of personnel employed by the corporations.

Of course, in some cases the failure to delineate between operations of the parent and the subsidiary may actually mislead third persons into believing they are dealing with the parent corporate entity. Most cases, however, impose liability whenever intermingling is present on a wide scale without inquiring whether the plaintiff was actually misled. As a result it is important in every "family" of corporations to maintain the maximum possible degree of separation. In most such families the ties are inherently very close: for example, the parent owns all the shares of the subsidiaries, they have common officers, they have common auditors or attorneys, they file consolidated returns for federal income tax purposes, they share common suites of offices in the same building, and they report their income on a consolidated basis. These close ties are basically consistent with the separate existence of the subsidiary; what creates problems are carelessness and casualness, such as transactions between parent and subsidiary that are not adequately documented, common officers and directors who do not specify on whose behalf an action is taken, the failure to maintain independent books and records for each corporation, and the failure of the parent to recognize that the subsidiary is theoretically an independent entity, e.g. by the board of directors of the parent making detailed decisions on behalf of one or more subsidiaries when in theory the decisions should have been made by the board of directors of the subsidiary.

Intermingling of assets is particularly dangerous. Separate accounts may be maintained, but informal transfers or "loans" may be made from time to time to meet the day-to-day needs of the business. Such conduct increases the risk of parental liability. If funds owned by the parent are needed by the subsidiary, the proper procedure is to establish a formal loan, preferably using a promissory note, and then to transfer the funds to the subsidiary's bank account. The corporate books of both parent and subsidiary then reflect the transaction accurately and the risk that the intermingling of assets will result in the two corporations being treated as one is reduced. Many parent corporations have established centralized cash management plans for their subsidiaries: each subsidiary is required to transfer excess cash on a daily basis to a central account managed by the parent where it may be invested, and each subsidiary may draw on this account on a daily basis as needed for its operations. If the cash management plan is properly approved and accurate records of all transfers of cash in both directions are kept, these plans should not be viewed as involving the kind of intermingling that gives rise to potential liability.

§ 6.6 The Concept of "Enterprise Entity"

"Enterprise entity" refers to the economic unity that is a single business enterprise. Courts are suspicious of attempts to divide a single economic enterprise among several different corporations with the intention of minimizing the assets subject to claims of creditors of each enterprise. Perhaps this is because it is not "playing fair" with creditors who may believe that the entire enterprise is a single unit; in any event, courts may well put the enterprise back together despite the shareholders' attempt to segregate it into separate corporate entities. In this kind of case, a "brother-sister" corporate relationship may be ignored as readily as a parent-subsidiary relationship.

Many large corporations are conglomerates consisting of several essentially discrete and independent businesses. The concept of enterprise entity does not apply to these operations. What is dangerous is taking a single business and separately incorporating its component operations. Of course, if one or more independent businesses are conducted as divisions of the parent corporation and are not separately incorporated, the parent is liable for the debts of those divisions.

§ 6.7   Choice of Law Issues in "Piercing the Corporate Veil" Cases

Until about 1980, the law of "piercing the corporate veil" appeared to be independent of the state in which the case arose. Courts resolving piercing cases freely cited cases from other jurisdictions without inquiry into whether different states were more or less liberal in imposing, or had different rules about, shareholder liability for corporate obligations. Indeed, the tests and rhetoric used by courts were so vague and amorphous that differences in formulation, even if they had existed, would have had little or no effect on the results reached. Thus, in the few cases in which courts did discuss whether the law of the state of incorporation, or the law of the state in which the activities giving rise to the claim on which shareholder liability was sought, should apply, a definitive resolution of this conflicts issue was found to be unnecessary.

As litigation in this area has continued to grow, however, different state policies or philosophies with respect to the imposition of shareholder liability have appeared. Some states now seem clearly to be more "liberal" than others in imposing such liability; some states have accepted the distinction between tort and contract cases suggested above, while others apparently have not. Texas has partially codified its law of piercing the corporate veil by enacting a statute that provides that in contract cases "actual fraud" is required for the imposition of liability, and failure to follow corporate formalities or procedures is not ground for imposing such liability. The development of such identifiably different principles by specific states means that the conflicts of law issue must be addressed.

Many corporations are of course incorporated in Delaware or other states of convenience and conduct their business primarily or entirely in other states. An argument may be made that the law of the state of incorporation should apply under the generally accepted rule that "internal affairs" of corporations should be governed by the law of the state of incorporation. The scope of shareholder liability for corporate obligations plausibly may be described as involving "internal affairs." On the other hand, there is a strong policy in favor of applying the law of the state with the most significant contacts with the litigation, particularly in torts cases. Consider, for example, a Delaware corporation that is wholly owned by Illinois residents; the corporation's entire business is conducted in Illinois, and a resident of Illinois is injured because of the negligence of the agents of the corporation. Certainly a strong policy argument may be made that the Illinois law of "piercing" rather than the Delaware law should be applied in such a case since all the important contacts are with Illinois and not with Delaware. The Delaware position with respect to "veil piercing" has been described as very conservative, though there is relatively little case law in that small state. If this turns out to be true, and Illinois law would permit "piercing" under the circumstances, it is unlikely that an Illinois court would deprive an Illinois resident of a remedy against another Illinois resident merely because of the Delaware corporation law. In a few cases of this type that have arisen, the court has simply applied local law without considering the possible application of the law of the state of incorporation, but the entire matter cannot be said to be free from doubt at the time this is written.

§ 6.8 The Federal Law of "Piercing the Corporate Veil"

An issue that is related to the choice of law issue discussed in section 6.7 is whether there is a federal law of piercing the corporate veil that is applicable in suits in which the United States is a party.

Clearfield Trust Co. v. United States (1943), held that federal law should govern questions involving the rights of the United States arising from nationwide federal programs. Acting under this general principle, federal courts have held, for example, that in a suit to recover overpayments from a provider of services under the Medicare Program, a federal law of piercing the corporate veil should be fashioned to determine whether shareholders of the provider are personally liable for such overpayments. Other cases agree with this general approach. In fashioning the federal law in this area, courts have generally relied on piercing cases that were in the federal courts because of diversity of citizenship. As a result, the federal law of "piercing" probably does not differ significantly from state law in most respects.

Mention should also be made of the Comprehensive Environmental Response, Compensation and Liability Act (CERCLA). This statute imposes broad responsibility for cleaning up toxic waste sites on both the "owner" and the "operator" of the site. Several cases arising under this statute have held that a controlling shareholder who manages the affairs of a subsidiary may have CERCLA liability as an "operator" of a site owned and operated by a subsidiary. Cases have also applied the Clearfield principle to develop a federal law of piercing the corporate veil in CERCLA cases that results in the parent being liable as an "owner" because its subsidiary owned the property. Either theory normally results in substantial environmental clean up responsibilities being imposed on the parent corporation. The scope of these alternative theories is still being developed by the federal courts.

§ 6.9   "Piercing the Corporate Veil" to Further Public Policy

Yet another type of piercing the corporate veil case involves the claim that a separate corporate existence should not be recognized because to do so would violate a clearly defined statutory policy.

To take an illustrative case, the statutes of several states prohibit branch banking. In other words in these states a banking corporation must stick to a single location and cannot open branches around the state. Accepting this statutory policy, may a banking corporation own the voting stock of another bank? Or, may a single holding corporation own a majority of, or all, the voting stock of several banks? Answers to questions such as these must be based on an evaluation of the strength of the state policy against branch banking rather than on policies underlying the separate existence of corporations. If the policy is a strong one, the recognition of a separate corporate existence may provide an unacceptable method of circumvention, and the separate corporate fiction must yield to the state policy. On the other hand, if the policy against branch banking does not appear to be a strong one, there is no reason for courts to find a fundamental conflict between the statute and the corporate form and hold invalid relationships that conform with the notion of separate corporate existence.

Public policy is also the critical question in the series of cases involving family corporations organized to obtain social security or unemployment benefits for owners who would not be eligible for such benefits if the business had continued to be conducted in noncorporate form. Several federal decisions have held that social security benefits may not be denied to a person who "incorporates" his or her business assets for the sole purpose of qualifying for the benefits, but decisions at the state level concerning temporary disability insurance, workmen's compensation, and unemployment compensation, are split. A clearer example involves the unemployment compensation statutes which provide for an exemption from the tax for employers having fewer than some designated number of employees, e.g., four. May a single business be divided into several separate corporate units each employing less than the statutory minimum to obtain the exemption for each? Courts have held, not surprisingly, that the state unemployment commissions may disregard the separate corporations, treat the business as a single unit, and impose the tax on it.

Generalization is difficult in such cases. Sometimes, assistance may be gained from statutory language that indicates that the policy should be applied to "direct or indirect" relationships. Nevertheless, delicate judgments are required in these cases, for the policies underlying regulatory statutes must be weighed against the policies supporting the concept of the corporate entity.

§ 6.10 "Piercing the Corporate Veil" in Taxation and Bankruptcy

Given the broad social and governmental policies involved in the federal income tax laws and the federal bankruptcy act, it is understandable that specialized tests have also evolved under these statutes for determining when the separate corporate existence will be disregarded.

Under the Internal Revenue Code of 1954 there is a need to preserve tax revenue and to be able to set aside fictional transactions which have as their sole purpose the minimization of taxes. A corporation's separate existence generally will be recognized for tax purposes if it is in fact carrying on a bona fide business and is not merely a device created for the purpose of avoiding taxes. The taxpayer, however, must accept any tax disadvantages of the corporate form if he or she has elected to choose that form. Further, even if the corporate form is adopted and carefully followed, the Commissioner has broad powers to disallow deductions or exemptions, or reallocate items of income to clearly reflect income.

Entirely different policies are involved in the bankruptcy area. Bankruptcy courts have considerable flexibility in dealing with controlling or dominant shareholders of bankrupt corporations. The bankruptcy court may:

(1) "Disregard the corporate entity" and hold the shareholder personally liable for the corporation's debts if the shareholder's conduct is within the rather vague tests of piercing the corporate veil. The effect of this conclusion is that the controlling shareholder may be responsible for all corporate obligations; all payments made by the corporation to the shareholder before bankruptcy may also be recovered by the trustee since essentially the corporation and shareholder are treated as a single unit.

(2) Refuse to recognize claims by shareholders against the corporation as bona fide debts provable in bankruptcy. If the claim is based on services or intangible benefits provided to the corporation, the claim may be disallowed in its entirety as fictitious or "not proved." If it involves infusions of capital or tangible property, the bankruptcy court may consider them as contributions to capital rather

than as a debt. This treatment of shareholder debt is usually limited to loans made at or shortly after the formation of the corporation when the corporation is inadequately or thinly capitalized, and simply reflects that what in fact is equity capital may have to be treated as equity capital in bankruptcy proceedings. A number of decisions follow this approach and there are analogous holdings in the tax field. Yet the application of this principle is elusive: there is no easy way to determine when a corporation is in fact under capitalized, and while most courts have treated the issue on an "all or none" basis and reclassified all the debt as equity, it is arguable that it should reclassify only that portion necessary to make the capitalization adequate. As a general test, where the corporation enters into a new business with sufficient capital so that it can borrow the balance of the needed capital from a bank or other independent source of funds, the original capitalization for that business is deemed "adequate"; if the shareholder rather than the third party makes the loan under such circumstances, that transaction should be accepted by the bankruptcy court as a bona fide loan.

(3) Under the "Deep Rock" doctrine—so named from the Deep Rock Oil Corp., the subsidiary involved in the leading case of Taylor v. Standard Gas & Electric Co. (1939)—the court may subordinate claims presented by controlling shareholders to the claims of other creditors or preferred shareholders on the ground that the shareholder acted inequitably or unfairly. Examples of inequitable claims include taking unreasonable amounts as salary, manipulation of the affairs of the corporation in disregard of standards of honesty, or selling assets to the corporation at inflated prices. The type of conduct that will result in subordination under the Deep Rock doctrine can only be stated in general terms: the doctrine is based on general principles of equity and fair dealing. It is not necessary to show that the indebtedness was a sham or fiction, since

technically what is involved is the order of payment of debts rather than total rejection of the claim. The theory is that a person who has acted unfairly in his or her management of the corporation should step aside so that other creditors may be first satisfied. Of course, usually the assets of the bankrupt estate are inadequate to satisfy all claims and subordination therefore results in the shareholder receiving nothing on his or her claim. Despite this underlying theory, in at least one case the Deep Rock doctrine was applied when the controversy was between innocent creditors of the bankrupt subsidiary and the equally innocent creditors of the bankrupt parent.

The type of conduct that triggers these doctrines differs only in degree rather than kind. In a sense these are alternative weapons in the bankruptcy court's arsenal.

§ 6.11 Other Generalizations About "Piercing the Corporate Veil"

Three final observations should be made about the confusing and result-oriented doctrines discussed in this chapter. First, there is no inherent reason to assume that ignoring the separate corporate existence must be an all-or-nothing affair. Particularly if the dominant question does not involve public statutory policies but merely liability for corporate obligations, a corporation may be viewed as existing for some purposes but not for others. There is some case authority, for example, for piercing the corporate veil to hold shareholders active in the business personally liable, but recognizing the same corporation's separate existence to protect passive investors from the same liabilities. Second, there is a strong judicial feeling that when a person elects to do business in corporate form he or she must take the bitter with the sweet, and cannot later argue that the separate corporate existence should be ignored when it is to his or her benefit. The doctrine of piercing the corporate veil, in other words, is not available for the benefit of shareholders, but only against shareholders. This view is particularly strongly developed in the tax cases. Finally, where the considerations are not strongly weighted one way or the other, a presumption of separate existence of the corporation should be respected. The fiction of separate corporate existence, in other words, should be the rule not the exception.

[For unfamiliar terms see the Glossary]

CHAPTER SEVEN

FINANCING THE CORPORATION

§ 7.1 Introduction

Perhaps no other area of corporation law is more confusing to law students without prior business backgrounds than corporate securities such as shares of stock, bonds and debentures. The language is new and unfamiliar, the concepts seem mysterious and sometimes illogical, and everything seems to build on historical concepts of dubious relevance today.

While this has been traditionally true, in the 1990s new winds are blowing through the area of corporation finance. The Revised Model Business Corporation Act and the statutes of about twenty states have eliminated the historic concept of par value and have developed new and simplified rules relating to the issuance of stock. These states have also adopted new rules relating to the validity of distributions. The advantages of this new approach are so obvious that it is likely that ultimately all states will abandon the older historical concepts. However, for the foreseeable future, a significant number of states, and attorneys practicing in them, must cope with the historical rules.

The basic purposes of this chapter are to dispel the mystery of the older historical statutes and introduce the modern approach by describing the provisions of the Revised Model Business Corporation Act. The discussion of the older statutes proceeds one simple step at a time. It begins with the issuance of shares of common stock by a newly formed corporation. It then briefly considers other classes of stock that corporations may issue, the use of borrowed capital—that is, debt—as a substitute for contributed capital, and finally, the issuance and reacquisition of shares of stock by an ongoing corporation. Reserved for a later chapter are issues related to the payment of dividends and the making of other distributions to shareholders (Chapter 16 of this Nutshell).

§ 7.2 Basic Definitions: Common Stock; Authorized and Issued Shares

Shares of common stock are the fundamental units into which the proprietary interest of the corporation is divided. If a corporation issues only one class of shares, they may be referred to by a variety of similar names: common shares, capital stock, common stock, or, possibly, simply shares or stock. Whatever the name, they are the basic proprietary units of ownership and are referred to here as simply common stock.

Section 6.01(b) of the RMBCA defines the two fundamental characteristics of common stock: they are entitled to vote for the election of directors and on other matters coming before the shareholders and they are entitled to the net assets of the corporation (after making allowance for debts and senior securities) when distributions are to be made, either during the course of the life of the corporation or upon its dissolution. One important innovation of the RMBCA is that it permits these two fundamental characteristics to be divided or split between different classes of stock (so there may not be a single class that has both of these residual characteristics and, therefore, no class of stock that is unambiguously common stock), but section 6.03(b) requires that at least one share of each class with these basic attributes must be outstanding.

Assuming that a new corporation is going to have only a single class of shares, the articles of incorporation must state the number of shares of common stock the corporation is

authorized to issue. This number is known, not surprisingly, as the corporation's "authorized capital" or "authorized
stock." In states with older statutes, the articles of incorporation must also set forth the "par value" of the authorized
shares or a statement that the shares are "without par
value." The limited significance of "par value" is discussed
in the following sections. There is no limitation on the
number of shares that may be authorized and no requirement that all or any specific fraction of the authorized shares
be actually issued. Why, then, doesn't every corporation
authorize millions and millions of shares? In many states
there are practical constraints. Some states impose franchise
or stock taxes on the basis of authorized shares; in these
states to authorize many more shares than there is an
intention to issue simply increases taxes with no offsetting
benefit. Also, authorizing a large number of shares may
create concern on the part of investors since authorized
shares may be later issued merely by the board of directors
without shareholder approval. On the other hand, it is
generally believed desirable to authorize some additional
shares over and above what is presently planned to be issued
for unexpected contingencies and to avoid the need for
amending articles of incorporation if more capital is later
needed.

The capitalization of a corporation is based on the number
of shares actually issued and the capital received therefor,
not on the number of authorized shares. Capital received in
exchange for issued shares is usually referred to as the
corporation's invested capital (or sometimes its "contributed" capital) and is viewed as being invested in the corporation permanently or indefinitely.

§ 7.3 The Price of Common Shares

Let us assume that a new corporation is authorized to
issue 1,000 shares of common stock and it has been agreed

that the two investors, A and B, will each contribute $5,000 for 50 percent of the stock. How many shares should be issued and for what price?

Within a broad range, the number of shares and price per share in such a situation can be set at any level. For example A and B might purchase one share each for $5,000, or 10 shares each for $500 per share, or 100 shares each for $50 per share. It is important, of course, that A and B each pay the same amount for each share and receive the same number of shares; however, as between themselves it makes no difference what that amount is per share. It would be undesirable, however, to issue 500 shares each at $10 per share, since that would exhaust the entire authorized capital and would require an amendment to the articles of incorporation if more capital was needed at a later date.

In this simple example it was assumed that the two shareholders had agreed in advance as to how much would be contributed by each investor. That is often true in the case of a start up business. In the case of an ongoing business that decides that it needs additional capital to be obtained by the issuance of more stock, negotiation will usually be necessary. This negotiation will often be between corporate officers or directors, on one side, and potential investors, on the other. If the price is set too high, the new investor pays more than the proportionate interest he or she is obtaining is worth; if it is set too low, the interest of the current shareholders is being diluted and the new investor is obtaining a bargain. Usually the price that yields total fairness between the old and the new is uncertain or subjective so that any price agreed upon by arms-length negotiation should be acceptable. Problems may arise, however, if the contributor of the new capital is already a shareholder, officer or director of the corporation.

Usually the board of directors of the corporation determines the price at which new shares are to be issued (subject of course to the willingness of potential investors to pay this price). See RMBCA § 6.21(b). State statutes, however, authorize the shareholders to reserve this power to themselves by appropriate provision in the articles of incorporation. See RMBCA § 6.21(a). As a practical matter, it is unusual for the shareholders to reserve this power to themselves; the board of directors typically sets the price at which shares are to be issued.

If only common sense were involved, the pricing of common shares would end at this point. However, the par value statutes in effect in most states impose an elaborate system of rules relating to the issuance of common shares which have substantive as well as accounting implications for this apparently simple transaction. These rules dealing with par value are the subject of the following four sections.

§ 7.4 Par Value, Stated Capital and Related Concepts

Older state statutes assume that shares will have a "par value" or "stated value" (which is the same thing). The possibility that a corporation may issue "no par" shares or shares "without par value" should be put to one side for the moment since in most states the treatment of such shares is based on the treatment of par value shares. Par value of a share of common stock is simply the dollar amount designated as par value by the draftsman of the articles of incorporation. It may be one mill, one cent, one dollar, ten dollars, whatever the draftsman designates. The par value designation is made in the articles of incorporation as part of the description of the authorized capital, e.g. "The number of shares the corporation is authorized to issue is 1,000 shares of common stock with the par value of $1.00 per share;" the share certificates then describe the stock represented by the certificate as involving both "common shares" and a "$1.00 par value," both usually in large and conspicuous type.

At one time par value had considerable importance because it was widely viewed as the amount for which the shares would be issued: shares with a par value of one hundred dollars could be subscribed for at one hundred dollars per share with confidence that all other identical shares would also be issued for $100. This practice, however, long ago fell into disuse. Today, par value serves only a minor function and is in no way an indication of the price at which the shares are issued, with this one exception: The one basic rule about setting the price for shares of common stock with a par value is that the price must be equal to or greater than par value. If this rule is violated and shares are issued for less than par value, the recipient shareholder in most states is automatically liable to the corporation for the difference. This liability is usually called a "watered stock" liability and is discussed in greater detail in § 7.7 of this Nutshell. In par value states today, most attorneys use "nominal par value," in which a low (or "nominal") par value is set but the shares are issued for a significantly higher price. For example, shares with a par value of ten cents per share may be issued for $10.00 or $50.00 per share. In such states, "no par" shares may be used but they have not attained the nearly universal acceptance of nominal par value shares. For several reasons the current practice in states with par value statutes runs strongly in the direction of using a "nominal" par value.

Several factors caused the gradual movement away from par value as a representation of the purchase price of shares and the development of nominal par value shares. One factor was the loss of flexibility of pricing shares. When a secondary market for shares develops, a corporation raising capital by selling shares with a par value of $100 for $100 per share competes with that market and would have to stop selling shares if the market price of the previously-issued shares dropped below $100 per share. At that point potential investors could get a better price in the secondary market than they could from the corporation which was locked into the $100 price by the par value. A second factor was the federal documentary stamp tax on issuance of corporate securities (since repealed) which, until 1958, was based on the par or stated value rather than actual value. A nominal par value thus reduced taxes. Similarly, state franchise and stock transfer taxes also were (and to a limited extent still are) based on par or stated value; in these states a low par value reduces the corporation's tax liability. Another factor arose in the situation where property of uncertain value was being contributed; if high par value shares are given in exchange for such property, arguments may later arise that the property was not worth the par value of the shares received and the recipients might be sued for the difference on the theory that they had received watered stock. These various reasons provide adequate practical justification for abandoning high par value shares in every instance. Further, there is very little to be gained from using high par value shares; the principal advantages are possible benefits to the corporation because psychologically investors or creditors may feel more secure dealing with a corporation with a high par value stock. Such an advantage is not very persuasive, however, since there is no reason to believe that investors or creditors pay any attention to par value one way or the other. In any event there has been a virtually universal shift away from the use of high par value shares.

Par value serves an important function in addition to establishing a price floor below which shares may not be issued: it is an essential ingredient in determining the capital accounts of the corporation. In this and the following sections, the terminology of the 1969 Model Business Corporation Act will be followed. While not all states with par value statutes use this terminology, most states do (and those that do not embody similar concepts). In this terminology, par value is an essential ingredient in determining the "stated capital" and "capital surplus" of the corporation.

In order to understand "stated capital" and "capital surplus" and the issues that evolve from them, a brief excursion into fundamental accounting concepts is useful. The basic syllogism or truism on which financial statements are based is that *net worth* equals *assets* minus *liabilities*. That syllogism is obviously true for an individual such as you or me; it is equally applicable to a corporation that is treated as an entity or fictitious person. By simple arithmetical manipulation of the basic syllogism, assets also equal liabilities plus net worth. This is the formula used in a "balance sheet" where one side of the equation is placed on the left side and the balance on the right side of a ledger.

Assets	Liabilities
	+
	Net Worth

A balance sheet balances because it is simply a restatement of the basic equation.

Let us examine a balance sheet for a new corporation immediately after it has sold 100 shares of stock for 1,000 dollars in cash. The balance sheet shows:

Assets		Liabilities	-0-
Cash	$ 1,000	Net Worth	
	———	Common Stock	$ 1,000
	$ 1,000		$ 1,000

The concepts of stated capital and capital surplus relate to how the common stock item is shown on the right hand side of the balance sheet. Stated capital is defined to be the aggregate par value of all issued shares (plus or minus certain adjustments not relevant for present purposes) while capital surplus is defined to be the excess (if any) of capital contributed over the par value. Thus, if in our hypothetical the 100 shares of common stock had a par value of $1 per share and were sold at $10.00 per share the balance sheet would be as follows:

Assets		Liabilities	-0-
Cash	$ 1,000	Capital Accounts	
		Stated Capital	$ 100
		Capital Surplus	$ 900
	$ 1,000		$ 1,000

In this balance sheet, the phrase "capital accounts" has been substituted for "net worth" to somewhat more closely reflect accounting terminology used in the old Model Business Corporation Act, but its meaning is the same.

Under par value statutes, there is no requirement that any specific minimum amount be put in in the form of stated capital; even states that establish a minimum capitalization of $1,000 (or some other amount) require only an aggregate capital of the specified amount without differentiating between how much is stated capital and how much is capital surplus. Thus, in these states, it is theoretically possible to create a corporation with $0.01 of stated capital and $999.99 of capital surplus.

Now, a logical question that may be asked is what difference does it make if the capital contribution is recorded as stated capital or capital surplus. Rather surprisingly it does make a difference, which can best be appreciated if we first draw up a balance sheet after the corporation (1) has borrowed $1,000 from a bank and (2) has had two years of operations during which it has earned and accumulated an aggregate of $2,000 over-and-above all costs, taxes, etc. Further, for simplicity we will continue to assume that all of

the assets are held by the corporation in the form of cash.
The balance sheet looks like this:

Assets		Liabilities	$ 1,000
Cash	$ 4,000	Capital Accounts	
		Earned Surplus	$ 2,000
		Stated Capital	100
		Capital Surplus	900
	$ 4,000		$ 4,000

At this point the shareholders decide they want to distribute
to themselves some or all of the $4,000. If the balance
sheet is to continue to balance, every dollar taken from the
left-hand column must obviously be reflected by the reduction of a right-hand column entry. The right-hand entries
thus in effect limit or monitor the distribution of assets from
the left-hand column. For example, as described in a later
chapter, under the 1969 Model Act dividends may be
lawfully paid, "out of" earned surplus. This means that
amounts may be paid from the cash of the corporation as
dividends up to the maximum amount shown in the right-
hand column under "earned surplus," or $2,000 in the
above example. Of course, a dividend of, say, $500 paid
out of earned surplus would in the above example result in
the reduction of cash by $500 to $3500, offset by a reduction of earned surplus to $1,500, and the balance sheet will
still balance.

Under most state statutes based on the old Model Business Corporation Act, corporations have greater freedom to
make distributions from capital surplus than from stated
capital. In most states stated capital is "locked in" the
corporation and cannot be distributed except upon the
liquidation of the corporation; however, assets may be
distributed to the extent of capital surplus simply with the
approval of the holders of a specified fraction of the com-

mon shares. Such a distribution is not a dividend in the normal sense of the word but is called by various names, e.g., "liquidating dividend," "distribution in partial liquidation," or the like. (See § 16.1 of this Nutshell.) Also under these statutes, capital surplus but not stated capital may be used to repurchase or redeem outstanding shares previously issued by the corporation. (See § 16.6 of this Nutshell.)

If all the capital is put in the form of stated capital (i.e. the par value of the issued shares equals the consideration received) all the capital is "locked in;" if the bulk of the capital contributed is recorded as capital surplus rather than stated capital there is greater flexibility to distribute unneeded capital to shareholders or reacquire outstanding shares at a later date. In other words, there is greater flexibility in a corporation with this balance sheet:

Cash	$ 1,000	Liabilities		-0-
		Capital Accounts		
		Stated Capital	$	100
		Capital Surplus		900
	1,000			1,000

than there is in a corporation with this balance sheet:

Cash	$ 1,000	Liabilities		-0-
		Capital Accounts		
		Stated Capital	$	1,000
		Capital Surplus		-0-
	1,000			1,000

From the standpoint of the corporation such flexibility is a mildly positive feature and is an additional reason for the wide-spread use of nominal par value which leads to low stated capital and high capital surplus. Of course, a bank that lends money to a corporation might be unhappy if large amounts of capital surplus are available for distribution to shareholders since theoretically the capital of the corporation forms a "cushion" for the creditor and increases the possibility that the corporation will have the liquid assets to repay the loan when it comes due. Lenders, however, do not rely on the corporation statutes for protection against unwise distribution policies; they usually insist on contractual restrictions on the otherwise virtually complete freedom of corporations to distribute their assets. (See § 16.7 of this Nutshell.) Such restrictions are required so routinely by most lenders that they have almost totally replaced the corporation statutes as the operative restriction on the freedom of corporations to distribute their capital to their shareholders.

§ 7.5 No Par Shares

In the early period of corporate history, corporations were only permitted to issue shares with par value. No par shares are a relatively recent wrinkle, first permitted in New York in about 1915, and the rules relating to such shares were developed in the context of the established rules for accounting for par value shares. Obviously, the consideration for which no par shares are issued may be set without any reference to a minimum imposed by a par value. However, the capital received must still be allocated between stated capital and capital surplus. When no par shares are issued under most state statutes based on the old Model Business Corporation Act, the entire consideration fixed by the corporation for the shares constitutes stated capital. However, statutes generally permit the directors to allocate some portion or all of the consideration to capital surplus. Before 1969, the old Model Business Corporation

Act limited this power to 25 per cent of the consideration received, and a few states still retain this restriction. Such a restriction on creating capital surplus obviously reduces the attractiveness of no par shares to some extent. However, most states today permit allocation of "any part" of the consideration received for no par shares to either stated capital or capital surplus. Apparently under such a provision it is possible to create a corporation with as little stated capital using no par shares as with nominal par value shares.

For many years no par shares suffered from a tax disadvantage in that federal stamp taxes were computed on no par shares based on the issue price while par value shares were valued at par value for tax purposes. Where this valuation structure is in effect (and it continues to be in effect in some states) nominal par value shares obviously continue to offer a tax saving over no par shares. Perhaps this historical pragmatic reason explains why no par shares have never become the dominant practice. No par shares are also sometimes created where it is contemplated that the shares will be issued for property or for services which may be difficult to value. For the reasons discussed in the following two sections, it is unlikely that no par shares provide any real advantage over nominal par shares in this regard.

State statutes provide that the board of directors has the power to fix the consideration for which no par shares are issued but the articles of incorporation may expressly reserve this power to the shareholders. This option was originally based on the long since discredited idea that par value ensures equality of shareholders while no par shares do not. In the modern context, the option for shareholders to set the issuance price of no par shares does not differ in any significant way from the similar election that is available with respect to nominal par value shares. It is doubtful if either is ever elected today.

§ 7.6 Shares Issued for Property or Services

This section deals with the issuance of shares for property (other than cash) or services under both the older par value statutes and the Revised Model Business Corporation Act.

If shares are issued for cash on the barrel head, the cash price of each share is readily established, subject only to the limitation that the price must equal or exceed the share's par value, if any. If the shareholder-to-be is contributing property or services, however, the situation is more complicated.

In the first place, under most state statutes not all types of property or services may serve as acceptable consideration for the issuance of shares. State constitutions in some seventeen states and statutes in at least thirteen additional states provide, in varying language, that shares may be paid only "in whole or in part, in cash, in other property, tangible or intangible, or in labor or services actually performed for the corporation." This quotation is taken from § 19 of the old Model Business Corporation Act, but it is common language. In addition, many state statutes specifically provide that promissory notes or the promise of future services do not constitute permissible consideration. Shares issued for ineligible consideration under these statutes are not validly issued and may be cancelled or suit brought by other shareholders; or alternatively, persons receiving such shares may be compelled in a suit by creditors to pay in additional consideration on the theory the shares are "watered." (See § 7.7 of this Nutshell.)

It is important to note at the outset that these statutes are not part of the par value structure but are independent requirements. A state may eliminate the par value requirements and yet elect to retain these limitations on the types of eligible consideration for shares (as, indeed, California has done).

There is a fair amount of case law under these statutes that provides additional gloss on what is eligible consideration: preincorporation services are "services actually performed;" patents for inventions, "good will" of a going and profitable business, contract rights, or computer "software" constitute "intangible property" if they appear to have real value. On the other hand, a lease or contract right that is subject to a substantial condition may not constitute "property," at least if it is likely that the condition will not be fulfilled. Secret formulas, processes or plans that lack novelty or substantial value have also been held not to constitute "property." A note secured by a mortgage on real estate is usually considered to be eligible "property" rather than an ineligible "promissory note" in states that prohibit shares to be issued in exchange for promissory notes. Further, if shares are issued partially for services previously rendered and partially for services to be rendered in the future, the entire issue of shares is invalid since the court will not apportion it if the directors do not. Thus, shares to be issued to employees for services may be validly issued only at the end of the employment period.

The Revised Model Business Corporation Act rejects these limitations on eligible consideration. Under section 6.21(b) eligible consideration may consist of "any tangible or intangible property or benefit to the corporation, including cash, promissory notes, services performed, contracts for services to be performed, or other securities of the corporation." This major change in policy was based on a recognition that the traditional rules often led to anomalous results and that "in the realities of commercial life" there is sometimes a need for the issuance of shares for contract rights or intangible property or benefits. Assume, for example, that Jane Fonda agrees to make a film in exchange for a twenty-five per cent interest in the film. Even though a bank might well be willing to lend a new corporation $10,000,000 to make the film based solely on the Fonda contract, the traditional rule would not permit the corporation to issue Jane Fonda her shares until after she has performed the requisite services. Similarly, John D. Rockefeller cannot give his promissory note for shares even though his promissory note is "as good as gold." However, the prohibition against promissory notes presumably would not prevent a third person from using Rockefeller's promissory note as consideration for the issuance of shares to the third person.

One consequence of the provisions of the Revised Model Business Corporation Act is that corporations may issue shares immediately for promises of future service, promissory notes or future benefits that involve possible receipts in the future. What happens if things do not work out as contemplated and the services are never performed, the notes are not paid, or the future benefits are never received? The answer is simple: the shares are still outstanding and the corporation simply has whatever claims it can put forward for the future benefits or under the contract for services or on the promissory notes. If the corporation is not happy with this result, section 6.21(e) permits the corporation to escrow the shares until the services are performed, the benefits received, or the notes paid, and cancel them if there is a default. Alternatively, the corporation may restrict the transfer of the shares until the desired benefits are received.

A second requirement under the old Model Business Corporation Act and the statutes of many states, is that the "value" of the property or services must be determined. Section 18 of the old Model Act required the board of directors to "fix" the "consideration, expressed in dollars" that the corporation is to receive, and many state statutes have identical or analogous language. Furthermore section 20 of the old Model Act provided that "in the absence of fraud in the transaction," the judgment of the board of directors as to the value of the consideration "shall be conclusive." These provisions are equally applicable to par and no par value shares. Under these provisions, the resolution of the board of directors accepting property for shares must do two things: it must specify the specific property involved, and it must express or fix the value of the property in dollars. Of course, the value so expressed must exceed the par value of any shares being issued. The purposes of section 18 apparently were to assure compliance with par value requirements and to enable existing shareholders to determine whether their interests were being diluted; the purpose of the "in the absence of fraud" language of section 20 was to give certainty to purchasers of shares; they can invest in shares without concern that the validity of those shares may later be attacked for having been issued for property worth less than what the directors established. The language, however, was broader and might prevent shareholders whose interests were significantly diluted from attacking the valuation placed on property by the board of directors. Presumably, something close to actual fraudulent intent must be shown before the decision of a board of directors as to the value of property received can be overturned even at the suit of other shareholders when there are no subsequent purchasers involved.

The Revised Model Business Corporation Act also changes these rules substantially. The board of directors does not have to determine the value of property that is received; it need only determine "that the consideration received or to be received for shares to be issued is adequate." [RMBCA § 6.21(c)]. Further, that determination "is conclusive insofar as the adequacy of consideration for the issuance of shares relates to whether the shares are validly issued, fully paid, and nonassessable." This language is designed to narrow the conclusive nature of the directors' determination to situations in which questions might be raised about the adequacy of the consideration for which shares currently on the market were issued.

§ 7.7 Liability of Shareholders for Watered Stock

This section deals primarily with problems arising under the par value statutes. To a limited extent, however, a similar problem may arise under the Revised Model Business Corporation Act.

The term "watered stock" is a colorful common law phrase describing the situation where shareholders receive shares without paying as much for them as the law requires. The common law defines three classes of such shares—"bonus" shares, "discount" shares, and "watered" shares. "Bonus" shares are par value shares issued free when the shareholder fully paid for shares of another class; "discount" shares are par value shares issued for cash for less than par value; "watered" shares are par value shares issued for property that is worth less than the par value of the shares. All three of these types of shares are often indiscriminately referred to as "watered shares," a convenient generic phrase to describe these transactions.

Much of the early common law relating to watered shares concerned the liability of shareholders receiving watered shares to pay the additional consideration needed to "squeeze out the water." Two alternative theories by which creditors might hold shareholders liable appear in the early cases. The "trust fund" theory in effect treated the stated capital of the corporation as being a trust fund available for the payment of creditors, and failure to pay in the proper amount was actionable by any creditor. As pointed out in Hospes v. Northwestern Mfg. & Car Co. (1892), this theory is to a large extent a fiction since corporate capital lacks virtually all the elements of a true trust. The "holding out" theory in effect presumed (usually contrary to fact) that creditors relied on the stated capital in extending credit. On this theory, creditors with claims arising prior to the wrongful issuance, or subsequent creditors who were aware of the wrongful issuance, could not compel additional payments by the shareholders on account of the watered stock. Early courts wavered between these two theories, often referring to a trust fund theory, but reaching decisions more consistent with the holding out theory.

Many modern corporation acts now define the liability of shareholders in connection with the issuance of shares in precise though not always unambiguous terms. A widely adopted provision of the old Model Business Corporation Act states that "a holder of * * * shares of a corporation shall be under no obligation to the corporation or to its creditors with respect to such shares other than the obligation to pay to the corporation *the full consideration for which such shares were issued or to be issued."* [MBCA § 25.] In effect, this article (1) substitutes a statutory obligation running both to the corporation and its creditors for the obligation based on the trust fund or holding out theories of common law, and (2) measures the extent of the liability on the basis of "the consideration for which such shares were issued or to be issued" rather than par value. This section must be read along with section 18 of the old Model Business Corporation Act which authorizes par value shares to be issued "for such consideration expressed in dollars, not less than the par value thereof, as shall be fixed from time to time" by the directors. The similar provision for no par shares is essentially the same with the omission of the phrase "not less than the par value thereof."

Under these statutes it seems clear that a shareholder is liable to the corporation if he or she pays less for the shares than the consideration fixed by the directors, and this liability is measured by the difference between the fixed consideration and the amount actually paid. Further, if the consideration is improperly fixed by the directors at less than the par value of the shares to be issued, the shareholder is liable for the difference between whatever he pays and the par value of the shares. If nominal par value shares are used, it is unlikely that a shareholder will end up actually paying less than the par value of the shares; however, even if he or she pays more than par value, liability to the corporation will nevertheless exist if the amount paid is less than the consideration fixed by the directors. Virtually the same risk of liability exists if no par shares are used: there is no possibility that a shareholder will pay less than par, but liability may arise if he or she pays less than the consideration fixed by the directors for the issuance of the shares. Under these statutes there is thus little, if any, difference in potential liability between par and no par shares.

Considerable ambiguity may exist under these modern statutory provisions where property at an excessive valuation is contributed in exchange for either par value or no par value shares. Under the old Model Act, for example, when issuing shares for property, section 18 provides that the directors must set "the consideration expressed in dollars" or the "consideration expressed in dollars, not less than the par value thereof" for no par and par shares respectively. Under section 25, shareholders have no liability to the corporation with respect to shares "other than the obligation to pay to the corporation the full consideration for which shares were issued or to be issued." The key phrase in this section, the "full consideration" for which shares were issued may conceivably refer either to the designated property itself or to the dollar value placed on the property by the directors when it expressed the consideration "in dollars." This is a practical question that arises whenever a previously unincorporated business with lots of different kinds of property of uncertain values is incorporated, and is present where either nominal par or no par shares are used. To take an example, assume that the directors authorize the issuance of 1,000 shares of $1.00 par value stock for specified property which they value at $10,000. Assume further the valuation of $10,000 is fraudulent and the property is actually worth only $5,000. After the shares are issued, the balance sheet of the corporation looks like this:

Assets		Liabilities	-0-
Property	$10,000		
		Capital Accounts	
		Stated Capital	$ 1,000
		Capital Surplus	9,000

At common law the rule in this kind of situation appeared to be that the shares were not watered at all since the value of the property received exceeded the stated capital of the corporation. If the shareholder in such a case did not expressly promise to pay $10,000 but only to contribute the specified property there appeared to be no way to hold the shareholder liable for more than the property itself. Of course, there is something peculiar about this balance sheet because the value of the assets are greatly overstated and the "capital surplus" account contains $5,000 of "water." It may be that a representation that the assets are worth $10,000 to a creditor would be fraudulent in and of itself; however, there is no basis for recovery against the *shareholder* unless he or she actually makes such a representation.

If the statute, like the old Model Act, requires the directors to express the value of the consideration "in dollars," it is likely that the shareholder in the above example is liable for an additional $5,000 since the "full amount of the consideration fixed as provided by law" was $10,000 and he has only contributed property with a value of $5,000.

At common law the issuance of watered, bonus, or discount shares gave rise to liability on the shareholders receiving the shares, not liability on the directors authorizing such shares. It is possible, however, to devise common law theories of liability by which directors might be held liable for authorizing watered shares, particularly in suits brought by other shareholders or creditors who relied on the financial statements thereby created. Yet another possibility is a suit brought by existing shareholders to cancel watered shares as not being lawfully issued. In many states this appears to be the most common way in which watered stock questions arise.

Section 6.22(a) of the Revised Model Business Corporation Act is superficially similar to section 25 of the old Model Business Corporation Act. It provides that a purchaser of shares from a corporation is not liable to the corporation or its creditors "with respect to its shares except to pay the consideration for which the shares were authorized to be issued." Under this Act the consideration may consist of a promissory note or a contract to perform services in the future (see § 7.6 of this Nutshell); the Official Comment states that the phrase "with respect to its shares" was included to make clear that the shareholder remains liable on the promissory note or contract to perform services without regard to this section.

In a sense, the limited liability of shareholders with respect to shares is closely related to the fundamental concept of limited liability that is central to the modern corporation. The relationship is made explicit in section 6.22(b) of the Revised Model Business Corporation Act that states that with two exceptions "a shareholder is not personally liable for the acts or debts of the corporation." The two exceptions are first, that the articles of incorporation may provide for such personal liability, and second, that the shareholder "may become personally liable by reason of his or her own acts or conduct." This latter clause is designed to cover both consensual assumption of liability for specific obligations and principles by which shareholders may inadvertently become liable for corporate obligations under the doctrine generally known as "piercing the corporate veil," discussed in chapter six of this Nutshell, or possibly other doctrines as well.

§ 7.8   Treasury Shares as a Device to Avoid Restrictions on the Issuance of Shares

Treasury shares are shares of the corporation that were once lawfully issued but have been reacquired by the corporation (and held in its treasury, hence their name). The status of such shares is an uneasy one under traditional par value statutes. They are given an intermediate status between being issued and being unissued: they are not outstanding for purposes of voting, quorum determinations, or dividends (which would obviously create circularity), but since they were once issued they also are not subject to the restraints on issuance described in the previous sections. In other words they can be resold or reissued presumably without regard to the par value of the shares or the nature of the consideration being received for them. This anomalous result is not accepted in all jurisdictions. However, it is generally the position that treasury shares are not subject to the restrictions applicable to original issuance of shares, and many corporations maintain a supply of treasury shares in part to permit transactions the consideration for which might not qualify under the traditional rules.

Treasury shares differ in kind, not degree, from shares of other corporations which the corporation may own. Shares of other corporations are investments; on the other hand, it is incorrect to argue that treasury shares of a corporation are also an investment. When a corporation acquires some of its own shares, the assets of the corporation are reduced by the amount of the purchase price and all the other owners of shares have a somewhat increased proportional interest in the reduced assets. Treasury shares are economically indistinguishable from authorized but unissued shares. Thus, it is not meaningful to treat the acquisition of treasury shares as anything but a disproportionate distribution of corporate assets to the selling shareholders, or better, a disproportionate dividend. See § 16.4 of this Nutshell.

The Revised Model Business Corporation Act eliminates the concept of treasury shares and treats all shares reacquired by the corporation as authorized but unissued shares [§ 6.31(a)].

§ 7.9 Current Trends Regarding Par Value

When all is said and done, the concepts of par value and stated capital have relatively little to commend them in the modern era. At best they are historical oddities that provide little real protection to creditors and have been twisted by sophisticated attorneys to squeeze out the maximum flexibility for their corporate creations. At worst, they are confusing if not misleading.

The Revised Model Business Corporation Act eliminates the concept of par value (except to the limited extent discussed below) and all consequences that flow from a distinction between stated capital and capital surplus. The validity of corporate distributions to shareholders is measured by new insolvency and balance sheet tests. (See § 16.6 of this Nutshell.) Further, the RMBCA eliminates the restrictions on eligible consideration discussed in § 7.6 of this Nutshell as well as the concept of treasury shares discussed in § 7.8. The elegance and simplicity thereby created has much to commend it since it returns the issuance of common shares back to a simple, common sense set of rules.

The Revised Model Business Corporation Act does permit a corporation to elect to create par value for shares if it desires. [RMBCA § 2.02(b)(iv).] The Official Comment indicates that this provision permits parties to elect to be governed by par value provisions as a matter of contract if they so desire. Election of an optional par value may be useful if the corporation plans to transact business in a state in which franchise or other taxes are computed on the basis of par values.

Most practicing attorneys, of course, are familiar with par value statutes, having studied them in law school and practiced under them. In states that have adopted all or significant portions of the RMBCA provisions, there is a tendency by attorneys to follow familiar patterns and continue to use par value provisions. As time goes on, however, it is likely that more attorneys will take advantage of the flexibility and simplicity provided by the RMBCA provisions.

§ 7.10   Other Types of Securities: "Equity" and "Debt" Securities

Securities issued by a corporation may be broadly classified into "equity securities" and "debt securities." "Equity" in this sense is roughly synonymous with "net worth" or "ownership" and is derived from the following, quite common usage: if one subtracts a business's liabilities from its assets, what remains is the owners' "equity" in the business. Equity securities therefore refer to all securities that represent ownership interests in the corporation, while debt securities, such as bonds or debentures, represent interests that must ultimately be repaid. Common shares, of course, are the quintessence of an equity security since they represent the basic residual ownership of the corporation but preferred shares are also equity securities.

The distinction between "equity" and "debt" underlies much of the modern law and practice relating to corporation finance. At the simplest level the distinction is easy to grasp. A "debt" is something that must be repaid: it is the result of a "loan," the person making the loan is a "creditor," and if periodic payments are made, they are "interest." On the other hand, "equity" represents an ownership interest in the business itself. One thinks in terms of "shareholders," shares of "capital stock," voting, and "dividends" rather than "interest." It is sometimes not realized, however, that as a matter of economics, the distinction between debt and equity may not be at all clear in many situations. For example, a 100 year "debenture" with interest payable solely from income if and when earned, and repayment subordinate to other debts of the business is more like an equity security than a debt security. Corporations may create mixed or "hybrid" securities which have some of the characteristics of debt and some of equity. Despite the lack of clear distinction between debt and equity in these situations, legal consequences vary substantially depending on how a particular hybrid security is classified. A hybrid security may be treated as a debt security for some purposes and as an equity security for other purposes, e.g., for income taxation purposes, rights on bankruptcy or insolvency, and the right to participate in management. The classification of hybrid securities for tax purposes, in particular, has given rise to litigation.

§ 7.11 Characteristics of Debt Securities

Debt securities are important sources of capital for publicly held corporations. Typical debt securities are notes, debentures, and bonds. Technically a "debenture" is an unsecured corporate obligation while a "bond" is secured by a lien or mortgage on corporate property. However, the word "bond" is often used indiscriminately to cover both bonds and debentures and is so used hereafter. A "bond" is a long term debt security while a "note" is usually a shorter term obligation. Bonds are historically bearer instruments, negotiable by delivery, issued in multiples of $1,000 with interest payments represented by coupons that are periodically clipped and submitted for payment. Notes are usually payable to the order of a person and interest payments are contractual obligations not evidenced by a coupon. Bonds may also be registered with the issuer and transferable only by endorsement. Article 8 of the Uniform Commercial Code makes registered bonds negotiable. Increasingly, bond ownership is reflected solely by book entries on the records of brokerage firms and not by physical instruments.

Interest payments on debt securities are usually fixed obligations, due in any event, and expressed as a percentage of the face amount of the security. However, so-called income bonds, in which the obligation to pay interest is conditioned on adequate corporate earnings, are also known. Somewhat rarer are so-called participating bonds, where the amount of interest payable on the bonds increases with corporate earnings. The 1980s saw the development of novel interest provisions for bonds. "PIK" ("payment in kind") bonds pay interest in the form of promissory notes or additional bonds rather than cash for a stated period of years; cash interest payments begin on a specified date. "Reset" bonds contain provisions that require the issuer to adjust ("reset") the interest rate at a specified date in the future in the event the bonds are selling below face value so as to return the bonds' market value to their face value. These novel provisions have created difficulties for borrowers; in several instances, for example, reset bonds were selling at such a low price as the reset date approached that no adjustment in the interest rate could return the bonds' market price to their face value. In the case of such bonds, default or renegotiation of their terms was inevitable.

Debt securities are usually subject to redemption, which means that the corporation has reserved the power to call in and pay off the obligation before it is due, often at a slight premium over the face value. Securities chosen for redemption may be chosen by lot or by some other system. Many debt securities require the corporation to set aside cash, usually called sinking fund provisions, to redeem a part of the issue each year (or purchase securities on the open market and retire them), or to accumulate until the entire issue matures.

Debt securities may be convertible into equity securities, particularly common stock, on some predetermined ratio. This ratio is usually adjusted for stock splits, dividends, etc. The protection given by such adjustments is often referred to as protecting the conversion privilege from dilution. When convertible debentures are converted, they, and the debt they represent, disappear and the new equity securities (the "conversion securities") are issued in their place. Convertible debentures themselves are treated as equity securities for many purposes. Convertible debentures are also usually redeemable; when the value of the conversion securities exceeds the redemption price, it is obviously to the holders' advantage to convert when an announcement is made that the debentures will be called for redemption. Such a conversion is usually described as forced. Conversion in such situations is possible because a redemption privilege is exercisable only after notice is given as specified in the indenture (the underlying contract that defines the rights of the issuer, the holders, and the trustee) while the conversion privilege continues to exist until the instant of redemption. Litigation has arisen over the adequacy of the notice of redemption, the issue typically being whether the issuer need only give the minimum notice called for in the indenture or whether broader public notification must be given.

Some states authorize holders of bonds to participate in the selection of the board of directors either generally or upon specified contingencies, such as default in payment of interest. The inclusion of such powers, of course, blurs the distinction between debt and equity securities. The Revised Model Business Corporation Act does not permit debenture holders to be given the power to vote.

§ 7.12 Classes of Equity Securities; Preferred Shares

State corporation statutes give corporations broad power to create novel types of securities or specially tailored classes of common or preferred securities; this flexibility may be utilized to create innovative means of raising capital from third parties and to effectuate intracorporate agreements in closely held corporations. The emphasis in this section, like the preceding one, is essentially descriptive, concentrating on broad classes of equity securities including those used in the modern era by corporations to raise capital.

(1) *Preferred Shares.* Preferred shares differ from common shares in that they have preference over common shares in the payment of dividends and/or preference in the assets of the corporation upon the voluntary or involuntary liquidation of the corporation. "Preference" simply means that the preferred shares are entitled to receive some specified payment (either a dividend or a liquidating distribution, or both) before the common shares are entitled to anything. Most preferred shares contain preferences both as to dividends and liquidation.

The dividend preference may be described either in terms of dollars per share (the "$3.20 preferred") or as a percentage of par or stated value (the "five per cent preferred"). A dividend preference does not mean that the preferred is entitled to the payment in the same way that a creditor is entitled to payment from his or her debtor. A preferred dividend is still a dividend, and the directors may decide to omit all dividends, common or preferred, and this decision is in no way dependent on whether or not there is current income. Shares preferred as to dividends may be cumulative, noncumulative, or partially cumulative. If cumulative dividends are not paid in some years, they are carried forward and both they and the current year's preferred dividends must be paid in full before any common dividends may be declared. Noncumulative dividends disappear each year if they are not paid. Partially cumulative dividends are usually of the "cumulative to the extent of earnings" type so that such preferred shares continue to have first claim to actual earnings if not paid out as dividends. Unpaid cumulative dividends are not debts of the corporation, but a continued right to priority in future distributions. Since directors (who are elected by the common shareholders) may defer preferred dividends indefinitely if the directors are willing to forego dividends on the common shares as well, it is customary to provide that preferred shares may elect a specified number of directors if preferred dividends have been omitted for a specified period.

Preferred shares may also be participating, though typically they are not. Nonparticipating shares are entitled to a specified dividend before anything is paid on the common but no more, irrespective of the earnings of the corporation. Participating preferred shares are entitled to the original dividend, and after the common receives a specified amount, they may share with the common in any additional distributions. Such shares are sometimes referred to as "Class A common" or a similar designation reflecting that their right to participate is open-ended.

Like debt securities, preferred shares may be convertible into common shares at a specified price or specified ratio and redeemable by the corporation at a fixed price. Typically, the original conversion ratio is established so that the common must appreciate substantially before it is profitable to convert the preferred. When the price of the common rises above this level, the preferred shares will fluctuate in price as the price of the common fluctuates. The redemption privilege usually does not affect the price of the convertible preferred since the privilege to convert customarily continues for a limited period of time after a call for redemption. A conversion is "forced" when shares are called for redemption at a time when the value of the shares obtainable on conversion exceeds the redemption price. Also like convertible debt securities, convertible preferred usually contain elaborate provisions protecting the conversion privilege from dilution in case of stock dividends, stock splits, or the issuance of additional common shares. The statutes of some states prohibit the creation of a security which is convertible into shares having superior rights and preferences as to dividends or upon liquidation—in other words, a common may not be made convertible into preferred or into debt. State statutes also may limit the redemption privilege to securities that have a liquidation preference or permit redeemable common shares only if there is another class of common shares that are not subject to redemption. These limitations are virtually the only substantive statutory restrictions on the issuance of classes of shares in most states. The Revised Model Business Corporation Act does not contain either of these limitations. See § 6.01, and particularly the Official Comment.

The high interest rates of the early 1980s led to the development of novel financing devices, many of which involved preferred stock. For example, many corporations issued preferred stock that was redeemable at the option of the holder, or that became redeemable upon the occurrence of some external event, such as a change in interest rates or the lapse of a specified period of time. Still other corporations issued preferred with floating or adjustable dividend rates that depended on interest rates or some similar measure. Most of these novel preferreds were designed to give corporate holders of the preferred the benefit of the exclusion for intercorporate dividends while at the same time giving the holders most of the benefits of traditional debt. Classes of preferred shares with "PIK" and "reset" provisions also appeared. The validity of some of these novel types of preferred may be questionable under some state statutes; the Revised Model Business Corporation Act contains provisions designed to assure their validity. See § 6.01(c).

Articles of incorporation may also authorize preferred shares to be issued in *series.* The articles of incorporation in effect create a class of shares without any substantive terms and authorize the board of directors to create "series" from within that class from time to time and to vary any of the substantive terms of one series from another. Where preferred shares in substantial amounts are to be sold by a corporation from time to time to raise capital, the privilege of issuing preferred in series simplifies financing since the price, dividend, liquidation preference, sinking fund provision, voting rights, and other terms of each series may be tailored to then-current market conditions and the need for a special shareholders' meeting is eliminated. Shares of different series have identical rights except for the specified business terms which may be varied. Before a series of preferred shares is created, a public filing with the Secretary of State describing the terms of the new series is required. The importance of the power to create series escalated in the 1980s with the development of the so-called "poison pill" defensive tactic against unwanted takeover attempts, which involves the creation of one or more series of shares that have powers dependent on external events, typically the acquisition of some percentage of the corporation's voting shares by outsiders.

There is little or no difference between a "series" or a "class" of shares except their manner of creation—by the articles of incorporation in the case of a class and by action of the board of directors in the case of a series. In recognition of this, section 6.02 of the Revised Model Business Corporation Act and the statutes of a few states allow the creation of either "classes" or "series" by the board of directors if authority to do so is given in the articles of incorporation.

The various provisions defining the rights of preferred shareholders appear in the corporation's articles of incorporation, bylaws, or directors' resolutions. Collectively they are referred to as the preferred shareholders' "contract" with the corporation and with other classes of shareholders. Rights of preferred shareholders are generally limited to those set forth in this "contract."

(2) *Classes of Common Stock.* State statutes also give corporations broad power to create classes of common stock with different rights or privileges. Such classes are usually designated by alphabetical notations: "Class A common," "Class B common," and so forth. In closely held corporations, classes of common stock are primarily used to effectuate control, voting, or financial arrangements. The following examples illustrate the variety and flexibility that classes of common stock may provide:

(a) A Class A common may be created that is entitled to twice the dividend per share of Class B common, but in all other respects the two classes are identical.

(b) A Class A common may be created that has two votes per share while Class B common has one vote per share (this is permitted under the RMBCA and in most but not all states; some state statutes still have a "one vote per share" principle).

(c) A Class A common may be created that has the power to elect two directors; the holders of Class B common may have the power to elect one, two, or more directors, irrespective of the number of shares of each class outstanding.

(d) It may be required that the president of the corporation be a holder of Class A shares and the vice-president and treasurer be holders of Class B shares.

Classes of common stock may also be used to solve financial, control, or dividend problems in publicly held corporations, though such use is not common. When the Ford Motor Company went public in 1946, it created a special class of common shares to be held by the Ford Foundation. The special shares were convertible into regular common shares when sold by the Foundation. These shares were nonvoting so they permitted control of the corporation to be vested in the public without requiring the

Foundation to abruptly liquidate its huge interest in the corporation.

In the 1980s, several publicly held corporations in which specific families had long been associated in a control capacity sought to combat potential takeover attempts by creating a special class of shares with super voting rights to be issued solely to family members. The terms of this special class provided that shares lost their special voting privileges if they were sold or conveyed to non-family members. Among the corporations adopting this device were the publishers of the New York Times and the Wall Street Journal. The special class assured that voting control resided in the family even though most of the shares were publicly held. In 1988 the SEC adopted rule 19c–4 (usually known as the "one share one vote" rule) designed to prevent such unequal divisions in voting power in the future, though the rule "grandfathered" existing capital structures. This rule was held invalid in The Business Roundtable v. SEC (1990).

(3) *Non-voting Shares.* In most states, the articles of incorporation may limit or deny the right to vote to a class of shares. Preferred shares are usually non-voting shares, but the privilege to vote may be extended to such shares, either with the common shares or as a separate class.

In the closely held corporation, non-voting shares may serve a planning role. For example, the right to vote may be limited or denied to classes of common shares in the election of directors, on other subjects normally submitted to shareholders, or both. In such corporations there seems to be no reason why a specific limitation on voting should not be part of the shareholder's overall "contract" with the corporation.

In publicly held corporations, non-voting shares have been treated with greater suspicion. Such shares are somewhat analogous to perpetual voting trusts, and have been criticized on policy grounds for this reason. (See § 9.7 of this Nutshell.) Corporations with non-voting shares held by the public are ineligible for listing on the New York Stock Exchange, and may suffer market and other disadvantages as well. In the early years of this century, many corporations were capitalized by the issuance of non-voting shares to the public while the voting shares were held by the members of the family which founded or controlled the corporation. This practice has declined in importance in recent years. Several corporations that had issued non-voting shares for this reason later converted the non-voting shares into voting shares. This decision itself creates subtle issues as to the relative value of the right to vote and the fairness of the terms on which the privilege to vote is granted to the non-voting shares.

Under most state statutes, even non-voting shares are entitled to vote in connection with certain mergers, share exchanges, and other extraordinary events that may affect the class of nonvoting shares as a class.

(4) *Options.* Options to purchase shares may be used as a capital raising device, to provide employee incentives, and to a lesser extent as part of control devices. Of course, shares under option are not deemed issued and may not be voted until the options are exercised and the purchase price paid, or in some states, a firm commitment to pay the purchase price in the form of a promissory note has been delivered to the corporation.

Many state corporation statutes contain provisions that authorize the issuance of shares in connection with employee stock purchase or stock option plans by the board of directors, and provide that in the absence of fraud the determination by the board of the consideration for such shares shall be conclusive. (RMBCA § 6.24).

"Warrants" are transferable options to acquire shares from the corporation at a specified price. Warrants have many of the qualities of an equity security since their price is a function of the market price of the underlying shares and the specified issuance price. Warrants frequently are issued as "sweeteners" in connection with the distribution of a debt or preferred stock issue; they may be issued in connection with a public exchange offer, or as compensation for handling the public distribution of other shares. Sometimes they are issued in a reorganization to holders of a class of security not otherwise recognized in the reorganization. Warrants may be publicly traded; warrants issued by a number of corporations are listed from time to time on the New York Stock Exchange or other exchanges. "Rights" are in effect short term warrants. They may also be publicly traded and listed on securities exchanges. Rights may be issued in lieu of a dividend, or in an effort to raise capital from existing shareholders.

§ 7.13 The Advantages of Debt Financing

It is usually advantageous for a corporation to engage to some extent in debt financing. The notion that the best business is a debt-free business, while sounding attractive, is not consistent either with the minimization of income taxes or with the maximization of profits.

(1) *Tax Advantages of Debt.* There are tax advantages for individual shareholders to lend to a C corporation a portion of their investment in the corporation rather than to contribute it outright. Where the shareholders are individuals, such debt reduces the double taxation problem of C corporations discussed earlier. (See § 2.3 of this Nutshell.) Interest payments on such debt are deductible by the corporation whereas dividend payments on equity securities are not. Further, repayment of a debt may be a non-taxable return of capital, while a purchase or redemption of equity securities from a shareholder by the corporation is ordinarily a taxable event. When a shareholder lends a portion of a

contemplated investment to the corporation, he or she is hopefully reserving the option of recovering this portion tax free at some later date if the corporation is successful.

There is no tax advantage in debt owed to individuals other than shareholders. However, the deductibility of interest payments to third persons may significantly reduce the cost of borrowed capital as compared to the cost of capital raised through the sale of equity securities. Indeed, the systematic cost advantage that borrowed capital has in the modern American economy has significantly affected the capital structure of all domestic corporations.

Where the contributor of capital is another corporation, somewhat different rules apply. The exclusion of 80 per cent or more of intercorporate dividends may make an equity investment attractive even though the dividend payments are not deductible by the borrowing corporation.

The tax advantages of debt financing have been so substantial for small closely-held corporations in the past that a substantial amount of case law has developed dealing with the question when debt in the corporate structure is excessive so that the Internal Revenue Service may treat the debt as a kind of equity, and disallow interest deductions or treat its repayment as a taxable dividend. (See § 7.14 of this Nutshell.) This problem has diminished in importance with the increased popularity of the S corporation election for such corporations.

(2) *Non-tax Advantages of Debt.* In the non-tax area debt owed both to third persons and to shareholders may be advantageous to a corporation, but for entirely different reasons.

(a) Debt owed to third persons is desirable because of the factor of *leverage.* Leverage arises when the corporation is able to earn more on the borrowed capital than the cost of the borrowing. The entire excess is allocable to the equity accounts of the corporation, thereby increasing the rate of return on the equity invested in the corporation. An example should help to make this clear. Let us assume that a person is considering the purchase of a business which will yield $25,000 per year over and above all taxes and expenses. The purchase price is $200,000. If the person simply buys the business using only his or her own capital, the annual return is 25,000/200,000 or 12½ per cent.

Let us assume that the same person can borrow 80 per cent of the purchase price at an interest cost of 10 per cent per year. The person will then invest $40,000 of his or her own capital (20 per cent of $200,000), and borrow the remaining $160,000 (80 per cent of $200,000). The interest cost of the loan is $16,000 per year (10 per cent of $160,000). Since the business still makes $25,000 per year, the net profit after interest costs is $9,000 on a net investment of $40,000, and the return on the investment is 9,000/40,000 or 22.5%. In other words, by borrowing 80 per cent of the purchase price, the return per equity dollar invested is increased from 12.5 per cent to 22.5 per cent. If there were five such simultaneous opportunities, a rational investor would take his or her initial $200,000 and invest $40,000 in each of the five rather than buying only one debt-free business. By buying five businesses with 80 per cent loans, he or she will make $9,000 × 5 = $45,000 rather than $25,000. This is leverage, a device well understood by real estate syndicates and promoters who seek to obtain the largest possible mortgage and the smallest possible equity investment of their own. The reason that it is desirable to leverage in the hypothetical is that each dollar invested earns 12½ per cent but the cost of borrowing is only 10 per cent. The 2½ per cent difference on every borrowed dollar is allocable to the equity investment—the 20 per cent—thereby increasing the overall return on the equity. The risk involved with the extensive use of leverage, of course, is that the income from the project may not be sufficient to cover the fixed interest charges. The investor would then quickly see his or her return reduced to zero; it is possible that a "negative cash flow" would result and the investor might then have to invest additional amounts to cover the shortfall of income over expenses. Certainly, the investor may be wiped out much more quickly in a leveraged investment than if no part of the purchase price were borrowed.

Since World War II, the United States has suffered an inflationary spiral which may or may not continue in the future. If inflation continues, debt financing is also attractive because the loans will ultimately be repaid with inflated dollars. Of course, the competition for loans in such circumstances may cause high interest charges which will offset, either wholly or partially, this advantage of debt financing.

The Miller–Modigliani theorem states (with certain simplifying assumptions, including elimination of the tax advantage of debt) that the aggregate value of a corporation's securities (the market value of its equity securities plus the market value of its debt securities) is independent of the amount of debt in the corporation's capital structure. In other words, in a perfect world any enhanced value of common stock because of the advantages of leverage is precisely offset by a decline in the market value of the indebtedness.

(b) Leverage can be obtained only by the use of other people's money. Nevertheless, it is often advantageous for non-tax business reasons for shareholders to advance a portion of their investment in the business in the form of loans rather than capital contributions. (The tax advantages of doing this in a C corporation have previously been discussed.) As a creditor, a shareholder may have greater rights upon bankruptcy or insolvency than he or she would have as a mere shareholder. However, if the loans are made as part of the original capitalization of the company, there is a substantial risk that such loans will be subordinated to the claims of general creditors in a bankruptcy proceeding. (See §§ 6.8, 7.15 of this Nutshell.) The basic test in this area is whether the capitalization is such that a third person would have made an arms length loan. If so, the loan by the shareholder should be treated as a loan for bankruptcy purposes. Loans for subsequent business needs also may fare better and stand a good chance of being recognized as bona fide loans.

§ 7.14 Tax Consequences of Excessive Debt Capitalization in C Corporations

The substantial tax advantages of shareholder debt financing in C corporations have led to a large amount of tax litigation as to whether ostensible debt should be reclassified as equity for tax purposes. The judicial decisions in this area do not establish a simple, easily understood test as to when a reclassification from debt to equity is proper. The diversity of possible factual situations is substantial, and there is less than total agreement in the cases as to the applicable legal principles. Perhaps Judge John R. Brown was being somewhat ironic when, in the leading Fifth Circuit case on the question, he stated: "Although the results are diverse, sometimes favoring the taxpayer, sometimes the Government, the cases are in accord in applying with an even hand the controlling legal principles for determining the outcome * * * ." Tomlinson v. 1661 Corp. (1967).

Two interrelated ideas appear to underlie the judicial reasoning in the numerous cases in this area: first, are the legal incidents of the relationship between corporation and shareholder more similar to an equity investment or to a debt relationship? And second, even where the principal incidents of debt exist, is there some paramount policy of federal tax law which requires that particular debt interests be treated as equity investments?

Certainly, many cases may be explained on the ground that despite the label "debt" attached to an interest, the shareholder really created an equity interest. Some of these cases adopt a test of the "intention" of the shareholder in making the investment, but state that this "intention" may be inferred from the provisions of the debenture itself or from surrounding circumstances. The following factors tend to indicate an "intention" to make an equity or capital contribution: (a) use of initial payments, both capital and "loans," to acquire capital assets; (b) proceeds used to start up the corporate life; (c) subordination to other indebtedness; (d) an "inordinately postponed due date;" (e) provision for payment of "interest" only out of earnings; and (f) an express or implied agreement not to enforce collection of the "debt."

At one time it was thought that the talismanic test was the ratio between debt and equity. It was intimated in the Supreme Court decision in John Kelley Co. v. Commissioner (1946) that a ratio of 4:1 (debt equal to four times equity) or more automatically led to the reclassification of the debt as equity. A corporation with a high debt/equity ratio is often called a "thin" corporation. Later cases, however, have rejected the suggestion that the test is a mechanical one based on an arithmetic calculation. In other words, courts have rejected in strong terms the argument by the government that a high ratio of debt to equity automatically indicated an objectionable avoidance of taxes, and therefore grounds for treating the debt as equity. However, high debt/equity ratios are relevant and it is not surprising that most cases in which debt has been reclassified as equity involve debt/equity ratios higher than 4:1, and often higher than 10:1.

§ 7.15   The Deep Rock Doctrine Revisited

The so-called Deep Rock doctrine has been discussed in a previous chapter (see § 6.8 of this Nutshell). The doctrine, evolved in bankruptcy cases, permits subordination of shareholder-owned debt to the claims of general creditors when the court believes it is fair to do so. It is therefore the bankruptcy analogue to the "thin corporation" problem in tax law described in the last section. The shareholder claims which are subordinated may be either secured or unsecured: under this doctrine the court may treat secured shareholder claims either as on a parity with general unsecured claims or as inferior to all other such claims. Obviously, this doctrine, when applied, has the effect of eliminating one major advantage of shareholder indebtedness.

The doctrine has generally been applied in Federal bankruptcy cases, and it has also been recognized in some state insolvency proceedings.

Some cases have held that a mere showing of inadequate capitalization is not enough for disallowance or subordination in the bankruptcy area and that there must be some additional showing of unfairness, fraud, or misrepresentation. The shareholder involved may have the burden of showing "the inherent fairness and good faith of the transactions involved." One court has suggested that "[i]t is only where the conduct of a stockholder or officer toward his or her corporation can be challenged as being detrimental to the creditors that there is any duty on behalf of the [bankruptcy judge] or the courts to recast the voluntary acts of the corporation into something different from what they have in good faith undertaken to engage in." As a practical matter, however, if the initial capitalization is grossly inadequate, some other element of unfairness can usually be found which under this test will permit the court to subordinate the shareholder indebtedness. Also the case law is in disagreement as to whether the adequacy of the initial capital is to be judged in the light of the needs of the particular business, or on an abstract basis of substantiality.

As in the case of tax controversies, subsequent loans needed to keep the business afloat are likely to be accepted by the courts as true loans for bankruptcy purposes, though unfair attempts to obtain security for such loans may still be attacked under the Deep Rock doctrine.

§ 7.16   Equalizing Capital and Services When Forming a Corporation

A recurring problem in financing a close corporation involves the situation where investors have agreed to contribute capital or provide services in varying amounts, and shares are to be issued in some different agreed ratio. Assume, for example, that A and B have agreed to go into business with A providing the necessary capital of $100,000 with B to work exclusively for the new venture for at least three years. The parties have also agreed that A is to receive 60 per cent and B 40 per cent of the voting shares. The state in question has eliminated par value from its statute but has retained the restrictions on the types of eligible consideration for shares described in § 7.6 of this Nutshell. How can the arrangement be worked out?

(1) B cannot be issued shares immediately upon the execution of a long-term employment contract, since "future services" are not valid consideration for shares.

(2) There is no obstacle, however, to issuing shares for past services. Hence the arrangement may be worked out by issuing A 60 shares for $100,000 immediately, and issuing B 40 shares when the period of employment ends three years from now. Possible disadvantages are (i) until B has completed the services, A is the sole shareholder with total power over the corporation and may exclude B at any time (though such an exclusion may constitute a breach of contract); (ii) B may have to provide services for an extended period without receiving dividends or a salary to live on; and (3) B will have to pay income tax on the value of the shares but will not have received any money from the corporation to do so.

(3) B may propose that he or she sign a promissory note for the $66,667, have the 40 shares issued to him or her immediately, and pay off the note by rendering services under an employment contract. While some states that prohibit contracts for future services to serve as consideration for shares permit promissory notes to serve as consideration, most do not.

(4) Another solution is to issue shares at different prices. A may be issued 60 shares for $100,000 and B 40 shares for $40.00. There is no statutory requirement that all shares of the same class be issued for the same consideration. However, this suggestion is manifestly unfair to A if the business does not do well and the parties desire to liquidate since B in effect has an immediate 40 per cent interest in A's capital.

(5) A more reasonable solution, at least where the S corporation election is not to be made, is to create two classes of common stock with identical rights on dissolution:

(a) Class A common, one vote per share; 6,000 shares issued to A for $100,000 in cash (or $16.67 per share).

(b) Class B common, one hundred votes per share, 40 shares issued to B for $667.00 (or $16.67 per share). If dividends are to be paid on a 60–40 ratio, the dividends on each share of class B stock would have to be set at one hundred times the dividend on each share of class A stock.

This solves the premature liquidation problem. However, multiple votes per share are not permitted in some states. Essentially the same pattern could be created by giving A shares with a fraction of a vote per share, if that is permitted under the specific state statute.

(6) Another solution is to issue A 60 common shares for $60 and B 40 common shares for $40, and have A lend the corporation $99,940. This solves the corporate law and premature dissolution problems but creates others. There is a risk that the debt would not qualify as "straight debt" under the S corporation election, and make the corporation

ineligible for that desirable tax election. If the corporation is taxed as a C corporation, it would be viewed as a "thin" corporation for tax purposes, and an attempt by the corporation to deduct interest payments on the $99,940 "debt" would be disallowed. A also would probably not be able to maintain creditor status in a bankruptcy proceeding under the "Deep Rock" doctrine. B might also object that A should not have a creditor's claim to all his or her capital while B is contributing services for which he or she has no claim at all.

(7) Perhaps the best solution, where the S corporation election is not essential, is this: A receives 60 common shares, for $60.00 ($1 per share) and B receives 40 common shares, for $40.00 ($1 per share). A also receives 500 preferred shares for $50,000 ($100 per share) and "lends" the corporation the remaining $50,000. Since the aggregate capitalization is now $50,100 (combining all the consideration received for the common and preferred), debt is less than 50 per cent and the debt/equity ratio is about 1:1. The chances of applying the "thin" corporation or "Deep Rock" doctrines are therefore greatly reduced. This pattern was essentially upheld in the Maryland case of Obre v. Alban Tractor Co. (1962), involving a state insolvency proceeding. It may be noted that the dividend preference of the preferred is not specified. Under the circumstances, that is a matter of negotiation between A and B.

If this problem were to arise in a state with a par value requirement, the shares of stock would have to be assigned a par value that is less than the lowest consideration for which the shares are to be issued.

§ 7.17   Issuance of Shares by a Going Concern: Preemptive Rights

The issuance of authorized but previously unissued shares by a going concern must meet the same requirements as to kind and amount of consideration as on the original formation and capitalization of the corporation. The number of shares to be sold and the consideration therefor is set by the board of directors. In addition, however, the issuance of new shares may affect the financial and voting rights of existing shareholders, and as a result additional legal requirements may be applicable. If shares are issued to the current shareholders in strict proportion to their shareholdings, the relative position of each shareholder is obviously unaffected though the aggregate capital invested in the corporation has increased. However, if shares are issued to third persons or to existing shareholders not in strictly proportional amounts, the voting power of some shareholders will necessarily be reduced. Further, if the shares are issued disproportionately and for less than current value (a term that need not here be precisely defined), the financial interest of some shareholders in the corporation will necessarily be diluted.

A "preemptive right" permits existing shareholders, subject to several important exceptions, to subscribe—in preference to strangers and pro rata with other existing shareholders—for their relative proportion of new shares to be issued by the corporation. Ideally, the preemptive right of each existing shareholder protects him or her from injury resulting from the issue of shares. However, in practice it often does not work out that way. For one thing, preemptive rights under modern statutes are permissive rather than mandatory and corporations may limit or deny such rights by provisions in the articles of incorporation. However, even if preemptive rights are excluded, equitable principles may limit the power of corporations to dispose of new shares on an unfair basis.

Shares sold by a going corporation may come from three sources. They may be shares that are newly authorized by the corporation by an amendment to the articles of incorporation. Or, they may be shares that were previously authorized in the articles but never previously issued. Or they may be "treasury shares," that is, shares that have been issued and subsequently reacquired by the corporation. Even though the issuance of any additional shares, no matter what the source, has the same dilutive effect, different legal principles may be applicable depending on the source of the shares and the precise language of the state statute defining the shareholder's preemptive right.

At common law and under the statutes of many states the preemptive right did not extend to the following types of transactions:

(1) Shares that were originally authorized but unissued. The rationale for this exception was that an implied understanding existed between the original subscribers that sale of the remaining authorized shares to obtain necessary capital may be completed. However, this rationale is not persuasive today in light of the modern practice of authorizing additional shares that are not planned to be sold as part of the original capitalization. As a result some states do not recognize this exception.

(2) Treasury shares. The rationale for this exception is that shareholders are not injured since the shares had previously been issued and their reissuance simply restores a dilution that had existed previously. Again this may not be persuasive, depending on the particular factual situation under consideration.

(3) Shares issued for property or services rather than cash or shares issued in connection with a merger. The theory underlying these exceptions is that preemptive rights in such situations would frustrate or render impractical desirable transactions, or are impossible to work out since existing shareholders may not own, and therefore cannot contribute, property on a proportional basis.

(4) Shares issued to satisfy conversion or option rights.

(5) Shares issued pursuant to a plan of reorganization or recapitalization under court supervision.

Some recent decisions have refused to apply these exceptions mechanically and have looked to the realities of the particular situation. One court, for example, held that preemptive rights should not be denied when property is the consideration for shares except where, because of peculiar circumstances, the corporation has great need for the particular property, and issuance of shares therefor is the only practical and feasible method by which the corporation can acquire it. In many situations, the corporation may pay cash to acquire the needed property; to allow the corporation to acquire it with shares, it was argued, defeats the preemptive right that would exist if shares were issued for cash and the cash used to acquire the property.

Modern state statutes change the common law preemptive right in several respects:

(1) At common law it was generally held that a shareholder's preemptive right was an integral part of the ownership of shares. However, all modern statutes give corporations the privilege of dispensing entirely with preemptive rights if they so choose. The choice must be made by a specific provision in the corporation's articles of incorporation. Statutes may grant preemptive rights unless they are specifically negated in the articles (an "opt-out" clause), or preclude preemptive rights except to the extent specifically granted in the articles (an "opt-in" clause). Section 6.30 of the Revised Model Business Corporation Act adopts an "opt in" clause, but simplifies the drafting problem faced by an attorney desiring to create preemptive rights by establishing a "standard form" for electing preemptive rights in section 6.30(b). This standard form, which covers such matters as the scope of the preemptive right, waiver, and the duration of the right, may be modified as desired.

(2) They sometimes give preemptive rights more broadly than the common law, e.g., they may extend the right to "authorized but unissued shares," "treasury shares," and securities convertible into common shares, all types of shares to which the common law preemptive right did not extend.

(3) They provide specifically that preemptive rights do not exist between different classes of shares, e.g., holders of preferred do not have a preemptive right to acquire common. The RMBCA standard form of preemptive rights, however, seeks to preserve voting power by providing that common shareholders have a preemptive right to acquire voting or convertible preferred shares.

(4) They provide that shares issued pursuant to employee incentive or compensation plans are not subject to preemptive rights if the plan was originally approved by the shareholders. The RMBCA standard form of preemptive rights does not include this proviso.

What considerations enter into the decision to limit or deny preemptive rights? The argument in favor of preserving preemptive rights is that the shareholder who subscribes for a given percentage of the original issue of the shares of a corporation should be entitled to maintain his or her percentage interest provided he or she is willing to subscribe for the proportion of the additional issue. This sounds like a democratic principle and undoubtedly it is in many cases. There are situations, however, in which preemptive rights are more a nuisance than anything else. Suppose for example that a corporation with a fairly large number of shareholders is in need of immediate funds and can obtain them only by a prompt sale of additional shares to bankers or underwriters. It may well find that compliance with and satisfaction of the preemptive rights of its existing shareholders will be expensive, time-consuming, and only partially successful.

If it is anticipated that the corporation will for some time remain a close corporation, preemptive rights may be retained so as to give each shareholder the maximum protection against dilution, though it is safer to provide such rights by shareholder agreement than by reliance on the state statute. But, if it is anticipated that the corporation will in the near future engage in public financing or will seek to acquire other companies or properties by the issuance of its shares, preemptive rights are often eliminated to avoid legal complications when the time arrives for the sale of additional shares or the acquisition of other companies or properties. In any event, preemptive rights serve little purpose where shares are publicly traded, since additional shares can usually be bought on the open market if desired. Where preemptive rights have been excluded, the directors may always later decide to offer additional shares pro rata to existing shareholders. In fact, in many corporations, existing shareholders are the most logical market, and the one likely to be pursued.

§ 7.18　Oppressive Issuance of Shares

Additional shares of stock may be issued oppressively to dilute the interests of other shareholders in the corporation. Misuse of this power is often referred to as a "squeeze out" or "freeze out."

A number of cases attest that corporate management has a fiduciary duty of taking corporate action according to the best interests of the corporation rather than for personal advantage. This principle amply covers situations where, in the absence of preemptive rights, management dilutes the interests of shareholders simply by issuing additional shares to itself at a bargain price. This principle may also cover situations where management issues shares to itself at a fair price to ensure retention of control without offering the shares more broadly. In the first situation there is dilution of both financial and voting interests; in the second there is only dilution of the voting power.

Much more difficult are cases involving a combination of legitimate and self-serving purposes. Shares may be issued to friendly persons for apparently worthwhile purposes and entirely in accordance with statutory requirements, but the minority shareholders complain that the real purpose and principal effect of the transaction is to freeze them out or dilute their interest. Most cases have permitted such transactions to stand, at least where the ostensible purpose does seem to have substance. Courts are naturally reluctant to second guess decisions by directors and interfere in intracorporate disputes, but will do so if they feel that the ostensible purpose is a sham, and the real purpose of the transaction is simply to benefit management.

Preemptive rights give shareholders considerably less protection against such tactics than is often thought. Indeed, as a practical matter, the protection provided by preemptive rights is often illusory. A minority shareholder may be frozen out if he or she lacks the financial ability to exercise the preemptive right and purchase the additional shares in order to protect his or her proportionate interest. Often, the majority or dominant shareholders may purchase their allotment by offsetting indebtedness owed to them by the corporation (thereby exercising their preemptive rights without further financial investment) while other shareholders have to invest substantial amounts of cash just to stay even. In one case, for example, the court refused to intervene when a shareholder was given the choice of investing an additional $136,000 to preserve his twenty per cent interest or permitting his interest in the corporation to be diluted to less than one per cent. Hyman v. Velsicol Corp. (1951). In another case, where the reduction was from about 32 per cent to less than one per cent, the court applied the test whether the issuance of shares seemed to serve a substantial corporate purpose or whether it was designed simply to benefit management, and over one dissent, concluded that the issuance of shares should be set aside. Browning v. C & C Plywood Corp. (1967). The issue in these cases may come down to an evaluation of the existence of a valid business purpose for the transaction: e.g. the need of the corporation for the additional capital, or where indebtedness is cancelled and the corporation receives no additional cash, whether the improvement in the balance sheet caused by the cancellation of indebtedness is a bona fide purpose. There appears, however, to be a trend toward giving minority shareholders protection against the unfair issuance of shares despite the presence of a nominal business purpose on the theory that the majority shareholder owes a fiduciary duty to the minority. See § 16.11 of this Nutshell.

§ 7.19 Circular Ownership of Shares

As indicated earlier, treasury shares—shares of a corporation which have been issued but subsequently reacquired by and belong to the corporation—have an intermediate status in most states. They are treated as issued but not outstanding and may not be voted or be counted in determining the number of shares outstanding.

Shares that are owned by a wholly- or majority-owned subsidiary of the issuing corporation are usually called circularly owned shares. Even though they are not technically treasury shares, they are treated in an analogous fashion. They may not be voted or considered as outstanding for purposes of a quorum. See RMBCA § 7.21(b). In other words, circular control is prohibited under most statutes. On a similar theory, shares held by the issuing corporation in a fiduciary capacity also have sometimes been barred from being voted or counted in determining the number of shares outstanding, though section 7.21(c) and the statutes of a number of states permit such voting.

§ 7.20   A Cautionary Postscript: The Risk of Violating Securities Acts While Raising Capital

The Federal Securities Act of 1933 and state statutes, called "blue sky laws," require corporations to register issues of securities with governmental agencies before they are sold publicly. (The picturesque name, "blue sky laws," is reputedly derived from the practice of certain turn-of-the-century promoters of selling "lots in the blue sky in fee simple absolute.") Registration under these statutes, considered at length in advanced courses on securities regulation, is expensive, difficult, and time consuming. Further, selling shares without registration when required gives rise to substantial civil liabilities and may lead to criminal prosecution as well.

When corporations raise capital by selling shares, it is important that the offering not become inadvertently a public one, thereby triggering the registration requirements of these statutes, or that some exemption from registration under these statutes is available. The definition of a "public offering" and the scope of exemptions from registration are often complex legal issues. As a result, the risk of an inadvertent violation of these statutes is often a real one.

When a corporation first registers securities under these statutes it is often said to "go public."

[For unfamiliar terms see the Glossary]

CHAPTER EIGHT

THE DISTRIBUTION OF POWERS WITHIN A CORPORATION: THE SPECIAL PROBLEMS OF THE CLOSELY HELD CORPORATION

§ 8.1 The "Statutory Scheme"

Each state business corporation act envisions a particular model or norm of management and control within the corporation. This model is referred to as the "statutory scheme," or "statutory norm." The statute assumes that every corporation has certain characteristics, even though manifestly not all corporations in the real world possess these characteristics. For example, the statute assumes that shareholders will hold meetings to select directors who in turn elect or appoint officers. A corporation with only a single shareholder does not fit this scheme very well. Rather surprisingly, a large, publicly-held corporation also may not fit this scheme very well either since shareholders in a public corporation may be so diverse and poorly organized that their principal function is ratifying the selection of directors by "management," a group of persons who control the corporate destiny but have a small financial investment in the corporation. It is probable, however, that the statutory scheme more or less accurately describes the control relationships in many intermediate corporations in the continuum between the very small and the very large.

A question that is often critically important is the extent to which the statutory requirements relating to management and control may be varied by agreement among the parties. This question usually arises in the context of small, closely held corporations which in practice more closely resemble partnerships than publicly held corporations. A person not versed in corporation law might well conclude that in the absence of harm to some class of persons, businessmen should be permitted to vary the statutory norms to fit the needs of their particular business relationship. Such freedom is generally available in partnerships, and there seems to be no reason why it should not be equally available in corporations. While the trend is clearly in the direction of providing increased freedom within the corporation, it is still not available to the same extent as it is in a partnership. The reason is the survival of the theory that the granting of the privilege of limited liability and permission to conduct business in the name of a fictitious entity is a concession by the State: In order to gain the concession one must follow the procedures and rules set forth in the business corporation statutes. (See generally § 1.2 of this Nutshell). Despite criticism of this theory as pure formalism, vestiges of it remain embedded in the thinking of judges, and it is therefore unsafe to attempt by agreement substantial variations from the statutory norm that are not expressly authorized by statute. Legislation is the ultimate solution if greater freedom is felt to be necessary, and indeed there is a trend toward relaxing the statutory norms discussed in this Chapter both by general legislation in business corporation statutes and the enactment of special statutes (discussed in Chapter 12 of this Nutshell) to relieve closely held corporations from the strictures of the statutory scheme. Even then, however, it is still unsafe to attempt to vary the statutory norms in a way not contemplated by these statutes.

§ 8.2 The Statutory Scheme: Shareholders

The shareholders in the statutory scheme are the ultimate owners of the corporation, but have only limited powers to participate in management and control. The statutes contemplate that they may act through four main channels:

(1) Election and removal of directors;

(2) Approval or disapproval of corporate operations which are void or voidable unless ratified;

(3) Approval or disapproval of amendments to articles of incorporation or bylaws constituting the "contract" between the corporation and its shareholders; and

(4) Approval or disapproval of fundamental changes not in the regular course of business (mergers, compulsory share exchanges, dissolution, or disposition of substantially all the corporate assets).

This list, however, does not fully exhaust the shareholders' powers in fact. For example, statutes also grant shareholders miscellaneous incidental powers, perhaps the most important of which is the right to inspect corporate books and records. See, for example, Chapter 16 of the Revised Model Business Corporation Act, discussed in Chapter 15 of this Nutshell. Section 8.03 of the RMBCA requires shareholder approval of certain major changes in the size of the board of directors. The RMBCA and most state statutes also authorize shareholders to file derivative suits on behalf of the corporation (RMBCA §§ 7.40—7.47) or suits to enjoin ultra vires acts (RMBCA § 3.04). State statutes that embody the traditional par value corporation finance concepts also grant shareholders other powers, e.g., a veto power over repurchases of corporate shares out of capital surplus, a veto power over dividends payable in the shares of the corporation, and the power to approve the consideration for which no par shares are issued. It is also well established that shareholders may adopt resolutions making recommendations to the board of directors, and because of the power to select and remove directors, it is probable that the directors will listen carefully to the views of a majority of the shareholders. (See § 8.7 of this Nutshell.) Further, some matters such as the selection of independent accountants have been vested in the shareholders either by tradition or because of regulations by the Securities and Exchange Commission. Nevertheless, the fact remains that the shareholders have only limited powers to participate in management and control: their principal function is to select other persons—the directors—to manage the business of the corporation for them.

§ 8.3   The Statutory Scheme: Power of Shareholders to Remove Directors

At common law, a director had considerable security of office for the period of his or her election. He or she could be removed only for cause, a procedure technically known as "amotion." Further, a director, threatened with removal for cause, was entitled to some minimal elements of due process including notice of charges, an opportunity to be heard, and a hearing. Of course, in a corporation with shares widely held by the general public, a "trial" of a director by the shareholders at a meeting was unwieldy and impractical. Decision was made in fact by the granting or withholding of a proxy appointment, a fact that was recognized by courts which required that the imperiled director be given access to the proxy machinery to conduct his or her defense. There was also some case law questioning the power of a court to remove a director even for cause if a majority of the shareholders refused to do so. These various common law rules are, of course, basically consistent with the principle that directors' independence of judgment cannot be restricted or interfered with by shareholders.

These common law rules have been virtually totally superseded by statute. Modern corporation statutes permit shareholders to remove directors without cause (see RMBCA § 8.08), though in a few states such a power exists in all circumstances only if specifically reserved to the shareholders in the articles of incorporation. Furthermore, a number of states expressly permit a court to remove directors upon a judicial finding that the director "engaged in fraudulent or dishonest conduct, or gross abuse of authority or discretion," and that removal is in the best interest of the corporation. See RMBCA § 8.09. The power to remove a director by judicial act is appropriate in two circumstances: (1) where the director possesses sufficient voting power as a shareholder to prevent removal, and declines to vote for his or her own removal, and (2) in publicly held corporations where the director refuses to resign despite requests to do so, and the cost of a special shareholders' meeting to remove him or her is substantial.

The statutes permitting the removal of directors without cause subtly change the relation between shareholders and directors. The power to remove for policy or personal reasons (not involving "cause" in the legal sense of misconduct) may be important in several areas, for example:

(1) Where a person has recently acquired a majority of the outstanding shares (or at least working control) and desires to put "his own people" in control of the corporation immediately;

(2) In closely held corporations where a majority (or sole) shareholder may wish to elect friends as directors but ensure their continued loyalty. An unlimited power of removal without cause goes a long way to ensuring that loyalty.

Of course, under modern statutes a corporation may voluntarily elect to grant directors the tenure they possessed at common law. Such provisions are not uncommon. For example, a number of publicly held corporations have granted directors this security as part of a defensive plan to make takeovers more difficult, the theory being that a potential purchaser of a working majority of the corporation's voting shares may be deterred if the purchaser is unable to obtain immediate control of the corporation's decision-making power. Similar provisions may also appear in closely held corporations as part of a plan to assure continued minority shareholder representation on the board of directors.

A question may exist as to whether an amendment to bylaws granting (or restoring) the power to remove directors without cause may be made effective against incumbent directors who were elected under bylaws that guaranteed them greater security of office. A court may be tempted to argue in this situation that a change in the bylaws during the term of a director is an invalid deprivation of a vested right.

§ 8.4   The Statutory Scheme: Directors

The traditional language of business corporation acts defining the role of the board of directors is that "the business and affairs of a corporation shall be managed by the board of directors." The word "shall" has a mandatory ring, and it is pursuant to this provision that courts have sometimes struck down, as against public policy, agreements between businessmen which purport to dictate how persons shall vote as directors.

In the very large corporation with billions of dollars of assets, it is not realistic to expect the directors actually to manage the day-to-day affairs of the business. That is management's responsibility. In recognition of this, section 8.01(b) of the Revised Model Business Corporation Act and the statutes of some states have modified the basic obligation of directors to read: "all corporate powers shall be exercised by *or under the authority of,* and the business and affairs of the corporation *shall be managed under the direction of,* its board of directors, subject to any limitation set forth in the articles of incorporation." The final "subject to" clause, it may be noted, authorizes limitations on the scope of the traditional power of directors.

The scope of the phrase "business and affairs" is not defined in the statutes. Generally, in closely held corporations directors formulate the policy of the corporation, and authorize the making of important contracts. They may delegate details of the actual daily operation of the corporation to officers and agents, but oversee those activities. In the publicly held corporation, actual management is delegated to corporate officers subject to the general direction of the board of directors.

Directors have specific statutory authority in numerous areas. For example, the decision to declare dividends is specifically a directoral function, as is the determination of the consideration for which shares are to be issued. Even in the case of important corporate changes, such as mergers or amendments to articles of incorporation, which require shareholder approval, the directors have the responsibility to formulate the proposed change, approve it, and submit it to the shareholders for approval or disapproval. See § 8.8 of this Nutshell.

The power of directors with respect to the business and affairs of the corporation in a sense flows from the statute rather than from the shareholders who elected them. Directors may, if they wish, disregard the expressed desires of a majority of the shareholders and act as they think best— subject of course, to the ultimate power of the shareholders to select different directors next time. However, there are only a few recorded illustrations of the exercise of this independent power. As a practical matter, the power of selection and removal of directors is a powerful brake on boards of directors acting independently of the expressed wishes of a majority of the shareholders. In addition, there is perhaps a partially articulated notion that such independence of action is inconsistent with shareholder democracy in publicly held corporations. This problem occasionally arises immediately after a successful corporate takeover where the shareholders do not possess the power to remove sitting directors.

The relationships between directors, shareholders and the corporation are *sui generis*. The shareholders elect directors who are granted broad authority with respect to the corporation and its property. Further, responsibility accompanies power. The directors owe fiduciary and other duties to the corporation and to the shareholders. Such duties include specified statutory liabilities for director misconduct plus broader common law duties—due care, loyalty, corporate opportunity, and the like. A director may be liable for misconduct even though he or she is following the wishes of a majority of the shareholders of a corporation. Because of this risk of directoral liability, cases involving the role of directors place great importance on their unimpaired independence of decision. Shareholder agreements on matters that are reserved to the discretion of directors are often referred to by courts in antagonistic terms: they are against public policy because they "fetter" the discretion of directors, or in extreme cases, "sterilize" the board.

§ 8.5 Elimination of the Board of Directors

Until relatively recently it was an accepted premise of corporation law that every corporation had to have a board of directors. The first important exception to this principle occurred in the special close corporation statutes described in Chapter 12 of this Nutshell. The reason underlying the decision to permit such corporations to dispense with a board of directors and have their affairs conducted directly by shareholders runs along the following lines. Why should a corporation with a few shareholders—perhaps only one or two—have to have a board of directors? Why should not such a corporation be permitted to dispense with a board of directors entirely and simply conduct business directly through shareholders? In fact, that is almost always what happens, with the shareholders donning their "director hats" when their lawyer tells them to. There seems to be no good reason why such a corporation should not be able to have its formal structure reflect the reality of the way the business is run, and a number of states enacted close corporation statutes authorizing such a management form.

The close corporation statutes generally require an election by the corporation to adopt those statutes. Should the option to dispense entirely with the board of directors be limited to corporations that have made that election? If a non-electing corporation has only one or two shareholders, why should it not also be entitled to dispense with its board of directors? It was on the basis of reasoning implicit in these questions that the draftsmen of the Revised Model Business Corporation Act added section 8.01(c) that permits any corporation with 50 or fewer shareholders to elect to dispense with or limit the authority of the board of directors. It is too early to tell whether this innovative provision will be widely used; certainly it represents a sharp departure from the traditional mores of the corporate form.

§ 8.6 The Statutory Scheme: Officers

Corporation statutes generally do not attempt to define the authority and role of officers. A typical statutory provision merely states that each officer of the corporation "has the authority and shall perform the duties set forth in the bylaws or, to the extent consistent with the bylaws, the duties prescribed by the board of directors or by direction of an officer authorized by the board of directors to prescribe the duties of other officers." (RMBCA § 8.41). In theory, corporate officers administer the day-to-day affairs of the corporation subject to the direction and control of the board of directors. In fact, of course, their authority is often considerably greater, particularly in larger publicly held corporations. Further, the precise scope of the implied authority of officers vis á vis third persons—particularly the president—is somewhat broader, but varies from state to state. (For a discussion see § 11.2 of this Nutshell.) The basic point for present purposes, however, is that corporate officers are visualized in the statutory scheme as agents carrying out policies established by the board of directors.

§ 8.7   Shared Responsibility With Respect to Corporate Operations

As indicated previously, the directors have responsibility for the management of the business and affairs of the corporation. Shareholders also may have a limited role on business matters. For example, shareholders of publicly held corporations may be called upon to review and approve the selection of accountants, auditors or attorneys who are to evaluate the stewardship of the directors. Also, shareholders are sometimes called upon to approve or refuse to approve specific corporate operations or corporate transactions. Shareholder ratification usually involves transactions in which management is personally interested (see § 14.7 of this Nutshell) or requests by officers or directors for indemnification against liability or litigation costs (see § 14.20 of this Nutshell). It has become almost standard operating procedure, for example, for publicly held corporations to submit incentive compensation plans for officers and high level employees (profit sharing plans, stock option plans, "phantom stock" plans, and the like) to the shareholders for approval. Approval of transactions by shareholders does not totally immunize the transaction from attack since a court may subsequently decide that it involves waste or a gift of corporate assets. Approval by shareholders, however, probably prevents shareholders who voted to approve the plan from later attacking it; approval may also prevent other shareholders from attacking the fairness of the transaction or shift the burden of proof from management to the attacking shareholders. Ratification or approval of transactions, however, does not validate fraudulent, oppressive or manifestly unfair transactions involving officers or directors.

Shareholders are sometimes asked to approve a blanket resolution covering all business and other transactions by management during the period since the last meeting. Such resolutions do not validate improper transactions of which the shareholders have no knowledge.

Shareholders also may make recommendations to the board of directors on corporate matters. While without legal effect, such resolutions express the views of the ultimate owners of the corporation, and are usually followed. For example, in one leading case, Auer v. Dressel (1954), it was held proper for shareholders to vote upon a resolution approving the administration of an ousted president and demanding his or her reinstatement. The Court said, "The stockholders, by expressing their approval of Mr. Auer's conduct as president and their demand that he be put back in that office, will not be able, directly, to effect that change in officers, but there is nothing invalid in their so expressing themselves and thus putting on notice the directors who will stand for election at the annual meeting."

§ 8.8 Shared Responsibility: Approval of Fundamental Corporate Changes

Shareholders have the specific statutory power to approve or disapprove fundamental changes in the corporation's structure proposed by the board of directors. In a few states, shareholders have the power both to propose and to adopt such changes, but in most states the responsibility is shared by shareholders and directors. While changes subject to shareholder approval vary to some extent from state to state, most states require shareholder approval of the following:

(1) Amendments of articles of incorporation.

(2) Mergers and consolidations.

(3) Dissolution.

(4) Sale of all or substantially all of a corporation's assets not in the ordinary course of business.

(5) Statutory share exchanges where a decision to make an exchange is binding on all holders of shares.

In most states, a majority of all the outstanding voting shares must approve the proposed transaction, though several states retain the older requirement (almost universal thirty years ago) that two-thirds of the outstanding shares (both voting and nonvoting) must approve the proposed transaction.

Under the Revised Model Business Corporation Act and the statutes of many states, the board of directors has a "gatekeeping" function with respect to such transactions: the shareholders may consider such transactions only if the board of directors decides it is appropriate for them to do so. If the board of directors refuses to recommend the transaction to the shareholders, they may not take the proposal upon their own motion. Thus, decisions on such basic matters in most states are shared between shareholders and directors, and both must concur in the proposal. In a handful of states, including Massachusetts, shareholders have power to effectuate basic corporate changes without the concurrence of the directors, but that is the exception rather than the norm.

In addition to these fundamental changes, state statutes may provide for shareholder approval of less substantial transactions, including distributions in partial liquidation out of capital, reductions of stated capital, or the purchase of corporate shares out of capital surplus.

§ 8.9   Shared Responsibility: Bylaw Amendments

In most states, the initial bylaws of a corporation are adopted by the board of directors or incorporators, whichever group completes the organization of the corporation. Thereafter, the power to amend or repeal bylaws may be vested in either the shareholders or the directors, or very commonly in both organizations. The 1969 Model Act contained a skeletal and rather ambiguous provision that appears in the statutes of many states; it provides that the power to amend is vested in the board of directors "unless reserved to the shareholders by the articles;" further the shareholders may "repeal or change" bylaws adopted by the directors. (1969 MBCA § 27, second sentence)

The Revised Model Business Corporation adopted in 1984 devotes three entire sections to bylaw amendments. Section 10.20 is the basic section: it provides that directors may adopt, amend, or repeal bylaws unless (a) the bylaw deals with a subject that the statute or the articles of incorporation reserve exclusively to the shareholders, or (b) the shareholders have previously amended or repealed a bylaw on the same subject and have provided expressly that their action is not subject to change by the directors. Further, section 10.20(b) makes it clear that the shareholders' power in this area is primary since the directors may not declare any bylaw off-bounds to the shareholders in the same way that shareholders can with respect to future action by the directors. Section 10.21 deals with bylaw provisions increasing quorum or voting requirements for shareholders while section 10.22 deals with bylaw provisions relating to quorum or voting requirements for directors.

There are wide variations in the state statutes dealing with the power to amend or repeal bylaws. Generally, the power is shared but the primacy of shareholders in this regard is usually recognized. In a few states directors may not repeal or amend bylaws adopted by shareholders; in others the shareholders may designate bylaws that may not be amended by the board of directors.

§ 8.10 May the Statutory Scheme Be Varied? The Problem of the Close Corporation

Experience has shown that in the real world the participants in a business venture often wish to divide up the powers of management and control in a way that is difficult to fit within the statutory scheme. Doubtless the greatest strain on the statutory scheme occurs in corporations with relatively few shareholders—"close corporations" or "incorporated partnerships." But similar problems also may occur in joint venture corporations and even in publicly held corporations. This section considers the developing law as to the extent to which the statutory scheme can be varied by agreement.

As noted earlier, if two or three persons own a business which is being conducted in corporate form, each person active in the business usually will be simultaneously a shareholder, a director, and an officer. While it is possible for the participants to indicate which hat each is wearing at any particular time, the rigid tripartite separation of levels of control and ownership required by the statutory scheme is apt to be considered silly and formalistic. This problem of informality and overlapping role is addressed in part by the close corporation statutes referred to earlier and discussed in a later section of this Nutshell (§ 12.8). Many states, however, have not enacted such statutes, and in those states, close corporation problems must continue to be worked out in the context of regular corporation statutes. And, even in states that have adopted close corporation statutes, most attorneys do not take advantage of them. As a result, the close corporation statutes are not a complete answer to the problem of varying the statutory scheme.

Section 8.01(b) of the Revised Model Business Corporation Act provides for the power of the board of directors to direct (or oversee the direction of) the business and affairs of the corporation "subject to any limitation set forth in the articles of incorporation." This provision should authorize all variations to the statutory scheme discussed in this section so long as the appropriate provision appears in the articles of incorporation.

The prototype situation involving agreements varying the statutory scheme occurs when a person with a minority position in a close corporation wishes to have protection against abuse of power by his or her "partners" which are difficult to fit into the statutory scheme. For example, a shareholder in a closely held corporation may desire to retain a veto over the corporation borrowing money in excess of some stated amount. In one case the shareholders agreed that two small corporations would not borrow more than $10,000 and $40,000 respectively except by unanimous approval of the shareholders. The agreement also stated that each party "binds himself to vote as stockholders and directors in such a manner as to carry out bona fide the purposes and intent of this agreement." This provision obviously fettered to some extent the discretion of a majority of the directors, and thereby departed from the statutory scheme. The court invalidated the portion of the agreement relating to the directors: "An agreement by which directors abdicate or bargain away in advance the judgment the law contemplates they shall exercise over the corporation is void. The agreement of the parties to bind themselves as directors is void." Burnett v. Word, Inc. (1967). In a more recent case, the New York Court of Appeals upheld by a closely divided vote a provision that a corporation would not enter into specific transactions or new business without the consent of both shareholders. Zion v. Kurtz (1980). Cases such as these, whether or not correctly decided, illustrate the pervasive impact of the statutory scheme on judicial thought and the danger of assuming that simply because all parties in interest agree to a variation in the statutory scheme, the variation is valid. It may be noted in passing that the agreement in Burnett v. Word, Inc. was upheld to the extent it constituted an agreement by share-holders to vote as shareholders in a specified manner. In other words, the danger lies in directors' agreements, not agreements between shareholders as to how shareholders will vote as shareholders.

Some courts have upheld variations on the statutory scheme, and the modern trend distinctly appears to be running in the direction of upholding such agreements and away from the strict position of Burnett v. Word, Inc. The leading line of cases arose in New York. In McQuade v. Stoneham (1934), the Court invalidated an agreement be-tween the majority shareholders that they would maintain themselves as officers at specified salaries. The Court said, "We are constrained by authority to hold that a contract is illegal and void so far as it precludes the board of directors, at the risk of incurring legal liability, from changing officers, salaries or policies or retaining individuals in office, except by consent of the contracting parties. On the whole, such a holding is probably preferable to one which would open the courts to pass on the motives of directors in lawful exercise of their trust." (An independent ground for this decision also existed.)

Two years later the same problem again came before the highest New York court in the case of Clark v. Dodge (1936). Clark owned 25 per cent and Dodge owned 75 per cent of the stock of two corporations manufacturing medic-inal preparations by secret formulae. Dodge did not active-ly participate in the management of the business; the secret formulae were known only to Clark, who actively managed the business. In 1921, Dodge and Clark entered into an agreement by which Dodge agreed to retain Clark as gener-al manager of the business and to pay him one-fourth of the income either in the form of salary or dividends. The agreement was to continue so long as Clark remained "faithful, efficient and competent to so manage and control the said business." Clark, in turn, agreed to disclose the secret formulae to Dodge's son and upon Clark's death without issue to bequeath his 25 per cent interest in the corporation to the wife and children of Dodge. This entirely sensible business arrangement appears to run afoul of the McQuade principle, since Dodge was in effect agreeing to vote as director to retain Clark as general manager and to pay twenty-five per cent of the earnings to him in the form of salary or dividends. The Court nevertheless upheld the agreement:

Are we committed by the McQuade case to the doctrine that there may be no variation, however slight or innocuous, from [the statutory] norm, where salaries or policies or the retention of individuals in office are concerned? There is ample authority supporting that doctrine * * *. [S]omething may be said for it, since it furnishes a simple, if arbitrary test. Apart from its practical administrative convenience, the reasons upon which it is said to rest are more or less nebulous. Public policy, the intention of the Legislature, detriment to the corporation, are phrases which in this connection mean little. Possible harm to bona fide purchasers of stock or to creditors or to stockholding minorities have more substance; but such harms are absent in many instances. If the enforcement of a particular contract damages nobody—not even, in any perceptible degree, the public—one sees no reason for holding it illegal, even though it impinges slightly upon the broad provision [vesting directors with the powers of management]. Damage suffered or threatened is a logical and practical test and has come to be the one generally adopted.

Where the directors are the sole stockholders, there seems to be no objection to enforcing an agreement among them to vote for certain people as officers * * * .

If there was any invasion of the powers of the directorate under that agreement it is so slight as to be negligible; and certainly there is no damage suffered by or threatened to anybody. The broad statements in the McQuade opinion, applicable to the facts there, should be confined to those facts.

The Clark opinion arguably rests on two different grounds:

(1) The Court emphasized that in *Clark* all the shareholders were parties to the agreement. In *McQuade,* there were shareholders who were not parties to the agreement. Certainly, non-consenting shareholders may be injured if directors fail to exercise their "honest and unfettered" judgment, and hence it seems reasonable to reconcile the two cases on this ground. On the other hand, the agreement in *McQuade* was not being attacked by a non-consenting shareholder, but by a person who was a party to the agreement and was not living up to it. No emphasis was placed on the presence of non-consenting shareholders in the *McQuade* decision.

(2) The Clark opinion stresses that the arrangement harmed no one, and that "damage suffered or threatened" is a logical and practical test. If this were the sole test adopted in Clark v. Dodge, the courts might accept very substantial variations from the statutory norm—possibly to the extent of permitting the total abolishment of the board of directors. However, subsequent cases in New York indicate that this is too expansive a reading of Clark v. Dodge and that as much stress should be placed on the statement that the impingement in that case was "slight" or "innocuous" as on the language that no damage was "suffered or threatened." Hence the common law rule in New York following these two famous cases, and probably in most other states as well, is that only "slight impingements" that damage no one will be accepted.

In 1982, the New York Court of Appeals put a rather bizarre twist on these cases, which, if accepted generally, may eliminate most of the problems in this area. Zion v.

Kurtz (1980), involved a complex financing arrangement in which the creditor obtained as part of the security for a loan a minority interest in a closely held corporation and a commitment from the dominant shareholder that the corporation would not enter into transactions or new business without the consent of the creditor. Under the law of Delaware, such an agreement might validly be entered into by a corporation electing statutory close corporation treatment; however, to be eligible for such treatment the corporation in its articles of incorporation had to expressly elect close corporation status and refer to the agreement limiting the discretion of directors. The corporation involved in Zion v. Kurtz had done neither. The court nevertheless viewed these omissions from the articles of incorporation as "technical" defects and within the power of the court to correct by an order of reformation. Three justices dissented vigorously on the ground that the whole theory of close corporation election was that public notice should be provided in the articles of incorporation, and the reasoning of the majority vitiated this important principle. Nevertheless, if the reasoning of the majority is accepted, most problems of shareholders' agreements in states with close corporation statutes should disappear.

The leading case outside of New York that rejects the rather narrow view of McQuade and similar cases is Galler v. Galler (1964), a decision which enforced a complex shareholders' agreement containing numerous "impingements" of varying degrees of seriousness on the statutory scheme. After drawing sharply the distinction between closely held and publicly held corporations, the Court called for statutory recognition of the special problems of the closely held corporation, and concluded that "any arrangements concerning the management of the corporation which are agreeable to all" should be enforced if (1) no complaining minority interest appears, (2) no fraud or apparent injury to the public or creditors is present, and (3) no clearly prohibitory statutory language is violated. While this decision has generally been approved and applauded, a subsequent Illinois case refused to extend Galler to validate a shareholders' agreement that more or less squarely contradicted a specific statutory provision; because of this qualification in the Galler opinion, there is some lingering doubt as to whether all shareholders' agreements will be upheld.

§ 8.11   Delegation of Management Powers and the Statutory Scheme

Interference with the discretion of directors has also been used to attack broad management agreements between the corporation and outsiders by which the sole power of management appears to be taken from the board and vested in the managers. Similar arguments have been applied to invalidate agreements between shareholders which provided that the sole power to manage a portion of the corporation's assets is vested in one shareholder. Potentially over-broad delegation to an executive or other committee of the board may also be attacked on this ground, though that question is now usually dealt with by statute. (See § 10.10 of this Nutshell.) The test in all these cases is whether the agreement "sterilizes" the board so that it has no managerial role at all or whether reasonable powers of oversight are preserved to the board.

[For unfamiliar terms see the Glossary]

CHAPTER NINE

SHARES AND SHAREHOLDERS

§ 9.1 Annual and Special Meetings of Shareholders

Every state statute contains more or less routine provisions about meetings of shareholders. The Revised Model Business Corporation Act, for example, provides that a meeting shall be held "annually at a time stated in or fixed in accordance with the bylaws," [RMBCA § 7.01(a)], that notice of an annual or special meeting shall be given not less than ten nor more than sixty days before the meeting [RMBCA § 7.05(a)], and so forth. The failure to hold an annual meeting does not "affect the validity of any corporate action" [RMBCA § 7.01(c)], though any shareholder may obtain a summary court order to hold an annual meeting if one is not held "within the earlier of 6 months after the end of the corporation's last fiscal year or 15 months after its last annual meeting" [RMBCA § 7.03(a)(1)]. So far as notice is concerned, statutes permit written waivers that may be executed before, at, or after the meeting in question [RMBCA § 7.06(a)].

The principal purpose of an annual meeting is the annual election of directors, but the annual meeting may act on any relevant matter and is not limited to the purposes set forth in the notice. Indeed, under the Revised Model Act [RMBCA § 7.05(b)] and the statutes of most states, no statement of purposes at all need appear in the notice of annual meeting.

A special meeting is any meeting other than an annual meeting. It may be called by the persons specified in the statute or in the bylaws of the corporation. Typically, such a meeting may be called by the board of directors, the holders of some specified percentage of the outstanding shares of the corporation, or by certain officers. In the Revised Model Business Corporation Act, holders of ten per cent of the votes eligible to be cast at the meeting may compel the holding of a special meeting [RMBCA § 7.02(a)(2)]; this type of provision is controversial since it may result in a shareholders' meeting being held on matters which management might prefer not be considered or even on matters on which it is clear that there is no chance of passage. There is also the possibility that repetitive or unnecessary meetings might be called by small factions of shareholders. The Official Comment to RMBCA § 7.02 suggests that the board of directors has some discretion in calling special meetings at the request of shareholders to meet this last problem.

Unlike the annual meeting, the only subjects that may be considered at a special meeting are matters described in the notice of meeting. RMBCA §§ 7.05, 7.02(d).

A quorum at any annual or special meeting consists of a majority of the outstanding shares, except that the quorum requirement may be increased or decreased by provisions in the articles or bylaws. Statutes usually prescribe a minimum below which the quorum may not be reduced. The most popular figure is one-third, based on old MBCA § 32; the Revised Model Business Corporation Act does not contain any statutory minimum. Statutes do not prescribe a maximum number to constitute a quorum, and it is therefore possible to require the presence of all outstanding shares to conduct business at a shareholders' meeting. Such a provision is sometimes adopted in close corporations as a planning device, even though it increases the risk of a deadlock since a single shareholder, no matter how small his or her holding, may prevent the existence of a quorum.

Most state statutes provide that where a quorum is present, the affirmative vote of a majority of that quorum is necessary to bind the corporation. Such statutes may lead to questionable results in situations where votes are present (and counted toward the quorum) but abstain from voting on an issue. Under the traditional statutes abstentions are in effect treated as negative votes since an action can be adopted only if a majority of all the votes that are present vote in favor of the measure. The Revised Model Business Corporation Act changes the traditional rule: it provides that if a quorum is present a measure is approved "if the votes cast * * * favoring the action exceed the votes cast opposing the action" [§ 7.25(c)]. The example used in the Official Comment to explain why this is preferable posits a meeting of a corporation with one thousand shares outstanding. A quorum is, of course, 501 in the absence of a specific provision in the articles of incorporation. Assume that 600 shares are represented at the meeting and the vote on an action is 280 in favor, 225 opposed, and 95 abstaining. Under the traditional statute, the measure fails since 301 votes were necessary (a majority of the quorum); under the RMBCA, the action would be approved, 280–225. It may be noted that if the 95 abstaining shares were not present at all, the action would have been approved under both types of statutes.

Somewhat different rules of shareholder voting are often applicable to elections of directors. These rules are discussed in § 9.4 of this Nutshell.

If a quorum is initially present, a disgruntled faction may sometimes lose a vote, and thereafter leave the meeting seeking to "break" the quorum and prevent the victorious faction from conducting further business. The general rule is that a quorum, once present, continues, and the withdrawal of a faction does not disable the remaining shareholders from continuing. The position that a minority faction of shareholders cannot "break" a quorum once it is established is codified in § 7.25(b) of the Revised Model Business Corporation Act. Because of this rule, a faction that knows it will be in the minority but believes that a quorum will not exist without their presence, should stay entirely away to prevent a quorum from ever being present, rather than appearing and later withdrawing in an attempt to break the quorum.

Virtually all states authorize shareholders to conduct business by unanimous written consent without a meeting. Such a provision is particularly helpful in closely held corporations, where most shareholders' decisions are unanimous, and the formality of a meeting may be dispensed with. About a dozen states, including Delaware, have gone a step further and authorized holders of the number of shares needed to act on a matter to act by written consent without a meeting. (Del.Gen.Corp.Law, § 228.) As discussed in the chapter on proxy voting in publicly held corporations, elimination of the unanimity requirement is not as radical a proposal as might first be thought since most shareholder votes in such a corporation are cast by proxy in any event, and the same information must be provided for either a vote by proxy or an action by consent. (See § 13.7.) In smaller corporations, however, majority consent provisions do not contain the same built-in safeguards. And even in publicly held corporations, the majority consent provision has had some unexpected consequences since it enables a successful aggressor which acquires a majority of the target's voting shares to make immediate changes in management without having to request that the board of directors call a special meeting of shareholders.

§ 9.2   Eligibility to Vote: Record and Beneficial Ownership

Every corporation retains records of the persons in whose name shares have been issued and every share certificate that is issued refers by name to that person. This person is called the "record owner" and generally the corporation may deal with the record owner as though he or she were the sole owner of the shares. The theory is that when the record owner sells shares, he or she normally hands over the certificate to the purchaser with the endorsement on the reverse side of the certificate properly executed; the purchaser may then submit the endorsed certificate to the corporation with a request that a new certificate be issued in a designated name. The old certificate is cancelled and a new certificate is issued in the name of the purchaser (or another name designated by the purchaser) who then becomes the new record owner. While modern practice in the transfer of shares of publicly held corporations is quite different from the theory, the theory of record ownership continues to apply to all corporations. The corporate records of the names and addresses of record owners are usually called the "stock transfer books" or "share register" (though they may consist simply of stubs formerly attached to share certificates). The corporation deals only with record owners on matters such as dividends, voting, and notices of meetings. A purchaser who does not obtain the issuance of a new certificate is only the "beneficial owner" of those shares; while corporations do not accord beneficial owners the rights of ownership (since they deal only with record owners), the beneficial owner is the "real" owner and can compel the record owner to turn over dividends or to execute appropriate documents to permit the beneficial owner to exercise the power to vote or to become the record owner.

Obviously every publicly held corporation with active trading in its shares must not only have available a large number of new certificates to issue to transferees but also must take steps to ensure that transfers are properly recorded, that new certificates refer to the same number of shares as old certificates, and so forth. These mechanical functions of registering share transfers are handled by "transfer agents" who keep exact records of all shareholders, their names, addresses and number of shares owned. Publicly held corporations also use "registrars," whose function is to make sure the corporation does not inadvertently overissue shares. In an earlier era, the mechanical functions of registration of transfer of shares were quite onerous. However, new devices that simplify the ownership and transfer of publicly held shares have greatly reduced the practical problems faced by transfer agents and registrars in this area. See § 13.5 of this Nutshell.

Once the possibility of share transfers is recognized, some rule must be established to determine the point in time that eligibility to vote is determined. This is normally done by corporations establishing a "record date" in advance of the meeting. A record date may be established directly by bylaw provision, but it is more customary to authorize the board of directors to set a record date. Section 7.07 of the Revised Model Business Corporation Act requires such a date to be established in advance and to be not more than seventy days before the meeting. The record date is usually specified in the resolution of the board of directors calling the meeting. If a record date is established, the corporation continues to register transfers and issue new certificates to transferees, but the persons eligible to vote are those in whose name the shares were registered on the record date.

If the board of directors does not formally set a record date, the corporation is deemed to set a record date as of the date the notice of the meeting is mailed, and eligibility to vote is determined as of that date.

Older statutes also usually permit the board of directors, rather than establishing a record date, to order the stock transfer books closed for a stated period, which the old Model Act set as at least ten days but not more than fifty days before the meeting (MBCA § 30). If the stock transfer books are closed, the corporation refuses thereafter to register transfers of shares and eligibility to vote is determined by the closed books. In effect the corporate records are frozen, though, of course, individual shareholders may endorse and deliver certificates to purchasers during the period. This alternative is obsolete since the record date alternative is so much simpler. Certainly in publicly held corporations, it would be completely impractical to allow requested transfers to pile up unrecorded for an extended period before a meeting. The RMBCA does not refer to closing the transfer books as an alternative to setting a record date.

The record date provisions are obviously for the benefit of the corporation. They permit the corporation to give proper notice of the meeting, to prepare a voting list, and to establish precisely who is entitled to vote. They also permit management and other shareholders to solicit votes before the meeting.

Analogous record date provisions are authorized by the Revised Model Business Corporation Act for a variety of other shareholder actions: who is entitled to receive corporate dividends as between transferor and transferee (§ 16.5 of this Nutshell), who may demand a special meeting, and so forth.

§ 9.3 Preparation of Voting List

A voting list of shareholders eligible to vote must be prepared before each shareholders meeting. Section 7.20 of the Revised Model Business Corporation Act contains fairly detailed rules about how this list should be compiled and where it must be kept before and during the meeting. Like the statutes of a number of states, it also requires that this list be available for inspection by shareholders before the meeting; the RMBCA requires that it be available for inspection beginning two business days after the notice of meeting is given. (The theory is that the corporation must compile a list of shareholders entitled to receive notice of the meeting before the notice is actually given and so it is no burden to prepare the voting list at the same time.)

Not all states require that the voting list be available in advance of the meeting; the 1969 Model Act only required that it be available at the meeting itself, though an even earlier version of the Model Act required that it be available for inspection for ten days before the meeting.

Every shareholder has an absolute right to inspect the voting list, and this right is not subject to the qualifications imposed upon a shareholder's right to inspect other books and records of the corporation. (See Chapter 15 of this Nutshell). While the failure to prepare the voting list does not affect the validity of any action taken at the meeting [RMBCA § 7.20(e)], such a failure may lead to a summary court order to create the list and postponement of the meeting.

At the meeting, the share transfer books (rather than the voting list) determines who are the shareholders entitled to vote.

§ 9.4   Election of Directors: Cumulative or Straight Voting

Directors are elected each year at the annual meeting of shareholders. The most common statutory provision is simply that directors are elected by a vote of a majority of the shares (1) present at the meeting and (2) entitled to vote, assuming that a quorum is present. This formulation does not address the situation of three or more factions contending for election (in which case it is quite likely that no faction will obtain a majority of the votes present at a meeting). Section 7.28(a) of the Revised Model Business Corporation Act handles this possibility by making the standard for election "a plurality of the votes cast by the shares entitled to vote in the election at a meeting at which a quorum is present."

Like in political elections, shareholders may only vote in favor of candidates. They may not cast negative votes against candidates.

The articles of incorporation, and in some states, the bylaws, may increase, but may not decrease, the percentage of the shares required for election. In close corporations it is not uncommon to exercise this privilege and require unanimity as a planning device, even though the possibility of a deadlock in the election of directors is thereby obviously increased.

The other important question relating to the election of directors is whether shares may be voted "cumulatively" or must be voted "straight." Cumulative voting (the mechanics of which are described immediately below) has historically had a strong emotional appeal. In several states cumulative voting is mandatory by state constitution or provisions in the state corporation statute. Most states today, however, give a corporation an option to exclude cumulative voting; usually this option requires a specific exclusion in the articles of incorporation (an "opt out" election) though in some states, cumulative voting is not permitted unless specific provision for it is made in the articles of incorporation (an "opt in" election). The Revised Model Business Corporation Act adopts the latter course [RMBCA § 7.28(c)].

The workings of cumulative voting can be most simply described by an illustration. Let us assume a corporation with two shareholders, A with 26 shares, and B with 74 shares. Further, let us assume that there are three directors and each shareholder nominates three candidates. A critical point is that candidates do not run for specific places. The three candidates with the most votes in this election are the winners. If only "straight" voting is permitted, A may cast 26 votes for each of any three candidates, and B may cast 74 votes for each of any three candidates. The result, of course, is that if they do not agree on any candidates, all three of B's candidates are elected. If cumulative voting is permitted, the total number of votes that each shareholder may cast is first computed and each shareholder is permitted to distribute these votes as he sees fit over one or more candidates. In the example above, A is entitled to cast a total of 78 votes (26×3) and B is entitled to cast 222 votes (74×3). If A casts all 78 votes for herself, she is assured of election because B cannot divide 222 votes among three candidates in such a way as to give each candidate 79 or more votes and preclude A's election. (If B gives 79 votes to himself and 79 votes to B_1, he will only have 64 votes left for B_2.) Obviously, the effect of cumulative voting is that it increases minority participation on the board of directors. In straight voting, the shareholder with 51 per cent of the vote elects the entire board; in cumulative voting, a relatively small faction (26 per cent in the above example) obtains representation on the board.

The difference between cumulative and straight voting may be vividly illustrated by the deadlock situation where all shares are owned equally by two shareholders—say fifty shares each. If only straight voting is permitted and each shareholder votes only for his or her own candidates a deadlocked election is inevitable. If there are two places to be filled A will vote 50 shares for herself, and 50 shares for A_2; B will vote 50 shares for himself, and 50 shares for B_2. Thus, four candidates will each have 50 votes for two positions, and the result is that no one is elected. If cumulative voting is permitted on the other hand, A may cast 100 votes for herself and she will be guaranteed election (since B obviously cannot give two candidates more than 100 votes each.) If there are an odd number of directors to be elected (say 3) straight voting still leads to deadlock: A_1–50, A_2–50, A_3–50, B_1–50, B_2–50, B_3–50. If cumulative voting is permitted, A and B may each elect one director but the situation is unstable: a deadlock will be created if each tries to elect the tie-breaking director and the other votes rationally. However, the strategy and counter-strategy can become complex. If A gives A_1 76 votes, A_1 will be guaranteed of election since B has only 150 votes and obviously cannot prevent A_1's election; similarly, if B gives B_1 76 votes, A cannot prevent B_1's election. If both shareholders follow this conservative strategy, the result will be A_1-76, A_2-74, B_1-76, B_2-74, with A_1 and B_1 each being elected and a tie existing between A_2 and B_2. However, if B knows that A will follow this strategy in voting, B might be tempted to divide his vote equally between two candidates in order to elect two of the three directors: A_1-76, A_2-74, B_1-75, B_2-75, with A_1, B_1, and B_2 all being elected. A may counter this strategy by also giving her two candidates 75 votes each, thereby creating a four way tie and electing no one. Indeed, it is disastrous if either shareholder deviates from these very precise voting patterns. If B decides to vote only slightly illogically, for example, B_1-77, B_2-73, he delivers control of the corporation over to A even if A follows the conservative strategy of guaranteeing the election of one director: B_1-77, A_1-76, A_2-74, B_2-73, with B_1, A_1 and A_2 elected. In these and the following illustrations it is assumed that A or B, once they have adopted a strategy and cast their votes, cannot thereafter change them. This is true only to a limited extent in the real world. Balloting for directors is by written ballot rather than voice vote so that each shareholder must establish his or her voting strategy without being sure of an opponent's strategy; however, until the vote is announced, a shareholder may recast his or her votes and thereby correct mistakes in the voting strategy adopted.

As the preceding discussion illustrates, one undesirable aspect of cumulative voting is that it tends to be a little tricky. If a shareholder casts votes in an irrational or inefficient way, he or she may not get the directorships a different voting strategy would have guaranteed; when voting cumulatively it is relatively easy to make a mistake in spreading votes around. The most graphic illustration of this are the cases where a majority shareholder votes in such a way that he or she elects only a minority of the directors. This is most likely to occur when one shareholder votes "straight" and another cumulates. For example, if A has 60 shares and B only 40, with five directors to be elected, B may nevertheless elect a majority of the board if A votes "straight," and B knows that A is doing so. The result might look like this:

A_1–60, A_2–60, A_3–60, A_4–60, A_5–60, B_1–67, B_2–66, B_3–65, B_4–1, B_5–1.

This strategy is daring of B because he is spreading his vote over three persons when he can be sure only of electing two. If A knows that B will try to elect three persons, A, by properly cumulating her votes, can elect four directors, in effect "stealing" one of B's. The results of such an election might be as follows:

A_1–73, A_2–74, A_3–75, A_4–76, A_5–2, B_1–67, B_2–66, B_3–65, B_4–1, B_5–1.

A shareholder generally should not create tie votes among his or her own candidates. If he or she does so, and the tied candidates come in fifth and sixth in an election for five directorships, say, the tie may be broken by a new election for only the fifth seat; the other shareholders may be able to vote their shares in the new election for their own candidates, thereby causing the other shareholder to lose a seat.

Section 7.28(d) of the Revised Model Business Corporation Act and the statutes of many states require shareholders to give advance notice before the meeting if they plan to vote cumulatively. Such a requirement seems plainly desirable because the last illustration graphically demonstrates that election results are illogical if some shareholders vote cumulatively while others do not.

The following formula is useful in determining the number of shares needed to elect one director:

$$\frac{S}{D+1} + 1.$$

Where S equals the total number of shares voting, and D equals the number of directors to be elected. The analogous formula to elect n directors is:

$$\frac{nS}{D+1} + 1.$$

A minor modification may sometimes be necessary. The first portion of the formula, $\frac{S}{D+1}$, establishes the maximum number of shares voted for a single person which is insufficient to elect that person as a director. Any share, or fraction thereof, in excess of that amount will be sufficient to elect a director. The formula set forth in the text ignores fractional shares which sometimes may lead to a one share-error. For example, where there are 100 shares voting and five directors to be elected, the first portion of the formula is $\frac{100}{5+1}$, or $\frac{100}{6}$. In this example, 16 shares will not elect a director, but 17 shares will, since the first part of the formula yields $16\frac{2}{3}$. The above formula mechanically yields an answer of $17\frac{2}{3}$.

The reason that several states have mandatory constitutional or statutory cumulative voting is that it is believed to be democratic in that persons with large (but minority) holdings should have a voice in the conduct of the corporation. Also, arguably, it may be desirable to have as many viewpoints as possible represented on the board of directors; and the presence of a minority director may discourage conflicts of interest by management since discovery is considerably more likely. Arguments in opposition to this point of view include: (1) the introduction of a partisan on the board is inconsistent with the notion that the board should represent all interests in the corporation; (2) a partisan director may cause disharmony which reduces the efficiency of the board; (3) a partisan director may criticize management unreasonably so as to make it less willing to take risky (but desirable) action; (4) a partisan director may leak confidential information; and (5) cumulative voting is usually used to further narrow partisan goals, e.g. to give an insurgent group a toehold in the corporation in an effort to obtain control.

As a practical matter, cumulative voting in a close corporation may be of considerable importance. In the large, publicly held corporation, it is traditionally considered more of a nuisance than anything else because it complicates voting by proxy, and usually does not affect the actual outcome of an election. It should be observed, however, that where large boards are involved, cumulative voting simplifies the task of institutional investors or "public interest" or other groups whose goal is merely to obtain representation on the board rather than to take over control of the corporation. For this reason, some groups have advocated that public corporations be required to adopt cumulative voting. And, of course, it is likely that this is the underlying reason why management in such corporations tends to oppose cumulative voting, even though the overt arguments stress the mechanical and technical complexities of such voting.

In states where cumulative voting is mandatory, and sometimes in corporations formed in other states as well, it is not uncommon to employ devices that minimize the effects of cumulative voting. One device that reduces the impact of cumulative voting is the "classification" (or "staggering") of the board of directors if the board consists of nine or more members. Under section 8.06 of the Revised Model Business Corporation Act and most statutes, the directors of a large board may be divided into two or three classes of as nearly equal numbers as possible, and one class may be elected each year. In a classified board, each director serves for two years (if there are two classes) or three years (if there are three classes). The theoretical justification for classification is that it ensures "experience of service" on the board, since only one-half or one-third of the board may be replaced each year. However, experience of service is usually not a major motivating factor for classifying a board, since as a practical matter, experience of service is usually provided by the simple process of reelecting the same persons as directors year after year. Even where a take-over attempt has been successful, or where a controlling interest in a corporation has been sold to outsiders, there is often a period during which some directors are continued in office to provide the necessary continuity and experience. Staggering has two basic effects:

(1) It makes it more difficult for a minority faction to elect a director when there is cumulative voting. For example, if there are nine directors elected each year, ten per cent of the stock can elect a director; if the nine directors are classified and three are elected each year, it takes twenty-five per cent of the stock to elect a director. (If you do not believe these percentages, try them out on the formulas set forth above.)

(2) It makes take-over attempts more difficult when directors can be removed only for cause. Where the board consists of three classes, a person becoming a majority shareholder cannot be assured of electing a majority of the board for more than two full years. In some instances classification has been proposed in publicly held corporations primarily for this reason even though the corporation does not have cumulative voting.

Other devices also limit the impact of cumulative voting. Reduction of the size of the board of directors has much the same effect as staggering the election of directors. Shares may sometimes be tied up in voting trusts or voting agreements; in many states non-voting shares also may be used consistently with a cumulative voting requirement. The influence of minority directors may be minimized by having informal director discussion in advance of meetings, scheduling board meetings at inconvenient times or places, and delegating functions to committees composed entirely of management directors. Also, it may be possible to remove the minority director without cause and replace him or her with a more congenial person, at least until the next election. Section 8.08(c) of the Revised Model Business Corporation Act and the statutes of many states, however, prohibit the removal of a minority director elected by cumulative voting unless the votes in favor of removal would have been enough to prevent the original election of the director in an election for directors.

Of course, in states where cumulative voting is permissive, it may be eliminated by an amendment to the articles of incorporation in the same way as any other attribute of shares. (See § 18.1 of this Nutshell.)

§ 9.5 Voting by Proxy

A proxy is a person who is authorized by a record shareholder to vote his or her shares. The relationship is one of principal and agent. Some confusion may arise in terminology since the single word "proxy" may interchangeably be used to designate the document that creates the authority, the grant of authority itself, and the person granted the power to vote the shares. The Revised Model Business Corporation Act limits the use of the word "proxy" to the person with the power to vote; it refers to the grant of authority as the "appointment" of a proxy, and the document creating the appointment as an "appointment form." The law of proxy regulation rather neatly divides itself into two areas. On the one hand is the skimpy—almost nonexistent—state law dealing with the legal requirements and duration of a proxy appointment. Under state law, perhaps the most lively issue is whether a proxy appointment that is stated to be irrevocable is in fact irrevocable. That this is not an earth shaking issue is attested to by the fact that the virtual absence of reported litigation on this question. On the other hand is the burgeoning law of federal proxy regulation in publicly held corporations subject to the reporting requirements of the Securities Exchange Act of 1934. This is discussed in a later chapter of this Nutshell (see § 13.7).

The standard state statutory provision relating to proxies merely states that a shareholder may vote either "in person or by proxy." RMBCA § 7.22(a). No particular form of proxy appointment is required under this section. Proxy appointments have been ruled valid despite omission of the name of the proxy, the date of the meeting, or the date of the proxy appointment. However, the proxy appointment must be in writing, a provision of obvious benefit to the inspector of elections and the corporation. A proxy need not be a shareholder.

The usual state statutory provision relating to duration of a proxy appointment provides in effect that an appointment "is valid for 11 months unless a longer period is expressly provided in the appointment form." [RMBCA § 7.22(c).] The theory of the eleven-month provision is that a new appointment form should be executed before each annual meeting. However, there is nothing to prevent the parties from agreeing that a much longer period shall be applicable to a specific proxy appointment. Since a proxy is an agent, his or her appointment is normally revocable at the pleasure of the record owner. Thus, even if a long period is designated as the duration of the proxy appointment, it still may be revoked by the record owner.

A proxy appointment may be revoked either expressly or by implication. For example, the execution of a later proxy appointment constitutes a revocation of an earlier, inconsistent appointment. Personal attendance at a meeting may also constitute revocation of an earlier proxy appointment, though this depends on the intention of the shareholder.

Since later proxy appointments revoke earlier ones, it is important that appointment forms be dated as of the time of execution. Inspectors of election, where there is a contest, must determine which is the latest appointment form executed by a specific shareholder in order to determine how the shares are to be voted.

Certain proxy appointments may be irrevocable. Generally a mere recitation that a proxy appointment is irrevocable does not make it so; such an appointment is usually as revocable as any other agency appointment. The general rubric for determining whether a proxy appointment is truly irrevocable is whether it is "coupled with an interest." This phrase, which has its origin in the agency case of Hunt v. Rousmanier's Adm'rs (1823), has no inherent meaning of itself and must be fleshed out with examples and further analysis. It is not enough that the proxy appointment merely be supported by consideration. The clearest example of this is a purchase of a proxy appointment for cash by a shareholder seeking to obtain control of the corporation. Such a purchased vote almost certainly would be held to be against public policy and unenforceable; rather than being irrevocable, such a proxy appointment might not be enforceable at all. On the other hand, if a person lends a shareholder money and takes a lien on the shares as security, an irrevocable appointment of the creditor as proxy almost certainly would be enforced against the shareholder. What is the difference between these two situations? A person who purchases a vote presumably intends to recoup his or her investment in the vote by exercising the power to vote in some way. This power may very well be exercised in a manner adverse to the corporation: the proxy's interest is in recouping a personal payment, and in a sense is antagonistic to the corporation. The creditor's interest, on the other hand, is to preserve or increase the value of the shares which constitute the security for the loan. Thus the creditor has a financial interest consistent with that of the corporation which the vote purchaser does not.

An irrevocable proxy appointment separates the ownership from the voting power. Because of the possibility of injury to the owners by the abuse of a naked voting power unconnected with a financial interest in the corporation, the courts have generally refused to recognize the irrevocability of a proxy appointment except where there appears to be little likelihood that the power to vote will be abused. This is the nub of the notion of "coupled with an interest." The following types of proxy appointments have been held to be "coupled with an interest":

(1) A proxy appointment given to a pledgee under a valid pledge of the shares;

(2) A proxy appointment given to a person who has agreed to purchase the shares under an executory contract of sale;

(3) A proxy appointment given to a person who has lent money or contributed valuable property to the corporation;

(4) A proxy appointment given to a person who has contracted to perform services for the corporation as an officer; and

(5) A proxy appointment given in order to effectuate the provisions of a valid pooling agreement (described in the following section).

Some courts have upheld irrevocable proxies which do not squarely fall within any of the above categories.

There appears to be a slow trend toward statutory codification of the common law proxy appointment "coupled with an interest" doctrine. New York and California have statutes which define the five situations described above as those in which an irrevocable proxy appointment should be recognized [N.Y.Bus.Corp.Law, § 609(F); Cal.Corp.Code, § 705]. Such a statute resolves possible future disputes very simply, but there is some danger that a reasonable irrevocable proxy appointment might be invalidated because it does not fit squarely into any of the above categories. It was for this reason that section 7.22(d) of the Revised Model Business Corporation Act, while based generally on the language of the New York statute, makes the list non-exclusive.

§ 9.6 Shareholder Voting Agreements

A shareholder voting agreement is a contract among the shareholders, or some of them, to vote their shares in a specified manner on certain matters. Such an agreement is usually called a "pooling agreement" because it results in the shares of the participants being voted as a pooled unit. The purpose may be to maintain control, or to maximize the voting power of the shares where cumulative voting is permitted, or to ensure that some specific objective is obtained. The manner in which the shares are to be voted, that is for or against a specified proposal or motion, may be specified in the agreement itself, or be the subject of subsequent negotiation and decision of the shareholders with some method of determining how the shares are to be voted in the event of a failure to agree. The shareholders' pooling agreement extends only to voting on matters that are within the province of shareholders, such as the election of directors, and should be sharply distinguished from agreements that attempt to resolve matters that are vested in the discretion of directors. The latter type of agreement raises serious questions of validity (see § 8.10 of this Nutshell). The pooling agreement does not.

In a pooling agreement, the shareholders retain all the indicia of ownership of shares except the power to vote. In this respect, a pooling agreement differs from a voting trust (discussed in § 9.7 of this Nutshell) which contemplates that legal title to the shares be transferred to the trustees.

Generally, the advantages of a pooling agreement over a voting trust are that it is less formal, easier to establish, and there is no disruption of other ownership attributes.

The pooling agreement is generally recognized as a valid contract, subject only to the rules applicable to the validity of contracts in general. A few states have adopted statutes regulating pooling agreements, often limiting the period during which a pooling agreement may continue (e.g. to ten years), requiring that copies of the pooling agreement be deposited at the principal office of the corporation, and so forth. However, in most states, the pooling agreement is essentially an unregulated contractual voting device that may continue for long periods of time. Section 7.31 of the Revised Model Business Corporation Act basically codifies the common law rules applicable to pooling agreements.

A basic part of a pooling agreement is the manner of resolution of possible disagreements in the future. While the parties to the agreement are presumably in complete accord as to how their shares should be voted today, there is no assurance that there will be such accord tomorrow. Pooling agreements usually specify that participants will consult in advance of the meeting as to how the pooled shares should be voted, and that the shares will be voted as a majority or some other percentage specify. For example, in an important Delaware case, the agreement provided that the six participants in the pool could select eight agents (most selecting one, some two) and the shares would be voted as any seven agents specified. Abercrombie v. Davis (1957). Arbitration was provided for in the event seven agents were unable to agree. While this agreement ultimately was held to constitute an invalid voting trust rather than a pooling agreement, the method of dispute resolution is interesting in that it required a high degree of consensus by the participants. Resolution of disagreements is usually by arbitration or by a decision of some person mutually trusted by all the participants. However, if the pooling agreement covers enough shares to constitute working control of the corporation, arbitration may in fact vest control of the corporation in the hands of the arbiter, a person with no financial interest in the enterprise. A "runaway" arbiter is unlikely because the shareholders may, by agreeing among themselves, retake control over the voting of the pooled shares. Pooling agreements also often provide that the participants in the pool may substitute arbiters by mutual agreement. Instead of arbitration, a pooling agreement may give a participant the option of withdrawing his or her shares if disagreement continues over a period of time. Such a provision, of course, in a sense defeats the original purpose of a pooling agreement.

Enforcement of a pooling agreement creates special problems since the shares are registered in the names of the individual shareholders. Many courts will enforce a pooling agreement by decreeing specific performance. It is not always certain, however, that specific performance will be available. In Ringling Bros.-Barnum & Bailey Combined Shows v. Ringling (1947), the leading Delaware case involving pooling agreements, the agreement itself did not specifically appoint anyone to vote the shares of an objecting shareholder who refused to follow the arbiter's instructions. Nevertheless, the Chancellor (1946) found by a process of implication that a proxy appointment existed in favor of the other shareholder. On appeal, the Supreme Court held that the proper remedy was simply not to count votes cast in contravention of the instructions of the arbiter. Under the circumstances, the result was to defeat utterly the purpose of the pooling agreement, since the minority shareholder who was not a party to the pooling agreement had a majority of the remaining shares after giving effect to the disqualification.

Some state statutes specifically address the enforcement issue either by authorizing irrevocable proxy appointments in connection with pooling agreements or by stating expressly that pooling agreements are specifically enforceable. New York, for example, validates and makes irrevocable a proxy granted in connection with a pooling agreement [N.Y.Bus.Corp.Law §§ 609(e), 620], while section 7.31(b) of the Revised Model Business Corporation Act simply states that a pooling agreement "is specifically enforceable." The New York statute was thought to be less desirable since, to take advantage of that statute, the agreement probably should specifically appoint a proxy. Enforcement of pooling agreements under the New York statute might also create practical problems for inspectors of corporate elections who must decide who is entitled to vote shares based on a construction of the pooling agreement. In such circumstances, an inspector probably would insist that a court decree be first obtained determining how the shares should be voted—a result that the Revised Model Business Corporation Act formulation clearly contemplates.

§ 9.7 Voting Trusts: Purpose, Operation, and Legislative Policy

A voting trust differs from a pooling agreement primarily in that legal title to the shares is vested in trustees, and the shares are registered in the names of the trustees on the books of the corporation. Voting trust agreements usually provide that all dividends or other corporate distributions be passed through to the equitable owners of the shares. The trustees may also issue transferable voting trust certificates representing the beneficial interests in the shares and such certificates may be traded much as shares of stock are traded. While voting trust agreements may limit the power of trustees to vote on certain matters or to transfer the shares held by them to third parties without the consent of the beneficial owners, nevertheless, in a voting trust the legal title to the shares, and usually the entire power to vote, is separated from the equitable ownership of the shares.

At common law there was great suspicion of voting trusts. One commentator described a voting trust as "little more than a vehicle for corporate kidnapping." This attitude has largely disappeared. State statutes now uniformly recognize the validity of voting trusts and they have received a more hospitable judicial reception. Section 7.30 of the Revised Model Business Corporation Act states that a voting trust may be created subject to minimal requirements:

(1) The agreement may not extend beyond ten years;

(2) The agreement must be in writing and signed by one or more shareholders who transfer their shares to the voting trustee on the books of the corporation; and

(3) The voting trustee must prepare a list of the persons with beneficial interests in the voting trust and deliver that list and a copy of the agreement to the corporation at its principal office. These documents are thereafter available for inspection by shareholders.

Section 7.30(c) deals with the matter of extending a voting trust beyond its ten year maximum life. The statutes of several states permit an extension during the last year of the life of a voting trust; section 7.30(c) adopts the somewhat simpler rule that a voting trust may be extended at any time during its life for a period of ten years running from the date the first shareholder signs the extension of a voting trust. Of course, an extension is binding on shareholders who agree to the extension; a person objecting to the extension is entitled to a return of his or her shares upon the termination of the original term of the voting trust.

Some states have imposed a further substantive requirement on voting trusts that the essential purpose of the trust must be a proper one. For example, a trust created solely for the purpose of securing control of or lucrative employment with a corporation would be invalidated in some states. Obviously, proof of such motives depends on subjective testimony; the cautious, close-mouthed creator of a voting trust in such states may create an enforceable voting trust despite wrongful motives, while a garrulous person with basically good motives may inadvertently make damaging statements about the underlying purpose of the trust. In a majority of the states, the purpose of a voting trust is not inquired into; a voting trust is valid if it complies with all statutory requirements.

A voting trust agreement that fails to comply with all statutory requirements is considered invalid in its entirety in most states. Even though these requirements are basically simple ones that may be easily complied with, a number of cases have arisen in which these requirements have been ignored. Some states take the position that a voting trust that is not by its terms limited to ten years is invalid because it does not meet the statutory requirements; under the RMBCA, a trust that contains no specified term is valid for ten years only.

§ 9.8 Voting Trusts: Use in Public Corporations

A voting trust, unlike most of the other control arrangements discussed in this Chapter, may be used in publicly held corporations as well as in closely held corporations. For example, a voting trust may be used in connection with the capitalization or reorganization of a corporation to provide for temporary stability of management. A temporary voting trust may be ordered where as a result of the reorganization the voting power is lodged in a large, unorganized group of bondholders who previously had no power to control the corporation. Another possible use is in connection with divestiture orders under the Federal antitrust laws, where the court desires to order an immediate termination of control, but where the financial details of the divestiture may take a long period to work out. A voting trust may also be used by creditors of a publicly held corporation to remove holders of large blocks of stock

whom the creditors mistrust from the control of the corporation. An outstanding example of this use was a 1960 loan
of $165,000,000 to Trans World Airlines by a consortium
of banks. As a condition to the loan, Hughes Tool Co.,
then wholly owned by Howard Hughes, was required to
place its shares of TWA (amounting to 75 per cent of the
outstanding shares) into a voting trust with the banks desig-
nating the trustees. In this way, Mr. Hughes was isolated
from the actual management of the debtor corporation.

§ 9.9 Voting Trusts: Powers and Duties of Trustee

Voting trusts usually contain precise provisions defining
the powers and duties of the trustees. Voting trustees may
have working control of the corporation for extended periods of time, but may have little or no financial interest in
the corporation. Problem areas that have arisen include:

(1) May the trustees elect themselves as directors and/or
officers? The wisdom of permitting dual offices is debatable since it is unlikely that a voting trustee would vote to
remove himself or herself as a director.

(2) May the trustees remaining in office fill a vacancy in
the trustees? Trustees are often given this power, though it
may also be vested in the holders of voting trust certificates.

(3) May the trustees vote on major corporate changes,
such as mergers, dissolution, or the sale of substantially all
of its assets? Arguably, consent of the holders of voting
trust certificates should be obtained on such major matters,
but voting trust agreements often provide that the trustees
may vote on such matters as they see fit.

(4) May the trustees dispose of the shares subject to the
voting trust? Voting trust agreements often provide that no
sale of underlying shares may be effected without the prior
consent of all, or a designated percentage, of the holders of
voting trust certificates.

(5) Should the trustees be relieved of liability for errors in business judgment or nonfeasance? Trustees typically desire broad exculpatory clauses, but such clauses may be inconsistent with the legitimate interest of depositing shareholders. Also, courts may decline to enforce broad exculpatory clauses applicable to fiduciaries or read such clauses very narrowly.

(6) What deductions, if any, may the trustees make from dividends received by them before paying them over to the equitable owners?

(7) Are the trustees entitled to compensation, and if so, in what amount?

(8) What provision, if any should be made for the eventuality that the trustees may disagree among themselves as to how the shares should be voted? Normally, the rule should probably be that majority vote controls, but it is possible that the creators of some voting trusts might prefer a rule of allocating the voting power proportionately among the voting trustees. Provision may also be made for the eventuality that the voting trustees might themselves deadlock on some specific issue.

Generally, courts tend to construe voting trust agreements narrowly or to imply a broad fiduciary duty by which trustees' actions may be tested.

§ 9.10 Creation of Floating Voting Power Through Different Classes of Shares

The common law treated with some suspicion various devices that effectively divorce the privilege of shareholder voting from the ownership of shares: irrevocable proxies (§ 9.5 of this Nutshell), shareholder pooling agreements (§ 9.6 of this Nutshell), and voting trusts (§§ 9.7–9.9 of this Nutshell). While these devices are valid and enforceable within their limited spheres, they are hedged with restrictions or limitations. One device that apparently permits the effective divorce of voting power from ownership of any significant financial interest in the corporation is the creation of classes of shares with disproportionate voting and financial rights. In most states, no limitation is placed on the creation of classes of shares without voting rights, with fractional or multiple votes per share, with power to select one or more directors, and with limited financial interests in the corporation. The leading case involving the use of special classes of stock to create a floating voting power without a significant financial interest in the corporation is Lehrman v. Cohen (1966). Two families, the Lehrmans and the Cohens, owned equal quantities of the voting stock of a major grocery chain. The shares were divided into two classes, denominated AL and AC, and each could elect two directors. Because of internal disputes and disagreements that could not be resolved because of the make-up of the board, both families agreed to the creation of a third class of voting stock, AD stock, consisting of one share with the power to elect one director. The par value of the one share of AD stock was $10; this stock was not entitled to receive dividends, and on liquidation was entitled to receive back only its par value. Further, it could be redeemed or called at any time upon the vote of four directors upon the payment of the par value to the holder.

For several years, this tie-breaking mechanism worked well. The holder of the one share of AD stock was the attorney for the corporation; he elected himself director and participated actively in the meetings of the board. Eventually, the holder of the AD stock allied himself with the Cohen family and together they made the attorney the chief executive officer of the corporation pursuant to a long term employment contract. Despite the fact that the AD stock was little more than a floating vote or tie-breaking mechanism with only a nominal financial interest in the corporation, its validity was upheld against the contentions that it constituted a voting trust or an invalid voting arrangement. One plausible justification for the result upholding the validity of the Class AD stock in this case is that it seems impossible to draw a line between permissible and impermissible classes of shares. The statute gives virtually total freedom to vary voting and financial interests; one cannot say that $10 is too little, but that some other financial interest is enough.

While there has not been very much litigation on this type of arrangement, what there is tends to support the basic conclusion of the Delaware Supreme Court.

§ 9.11 Share Transfer Restrictions: Purposes, Operation, and Effect

In the absence of specific agreement, shares of stock are freely transferable. However, restrictions on free transferability of shares may be of vital importance in both closely held and publicly held corporations.

A. *Closely Held Corporations.* In the closely held corporation share transfer restrictions typically constitute contractual obligations to offer or to sell shares either to the corporation or to other shareholders, or to both successively, on the death of the shareholder or when the shareholder decides he or she wishes to retire or leave the venture. The restriction may take the form of (1) an option in the corporation or shareholders to purchase at a designated price, (2) a mandatory buy-sell agreement obligating the corporation or shareholders to purchase the shares, or (3) merely a right of first refusal, giving the corporation or the shareholders an opportunity to meet the best price the shareholder has been able to obtain from outsiders. The choice between these three forms of share transfer restrictions depends on the business needs of the shareholders. Obviously, an option or a right of first refusal does not guarantee the shareholder a specified price, whereas a buy-sell agreement does. Since investors or participants wish to avoid being "locked in" to an investment, most closely held corporations adopt buy-sell agreements.

In closely held corporations, share transfer restrictions not only enable participants in the venture who wish to leave to liquidate their interests but also enable the continuing participants to decide who shall thereafter participate in the venture. In effect they achieve the corporate equivalent of the partnership notions of dissolution-on-demand and *delectus personae.* They also may ensure a stable management and protection against an unexpected change in the respective proportionate interests of the shareholders which might occur if one shareholder is able to quietly purchase shares of other shareholders. A further advantage of share transfer restrictions in a closely held corporation is that they may materially simplify the estate tax problems of a deceased shareholder. If the corporation or other shareholders are obligated to purchase the shares owned by the deceased shareholder (a buy-sell agreement) the estate is assured that a large, illiquid asset will be reduced to cash. Further, either an option or a buy-sell agreement, if established in good faith, will be accepted by the Internal Revenue Service as establishing the value of the shares for federal estate tax purposes, thereby avoiding a potentially serious dispute with the tax authorities. Since closely held shares have no market on which value can be based, the Internal Revenue Service is apt to take a very optimistic attitude as to the value of such shares in the absence of an agreement establishing the value.

Share transfer restrictions in closely held corporations may also be imposed to ensure the continued availability of the S corporation election (see § 2.3 of this Nutshell). Restrictions on transfer for this purpose may be necessary to ensure that the thirty-five shareholder maximum is not exceeded and that shares are not transferred to an ineligible shareholder such as a corporation or trust that would cause the loss of the election.

B. *Publicly Held Corporations.* In a publicly held corporation, share transfer restrictions are usually used to prevent violations of the Federal Securities Act where the corporation has issued unregistered shares, e.g., in connection with the acquisition of another business. In order to prevent the unregistered shares from immediately being resold in the public market, share transfer restrictions are imposed on the unregistered shares and instructions may be placed with the transfer agent to refuse to accept unregistered shares for transfer unless accompanied by an appropriate attorney's opinion. Share transfer restrictions may also be used to ensure the continued availability of an exemption from registration which may be lost, for example, if the shares are offered for resale to nonresidents. The availability of several exemptions from registration under regulations adopted by the Securities and Exchange Commission are expressly conditioned upon the corporation imposing restrictions on the transfer of shares issued in reliance upon the exemption.

Share transfer restrictions in publicly held corporations differ in nature as well as purpose from share transfer restrictions in closely held corporations. In the latter, restraints usually are of the option or buy-sell variety which require the shareholder to offer or sell his or her shares to the corporation or to other shareholders. In the publicly held corporation on the other hand, restrictions usually take the form of flat prohibitions on transfer unless the transferor can establish that the transfer is consistent with the securities laws or regulations. This may require an opinion of counsel, affidavits by the purchaser or transferee, and the acceptance of further restrictions on transfer by the purchaser or transferee. Such uses of share transfer restrictions are considered fully in courses on securities regulation.

§ 9.12 Share Transfer Restrictions: Scope and Validity

Most courts take the position that share transfer restrictions are restraints on alienation and should therefore be strictly construed. As a result it is important to specify clearly and unambiguously the essential attributes of the restrictions and the events that trigger the restraint. In option or buy/sell agreements for example, the death, divorce, or bankruptcy of a shareholder may trigger the restriction. A desire to sell or donate the shares to a third person will also usually trigger the restriction but a transfer by gift to children or grandchildren may be excluded from the restriction. Careful drafting is essential. It has been held, for example, that a restriction against sales "to the public" does not prohibit a sale to another shareholder, or that a prohibition against sale to an "officer stockholder" does not cover a sale to a corporation owned by an officer stockholder. Obviously, such holdings tend to defeat rather than further the basic purpose of share transfer restrictions.

The common law legal test as to the validity of a share transfer restraint is that it "does not unreasonably restrain or prohibit transferability." Under this test, an outright prohibition on transferability would certainly be held invalid. Also dangerous are restrictions which prohibit transfers unless consent of the directors or other shareholders is first obtained; the possibility that consent may be arbitrarily withheld may invalidate the restraint. Other questionable types of restrictions include restrictions barring transfers to competitors or to a distinct class, such as aliens; restrictions imposing a penalty, such as a loss of vote or loss of dividend as a consequence of the transfer; or the creation of callable common shares.

The niggardly common law view about the enforceability of share transfer restrictions reflected in the preceding paragraphs has caused several states to adopt legislation broadening the types of restrictions that may be enforced. Section 6.27 of the Revised Model Business Corporation Act builds on these provisions; it is a carefully drafted statute that attempts to eliminate most of the undesirable restrictive features of the common law. It distinguishes between the purpose of a restriction (subsection (c)) and the type of restriction (subsection (d)). Section 6.27(c)(3) provides that generally the purpose of a restriction must be "reasonable," but restrictions described in subparts (1) and (2)—to maintain the status of the corporation when it is dependent on the number or identity of shareholders and to preserve exemptions under federal or state securities law—are valid without investigation into the reasonableness of the purpose. Phrased differently, the purposes set forth in subparts (1) and (2) are conclusively presumed to be reasonable. Section 6.27(d) lists four types of restrictions—buy-sell requirements, options, consent restrictions, and prohibitory restrictions. The last two are valid if "the requirement is not manifestly unreasonable." This last clause is taken directly from section 202 of the Delaware statute. (Del.Code Ann. Tit. 8, § 202.) Several other states have adopted similar statutes.

Restrictions are sometimes imposed after the corporation has been created and shares issued. In these situations the question may arise as to whether the shares previously issued are subject to a restraint which is inserted in the articles of incorporation or bylaws. In the absence of statute, the case law has split on whether the restrictions may be imposed retroactively; section 6.27(a) of the Revised Model Business Corporation Act provides that restrictions are not applicable to previously issued shares unless the holders of the shares are parties to the agreement creating the restrictions or voted in favor of imposing them.

§ 9.13 Share Transfer Restrictions: Duration of Restraints

Unlike voting trusts, which usually have a statutory duration of ten years or less, there is no express restriction on the duration of share transfer restrictions. So long as the type of restriction is limited to the traditional option or buy-and-sell agreement, it is probable that the restriction remains enforceable without regard to the rule against perpetuities or equitable notions of "reasonableness." Less orthodox types of valid restraints normally continue so long as the need or justification for them exists.

Share transfer restrictions may terminate prematurely in one of two ways: by express agreement of the shareholders involved (e.g., when all decide to sell their shares to an outside purchaser despite a restriction against such sales), or by abandonment or disuse. If shares are sold or transferred without compliance with the restrictions and without objection by the various parties, a court may conclude that the restrictions have been abandoned and are no longer enforceable. Isolated sales in violation of the restriction may not be sufficient to support such a conclusion, though a person objecting to the current sale may be estopped if he or she participated in the earlier transaction.

§ 9.14 Share Transfer Restrictions: Procedural Requirements

In creating share transfer restrictions it is important that the proper formalities be followed and that the requirements of the relevant business corporation act be complied with. Most restrictions appear in the articles of incorporation or bylaws of the corporation, though some may be imposed by simple contract between the corporation and shareholders or between the shareholders themselves. Statutes generally require that a reference to any restriction imposed in corporate documents must also be placed or "noted" on the face or back of each share certificate which is subject to the restriction [RMBCA § 6.27(b)]; generally, however it is not necessary for the full text or a complete description of the restriction to appear on the certificate. Section 6.27(b) also requires the notation to be "conspicuous," a term that is defined in section 1.40 as meaning "so written that a reasonable person against whom it is to operate ought to have noticed it. For example, printing in italics or boldface or contrasting color, or typing in capitals or underlined, is conspicuous. A printed heading in capitals * * * is conspicuous. Language in the body of a form is 'conspicuous' if it is in larger or other contrasting type or color." The requirement of conspicuous notation also appears in article eight of the Uniform Commercial Code, and in many states that is the only place where a "conspicuous" requirement appears.

Unless the procedural requirements described in the previous paragraph are complied with, the restriction is unenforceable against a person who is unaware of the restriction; a person who knows of the restriction at the time the shares are purchased is bound by the restriction whether or not these procedural requirements have been met.

§ 9.15 Option or Buy/Sell Agreements: Who Should Have the Right or Privilege to Buy?

Share transfer restrictions that constitute option or buy/sell agreements to purchase the shares may run either to the corporation or to some or all the other shareholders. The choice is a matter of convenience, though usually it is preferable for the restriction to run to the corporation. The advantages of this are two-fold: the corporation may be able to raise the necessary cash more easily than the shareholders individually, and the proportionate interests of the remaining shareholders are unaffected by a corporate purchase.

On the other hand, a repurchase of shares by a corporation is a distribution of assets to shareholders that must meet certain legal requirements; in par value states, the purchase may be lawfully made only if the corporation has the necessary earned or capital surplus at the time the purchase is to be made; under the RMBCA, such a transaction is a distribution and must meet the tests of RMBCA § 6.40 (see § 16.6 of this Nutshell). In order to take care of the possibility that the corporation may be legally barred from acquiring the shares, buy/sell agreements may require the shareholders or some of them to agree to buy the shares if the corporation is not legally permitted to do so.

If the share transfer restrictions run to the other shareholders, a problem arises if one or more of the shareholders are unable or unwilling to purchase their allotment of shares. Agreements usually provide that in that situation the shares not purchased should be reoffered proportionately to the remaining shareholders who may or may not be obligated to purchase the shares. The proportionate interests of the shareholders will necessarily be changed if one shareholder is unable or unwilling to purchase his or her allotment. However, the shareholders may not always desire that the shares be offered proportionately to the other shareholders. For example, a majority shareholder with a son and daughter may wish to provide that all shares be first offered to his or her son and then to his or her daughter (or vice versa) rather than be offered proportionately.

If the number of shareholders is large—more than four or five, say—the mechanics of having the restrictions run to the shareholders become complicated, and it usually is preferable for the restrictions to run to the corporation. Many share transfer restrictions provide for sale to the corporation, or then proportionately a sale to the other shareholders if the corporation is unable to purchase them. Finally, if life insurance is to be used to provide funds to purchase shares on the death of a shareholder, it is usually simplest to have the corporation pay the premiums and own the policies on the lives of each shareholder rather than having each shareholder attempt to insure the life of every other shareholder. If there were 25 shareholders, a complete cross-purchase arrangement with life insurance would require 600 policies!

§ 9.16 Option or Buy/Sell Agreements: Establishment of Purchase or Option Price

The price provisions of shareholder option or buy-sell agreements often raise the most difficult and important problems in drafting such agreements. Since closely held shares by definition have no market or quoted price, one simply cannot refer to a "fair," "reasonable," or "market" price; some definite method of valuation must be provided. Further, since it usually is impossible to know whose shares will be first offered for sale under such an agreement, everyone's goal in establishing such a mechanism is often to be as fair as possible. (Of course, this is not universally true; individualized circumstances may well exist which make it reasonably clear that one shareholder's interest will be retired first.)

The following methods are often used to establish a purchase price usually stated on a per share basis:

(1) A stated price;

(2) Book value;

(3) Capitalization of earnings;

(4) Best offer by an outsider;

(5) Appraisal or arbitration, either by expert, impartial appraisers or arbitrators, or by directors or other shareholders; or

(6) A percentage of net profits to be paid for a specified number of years following the event which triggers the sale.

It is impossible to state definitively which is the most desirable method, since it depends on the nature of the business and assets being valued. The simplest method is for the parties to fix a definite price in the agreement itself. This may be par value, original purchase price, or a price established by negotiation. In the absence of fraud or overreaching, courts have enforced agreements where the price is well below the value of the shares, though there is always a possibility that a court may deem a grossly inadequate price to constitute an unreasonable restraint on alienation or to be "unconscionable." Generally, it is desirable to provide for periodic reevaluation of the fixed price as the fortunes of the corporation rise or fall. One problem that may arise is what happens if the parties fail to agree on a new price, or if they fail to revise the price from time to time as contemplated by the agreement. A willful refusal by a younger shareholder to renegotiate the price under such an agreement might be considered fraudulent, as might be a convenient "forgetfulness" on the part of such a shareholder. It is also possible that a court might conclude that there is a sufficient fiduciary relationship between the shareholders to justify a court-ordered price reevaluation whether or not specific provision therefor was made.

By far the most popular method of valuation is "book value," which may be computed by a simple division of a balance sheet figure by the number of outstanding shares. Indeed, it is probable that book value is often used without serious consideration as to its advantages or disadvantages in connection with the specific business. Book value is based on the application of certain accounting conventions to corporate transactions and whether or not book value is a realistic estimate of value depends on the circumstances; it may be appropriate to require that book value be adjusted in certain ways before being used to establish a purchase price. For example, one accounting convention requires assets to be valued at cost and not be reappraised upward to reflect current market values. Thus, a corporation that owns real estate acquired decades earlier at low prices often will have a book value that considerably understates the true value of the assets. Similarly investments in readily marketable securities may be shown on the books at cost even though current market values may be obtained from the financial tables of any newspaper. In these instances, a restatement of such assets in terms of current market or appraised values may be more appropriate than "pure" book value. Accounting conventions also allow corporations to include certain things as assets which may never be realized; for example, costs of initial formation or of "good will" acquired in connection with the purchase of another business. It may be appropriate to eliminate such "assets" from the balance sheet before computing book value.

A number of accounting techniques have been developed for federal income tax purposes, and it may be undesirable to have a shareholder's interest in a corporation valued on the basis of such accounting principles. For example, if the corporation utilizes accelerated depreciation schedules for tax purposes, it may be desirable to specify that straight line depreciation should be used to compute book value for valuation purposes. Or, if inventory is valued on a LIFO basis, it may be desirable to require the inventory to be valued at a more realistic figure before computing book value.

Appraisal of the value of closely held stock has its own difficulties. Appraisers often prefer to value shares by capitalizing earnings or cash flow, or by making a direct appraisal of the market value of assets, or by a combination of the two, rather than relying on book value. Capitalization of earnings or cash flow is a fairly complex method of estimating the value of a business, though the basic idea is simple enough: if a corporation has average earnings of, say, $50,000 a year, and it is reasonable to capitalize those earnings at ten per cent, the corporation should be valued at

$500,000. If the reasonable capitalization ratio were eight per cent, the business would be valued at $625,000 (625,-000 × .08 = 50,000); if it were fifteen per cent, it would be valued at $333,333 (333,333 × .15 = 50,000). One may quite legitimately ask where both the $50,000 and the ten per cent figures came from, particularly since different earnings estimates or capitalization ratios have a significant effect on the overall valuation. An appropriate capitalization ratio may be justified on the basis of earnings ratios of comparable publicly held businesses, the appraiser's general experience with valuing businesses in the particular industry, or simply the appraiser's intuitive "feel" as to how risky a specific business is. Valuation based on capitalization of earnings may also be affected by different assumptions about the level of average earnings in the future, and whether different assets should be capitalized at different rates.

Normally, an appraiser or arbitrator will consider all the various possible methods of valuation, and in fact the price he or she sets may reflect an average of various possible values, for example, the average of book value, the capitalized value, and the estimated liquidation value if the assets were sold.

After the value of the overall business is obtained, the per share value is usually obtained by a simple division by the number of outstanding shares. However, complications may involve the basis on which senior securities are valued and whether a further discount from the per share value should be taken if the shares are an isolated minority block with no chance of sharing in control.

§ 9.17   Option or Buy/Sell Agreements: Life Insurance

The unexpected death of a shareholder may cause serious disruption in a close corporation. Two things are essential if the corporation is to pass smoothly through such difficult periods: planning and money. A properly drafted buy-and-sell agreement or option may provide the former; life insurance is often the simplest way of providing the latter. It is possible, of course, to provide that the estate of a deceased shareholder is to be paid out over a period of time from anticipated future earnings. This may not be satisfactory from the standpoint of an estate, faced with large tax liabilities and a desire to wind matters up promptly. Life insurance, usually owned by the corporation, may provide the necessary funds to allow the estate's interest to be retired promptly. Of course, this assumes that the shareholder is insurable and that his or her age is not such that the cost of premiums is prohibitive.

§ 9.18 Selection of the Purchaser in Deadlock Buyouts

A mandatory buy-sell arrangement is often recommended as the best solution in possible deadlock situations, where (usually) two equal shareholders own and manage the business but fear that there may be disagreements in the future. As described in some detail in a later chapter, (Chapter 12 of this Nutshell), the remedies for deadlock in the absence of agreement are not entirely satisfactory. In the event of significant, unresolvable disagreement, it seems much neater and cleaner that one shareholder should buy out the other. Important questions in working out such an arrangement are: who is to buy out whom if both desire to continue the corporate business? Often the senior should buy out the junior, though if the age discrepancy is large, it may be more sensible to reverse the order and have the junior buy out the senior. One variation, which somewhat resembles roulette, or the classic children's device for cutting up a pie evenly, is to have one shareholder set a price at which he or she is willing to buy out the other shareholder or to sell his or her own shares, at the election of the other shareholder. While there is nothing inherently improper with such devices, they should be utilized with caution since it may be necessary to persuade a court of their reasonableness in order to obtain judicial enforcement by a decree of specific performance. Another issue is precisely what events trigger the power to buy? Some kind of objective standard is usually desirable, such as the failure to agree on a slate of directors for some specified period. Another issue is which of the various pricing formulas should be used and which should be avoided? In light of the possible deadlock it seems important to choose a formula that does not rely on a cooperative effort to set the price; it also seems desirable to use a formula that will yield as "fair" a price as possible rather than one that appears to create a bargain for one faction or the other.

§ 9.19 Deferred Payment of the Purchase Price

Many share transfer restrictions provide that the purchase price of shares shall be paid in annual or more frequent installments extending over several years upon the retirement of a shareholder or on his or her separation from the business. The theory behind these provisions is that they enable the business to pay for the shares out of future profits or future cash flow without incurring indebtedness for this purpose. The withdrawing shareholder may or may not be entitled to interest on the deferred payments. Under modern statutes such debts are on a parity with general trade creditors. See § 16.11 of this Nutshell.

Where payments of the purchase price are deferred, the parties may also agree that the aggregate amount of the price may be adjusted upward or downward depending on the profitability of the business in the years following the exercise of the share transfer restriction. In effect, this is a form of "work out," widely used in connection with the purchase of businesses generally to adjust the purchase price to reflect the future success of the business.

[For unfamiliar terms see the Glossary]

CHAPTER TEN

DIRECTORS

§ 10.1 Number and Qualifications of Directors

Historically, virtually all statutes required that there be at least three directors, and many statutes required that each director have certain qualifications, such as being a shareholder or a resident of the state. Qualification requirements have been almost universally eliminated and an increasing number of states now permit boards of directors to consist of one or two directors. The privilege of having a board of one or two directors in many states is limited to corporations with one or two shareholders, but under section 8.03(a) of the Revised Model Business Corporation Act and the statutes of an increasing number of states, any corporation may elect to have a board consisting of one or two members without regard to the number of shareholders.

The notion that only corporations with one or two shareholders may have boards of directors consisting of one or two members seems superficially plausible. In some situations, however, such a requirement creates unnecessary problems. Consider, for example, a corporation that is owned entirely by one person, and the sole shareholder is the single director. Assume further that the shareholder desires to make gifts of stock to his or her two minor children. Under these statutes, the board of directors would have to be increased to three members when the first gift of stock is made since there are then three shareholders!

Under the Revised Model Business Corporation Act only "individuals" may serve as directors. RMBCA § 8.03(a).

In some countries, corporations or other entities may serve as directors; this practice has apparently never taken root in the United States.

The number of directors of a corporation may be "specified in or fixed in accordance with the articles of incorporation or bylaws." RMBCA § 8.03(a). It is quite common for the size of the board of directors to be set by the board of directors, either because the bylaws expressly give this power to the board, or because the number of directors is fixed in the bylaws and the board of directors has the general power to amend bylaws. (See § 8.9 of this Nutshell.) Section 8.03(b) restricts the power of the board of directors to fix its own size by requiring shareholder approval of changes in the board of directors that increase or decrease its size by 30 per cent or more. Alternatively, the articles of incorporation or bylaws may create a variable range size for the board of directors and the board of directors may set the size of the board within that range; shareholder approval is required for changes in the outer limits of that range or for a change from a fixed to a variable size board, or vice versa. RMBCA § 8.03(c). The purpose of these provisions is to give the board of directors power to add desirable members to the board without shareholder approval, or to decide not to fill a vacancy, but to prevent the board from manipulating its own size in a substantial way without shareholder approval.

Some cases have recognized that bylaws setting the number of directors may be amended informally, as for example by the shareholders electing four directors when the bylaws specify that the board shall consist of only three directors. However, that is not a desirable practice, injecting future uncertainty as to the number of directors to be elected and reducing the value of the written bylaws.

§ 10.2 Directors' Meetings: Notice, Quorum, and Similar Matters

Detailed provisions relating to directors' meetings appear in corporate bylaws and only skeletal provisions are set forth in business corporation statutes. Regular meetings of the board of directors may be held weekly, monthly, quarterly, or at any regular interval. The bylaws usually specify when such meetings are to be held, or may authorize the directors themselves to specify, by resolution, when regular meetings are to be held. It is customary to hold a regular meeting of directors either immediately before or immediately after the annual meeting of shareholders. Special meetings are meetings other than regular meetings. The principal difference between regular and special meetings is that a regular meeting may be held without notice, while a special meeting "must be preceded by at least two days' notice of the date, time, and place of the meeting." RMBCA § 8.22(b). However, even these modest notice requirements may be dispensed with by a corporation if an appropriate provision is placed in the articles of incorporation or bylaws. Directors may also waive notice (if such notice is required at all) in writing before, at, or after the meeting. RMBCA § 8.23(a).

Unlike a shareholders' meeting, any relevant business may be transacted at a special meeting of directors even though not referred to in the notice. The theory behind this distinction is that directors' meetings routinely consider a variety of business matters under varying degrees of urgency whereas shareholders meet only to consider a limited number of matters. As a result there is little practical difference between regular and special meetings of directors.

In a board of directors with a fixed size, a quorum consists of a majority of the number so fixed; if the board does not have a fixed size (i.e. it is a board with a variable range), a quorum consists of a majority of the directors in office immediately before the meeting. RMBCA § 8.24(a). The articles of incorporation or the bylaws, however, may authorize a quorum to consist of as few as one-third rather than a majority of the number described in the preceding sentence. RMBCA § 8.24(b). This provision is patterned after § 707 of the New York Business Corporation Law; in most states, a quorum of directors may not be set at less than a majority. The articles of incorporation or bylaws may also specify that a number greater than a majority constitute a quorum. RMBCA § 8.24(a). Where a quorum is present, the act of the majority of the directors present at the meeting is the act of the board, unless the articles of incorporation or bylaws require a greater number. RMBCA § 8.24(c). Under this section, the quorum must be actually present when the action is taken; it may be recalled that a different rule is applicable to meetings of shareholders: once a quorum is present at a shareholders' meeting it is deemed to exist throughout the meeting even if some shareholders withdraw in an effort to break the quorum. (See § 9.1 of this Nutshell.) The opposite rule is applicable to boards of directors in view of their management and fiduciary responsibility; it also encourages management to present important issues early in the meeting when a quorum is more likely to be present than toward the end of the meeting when some directors may have left.

Provisions that a quorum consists of all directors sometimes appear as control provisions in closely held corporations. Unanimity requirements for voting also sometimes appear as control provisions in such corporations. These provisions create potential deadlocks at the directoral level, since the refusal of a single director to attend or vote affirmatively on a matter prevents the corporation from acting.

With a single exception, if a quorum is not present the board of directors may not act. The only exception is where the directors are filling a vacancy; section 8.10(a)(3) of the Revised Model Business Corporation Act provides that "if the directors remaining in office constitute fewer than a quorum, they may fill the vacancy by the affirmative vote of a majority of all the directors remaining in office." Many state statutes contain a similar provision based on the language of the 1969 Model Act that a vacancy "may be filled by the affirmative vote of the remaining directors *though less than a quorum.*" Unlike the RMBCA, an ambiguity hides in the italicized language of the older statute. Even though there are vacancies, the number of directors in office may still be greater than a quorum. However, if two factions are vying for control, the smaller faction may stay away from a meeting called by the larger faction to prevent a quorum from being present. At such a meeting the directors present are less than a quorum even though the directors in office are greater than a quorum. The cases are split as to whether the faction present at such a meeting, "though less than a quorum," may fill the vacancies. In Tomlinson v. Loew's (1957) bylaw language similar to the phrase "though less than a quorum" was held to refer to the directors in office rather than to the directors present at the meeting. Several other cases, however, adopt the opposite construction.

§ 10.3 Compensation of Directors

The traditional view is that a director is not entitled to compensation for his or her ordinary services as director unless specific provision is made by the board of directors. The theory is that either directors are acting as trustees or that they are motivated by the prospect of increasing the return on their shares. However, a director may be entitled to compensation pursuant to contract entered into in advance or for extraordinary services beyond normal directoral functions, or for service as a corporate officer or agent.

These principles are based on tradition not legal power. In the early years of this century the practice developed in many corporations of paying small honoraria for attending meetings. With the increasing use of nonmanagement directors, particularly in publicly held corporations, the practice has grown of providing substantial remuneration ($50,-000 per year or more) to all directors who are not officers of the corporation. In addition, many corporations provide incentive plans (such as stock options) or "golden parachutes" to outside directors in order to induce them to serve. Many corporations believe such payments improve the quality and interest of directors.

A number of state statutes give express recognition to the modern practice of compensating directors. The Revised Model Business Corporation Act, for example, provides that "unless the articles of incorporation or bylaws provide otherwise, the board of directors may fix the compensation of directors." RMBCA § 8.11.

§ 10.4 Filling of Vacancies on the Board

Modern statutes authorize vacancies in the board of directors to be filled either by the shareholders or by the board of directors. RMBCA § 8.10(a). Directors elected to fill vacancies must stand for election at the next annual meeting of shareholders even if the term otherwise would continue beyond that meeting. RMBCA § 8.05(b). Some states follow earlier versions of the Model Act and provide that directors elected to fill a vacancy remain in office for the term of their predecessor. This has application only if the terms of the board are staggered. (See § 9.4 of this Nutshell.)

Older statutes distinguish between an "old" and a "new" vacancy. An "old" vacancy is created by the death or resignation of a director and may be filled by the remaining directors. A successor director in an "old" vacancy serves the unexpired term of his or her predecessor. A "new" vacancy, on the other hand, is created by an increase in the number of directors by amendment of the bylaws or articles. A "new" vacancy may be filled only by the shareholders, not the directors. The distinction between "old" and "new" vacancies arose in decisions from the State of Delaware, and was reflected in the 1950 version of the Model Act but was eliminated by an amendment in 1962. This history explains why section 8.10(a) of the Revised Model Business Corporation Act expressly treats a "vacancy resulting from an increase in the number of directors" the same way as other vacancies. Many but not all statutes reflect this simpler and more sensible approach.

A common device to ensure minority representation on boards of directors of closely held corporations is to provide that separate classes of shares are entitled to elect specific numbers of directors. Section 8.10(b) preserves this concept when vacancies are to be filled by limiting the shareholders authorized to fill vacancies to those that would be entitled to vote for the original election of the directors. Otherwise all shareholders might be able to vote on filling the vacancies. If such vacancies are filled by the board of directors, all directors, including those elected by other classes of shares, may vote on filling the vacancies. However, the damage this might do to the interests of the class of shares entitled to elect the original directors is limited because directors elected to those positions may be thereafter removed without cause solely by the class of shares entitled to vote in the original election under section 8.08(b). Section 8.10(c) makes it clear that a vacancy that will occur in the future, as by a dated resignation, may be filled immediately, with the resigning director participating in the decision. This provision may be of importance in corporations with closely divided or deadlocked boards of directors.

§ 10.5   Hold–Over Directors

Statutes provide that despite the expiration of a director's term, he or she continues to hold office until a successor is "elected and qualified." RMBCA § 8.05(e). As a result, the failure to hold an annual meeting does not affect the power of a corporation to continue to transact its business since the directors presently in office continue in office with power to act.

The hold-over director provision is particularly important in situations where the shareholders are deadlocked in voting power and unable to elect successors to directors whose terms have expired. In this situation, those who are "in" remain as directors apparently forever; however, the ultimate solution is the involuntary dissolution of the corporation (or a mandatory buyout of one faction's shares at a judicially determined price) if the deadlock cannot be broken. See Chapter 12, § 12.5 of this Nutshell.

§ 10.6   Necessity for Meeting and Personal Attendance

Numerous early cases refer to the rule that the "power invested in directors to control and manage the affairs of a corporation is not joint and several, but joint only," and that therefore action by directors must be "as a body at a properly constituted meeting." The underlying theory was that the shareholders were entitled to a decision reached only after group discussion and deliberation. Views may be changed as a result of discussion, and the sharpening of minds as a result of joint deliberation improves the decisional process. Several corollaries arise from this theory: first, the independent, consecutive approval of an act by each of the individual directors is not effective directoral action; second, directors may not vote by proxy; and third, formalities as to notice, quorum, and similar matters must be fully adhered to.

These corollaries make very little sense when applied to a close corporation where all the shareholders are active in the business, and even the requirement of a formal meeting of the directors in that situation is likely to be considered a meaningless formality. Further, rigid application of the doctrine often permits a corporation to use its own internal procedural defects as a sword to undo undesired transactions. This basic injustice is heightened because persons dealing with the corporation usually have no way of verifying that the formalities were in fact followed.

As a result, the broad principle was vitiated by judicially created exceptions even as it was being articulated. The basic exceptions are "estoppel," "ratification," and "acquiescence." Even though informal directoral action may be ineffective to formally authorize a transaction, it may be considered acquiescence in and ratification of the transaction. "Ratification" is usually applied where the corporation accepts the benefit of the contract without objection or where all the shareholders are aware of the contract and voice no objection. "Estoppel" is usually applied where the secretary of a corporation certifies that a meeting took place when it in fact had not; the corporation is estopped from questioning whether the requisite formalities were followed. While it is dangerous to assume that the historical principle that directors may act only at meetings is totally obsolete, it is probable that one or more of the exceptions will be found applicable in specific situations.

§ 10.7 Telephonic Meetings

The Revised Model Business Corporation Act contains a provision that authorizes the board of directors to permit members of the board of directors or a committee of the board to participate in a regular or special meeting through the use of a means of communication "by which all directors participating may simultaneously hear each other during the meeting." Most states have similar statutes that at least extend to the most ubiquitous "means of communication" that meets this requirement: the conference telephone call. The RMBCA, however, goes somewhat further than most of these statutes since it is broadly phrased in anticipation of possible advances in communications technology and expressly authorizes "a meeting" through the use of such technology at which no two directors are in the same room.

Participation through one of these "means of communication," the statute adds, constitutes presence in person at a meeting. This provision may be of considerable practical usefulness where directors are widely scattered, or where one or more of them are distant from the location where regular meetings are held. However, the fact that specific statutory authorization was felt to be necessary for a common sense idea such as telephonic meetings illustrates the persistence of the common law notion that directors can act only in meetings.

§ 10.8 Action Without a Meeting

Section 8.21 of the Revised Model Business Corporation Act permits directors to act by unanimous written consent without a formal meeting "unless the articles of incorporation or bylaws provide otherwise." Most states have similar statutes.

Action by written consent has the same effect as a unanimous vote and may be described as such in any document. RMBCA § 8.21(c). This modest and sensible provision solves most problems created by the rule requiring actions to be taken at directors' meetings. Problems still may arise, however. For one thing, obtaining a written consent signed by all the directors is itself a formality which may be overlooked by a careless attorney. There is also the problem of timing; action by consent is effective when the last director signs the consent under RMBCA § 8.21(b), so that it is difficult to argue that such a consent is retroactive. Of course, arguments may then be made based on the doctrine of ratification, but it is always possible that by the time the last director signs one or more other directors may have changed their minds. And, of course, the procedure is inapplicable if one of the directors objects to the transaction in question and refuses to execute the consent; a formal meeting is then essential.

§ 10.9 Directors' Objections to Actions

Directors are sometimes faced with the difficult problem of what to do when a majority insists on authorizing the corporation to enter into transactions which the director feels to be precipitate, risky, a breach of fiduciary duty, or outright illegal. The concern of such a director is not theoretical, since in some circumstances all acquiescing directors may be held personally liable even though some of them may have had serious mental reservations about the action. To avoid this result a director must make sure that his or her dissent appears in writing in one of the ways set forth in section 8.24(b) of the Revised Model Business Corporation Act: a dissent or abstention from the action is entered in the minutes of the meeting or the director delivers written notice of dissent or abstention "to the presiding officer of the meeting before its adjournment or to the corporation immediately after adjournment of the meeting."

Filing of a dissent not only eliminates liability, but also obviates later questions of proof and may have a psychological effect upon the other directors who realize that at least one director considers the conduct sufficiently questionable as to seek legal protection. Also, it affords notice to shareholders or others examining the records that at least one director questioned the propriety of a specific transaction.

Rather than filing a notice of dissent, directors may take other steps. For example, they may request that the corporation obtain an opinion of counsel as to the propriety of the proposed transaction. While directors may rely in good faith on the opinion of counsel [RMBCA § 8.30(b)(2)], an unqualified reliable opinion may be difficult to obtain as a practical matter if the transaction is questionable. Another option is that the director may announce his or her resignation from the board before the action is taken; if the resignation occurs after the transaction is approved, liability may be avoided only if the director files the appropriate dissent. Presumably, a written resignation because of disagreement over an action taken by the board of directors would be viewed as a dissent from that action.

Similarly, even though a meeting is called without proper notice, a director waives any objection to the notice by attending the meeting and participating in it. Indeed, any participation by such a director is likely to be considered a waiver even though the director objects at the outset to the lack of notice. Section 8.24(d)(1) also addresses this issue in part by providing that such a director must object "at the beginning of the meeting (or promptly upon his arrival) to holding it or transacting business at the meeting."

§ 10.10 Committees of the Board of Directors

Many corporations utilize committees of the board of directors to consider in detail technical matters, to consider corporate transactions that in some way affect the personal interests of one or more directors, and to make directoral decisions during periods when the board does not meet. In addition to the committees discussed here, some corporations have utilized committees that may be composed of directors (and sometimes outsiders) to provide advice and perspective to the board of directors. Corporations also may form committees of management personnel to consider business-related problems; these committees form part of executive management rather than part of the management structure of the board of directors. The committees discussed here are unlike either of these other types of committees; they are not purely advisory or part of management; they are committees of directors that have the power to act to some extent in lieu of the board of directors.

Where a board of directors is large and meets relatively few times per year, it may be convenient to appoint an executive committee to perform the functions of the board of directors between meetings of the full board of directors. Executive committees are usually composed of inside directors who are officers or employees of the corporation (or at least are likely to be available upon call or upon short notice). The executive committee is probably the best known type of committee of directors; the earliest corporation statutes that recognized the need for committees of the board of directors apparently had this type of committee in mind. The scope of the authority of an executive committee is discussed below.

During the decade of the 1970s, a strong trend developed toward creating additional committees within the boards of directors of publicly held corporations. The three most popular standing committees are the audit committee, the compensation committee, and the nominating committee; in many corporations they are primarily or exclusively composed of outside directors, i.e. directors not affiliated with management. In addition, special ad hoc committees may be created to consider the merits of specific issues, such as derivative litigation filed on behalf of the corporation, requests for indemnification for expenses incurred by directors or officers in connection with litigation, or on the ratification of conflict of interest transactions between a director and the corporation.

Many state statutes permit committees of directors to be formed only if there is express authorization to do so in the articles of incorporation. The Revised Model Business Corporation Act and more modern statutes permit the creation of such committees unless expressly prohibited by the articles of incorporation or bylaws. Many statutes require that the creation of such a committee be approved by an absolute majority of the directors (as contrasted with a majority of the directors present at a meeting at which a quorum is present, the test applicable to normal directoral decisions). See RMBCA § 8.25(b). The RMBCA and the statutes of many states require that a committee consist of at least two directors, though some statutes permit a committee to consist of one or more members.

A question that has received a fair amount of legislative attention is what limits should be imposed on the delegation of power to directoral committees. The early statutes dealing primarily with executive committees limited the authority of committees to routine matters relating to the business of the corporation. Many statutes also expressly negated the power of committees to act on behalf of the board on such important or extraordinary matters as approving mergers, declaring a dividend, and authorizing the sale of shares. The concerns apparently were to obviate the possibility of a "run away" committee and ensure that the full board of directors considered important matters. Section 8.25(e) of the Revised Business Corporation Act contains a list of prohibited functions that was developed on a somewhat different theory: delegation of authority to committees should be prohibited only where the actions substantially affect the rights of shareholders among themselves as shareholders and are irrevocable when completed, or are likely to become irrevocable within a brief period of time, or are likely to involve significant changes of position by others that cannot be rectified. The test basically is to prohibit delegation of important actions that cannot be overruled or overturned by the board of directors. Among the nondelegable matters listed in section 8.25(e) are authorizing distributions, filling of vacancies on the board of directors, amending bylaws, authorizing the repurchase of shares, authorizing the issuance of shares, or recommending approval of transactions that the statute requires be approved by the shareholders.

[For unfamiliar terms see the Glossary]

CHAPTER ELEVEN

OFFICERS

§ 11.1 Statutory Designations of Officers

Traditional corporation statutes require every corporation to have certain designated officers. Typically, such statutes require that each corporation have a president, one or more vice presidents, a secretary, and a treasurer. The apparent need for four different officers in even small corporations is significantly tempered by the further provision that any two offices (other than secretary and president) may be held by the same individual. The requirement that the president and secretary be different individuals is apparently based on the perceived need for two officers to execute contracts and other formal documents; some statutes that require designated officers allow all the offices to be held by a single individual. Even though these statutes designate the titles of the offices, most of them do not purport to define what the roles of these officers are or what the inherent powers of the various offices are.

The Revised Model Business Corporation Act, following the Delaware statute, eliminates all mandatory titled officers. Section 8.40(a) provides simply that each corporation shall have the officers described in its bylaws or appointed by its board of directors. The reasons underlying this change were that some corporations desire to have officers with different titles, and there seems to be no good reason to require such corporations to fit into the statutory mold in this regard. Also, there was some concern that implications of authority might be drawn from the statutory titles that might be inconsistent with the corporation's desires.

The Revised Model Business Corporation Act did find it necessary to define the duties of one corporate officer in section 8.40(c). The responsibility for preparing minutes of meetings and authenticating records referred to in that section are traditionally viewed as part of the responsibility of the secretary of a corporation, and the RMBCA uses the designation "secretary" in the statute when referring to the officer with those responsibilities. RMBCA § 1.40(20). However, it is not necessary that a corporation use this designation for the officer with this responsibility. The definition of "secretary" in the RMBCA is intended to be used only for internal cross references within the statute itself.

§ 11.2 Express Authority and Power to Act in General

The source of express authority of corporate officers should first be sought in the state's business corporation act, second in the corporation's articles of incorporation, third in the corporate bylaws and, fourth, in corporate resolutions adopted by the board. The first two sources rarely shed light on the authority of officers. As described above, even the older statutes that designate required offices do not typically describe the authority of those officers. A typical statutory provision (section 50 of the 1969 Model Act) simply provides that each designated officer "shall have such authority and perform such duties in the management of the corporation as may be provided in the bylaws, or as may be determined by resolution of the board of directors not inconsistent with the bylaws." Compare the similar language of section 8.41 of the Revised Model Business Corporation Act. Modern articles of incorporation generally do not refer at all to corporate officers, so that one is remitted to the bylaws and express resolutions of the board. Bylaw provisions are usually so general as to give little specific or reliable practical guidance (see § 11.3 of this Nutshell), so that as a practical matter express authority is apt to be found solely in authorizing resolutions of the board of directors.

In addition to express authority, corporate officers may possess implied actual or apparent authority, either from the nature of the office held or the manner in which business was conducted in the past. Finally, amorphous doctrines of "ratification," "estoppel," or "unjust enrichment" may sometimes allow third persons to hold corporations responsible for actions by officers despite the absence of express, implied, actual, or apparent authority when the action occurred. These various sources of authority are discussed in the sections that follow.

§ 11.3 Roles of Corporate Officers

The roles of corporate officers are usually outlined in corporate bylaws which may vary from corporation to corporation. The following descriptions are drawn from model bylaws intended for use under a statute that requires designated officers, and therefore represent normal "boilerplate" descriptions.

(1) The president is "the principal executive officer of the corporation" and, subject to the control of the board, "in general supervises and controls the business and affairs of the corporation." He or she is the proper officer to execute corporate contracts, certificates for securities, and other corporate instruments.

(2) The vice president performs the duties of the president in the absence of that officer or in the event of his or her death, incompetence, or inability or refusal to act. Vice presidents act in the order designated at the time of their election, or in the absence of designation, in the order of their election. Vice presidents may also execute share certificates or other corporate instruments.

(3) The secretary has several different functions: he or she keeps the minutes of the proceedings of shareholders

and the board of directors, sees that all notices are duly given as required by the bylaws, acts as custodian of the corporate records and of the corporate seal and sees that the seal of the corporation is properly affixed on authorized documents, keeps a register of the names and post office addresses of each shareholder, signs, along with the president or vice president, certificates for shares of the corporation, and has general charge of the stock transfer books of the corporation.

(4) The treasurer has "charge and custody of and is responsible for" all funds and securities of the corporation, and receives, gives receipts for, and deposits, all moneys due and payable to the corporation. The treasurer may be required to give a bond to ensure the faithful performance of his or her duties.

Traditional statutes also usually provide that the board of directors may assign additional duties to any statutory corporate officer, and the president may also assign additional duties to any vice president, the secretary, or the treasurer.

In states that designate titles of officers in the statute, corporations may create assistant secretaries, assistant treasurers, and other officers not specifically referred to in the statute. Such officers may have titles such as chief executive officer (CEO), chief operating officer (COO), chief legal officer (CLO), chief financial officer (CFO), comptroller, general manager, cashier, loan officer, or other designation. The chief executive officer, generally viewed to be the title of the individual ultimately in charge of the management of the business, may hold an office with a designation other than president, for example, chairman of the board of directors. Thus, even in states that designate officers, the person named to the statutory office of president may be an intermediate rather than the senior management position.

§ 11.4 Express Authority Delegated by Board of Directors

When a person negotiates with a corporation, he or she deals with a flesh-and-blood human being who may represent, either expressly or by implication, that he or she is authorized to bind the corporation. How does one make certain that the corporation—a fictional entity—will in fact be bound by a transaction so negotiated? It is possible, of course, to trust to appearances, implied authority, general descriptions of authority set forth in the previous section, blind luck, and the like, but that is very dangerous since litigation may be necessary to prove that the person in fact had authority to bind the corporation, and, because the doctrines are vague and amorphous, it is always possible that one may lose.

The simple and foolproof way to ensure that the corporation is bound by a transaction is to require the person purporting to act for the corporation to deliver, prior to the closing of the transaction, a certified copy of a resolution of the board of directors authorizing the transaction in question and directing the named officer to enter into the transaction on behalf of the corporation. The certificate should be executed by the secretary or an assistant secretary of the corporation, the corporate seal should be affixed, and the certificate should recite the date of the meeting (or a statement that the resolution was approved by unanimous written consent) and quote the resolution itself. There is no reason to go behind the certificate and attempt to ascertain whether or not the stated facts are true, since the corporation is estopped to deny the truthfulness of facts stated in the secretary's certificate relating to the records in his or her custody. Or to put the issue in a somewhat different way, keeping and certifying corporate records is within the actual authority of the secretary and the act of certification therefore binds the corporation. However, since the binding nature of the certificate rests on an estoppel, an inquiry into the background behind the certificate may possibly destroy the basis of the estoppel. And a third person who has reason to know that the facts recited in the certificate are not true may not be able to rely on the estoppel. However, in the absence of such knowledge, one can deal with a corporate officer with confidence upon the production of a duly executed secretarial certificate. Cautious attorneys have followed this procedure for many years. That it has not achieved universal acceptance probably is a result of two factors: ignorance, particularly on the part of laymen who may not realize that the inherent authority of a corporate president is very narrow in many states (see § 11.5 of this Nutshell), and the small size of many transactions, which may make any formality, no matter how simple, uneconomic.

Attorneys required to give an opinion that some transaction has been duly approved by a corporation will normally inspect the minutes of the meeting of the board of directors at which the action was taken. However, they normally rely on the certificate of the secretary of the corporation that the minutes accurately reflect who was present and what action was taken; such reliance is consistent with the attorneys' obligation to investigate with due diligence.

§ 11.5 Inherent Power of the Corporate President

Most non-lawyers are apt to think that the person holding the office of president of a corporation is the most important single person within the corporation and that he or she therefore must have authority to enter into normal business transactions, and probably has authority to enter into extraordinary transactions as well. In fact, these widely held views are often erroneous: the present state of the law in many jurisdictions is that the president has only limited authority which may not extend beyond minor, ordinary, routine transactions. Essentially, the focus of power to approve more significant transactions is in the board of directors, not the president.

This narrow construction of the president's authority may lead to injustice. Persons relying on reasonable appearances may discover that their reliance was ill-advised, and that the corporation is not obligated on a relatively routine transaction authorized by the corporate president. Persons aware of the rule are forced virtually to insult the president by demanding an exhibit of his or her authority.

Some courts have broadened the implied authority of the president or chief executive officer, and there appears to be a general trend in this direction particularly in large, publicly held corporations. Broader authority of the president is likely to be found in cases where the corporation later regrets the transaction and seeks to hide behind the lack of authority of its nominal chief officer. Some courts have concluded that a president presumptively has any powers which the board could give him or her. Others give that officer authority to enter into transactions "arising in the usual and regular course of business," and construe that phrase broadly. This may include, for example, the power to hire or discharge all employees. However, the inherent authority test is at best uncertain in its application to specific facts so that all unusual or extraordinary contracts should be authorized by the directors—including such matters as lifetime or long-time employment contracts and settlement of material litigation.

§ 11.6 Implied Authority, Apparent Authority, Ratification, Estoppel, and Unjust Enrichment

Even where the authority of the person purporting to act for a corporation has not been established by a previous action of the board of directors, the doctrines of ratification, estoppel, implied actual authority, or apparent authority may be available to a third person seeking to hold the corporation. These various doctrines are closely interrelated.

The board of directors of a corporation may learn that an officer has entered into a transaction in the past without being specifically authorized to do so. If the board does not promptly attempt to rescind or revoke the actions previously taken by the officer, it is probable that the corporation will be bound on the transaction on a theory of "ratification." Ratification may arise merely from knowledge of the transaction and failure to disaffirm or rescind it; usually, however, there are also elements of retention of benefits by the corporation and/or known reliance by the third party on the existence of the contract. "Estoppel" or "unjust enrichment" might equally well be found in such cases. Estoppel differs from ratification mainly in that attention is placed on the reliance of the third person, and the inequitableness of permitting the corporation to pull the rug out from under a person who reasonably relied on the corporation's silence.

Most problems involving implied authority of corporate officers arise when the third person seeks to hold the corporation on a current transaction by showing that the directors accepted or ratified prior similar transactions in the past. The argument is that the acquiescence of the board of directors indicates that an actual grant of authority was informally made. The same facts which support a finding of ratification of transaction A_1 may be used to conclude that a later similar transaction, A_2, was impliedly authorized. This is, of course, implied actual authority.

Apparent authority bears somewhat the same relationship to the concept of estoppel as implied authority bears to ratification. To show apparent authority, one must prove such conduct on the part of the principal as would lead a reasonably prudent person, using diligence and discretion, to suppose that the agent has the authority he or she purports to exercise. A third person, knowing that an officer has exercised authority in the past with the consent of the board of directors, may continue to rely on the appearance of authority, and the doctrine of apparent authority may protect such reliance. For apparent authority to exist, there must be some conduct on the part of the principal, i.e., the corporation, which creates the appearance of authority; a mere representation by an agent that he or she possesses the requisite authority is not sufficient. However, such conduct may consist of silence when the principal is aware that the agent represents the existence of authority, or it may consist of acquiescence in, and ratification of, acts performed in the past.

The principal practical difference between apparent authority and implied actual authority is that for apparent authority, the third person must show that he or she was aware of the prior acts or holding out and relied on appearances, while implied actual authority may be found even in the absence of knowledge or reliance on the part of third persons. However, the same conduct may often be cited to prove either implied actual authority or apparent authority.

In view of the close interrelationship between the various doctrines referred to in this section, it is not surprising to find that courts sometimes slip from one doctrine to another, sometimes perhaps not being fully aware of the differences.

The various doctrines discussed in this section may be applicable to situations other than silence and acquiescence. For example, a corporation may expressly ratify a transaction, or a corporation may be estopped to deny that a transaction was authorized if it expressly creates the appearance of authority but withholds actual authority. Similarly, implied authority or apparent authority may arise from a variety of affirmative circumstances as well as silence on the part of the directors.

Courts may be reluctant to find ratification of an unauthorized act by an officer where the act is fraudulent, unfair to minority shareholders, or against public policy. Often, in such situations, the court may conclude that the corporation lacked the requisite full knowledge to ratify the act. Of course, to avoid such an act the directors must offer to return any benefits obtained by the corporation.

§ 11.7 Fiduciary Duties of Officers and Agents

Corporate officers and agents owe a fiduciary duty to the corporation. The common law standard imposed involves a high degree of honesty, good faith, and diligence because corporate officers and agents render services for pay, and are often full-time employees. The officer or agent should act for the sole benefit of the corporation and give to it his or her best uncorrupt business judgment. Full disclosure of possibly conflicting transactions may be required, and the officer or agent may hold in trust for the corporation profits made personally in competition with, or at the expense of, the corporation. When all is said and done, however, general statements about the scope of fiduciary duties rarely decide specific cases.

Section 8.42 of the Revised Model Business Corporation Act imposes a standard of conduct for officers that is essentially identical to that imposed on directors. See Chapter 14 of this Nutshell. However, the scope of an officer's obligation to the corporation is determined in part by the nature of the performance required of him or her. The duty of subordinate officers or agents may be somewhat narrower than the analogous duty of a director. However, most of the litigation relating to fiduciary duties involve directors, and such cases are often relied on to establish the duties of high-level or managing corporate officers and agents.

A corporate officer or agent may also be liable to the corporation if he or she exceeds his or her actual authority and binds the corporation in a transaction with a third person. Such a transaction, of course, must be within the officer's or agent's apparent authority if the corporation is to be bound.

§ 11.8 Liability of Officers and Agents to Third Parties

A corporate officer or employee who acts within the scope of his or her authority as the corporation's representative in a consensual transaction is not personally liable on the transaction if he or she acted solely as an agent. This statement of basic principles of agency is little more than a truism; what is significant are ways in which a corporate officer or employee may, despite the general agency principle, make himself or herself liable on a corporate obligation. There are several possibilities:

First, the agent may expressly guarantee the performance by the corporation, intending to be personally bound on the obligation. Such a guarantee may be written or oral, and may or may not be supported by consideration, depending on the sequence of events and what is requested. Of course, to be enforceable, a promise must be supported by consideration. Whether or not it must also be in writing usually depends on the proper scope of the provision of the statute of frauds dealing with promises to answer for the indebtedness of another. For example, an oral promise by the president of a corporation to a supplier of merchandise that he or she would assume the obligation of payment if goods were delivered might be enforced despite the statute of frauds on the theory that the president was the primary obligor. Similarly, the so-called "main purpose" or "leading object" exceptions to the suretyship provision of the statute of frauds may in some circumstances make an oral guarantee by a corporate officer enforceable.

Second, the agent may not intend to be personally bound, but may in fact bind himself or herself by creating the impression that he or she is negotiating on an individual rather than corporate basis, or by executing the agreement in such a way as to indicate personal liability. If a person negotiates a transaction without disclosing he or she is acting on behalf of a corporation the actor is personally liable to the third person on general agency principles. Even if the existence of the corporation is disclosed, joint liability of the corporation and the officer may be created because of informality in the manner of execution. The proper manner for an officer to execute a document in the name of, and on behalf of, a corporation is as follows:

ABC Corporation

By:_____
        President

Any variation from this form is dangerous, since the mere designation of the corporate office may be deemed a description of the signing party rather than evidence that he or she signed as agent. For example, the following form of execution:

ABC Corporation

_____

President

is ambiguous since the corporation and the president may be either joint obligors or the president may have intended to sign only in a representational capacity. The word "president" does not resolve the ambiguity since it may be an identification of the individual obligor or an indication that he or she signed only as a representative. In cases involving ambiguous forms of execution courts appear to be more willing to allow corporate officers to testify about the "real intention of the parties" in executing general contracts than in executing promissory notes.

Third, if the agent is acting beyond the scope of authority, he or she may be personally liable on the transaction unless the corporation takes the agent off the hook by ratifying the transaction. A person acting as an agent generally warrants his or her own authority; this principle, of course, does not apply where the third person is aware the officer or agent lacks authority and the transaction must be submitted to the board of directors for approval.

Finally, liability may arise because imposed by statute. Failure to pay franchise taxes or to publish a notice upon incorporation may, in some circumstances, lead to individual as well as corporate liability on corporate obligations. The federal income tax statutes provide for a penalty of one hundred per cent of the tax for failing to pay over income taxes withheld from employees. This penalty tax may be imposed on "any person required to collect, truthfully account for, and pay over" the tax. (IRC § 6672.) There are perhaps other situations as well where personal liability is imposed by statute.

§ 11.9 Imputation of Knowledge to Corporation

In the foregoing discussion, there have been several references to "corporate knowledge" or understanding that appear to ignore the fictional nature of a corporation. Of course, a corporation can "know" or "have notice of" something only if one or more persons who represent the corporation know or have notice of the thing. Usually, knowledge acquired by a corporate officer or employee while acting in furtherance of the corporate business or in the course of his or her employment will be imputed to the corporation. Thus, if the president knows of a transaction, the corporation ratifies it if the corporation accepts the benefits of the transaction, even though one or more directors or other officers may not know all the details. Service of process on an authorized agent of the corporation will support a default judgment against the corporation even though the agent fails to forward the papers to the corporation's attorney.

Difficult problems arise when it is sought to impute knowledge of an agent to the corporation if the agent is acting adversely to the corporation. Generally information or knowledge may be imputed from an agent who has ultimate responsibility for the transaction to the corporation even if the agent is acting adversely to and in fraud of the corporation. Similarly, if a corporate officer learns that a low level employee is defrauding the corporation, the officer's knowledge may be imputed to the corporation even though the officer does not disclose the information to other officers or directors.

Generally, an agent's wrongful intention may be imputed to a corporation so that a corporation is subject to civil or criminal prosecution, including prosecution for traditional crimes such as murder or rape. Of course, for the corporation to be prosecuted such acts must be connected with, or be in furtherance of, the corporation's business.

§ 11.10 Tenure of Officers and Agents

Corporate officers and agents generally serve at the will of the person or board having authority to elect or appoint the officers or agents. Corporate officers are elected or appointed by the board of directors, and corporation statutes generally provide that they may be removed by the board of directors with or without cause. RMBCA § 8.43(b). So far as agents appointed by the president or general manager are concerned, the power to discharge is implicit in the power to employ. Corporate bylaws usually explicitly grant the power to remove or discharge as part of the power to appoint.

Many state statutes refer to the "election" or "appointment" of officers. The Revised Model Business Corporation Act uses only the word "appointment," reserving the word "election" for the selection of directors.

Of course, an officer or agent may be given an employment contract, and removal of such an officer or agent may give rise to a cause of action for breach of contract. However, the mere election or appointment of an officer or agent, even for a definite term, is not usually held of itself to give rise to a contract right. RMBCA § 8.44. The validity of such contracts in light of corporate bylaws is discussed in the following section.

§ 11.11   Long–Term Employment Contracts

Long-term employment contracts have given rise to a substantial volume of litigation in the context of closely held corporations.

(1) *Validity.* Corporate bylaws usually provide that specified named officers, such as the president, vice president, secretary, and treasurer, are to be elected or appointed by the board of directors for a term of one year. Does such a bylaw restriction limit the power of a corporation to grant such an officer an employment contract extending beyond the term of that office? Generally, the answer is "no" since, despite the contract, the officer or employee may be relieved of his or her duties at any time. Of course, the corporation may be liable for breach of contract for the premature termination of the employment period. RMBCA § 8.44(b). On a parity of reasoning, long-time contracts, e.g., leases, have been upheld despite the fact that they "bind" subsequent boards of directors. A second argument may also be made if the board has power, as most boards of directors do, to amend the bylaws. An employment contract for more than one year may be deemed to be an implied amendment of the bylaws by the board, since the board could first amend the bylaw and then enter into a long term employment contract. While some courts have

accepted this argument, there is a practical problem with implied amendments of bylaws since one cannot then rely on the written bylaws as being the current and complete rules governing the corporation's internal affairs.

(2) *Lifetime Employment Contracts.* The claim that a person has been given a life time employment contract by a corporation has been treated with hostility by the courts. Such contracts are usually oral and arise within the context of a family-run business. While such a contract is not within the statute of frauds, courts may feel that the factual basis for such an open-ended commitment is inherently implausible. Also, such contracts may subject a corporation to a substantial liability which may run for a long and indefinite period during which circumstances may substantially change. Most cases which have refused to enforce such arrangements have done so on the ground the officer making the arrangement had neither actual nor apparent authority to enter into such an arrangement.

(3) *Discharge for Cause.* It is clear that an officer or employee with a valid employment contract may nevertheless be discharged for cause. "Cause" may consist of acts of dishonesty, negligence, refusal to obey reasonable orders, refusal to follow reasonable rules, or a variety of other acts such as engaging in an unprovoked fight. In effect, such conduct constitutes a breach of an implied—if not express—covenant in the employment contract. Of course, since officers usually do not have employment contracts, it is usually unnecessary to determine whether or not "cause" exists.

(4) *Basis of Compensation.* Employees sometimes request that they be compensated on the basis of a percentage of corporate earnings or profits rather than at a flat rate. No particular legal problem is raised by such contracts, though questions sometimes arise as to how earnings and profits are to be measured. The simple phrase "net profits" is often ambiguous and its meaning may be elusive.

(5) *Miscellaneous.* Employment contracts for highly paid personnel in publicly held corporations often provide for deferred compensation, options to purchase shares, reimbursement of business expenses, and other tax-related benefits. In the closely held corporation, an employment agreement may be an integral part of the basic planning arrangement between shareholders. Terms relating to employment are often placed in shareholder's agreements so that they will be binding on all the other shareholders as well as the corporation. There also may be a greater possibility of specific performance of a shareholders' agreement than of a simple employment contract; specific enforcement may be significant in a close corporation where the right to participate in management may be important and the salary derived from the arrangement is the only available financial benefit.

[For unfamiliar terms see the Glossary]

CHAPTER TWELVE

THE CLOSELY HELD CORPORATION

§ 12.1 Close Corporations in Perspective

A "close corporation" or "closely held corporation" may be defined preliminarily as a corporation with a few shareholders. (See § 1.5 of this Nutshell.) Most states do not provide any special treatment for such corporations and they must comply with the various provisions of the state corporation statute the same way as any other corporation. Several states, however, have enacted special statutes dealing with such corporations. Also, the legal literature has long argued that such corporations have special problems and needs. As a result, a "jurisprudence" of closely held corporations is in the process of being developed.

A closely held corporation has certain unique attributes:

(1) Since it has only a relatively small number of shareholders, there is no public trading in, or public market for, its shares. Small blocks of shares may be unsalable; potential purchasers must be found among present shareholders, or rarely, among outsiders willing "to take a gamble." As a result, the market for small blocks of closely held shares is at worst non-existent and at best a buyer's market. There is usually no competition and therefore little incentive for buyers to offer prices for shares that the seller believes are reasonable. On the other hand, if the shares offered for sale constitute a majority interest, they are often readily salable at attractive prices to outsiders interested in running the business in which the corporation is engaged. It is common, in other words, for controlling shares to be worth

a great deal while otherwise identical minority shares are worth much less.

(2) The management of the corporation is closely associated with the principal shareholders, or with all the shareholders. The majority shareholders may name the board of directors, and through them, the officers and employees. If there is a disagreement between the majority and minority shareholders, the majority may exclude the minority totally from the corporation and its business, and without specific employment rights there is little that the minority shareholder can do about it.

(3) The majority shareholders usually have little interest in paying dividends. Rather, they may prefer to distribute earnings in the form of salaries or other payments to the shareholders, or some of them, that are tax deductible by the corporation. Even in S corporations where there is no tax incentive to minimize the "double taxation" of corporate income, majority shareholders may prefer to pay themselves substantial salaries and distribute only modest amounts, if that, to the shareholders generally. The ability of the majority to exclude the minority is, of course, part of the reason that control shares usually sell for more than minority shares.

(4) The management may wish to operate the business in an informal manner, often as though it were a partnership rather than a corporation.

(5) Shareholders usually desire a voice in determining who their fellow shareholders are, and may wish to limit the shareholders to persons active in the management of the corporation.

Because shares in a close corporation are not readily salable and minority shareholders ordinarily have no power to force a dissolution of the corporation, a person may be "locked in" a minority position for long periods of time, receiving little or no return on his or her investment and being unable to dispose of it at a reasonable price. Indeed, over a period of time in which deaths, withdrawals, or fallings out are likely, the possibility that adverse and hostile interests will develop within a closely held corporation is fairly high. It is for this reason that advance planning in the close corporation is essential if difficult and costly problems are to be avoided.

This chapter considers control arrangements within the close corporation. Such arrangements may be made to ensure control by a working majority, or to give a minority a greater voice in corporate affairs than it naturally has, or to give a minority shareholder some protection against the possible tyranny of the majority referred to in the preceding paragraphs.

§ 12.2 Traditional Control Devices in Closely Held Corporations

In the absence of special statutory treatment of closely held corporations, such corporations must establish control devices through the use of traditional and accepted techniques. An earlier section has discussed the limited validity of shareholders' agreements that restrict the discretion of directors (§ 8.10 of this Nutshell); that rule of law of uncertain scope obviously limits the usefulness of the simple contract as a control device. Accepted voting control devices such as shareholders' pooling agreements (§ 9.6 of this Nutshell), voting trusts (§§ 9.7–9.9 of this Nutshell), and irrevocable proxies (§ 9.5 of this Nutshell) have their place, but their inherent usefulness is often limited.

Of greater practical importance is the use of restrictions on the transfer of shares (§§ 9.11–9.19 of this Nutshell). Such restrictions not only ensure that shareholders have a voice in who is a shareholder in the corporate venture, but often of greater importance, a mandatory buy/sell agreement may be the best guarantee to a minority shareholder that his or her investment in the corporation may be liquidated under specified circumstances at a reasonable price (see § 9.11 of this Nutshell).

The most flexible and fool-proof device to establish desired control relationships within a continuing relationship involves the use of different classes of shares, usually different classes of common stock (see generally §§ 7.12, 9.10 of this Nutshell). The following examples illustrate the flexibility of this device:

(1) A corporation is to have two shareholders, one putting in $100,000, the other $50,000. They desire to share equally in control but in the ratio of their contributions (2:1) for financial purposes. The attorney suggests that an equal number of shares of two classes of common stock, Class A common and Class B common, be authorized. Each class is entitled to elect two directors, but the dividend and liquidation rights of the Class A are twice those of Class B. The corporation then issues all the Class A common to one shareholder for 100,000 dollars and all the Class B common to the other shareholder for 50,000 dollars. In this structure, the S corporation election would be unavailable because of the two classes of stock.

(2) Alternatively in the same situation, if shares with multiple votes per share are authorized in the particular state, the shares may be identical in all financial respects, with the class received by the smaller contributor having two votes per share and half the number of shares being issued. In this structure, the S corporation election is available, since different classes of stock do not disqualify a corporation from that election if the classes differ only in voting rights.

(3) A minority shareholder wishes to be assured of being treasurer of the corporation and to have a veto over all amendments to the articles of incorporation. The attorney suggests that a special class of common stock be issued to

the minority shareholder, and the articles of incorporation provide that (1) the treasurer must be a holder of that class of stock, and (2) the articles may be amended only by an affirmative vote of two-thirds of each class of stock, voting by classes. In other respects the classes have equal rights.

(4) There are three shareholders, each contributing the same amount of capital, but C is also contributing the basic idea and wants the same voting power as A and B combined. One simple solution is to issue voting and non-voting common stock (with equal dividend and liquidation rights) in the following amounts:

	Voting	Non-voting
A	50	50
B	50	50
C	100	-0-

Somewhat the same result may be obtained by the use of nonvoting preferred stock or indebtedness rather than non-voting common stock. If the classes of shares differ other than in voting rights the S corporation election is unavailable.

(4) A, B, and C are each contributing the same amount of capital, but A wants to be sure that B and C will not combine to oust him or her and cut off his or her income. The attorney suggests that A execute a five-year employment contract with the corporation guaranteeing him or her the specified income, renewable for a second five years at the option of A. To assure that A will be assured of a right to participate in the board deliberations, the attorney suggests that three classes of stock be created with identical financial rights but each with the power to elect one director. The S corporation election remains available to a corporation with this capital structure.

There seems to be little doubt about the validity of such control arrangements based on different classes of stock.

While there has been litigation on the outer bounds of the power to create specialized classes of stock, recent decisions appear uniformly favorable. In perhaps the most startling case, Lehrman v. Cohen (1966), the Delaware Supreme Court upheld a class of common stock which consisted of one share having a par value of $10; the share (1) could elect one of the five directors (the other four were elected by two equal factions), (2) was not entitled to receive dividends, (3) could share in the proceeds of dissolution only to the extent of the par value of the one share, and (4) could be redeemed by the corporation at any time by paying the shareholder the par value of the share, upon approval of four of the five directors. This share comes close to a naked vote completely divorced from ownership, yet was upheld. This one share class was designed to avoid a potential deadlock between the two principal shareholders and was issued to the attorney representing the corporation; after several years, the attorney and one of the other two shareholders combined forces to take over working control of the corporation, a situation which was cemented by a long term employment contract for the attorney. This arrangement was upheld in its entirety. (See § 9.10 of this Nutshell for a discussion of the same case in a different context.)

§ 12.3 Increased Quorum and Voting Requirements

Another useful device in effectuating shareholder control devices is increased voting requirements in order to give minority interests a veto power. This veto power may be applicable at the shareholder level, at the board of directors level, or both. In all states today, it is possible to increase the percentage needed to approve a measure to any desired number; usually unanimity is imposed, but in some circumstances a lesser percentage may be sufficient or have the same effect. While a requirement of unanimity was held invalid by a few courts, most notably Benintendi v. Kenton Hotel (1945), the language of modern statutes is broadly permissive, and there is no doubt today about the validity of increased voting requirements.

It is usually important to increase both the quorum requirement and the minimum vote requirement in order to make sure that it is impossible for the corporation to act without the assent of the minority shareholder. Where the quorum requirement has not been increased it is sometimes possible for the minority shareholder to prevent action by staying away from the meeting if that makes it impossible to obtain a quorum. In one case, such conduct was held to constitute a breach of fiduciary duty. Gearing v. Kelly (1962). This decision seems questionable given the dynamics of the closely held corporation.

If the increased voting requirement is set forth in the articles of incorporation or bylaws, the provision creating the increased voting requirement should itself expressly be made non-amendable except by the increased voting requirement. Some state statutes provide this protection automatically, but many do not. See RMBCA § 7.27(b).

§ 12.4 Fiduciary Duties of Shareholders

Until relatively recently it was generally accepted legal principle that shareholders in a closely held corporation did not owe greater duties to other shareholders than shareholders in corporations generally. The first indication of change in this regard occurred in judicial opinions and law review articles that referred to a closely held corporation as an "incorporated partnership" and urged greater use of this analogy in resolving disputes between shareholders of such corporations.

Decisions in Illinois, Galler v. Galler (1964), and Massachusetts, Donahue v. Rodd Electrotype Co. (1975), are the leading authorities that have used the partnership analogy in analyzing the duties of shareholders in closely held corporations, and similar language has appeared in a few other judicial opinions as well. The implications of this approach have been explored most fully in the post-*Donahue* decisions in Massachusetts. From these decisions it can be generalized that no court will fully accept the partnership analogy and impose analogous fiduciary duties on shareholders generally, but that fiduciary duties may be imposed on shareholders to invalidate unreasonable or hostile action that seems to serve no valid corporate purpose. Some recent decisions in other jurisdictions have declined to follow the Illinois/Massachusetts approach in this regard.

§ 12.5   Dangers of Dissension and Deadlock

A closely held corporation is often involved in dissension and deadlock. "Dissension" refers to internal squabbles, fights, or disagreements; "deadlock" to control arrangements that effectively prevent the corporation from acting. Many small corporations at one time or another in their history are wracked by such problems, and some advance planning may help to reduce or eliminate such disagreeable incidents.

In a typical close corporation, all the shareholders actively participate in the management of the business; it is easy to envision how disagreements may lead to distrust or friction. There may be good faith disagreement as to desirable business policies or a less than good faith suspicion that another shareholder is attempting a power grab or trying to obtain more than his or her "fair share" of the assets. The relationship of shareholders within a close corporation requires good faith and cooperation on all sides in much the same way as in a partnership; when this is lacking, serious disagreements are bound to arise.

Dissension within a close corporation creates more serious problems than in a partnership. If one faction has effective working control, the minority faction is in a weak if not helpless position. Arguments based on fiduciary duties of shareholders described in the previous section are obviously a last resort. Typically, the minority has no power to force dissolution and no right to share in the fruits of management (except to the extent the majority permits or a court is willing to apply fiduciary concepts to restore the minority's position). The minority may have the dubious recourse of trying to sell their shares to the majority. Where there is dissension, a majority group is often willing to pay something to eliminate the nuisance of a minority block and the threat of litigation. However, the majority may well decide to "soften up" the minority by removing them from salaried positions with the corporation, cease paying dividends, and letting them sit for a year or so. In this situation, attorneys often counsel minority shareholders to vigorously pursue whatever rights the minority shareholders possess, including particularly litigation based on theories of breach of fiduciary duty, mismanagement, usurpation of corporate opportunities, and breach of directors' duties, in an effort to improve their bargaining position. Other demands may be to inspect corporate records (to search for financial misconduct) or to compel the holding of shareholders' meetings. Of course, such tactics are likely to increase the enmity and friction within the corporation, though they may also make the majority more willing to pay a better price for the minority's shares.

Equally complex problems arise if neither faction has effective working control, since the corporation may become deadlocked. A corporation is potentially subject to deadlock if (1) two factions own exactly fifty per cent of the outstanding shares, (2) there are an even number of directors, and two factions each have the power to select the same number of directors, or (3) a minority shareholder has retained a veto power in one of the ways previously described. In each of these situations, the corporation may in effect be on dead center and unable to function as a corporation.

A deadlock may occur either at the shareholders' level or at the directors' level. If the shareholders are deadlocked, the corporation may continue to operate, since the board of directors in office when the deadlock arose will presumably remain in office indefinitely. A deadlock at the directoral level may prevent the corporation from functioning, though it is possible that the president or general manager may continue to operate the business, often to the complete exclusion of the deadlocked board of directors and the other faction of shareholders.

The most practical solution for the truly deadlocked corporation is usually for one faction to buy out the other in a negotiated transaction. It is ordinarily preferable to preserve a going corporation rather than to dissolve it. The business assets of a corporation, including intangible good will, are ordinarily worth more as a unit than fragmented. While it sometimes may be possible for deadlocked parties to work out a sale after the deadlock has arisen, the more logical solution is to address the problem when the parties are in amity and to work out an agreement in advance by which one faction should buy out the other at a fair price in the event of a deadlock. Such buy-sell agreements were discussed earlier (see § 9.18 of this Nutshell).

In the event there was no advance planning, and a buy-out after the dissension or deadlock arose cannot be worked out, the ultimate remedy is judicial action; the remedy usually provided by statute is involuntary dissolution (see § 12.6 of this Nutshell). Several state statutes, however, now provide a judicially imposed buy-out at an appraised price as an alternative to involuntary dissolution. These newer statutes are based on recognition that the remedy of involuntary dissolution often unreasonably benefits one faction of shareholders at the expense of another. And, in a modern development of considerable practical importance, courts have increasingly recognized a power under general equitable principles to order a judicially imposed buy-out even where the applicable statute refers solely to dissolution as the remedy for deadlocks.

The basic problem with the remedy of involuntary dissolution is that it often causes significant hardship to one party or the other on an erratic basis. For example, if a single shareholder's personal abilities largely explain the corporation's success, he or she may well desire liquidation of the corporation. By performing services for the corporation, the dominant shareholder is in effect sharing the fruits of his or her ability with other shareholders. If the corporation were dissolved, presumably the dominant shareholder could start up a new business that is virtually identical with the old one, capture the fruits of the good will that has been generated in the existing corporation, and not share those fruits with anyone. In most situations, the dominant shareholder cannot simply abandon the corporation and start a new business in competition with the corporation since such action might be deemed to constitute an usurpation of a corporate opportunity by the dominant shareholder. That argument would not appear to be applicable if the dominant shareholder were to start a new business following the involuntary dissolution of the old. A classic example of the attempted use of dissolution by a dominant shareholder in this manner is In re Radom & Neidorff, Inc. (1954). Whether or not dissolution unfairly benefits a shareholder in such a situation is debatable.

§ 12.6 Resolution of Intracorporate Conflict by Dissolution

The earliest general corporation statutes provided no special remedy for intracorporate conflict within a closely held corporation. As a result, minority shareholders were largely defenseless against abusive conduct. More modern statutes provide some protection by making the ultimate remedy of involuntary dissolution available at the request of a shareholder in the case of "illegal, oppressive, or fraudulent conduct" or actions constituting waste or misapplication of corporate assets. The language of § 14.30(2) of the RMBCA in this regard is typical. Under this section the sole remedy provided was involuntary dissolution, and a shareholder seeking that remedy must establish that

(1) The directors are deadlocked in the management of the corporate affairs, the shareholders are unable to break the deadlock, and that "irreparable injury to the corporation is threatened or being suffered, or the business and affairs of the corporation can no longer be conducted to the advantage of the shareholders generally, because of the deadlock;" or

(2) The directors or those in control of the corporation "have acted, are acting, or will act in a manner that is illegal, oppressive, or fraudulent;" or

(3) The shareholders are "deadlocked in voting power," and have failed, for a period that includes at least two consecutive annual meeting dates, to elect successors to directors whose terms have expired; or

(4) The corporate assets are being "misapplied or wasted."

Early cases state that there is no general common law right of dissolution. Hence the initial attitude toward these statutes was to construe them strictly and require strong showings of potential or actual abuse or harm before granting dissolution. Further, these statutes were construed as being addressed to the discretion of the court, so that a court might decline to grant dissolution even if the shareholder proved that conduct falling squarely within these provisions had occurred.

The early attitude toward strict construction of these statutes is disappearing and a much more flexible attitude developing. Courts have been willing to construe broadly language such as "oppressive" or "irreparable injury" in order to protect minority shareholders in a closely held corporation. "Oppressive," for example has been virtually equated with "fair dealing" or "fair play." Conduct may be "oppressive" upon a showing that action has been taken that is inconsistent with the expectations of the shareholders as to their roles in the corporation. Further, where oppressive or inequitable conduct has been demonstrated, courts are increasingly willing to provide remedies short of dissolution: a mandatory buyout of the interest of a minority shareholder at a judicially determined price being very common. In this respect, courts appear to be influenced by the flexible remedies provided in special close corporation statutes discussed in § 12.8 of this Nutshell, and in effect are extending these remedies to non-electing corporations by expansive construction of involuntary dissolution statutes.

In the absence of a contractual obligation, a dissatisfied shareholder does not have the power to compel other shareholders, on demand, to buy his or her shares at an appraised price. The remedies discussed in this section are available only in cases of significant misconduct by the dominant shareholders that injures the corporation or the interests of minority shareholders.

§ 12.7 Resolution of Intracorporate Disputes by Arbitration

Mandatory arbitration is sometimes used as a device to resolve intracorporate disputes. In most states today, arbitration is generally available to resolve future disputes without regard to their justiciability. Arbitration, of course, requires either a current willingness or a pre-existing agreement by the shareholders to submit the issues to arbitration.

In considering the desirability of arbitration for intracorporate disputes, two questions should be considered: first, what kinds of controversies is the arbitrator likely to face, and second, what kinds of solutions will he or she be permitted to adopt?

Certainly many intracorporate disputes involve personality conflicts or broad differences in policy. An arbitrator may have no criteria for resolving such disputes, and even if he or she does resolve a specific dispute, it is unlikely that the decision will have cured the basic disagreement which led to the specific dispute. In Application of Burkin (1956), a well-known New York case, a minority shareholder in a corporation sought arbitration of a claim that the majority shareholder should be removed as director. The corporation's governing documents required unanimity but the majority shareholder not unnaturally refused to vote in favor of his own removal. The court refused to order arbitration on the theory that the dispute was not justiciable, a result which was later overruled by statute. In this situation, the order of an arbitrator to remove the majority shareholder from the board of directors would in effect turn control of the corporation over to the minority shareholder, and as there was a unanimity requirement for the election of directors, the turnover of control would be permanent, at least until dissolution could be compelled pursuant to statute. Even if the majority shareholder had committed acts which might constitute cause for removal, it is doubtful whether an arbitrator should have power to favor permanently one faction over another in a pure struggle for control. There are other remedies of the minority shareholder to correct the acts which constitute cause for removal —e.g., a derivative suit—without turning the corporation over to the minority shareholder. Ultimately, if deep personal or policy conflicts continue, dissolution is the only suitable remedy because arbitration cannot cure the root cause of the disagreement.

The advantages of arbitration are speed, cheapness, informality (as contrasted with a court proceeding), and the prospect of a decision by a person with knowledge and experience in business affairs. Where the reason for deadlock is a question not involving a basic personal or policy matter, arbitration may satisfactorily resolve a dispute and permit the corporation to continue. For example, in Vogel v. Lewis (1967), the issue was whether a corporation should exercise an option to purchase contained in a lease of real property. The court held that this issue should be submitted to arbitration, a result which seems reasonable under the circumstances.

§ 12.8   Special Close Corporation Statutes

State statutes assume that corporations will be conducted with a degree of formality: shareholders will meet to elect directors who will in turn meet to elect or appoint officers and to direct the affairs of the corporation. Even a moment's reflection will indicate that these assumptions are unjustified for the small closely held corporation. With only a few shareholders, all or most of whom are active in the conduct of the business, corporate matters are likely to be resolved by unanimous consent with a minimum of formality and no regard for the statutory niceties. This entirely understandable practice creates several possible legal issues:

(1) Will the ignoring of corporate formalities give rise to an argument that the corporate veil should be "pierced" and the participants held personally liable on corporate obligations? (See Chapter Six of this Nutshell, particularly § 6.4.)

(2) Will the participants agree upon a control arrangement that is reasonable under the circumstances but violates the "statutory norms" so that the arrangement is legally unenforceable? (See § 8.10 of this Nutshell.)

(3) Will decisions made informally and without following the statutory norms be binding on the corporation and third parties? (See §§ 10.6–10.8 of this Nutshell.)

Special statutes relating to closely held corporations have been adopted in about a dozen states, including California and Delaware. These statutes are designed to permit such corporations to conduct their affairs with essentially the same formalities as if they were partnerships. While there is considerable variation in the state statutes relating to close corporations they generally provide the following:

(1) Agreements that restrict the discretion of directors and are therefore probably invalid under conventional principles (see § 8.10 of this Nutshell) are specifically validated.

(2) The corporation may elect to dispense with the board of directors entirely and have the business and affairs of the corporation conducted by the shareholders as though they were partners. If this option is elected, the liabilities otherwise imposed on directors are imposed on the managing shareholders.

(3) The corporation may elect special dissolution provisions that permit a minority shareholder, in specified circumstances, to compel the dissolution of the corporation. The close corporation supplement to the Revised Model Business Corporation Act also permits a corporation to elect a mandatory buy-out provision. These provisions, designed to eliminate the "locked in" feature of the close corporation (see § 12.1 of this Nutshell), are the principal substantive provisions of close corporation statutes that address the basic problem of the minority shareholder in a closely held corporation. However, they have only limited usefulness since they are applicable only when specifically agreed to.

(4) In the event of a deadlock at the directoral level, courts are specifically empowered to break the deadlock by the appointment of impartial "provisional directors." This provision is designed to provide a simpler, more flexible

and less drastic solution to deadlocked corporations than either the appointment of a receiver or involuntary dissolution. This provision is usually applicable to all electing close corporations and may not be opted out of; it is likely that the mere threat of the appointment of one or more provisional directors will be a strong stimulus to quarreling shareholders to make some kind of a mutual accommodation.

(5) All restrictions on share transfer restrictions are eliminated and standardized restrictions are established on an optional basis.

(6) In the event of deadlock or oppressive conduct, courts are invited to fashion a remedy that is suitable under the circumstances. The Model Close Corporation Supplement, for example, lists eleven different types of remedies that a court might invoke. Included are remedies that a court might be reluctant to grant under traditional statutes (see § 12.6), such as removal from office of any director or officer or the appointment of any individual as a director or officer.

Some close corporation statutes tend to be complex and prolix; much of the complicated language is usually addressed to problems such as determining which corporations are eligible to take advantage of these special provisions and what happens when an electing corporation loses its eligibility. Most close corporation statutes base eligibility on the number of shareholders: 15, 20, 35, 50 or some other maximum number. Some states also limit close corporation election to corporations that have never had a registered public offering, and to corporations whose shares are subject to a restriction on transfer. Since corporations form a continuum in terms of size and number of shareholders, lines must to some extent be arbitrary. A more complex problem is the possibility that an electing corporation might become ineligible because of events over which it has little control, e.g. a splitting up of a single shareholding into numerous small units. The problem of subsequent ineligibility is finessed by the Close Corporation Supplement to the Revised Model Business Corporation Act and the statutes of a few states by providing that once a valid election to come under the close corporation is made, it continues indefinitely, no matter what happens to the corporation and the number of its shareholders. The theory is that most corporations, if the number of shareholders increases above 50, will voluntarily conclude that the disadvantages of the close corporation election outweigh the advantages, and revoke the election voluntarily.

A few states originally made the special close corporation statutes applicable to all corporations that fell within a broad statutory definition, but the trend is clearly toward making the special provisions completely elective. The election is usually made by including a provision in the articles of incorporation simply stating that the corporation has elected to be a statutory close corporation. A few states also require that the name of the corporation reflect in some way the close corporation election; some states also require that a similar notation be placed on all certificates for shares of stock of the corporation which describes which special provisions the corporation has elected to make applicable.

Even though about a dozen states have adopted close corporation statutes, a rather limited sampling of the actual experience in several states indicates that they are not widely used. Florida even repealed its close corporation statute in 1975, placing many of the special provisions in its general corporation statute. While the reasons that attorneys have not taken advantage of these statutes are speculative, it is probable that most attorneys are able to work out basic control relationships under the general corporation statutes and therefore do not feel it is necessary to use or experiment with new and largely untried statutes. It is also possible that the sheer complexity of some of these statutes may have discouraged their widespread use.

[For unfamiliar terms see the Glossary]

CHAPTER THIRTEEN

THE PUBLICLY HELD CORPORATION

§ 13.1 The Publicly Held Corporation in Perspective

The most obvious difference between a publicly held corporation and the closely held corporations discussed in the previous chapter is that there is a public market for the shares of a publicly held corporation. That market may be the New York Stock Exchange, the American Stock Exchange, the vast over-the-counter market, or one or more regional exchanges. Nevertheless a shareholder of a publicly held corporation who desires to sell his or her shares may do so simply by calling a securities broker. An investor who decides to become a shareholder of a specific publicly held corporation also may do so simply by calling a broker and placing an order to buy.

Many publicly held corporations are huge economic entities with billions of dollars of assets, tens or hundreds of thousands of employees, and millions of shares outstanding. However, size is not a reliable criterion: many publicly held corporations are relatively small and a few closely held corporations rival the larger publicly held corporations in size. Nevertheless, the great bulk of this country's industrial wealth is owned by the 500 largest publicly held corporations.

In most publicly held corporations, shares are widely owned by thousands of different investors. Even though a significant fraction of the outstanding shares may be held by a relatively few institutional investors (described in section 13.4 of this Nutshell), the most common pattern is that the management of the corporation does not control, directly or indirectly, a majority, or even a substantial minority, of the outstanding shares. Even in corporations whose names are associated with individuals or families, it is relatively uncommon today to find that management control is based squarely on share ownership. The exceptions usually involve corporations that are relative newcomers on the public scene; they are often the modern success stories in which the founders of the business have decided to "go public" but have retained, singly or collectively, a majority interest in the corporation.

Another important distinguishing facet of the publicly held corporation is that it is subject to substantial disclosure obligations under regulations issued by the federal Securities and Exchange Commission and by the various securities exchanges. It has been stated that the management of a publicly held corporation operates in a goldfish bowl; that is an overstatement, but certainly such corporations have an obligation to make public disclosure of significant developments, both good news and news that the management would probably just as soon not be widely disseminated.

The number of publicly held corporations has been estimated to be in the range of only 10,000, or so. In contrast there are over a million closely held corporations. Nevertheless, in terms of wealth, power, and economic importance, the publicly held corporations far outweigh their much more numerous closely held counterparts.

§ 13.2 The "Chicago School" of Law and Economics

In the last two decades there has developed a law and economics analysis of the publicly held corporation that challenges many of the traditional beliefs about the role of management, the importance of takeover attempts by outsiders, and the efficacy of legal rules. This analysis has come to be associated with scholars at the University of Chicago and will be referred to here as the "Chicago school" of analysis since it was largely developed at that institution; it is appropriate to point out, however, that scholars with this analytic approach today teach at a number of different law schools and not only at the University of Chicago. Central to the Chicago school analysis is the treatment of the corporation as a "nexus of contracts" in which the shareholders are viewed as contributors of capital rather than ultimate owners of the business. Because management usually owns a small—or insignificant—portion of the common stock, the interest of management in maximizing its own interests conflicts to some extent with the interests of the providers of capital, particularly the common shareholders. The providers of capital must incur costs to monitor the performance of management and minimize the diversion of assets to them. These costs are usually referred to as "agency costs" and may include the cost of public outside auditors, bonding, and similar activities. These costs may also be reduced by establishing compensation schemes that tend to align management with the maximization of value to the holders of common shares—hence, the widespread popularity of stock option plans, stock purchase plans, and similar arrangements.

When approaching legal rules, members of the Chicago school do not usually start with an already-existing problem and seek to devise a rule that does substantial justice to the persons involved in that problem. This approach is usually referred to as an "ex post" establishment of rules; the Chicago school prefers to adopt an "ex ante" approach that assumes the rule is already in place and asks how the presence of the rule will affect prospective transactions or behavior. On the basis of this analysis, the members of the Chicago school have questioned the wisdom of many of the legal principles that are discussed in the balance of this, as well as the following, chapter.

§ 13.3   Role of the Small Shareholder in the Selection of Directors

The theoretical management structure of a corporation assumes that shareholders select directors who in turn select corporate officers to carry out their directives.   In some ways the large public corporation bears little resemblance to this theoretical structure.   Consider, for example, the role of the small shareholder in selecting directors in such a corporation.   He or she is presented with a list of candidates selected by the current managers of the corporation, and may vote for them or withhold his or her vote;   rarely does a small shareholder have a choice between competing directoral candidates.   Further, since the overwhelming majority of the shareholders are going to vote in favor of the persons proposed by management, it really does not make very much difference whether or not the small shareholder exercises the franchise or pitches the proxy solicitation form into the nearest trash basket.

For purposes of locating the real source of selection of directors, one must usually look not to the election process, but to some earlier point where an internal decision within the corporation was made as to which names should be presented to the shareholders for approval as the management's candidates.   This decision may have been made by the chief executive officer individually, or it may have been made by a committee composed of members of management, or by the standing nomination committee of the board of directors.   However it was made, it is important to recognize that this is the point at which the actual selection of directors occurs.   The role of shareholders in publicly held corporations is to ratify this selection.

Most shareholders routinely vote in favor of management. For one thing, they often have only the choice of voting in favor of management or not voting at all.   For another, many of the issues on which shareholders vote are routine and not controversial though it sometimes may be hard to tell since shareholders rarely hear competing points of view from management. Rather, management formulates its decision or recommendation and presents it as the experienced voice of those actually managing a complex business; usually no hint of possible internal disagreement or other independent voice is heard through the corporate machinery. Further, it is difficult for outsiders to address the shareholders as a body. The managers control the "proxy solicitation" machinery. They have the list of shareholders, and are not likely to make that list available to outsiders without a court proceeding. Persons seeking to challenge incumbent management on most issues coming before the shareholders thus face formidable if not impossible obstacles.

Another important reason for the pro-management bias of shareholders is that there is natural self-selection by shareholders. The presence of an active market in shares means that shareholders dissatisfied with the management of a corporation will be able to sell their shares and invest the proceeds elsewhere rather than having to fight city hall. Thus, by a process of self-elimination, shareholders unhappy with management tend to disappear, and the remaining shareholders tend to be pro-management, or at least not anti-management. The increased importance of institutional investors (described in the following section of this Nutshell) has also helped to solidify incumbent management. Institutional investors own large numbers of shares and usually vote as management recommends.

Management control, however, is not limitless. Indeed, one of the contributions of the Chicago school is recognition of the importance of the securities market as a disciplining device. The decisions by shareholders to sell their shares (often called the "Wall Street option") is in a sense a vote. A poor operating performance by management will result in depressed share prices and may lead indirectly to the ouster of management. This may occur by forced dispossession by proxy fight, public tender offer, or exchange offer. Or it may be the merger or voluntary acquisition by outside interests under the veiled threat of a tender offer if the proposed transaction is rejected. Or it may be the result of the power of large institutional shareholders to threaten to exercise the voting power inherent in their holdings to oppose rather than to support management. Or it may be the threat by other members of the financial community— commercial or investment bankers—to limit the sources of the corporation's long and short term financing unless operating improvements are made. In addition, a palace coup may be a possibility in extreme situations. Even where total ouster is unlikely other sources of pressure exist. The threat of shareholders' derivative suits produces pressure. The disclosure requirements of federal law also may exercise a cautionary effect on management. Widespread publicity produces pressure on the outside directors to take steps to correct current problems. While the threat that management will be turned out by an irate band of shareholders— as often occurs in political elections—is largely illusory in the large publicly held corporation, there is a very real possibility that incumbent management may lose the confidence of a majority of the directors and be forced to resign. The fear of being ousted from a position of power for less than optimal performance is not, in the modern scene, a purely theoretical fear.

§ 13.4 Institutional Investors

For many years the small shareholder described in the previous section was thought to epitomize the public shareholder. The predominant view was that share ownership of publicly held corporations was almost atomistic, and that as a result management had virtually a free hand. This was the position put forth by Berle and Means in an influential book written in 1931. It is doubtful that this view was ever entirely correct, but largely since World War II a development has occurred that puts quite a different complexion on share ownership patterns. Another type of public investor has grown tremendously in importance—the institutional investor. Institutional investors mainly collect and invest other people's money. They include life insurance companies, pension funds, investment companies (the "mutual funds"), bank trust departments, university endowment funds, brokerage firms, and similar organizations. These institutional investors invest significant amounts of capital in a large variety of securities traded on the major securities exchanges. As a group they were a modest force at the end of World War II but are now the largest single owner of publicly held corporations; their holdings in the aggregate are in excess of forty-five per cent of the outstanding shares of all companies listed on the New York Stock Exchange (NYSE). In 1988, it was estimated that institutional investors owned on the average fifty per cent of the outstanding securities issued by the 500 largest publicly held corporations listed on the NYSE, and in specific corporations the percentage ran as high as 80 per cent. In many companies, more than a majority of the outstanding shares were owned by 200 or less institutional investors, and in virtually all of them, institutional ownership was represented by less than 400 shareholders. It is clear that such investors are not only the predominant owners of American industry today but have the potential power to dramatically effect the governance of many corporations.

Since many institutional investors handle funds that ultimately belong to members of the general public in the form of pensions, life insurance proceeds, savings, or financial investments, their growth has been described as increasing the broad base of ownership of the means of production in modern society. However, in terms of potential control, the growth of institutional investors represent a concentration of the base, since a relatively few persons—the managers of the institutional investors—may determine how large blocks of shares are voted.

Even though institutional investors have the power, if they band together, to exercise influence over—if not effectively dominate and control—many large publicly held corporations, until the late 1980s virtually no attempt was made to exercise this power. Most institutional investors viewed their roles as purely investors and disavowed any interest in exercising control over or participating in the business and affairs of corporations. In part as a result of this attitude, institutional investors routinely voted their shares in favor of management; if they were dissatisfied with management, they preferred to sell their shares rather than engage in a struggle for control.

During the late 1980s, institutional investors became increasingly militant with respect to the governance of corporations in which they invested. This change in attitude was the result of two principal factors. First, institutional shareholdings had become so large that the simple sale of shares on the market had become impractical. If an institutional investor decided to exercise its "Wall Street option" and sell its shares, the block was so large that only other institutional investors had the capacity to absorb the shares without devastating effects on the market price. Institutional investors as a group had become "locked in" to investments because of their size. Second, the late 1980s was a period of extremely high levels of takeover activity in which large premiums of 50 per cent or more over current market prices were regularly offered by aggressors. Incumbent management bitterly opposed these takeover attempts and adopted increasingly sophisticated defensive tactics to avoid being taken over. See §§ 13.13, 13.14 of this Nutshell. Institutional investors faced with fiduciary duties to their members or participants usually desired takeovers to succeed so that they could take advantage of the extremely attractive prices that were being offered. Some institutional investors—most notably the California Public Employees Retirement System (CalPERS)—decided to oppose management's defensive tactics. In doing so, it quickly became apparent that management ignored recommendations or suggestions from individual institutional investors with respect to takeover defensive tactics. In response, some institutional investors instituted proxy solicitation campaigns and encouraged an organized, centralized approach to get management's attention. The extent and success of this organizational effort remains to be seen, but the probability of success appears good given the large holdings of institutional investors and the relatively small number of institutions involved in specific corporations.

The increased activity of institutional investors in the corporate governance area is reflected in other areas as well. Many institutional investors have formed committees to establish policies on how the investor should exercise its voting power or to consider how the investor should vote on specific proposals. CalPERS has submitted a large number of proposed changes to the SEC proxy regulations (described briefly in §§ 13.8 and 13.9 of this Nutshell) that are designed to simplify the institutional investors' organizational efforts. Despite these developments, however, most institutional investors still support management on most issues.

In proxy fights or struggles for control, where an unfriendly offer to purchase a majority of the voting shares has been made, the blocks controlled by institutional investors may be absolutely critical. The votes of institutional investors (or decisions whether or not to sell) may effectively determine who should ultimately control the corporation.

As indicated above, institutional investors often owe fiduciary duties to their beneficial owners which arguably require that the institutional investor maximize the short run gains of the owners. This concern for short run return by the largest and most important shareholders, it has been suggested, may have the undesirable effect of causing corporate management to concentrate on maximizing short term earnings to the possible detriment of longer range profitability. Whether or not this concern is justified is uncertain.

§ 13.5 Registration of Securities in Street Name or in the Name of Nominees; Book Entry

Institutional investors routinely record their ownership interests in publicly held corporations in the names of "nominees" rather than in their own names. Many firms and individuals that invest in securities on a speculative basis also do not register the transfer of shares into their own names. Many shares are also registered in the names of the major New York brokerage firms—"street name"—and endorsed in blank and transferred by delivery. Increasingly, shares are being registered in the name of Cede and Company, the nominee for the New York Depository Trust Company and ownership is reflected by book entry. These practices, described below, greatly simplify the trading of publicly held securities, but they have the effect of rendering largely irrelevant the record of shareholders maintained by transfer agents of publicly held corporations. These widespread practices developed for innocent reasons, but they also mask to a considerable extent the true ownership of a large part of publicly held securities. Indeed, the corporation itself may not know the identity of most of the beneficial owners of its securities.

Large institutional investors hold securities in the names of nominees, usually a partnership of employees using names such as "Abel and Company." This practice developed to avoid onerous transfer requirements placed on corporations or fiduciaries selling shares. Since some institutional investors use several different nominees, it is difficult to ascertain the actual ownership of securities from the corporation's records. In 1976, the Securities and Exchange Commission made an examination into this practice and concluded that it was consistent with the basic purposes of the securities acts administered by the Commission.

Beneficial owners of publicly traded securities today rarely hold record ownership to the securities. In the case of an owner who is an individual, the most common form of ownership is by simple book entry in the records of the brokerage firm with which he or she deals. Purchases and sales of securities are reflected solely by transaction confirmations and monthly statements from the brokerage firm to its customers. The brokerage firm, in turn, also does not hold record title to its customers' securities. It may hold shares in street name, but, assuming that it is a participant in the central clearing service maintained by the Depository Trust Company, increasingly shares owned by the firm and its customers are simply registered in the name of DTC's nominee Cede and Co. The firm's ownership is in turn reflected by book entry in DTC's records. Transactions with other brokerage firms within the central clearing service are reflected simply by book entries on DTC's records. The process does not record individual transactions in DTC's books; rather all transactions in a specific stock by customers of firm A—both purchases and sales—are netted together each day and only a single entry, plus or minus, is made on DTC's books. The same is true for firm B and for all other member brokerage firms of DTC. If a customer of firm A buys 100 shares of stock while another customer of firm A sells 100 shares of the same stock on the same day, no entry at all is made on DTC's records, though the books of the brokerage firm will, of course, reflect that a different customer now owns the 100 shares. This system of trading in undeniably efficient and it permits the recording of trades of hundreds of millions of shares each day with a minimum of paper flow. It also interposes two intermediaries—Cede and Co. and the brokerage firm—between the issuer of securities and the beneficial owner, and makes largely irrelevant the traditional learning on the rights of record holders.

The method of stock ownership described in the previous paragraph is usually called "book entry" ownership. More and more shares each year are being registered in the name of Cede and Co., and entering this form of ownership. Relatively few shares each year are withdrawn from the central clearing system and reissued in the name of a beneficial owner. Thus, fewer and fewer certificates are held by individuals, and the record owner who is also the beneficial owner is becoming more and more rare. The system is efficient not only for trading but also for the distribution of dividends, which are transferred by wire from the issuer to DTC to brokerage firms on the day the dividend is payable, and deposited into the accounts of customers on the same day. There are problems, however, in communicating through two sets of intermediaries for various types of shareholder actions, particularly actions that must be taken within narrow and clearly defined time limits. Even though book entry ownership is steadily becoming more important, there has been relatively little thought given as to how it may be most efficiently melded with the traditional rules with respect to the rights of record and beneficial owners.

§ 13.6 Directors of Publicly Held Corporations

In the large publicly held corporation, the business affairs of the corporation are usually run by the full-time management, not the board of directors. Management consists of a group of highly paid executives headed by a chief executive officer who may also hold the title of president, chairman of the board, or some other title. For simplicity, such person is usually referred to as the CEO in the legal literature. Similar designations may be used for the chief operating officer (COO), chief legal officer (CLO), chief financial officer (CFO), and possibly other high level officers as well.

The board of directors of a publicly held corporation usually consists partly of management representatives ("inside directors") and partly of persons who are not otherwise employed by the corporation ("outside directors"). Outside directors fall into two categories: "unaffiliated" directors, who have no significant business contact with the corporation (other than serving on the board of directors) and "affiliated" directors, who are not employees or officers of the corporation but are connected with investment bankers, law firms, suppliers, or others with business connections with the corporation. Retired members of management often serve on boards of directors and are also usually viewed as affiliated outside directors. Obviously, many outside directors have only limited detailed knowledge of corporate affairs. Since boards of directors meet only periodically and often are composed in large part of outside directors, it is not surprising that business management in fact rests with the corporate management, not the directors.

The Revised Model Business Corporation Act recognizes the theoretical role of the board of directors in the publicly held corporation in the following italicized language. "All corporate powers shall be exercised by *or under authority of,* and the business and affairs of the corporation managed *under the direction of,* its board of directors." RMBCA § 8.01(b). The actual role of boards of directors in many publicly held corporations is probably less than even the Model Act contemplates. One empirical study concludes that boards of directors in fact perform the following roles:

(1) They provide advice and counsel.

(2) They provide intellectual discipline for management which must appear before the board and present views and defend recommendations.

(3) They act in crisis situations, such as where the CEO unexpectedly dies or is incapacitated, or where the affairs of

the corporation are such that a change of CEOs seems desirable.

The same study concludes that by and large boards do not perform the following functions:

(1) They do not establish objectives, strategies, and policies of the corporation.

(2) They do not ask discerning or "tough" questions at meetings of the board.

(3) They do not select the CEO except indirectly as a form of "corporate conscience."

(4) They do not decide what the corporation or the board of directors does.

This study was made before the recent developments with respect to directoral liability for breach of duty, particularly in connection with takeovers. In recent years boards of directors have become more sensitized to the importance of their oversight roles and the consequence of acting in good faith and with due diligence in becoming informed and making decisions. In particular, in deciding whether or not to defend against an unwanted takeover, or to sell the company, the views of outside unaffiliated directors are given great respect by courts.

Historically, the boards of many public corporations consisted primarily or exclusively of inside directors. During the last twenty years, there has been a definite trend in the direction of increasing the number and influence of outside directors, and today it is unusual for a publicly held corporation to have a board of directors composed primarily of persons affiliated with management. This trend was caused in part by the widespread disclosures of corporate misconduct during the 1970s, in part by pressure on corporations by the Securities and Exchange Commission and the securities exchanges to "broaden" their boards, and in part by judicial decisions that gave greater weight and finality to the decisions of outside directors in conflict of interest and takeover situations. Whether or not this development has changed the locus of power within publicly held corporations is open to question, though, as indicated above, most directors today are increasingly sensitive to the importance of their positions.

The most popular source of outside directors today are present and retired chief executive officers of other publicly held corporations.

Along with the broadening of boards of directors by including more outside directors, a trend has developed toward wider use of committees of boards consisting primarily of outside directors. Audit committees are now virtually required for all corporations with shares listed on securities exchanges; many corporations have also formed nominating and compensation committees in an effort to provide greater review of issues in these areas by the non-management members of the board.

§ 13.7 Proxy Regulation in Publicly Held Corporations

Most modern law of proxy regulation is of federal rather than state origin. Section 14(a) of the Securities Exchange Act of 1934 makes it unlawful for any person to use the mails or any means or instrumentality of interstate commerce or the facilities of a national securities exchange "in contravention of such rules and regulations as the [Securities and Exchange] Commission may prescribe as necessary or appropriate in the public interest or for the protection of investors" to solicit any proxy appointment in respect of any security registered under section 12 of the Act. Pursuant to this broad grant of authority to regulate proxies, the SEC has issued comprehensive and detailed regulations that define not only the form of proxy solicitation documents but also require the distribution of substantial information about the backgrounds of candidates for directorships and other issues to be voted upon by shareholders.

Corporations subject to federal proxy regulation are those required to register a class of securities under section 12 of the Securities Exchange Act: all corporations a) with shares registered on a national securities exchange or b) having assets in excess of $5,000,000 and a class of equity securities held of record by 500 persons or more. It is not the total number of security holders that is significant, but the number of holders of the class of security for which registration is being considered. A corporation with 400 shareholders of record holding common stock, and another 400 shareholders of record holding preferred stock is not required to register either class under section 12, and therefore is not subject to proxy regulation (unless, of course, its shares are registered on a national securities exchange). However, once a corporation is required to register under section 12, its registration may be terminated only if (a) the number of shareholders of the class drops below 300, or (b) the assets drop below $5,000,000 and the shareholders of the class below 500.

The constitutional basis for federal proxy regulation is the use of the mails or an instrumentality of interstate commerce. As a practical matter, it is probably impossible to solicit proxies in connection with a security registered under section 12 without using the mails or facilities of interstate commerce.

The SEC proxy rules may be broken down into four broad categories—

(1) Requirements of disclosure of full information to shareholders relating to (a) proposals for action by shareholders presented by management through the proxy solicitation machinery, and (b) to a lesser extent, general information about the operations of the corporation.

(2) Prohibitions against the use of fraud or deceptive nondisclosure in the solicitation of proxies.

(3) Requirements that appropriate proposals submitted by shareholders be included in the proxy solicitation materials prepared by management, so that shareholders have an opportunity to consider them.

(4) Special requirements applicable only to proxy fights.

§ 13.8　Disclosure Requirements in Connection With Proxy Solicitations

The SEC proxy regulations (rule 14a–3) provide that with certain exceptions no solicitation of a proxy appointment may be made unless each person is furnished at the same time a proxy statement setting forth detailed information about the persons making the solicitation, about the background of all directors and nominees, about remuneration and other transactions with management and with others, and about any matter on which the vote of shareholders is sought. Proxy statements are not required for solicitations that involve less than ten persons, solicitations by brokers to beneficial owners to determine how to vote shares held in the name of the broker, and newspaper advertisements which merely describe how holders may obtain copies of the proxy statement. Proxy statements under rule 14a–3 are one of the major sources of shareholder information about corporate affairs.

The SEC conducts a presolicitation review process for proxy documents. Such documents and other soliciting materials (such as letters, press releases, and the like), must be filed with the SEC at least ten days prior to the date it is proposed to mail definitive copies to securities holders. Because the period for evaluation is short, as a practical matter the SEC review is based on an analysis of the filing and whatever else is in the Commission's files relating to the filing company. The SEC does not pass upon the accuracy of adequacy of the disclosures; however, it does indicate that revisions should be made if it concludes that some materials are inaccurate on the basis of information in its files. Most courts have recognized that this preliminary SEC review of proxy solicitation material should not be given great weight in subsequently evaluating the sufficiency of the disclosures.

The SEC disclosure requirements also indirectly require the distribution of annual reports. Rule 14a–3(b) provides that if a solicitation is made on behalf of management relating to an annual meeting of shareholders at which directors are to be elected, the proxy statement must be accompanied or preceded by an annual report of the corporation. This is the only basis in most states to require the distribution of an annual report, perhaps the most helpful informational document to shareholders generally.

All of these disclosure requirements assume that corporate management finds it necessary to solicit proxy appointments. In most cases this is necessary if there is to be a quorum at the meeting. (As a practical matter, the number of shares voted by shareholders who appear personally is likely to be numerically insignificant). In some corporations subject to registration under section 12, however, management may own enough shares to constitute a quorum without any solicitation of public shareholders. A special section of the Securities Exchange Act of 1934 requires even such corporations to supply shareholders with the same information that would have been required if a solicitation to its shareholders had been made. This section thus graphically illustrates that a major purpose of SEC proxy regulation is to ensure that significant information is made available to shareholders, whether or not they are requested to approve or disapprove some matter.

Section 13.5 of this Nutshell discussed the practice of holding shares in book entry form or in the names of nominees. This practice creates a problem for the SEC proxy disclosure process since the beneficial owners of such shares do not directly receive the proxy statements or annual reports (since they are not the record owners). SEC regulations require that brokers and dealers transmit proxy material to the beneficial owners of shares, and either (i) execute proxy appointment forms in blank, and deliver them to the beneficial owners so that the shares may be voted by them, or (ii) directly vote the shares as the beneficial owners direct. Stock exchange rules require brokers and dealers to transmit proxy forms if the solicitor of proxy appointments reimburses the expenses of the broker or dealer; in addition, regulations under the Securities Exchange Act require issuers to provide registered owners that are nominees with sufficient copies of the proxy material so that they can be transmitted to the beneficial owners. SEC regulations also require record holders and intermediaries to disclose the names of beneficial holders directly to the issuer (unless the beneficial holder objects) so that the issuer may communicate directly with the beneficial owners. Some brokerage firms recommend that their customers object to the disclosure of their identities.

Studies by the SEC have concluded that these indirect methods of distribution of proxy information work reasonably effectively. Nevertheless, section 7.23 of the Revised Model Business Corporation Act sets forth an alternative (and experimental) device that permits corporations to establish procedures to treat beneficial owners of shares as traditional registered owners.

SEC regulations also prescribe the proxy appointment form itself and prohibit certain devices such as undated or post-dated proxy appointment forms or broad grants of discretionary power to proxies in such forms. Shareholders must be given the option to vote for or against candidates for directors, and proxies must actually vote the shares as shareholders direct for the election of directors and on other issues presented for decision to the shareholders.

§ 13.9   Shareholder Proposals

Rule 14a–8 establishes a procedure by which shareholders may submit proposals for inclusion in the registrant's proxy solicitation material. If the proposal is an appropriate one for shareholder action, and is timely, registrant must include the proposal even if opposed to it. This is one of the few ways that small minority shareholders may communicate with fellow shareholders. Institutional investors have utilized this process in their effort to influence management decision-making (see § 13.4 of this Nutshell). The other principal users of this device are church, public interest, and advocacy groups in an effort to obtain support for their views on public issues, such as respecting the boycott of South Africa, questioning the compliance with the Arab boycott of firms trading with Israel, or ending the production of nuclear power, to name a few. Such proposals are openly political in nature.

If management does oppose a proposal (and management usually does), the proposing shareholder may include a statement of not more than 500 words in support of his or her proposal. A shareholder may submit only one proposal in a proxy statement. Even though the proponent is limited to 500 words, management may explain the basis of its opposition without limitation.

Because shareholders may seek action on proposals of dubious relevance or propriety, or simply for personal publicity, the SEC has imposed specific requirements and limitations on shareholder's proposals. The application of these requirements and limitations has resulted in some litigation, and a substantial body of administrative rulings by the SEC. The SEC has also issued policy statements from time to time with respect to issues raised by shareholder proposals.

Under present SEC regulations, a shareholder's proposal may be omitted if:

(1) It is not a proper subject for action by security holders under the law of the issuer's domicile;

(2) It requires the issuer to violate any state, federal or foreign law, if implemented;

(3) It is contrary to any of the SEC's proxy regulations;

(4) It relates to the enforcement of a personal claim or the redress of a personal grievance, against the issuer, its management, or any person;

(5) It deals with a matter that is not significantly related to the issuer's business;

(6) It deals with a matter that is beyond the issuer's power to effectuate;

(7) It deals with a matter relating to the ordinary business operations of the issuer;

(8) It relates to an election to office;

(9) It is counter to a proposal to be submitted by registrant;

(10) It has been rendered moot;

(11) It is substantially the same as a proposal by another shareholder which will be included in the proxy materials;

(12) Substantially the same proposal has previously been submitted to the shareholders within the previous five years and failed to receive specified percentages of the vote, depending on the number of times it was submitted previously;

(13) It relates to specific amounts of dividends.

Over the years the SEC has issued numerous rulings applying many of these exclusions; as a result, phrases such as "proper subject" or "ordinary business operations" have been given considerable practical content, and the tests are not as open-ended as the language might indicate. For example, the SEC has ruled that important business related proposals are "proper subjects" for shareholder action under state law if they are phrased as recommendations to the board rather than specific directions. See the discussion of state law on this subject in § 8.7 of this Nutshell.

Shareholder proposals presented by institutional investors deal with issues of direct concern to the electorate: requirement for secret ballot procedures, the adoption of cumulative voting, rotating the location of annual meetings, and actions with respect to "poison pill" defenses implemented by the board of directors without shareholder vote. These proposals have received substantial shareholder support, and have even carried in a few instances.

Virtually all proposals of a public interest nature which appear in the proxy solicitation material are rejected by substantial votes. Much the same is true of proposals by individuals that relate more directly to corporate matters. However, it is widely believed that even defeated proposals relating to corporate matters have an indirect educational effect and may call top management's attention to some problem area in the corporation's activities. Certainly some shareholder proposals decisively rejected at the polls have been subsequently accepted and implemented by management. Nevertheless, concern was expressed (before this device began to be used by institutional investors) that the costs imposed by the shareholder proposal rule outweighed the benefits of that rule.

§ 13.10　Private Actions for Violations of Federal Proxy Rules

Rule 14a–9 makes it unlawful to distribute proxy solicitation information that contains "any statement which, at the time and in the light of the circumstances under which it is made, is false or misleading with respect to any material fact, or which omits to state any material fact necessary in order to make the statements therein not false or misleading." This broad prohibition creates a private cause of action by shareholders. J. I Case Co. v. Borak (1964). The Court argued that rule 14a–9 created a private cause of action since, "private enforcement of the proxy rules provides a necessary supplement to Commission action. As in antitrust treble damage litigation, the possibility of civil damages or injunctive relief serves as a most effective weapon in the enforcement of the proxy requirements."

Since *Borak* there has been a substantial volume of private litigation under rule 14a–9. Such litigation is within the exclusive jurisdiction of the Federal courts so that state "security for expenses" statutes are inapplicable (see § 17.4 of this Nutshell). Rule 14a–9 litigation has largely been shaped by two subsequent decisions by the United States Supreme Court. In TSC Industries, Inc. v. Northway, Inc. (1976), in an opinion widely read as heralding a narrowing of the scope of the private cause of action under rule 14a–9, the Court defined a "material fact" as follows:

An omitted fact is material if there is a substantial likelihood that a reasonable shareholder would consider it important in deciding how to vote.

The competing test that was rejected would have defined material facts to include all facts "which a reasonable shareholder *might* consider appropriate." While the difference between the rejected and adopted tests may seem primarily semantic, the Court's distinction constituted a warning to lower courts to limit rule 14a–9 to substantial misstatements. Prior to this decision some courts had tended to find relatively minor misstatements or omissions to be "material" and therefore violations of rule 14a–9.

The other important case, Mills v. Electric Auto–Lite Co. (1970), involves the question of the required nexus between a material misstatement or omission and the approval of the proposal. It also discusses at some length the remedies available for a violation of rule 14a–9 after the transaction in question has been consummated, and the right of the plaintiffs attorney to recover attorneys' fees in rule 14a–9 cases.

In an appropriate rule 14a–9 case, the Court may, of course, issue a temporary restraining order (TRO), enjoining the distribution of proxy material, the voting by the proxies themselves, and the holding of the meeting, until after all misstatements or deficiencies in the proxy solicitation material under rule 14a–9 have been corrected. However, in many cases the plaintiff does not seek a TRO presumably because he or she is unable or unwilling to post the bond that may be required. In such a case, the meeting may be held, the proxies may vote, and the transaction consummated, all before there is a judicial determination of whether the proxy solicitation material violates rule 14a–9. That is essentially what happened in *Mills.* Merganthaler Linotype Corporation owned about 54 per cent of the outstanding Auto–Lite shares, and therefore named all the directors of Auto–Lite. Merganthaler decided to merge with Auto–Lite, but in order to do so it needed the favorable vote of a substantial number of minority shareholders of Auto–Lite. The Auto–Lite management solicited proxy appointments on the basis of a proxy statement that stated the Auto–Lite directors favored the proposed merger but did not disclose that these directors were all nominees of Mergenthaler. The merger proposed was approved and the merger consummated. Minority shareholders thereafter brought suit, claiming that the failure to disclose the relationship of the Auto–Lite directors to Mergenthaler constituted a material omission in violation of rule 14a–9. The lower courts agreed, but concluded that there was no showing that this violation of rule 14a–9 actually affected the outcome of the vote, and that since the terms of the merger were fair, no relief should be granted. The Supreme Court reversed without passing on the materiality of the omission. (This, it should be noted in passing, is the issue addressed in

TSC Industries.) It held that it was unnecessary to show a direct causal relationship between the violation and the vote, it was only necessary to show that the proxy solicitation was itself an essential step in the transaction under attack. The reason for this "rule of thumb" is that it is obviously impossible to inquire into the motivations of thousands of shareholders who voted to approve the merger. However, it does not necessarily follow that the merger should automatically be set aside. The remedy for a violation is in the discretion of the court, and unwinding the merger should be required only if "it would be in the best interests of the shareholders as a whole." If the merger is not to be set aside, a second possible type of relief may be money damages. The Court, however, made it clear that damages should be permitted only to the extent they can be proved, and as a practical matter, that may be impossible. If such proof is unavailable, and the merger should not be set aside, apparently the plaintiff/shareholder is left without remedy. However, in order to ensure that there will continue to be vigorous private enforcement of rule 14a–9, the Court then concluded that a court may award attorneys' fees when a proxy violation is found even though no monetary recovery is allowed. The possibility of champertous litigation, in the Court's eyes, was more than offset by the "therapeutic" effect vigorous enforcement of the proxy regulations has on fair and informed corporate suffrage. Later decisions by the U.S. Supreme Court on the right to attorneys' fees have limited this aspect of the Mills holding.

§ 13.11 Proxy Contests

A proxy contest is a struggle for control of a public corporation in which most of the high cards are typically held by management. In a proxy contest, a non-management group (usually referred to as "insurgents") compete with management in an effort to obtain sufficient proxy appointments to elect a majority of the board of directors and thereby obtain control. Management has several advantages in a proxy fight: (1) it has the current list of shareholders, while the insurgents may have to go to court to get it; (2) within a broad range, management may finance its solicitation from the assets of the corporation, while the insurgents must finance their campaign from outside sources; and (3) for the reasons discussed earlier, shareholders tend to have a pro-management bias. (See § 13.3 of this Nutshell.) For many years, these advantages appeared to be overwhelming and relatively few proxy fights were instituted. Insurgents wishing to take over another company preferred to use cash tender offers rather than proxy fights. With the growth of the shareholdings of institutional investors and their increased militancy (see § 13.4 of this Nutshell), however, there has been a resurgence in interest in the proxy fight as a device to get management's attention, if not to oust it outright. In these modern proxy fights, the roles of institutional investors are usually critical. The willingness of institutional investors to support insurgents in specific instances undoubtedly contributed to an increase in the number of such contests during the late 1980s.

In the classic proxy fight, an insurgent group, desiring to contest management control, usually first purchases a substantial block of shares in the open market before openly announcing its intentions. Under the Williams Act, a person or group acquiring more than five per cent of the voting stock of a registered company must file a disclosure statement within ten days after the acquisition that put it over the five per cent figure. The insurgents must then obtain a list of important shareholders in order to conduct what is essentially a political campaign to persuade shareholders to make proxy appointments in their favor. A court proceeding may be necessary to obtain the shareholders list, though a good deal of information is publicly available about the holdings of many institutional investors. Many such investors publish their entire portfolios on a regular basis, and if a limited solicitation of large shareholders is contemplated, the corporate shareholders' list may not be necessary. Specialized proxy contest firms are available to assist both management and insurgents in the campaign. Advertisements in the financial press are regularly used in an effort to reach smaller shareholders. Large shareholders are contacted individually. The process can be expensive, running into the hundreds of thousands or millions of dollars.

Proxy fights may be used in conjunction with tender or exchange offers. The aggressor may acquire a substantial minority position in the target by public tender offer and then seek to obtain control by a proxy contest to obtain sufficient additional votes to replace incumbent management. This tactic has been used when the aggressor lacked sufficient resources to acquire a majority of the target's shares outright because of the size of the target. It has also been used when management's defenses against a purchase-type takeover appeared to be impregnable, and the aggressor felt compelled to seek proxy appointments to force the dismantling of those defenses.

Proxy fights for public corporations subject to section 12 of the Securities Exchange Act of 1934 are subject to regulation by the Securities and Exchange Commission. Since this covers most proxy fights, state law on the subject tends to be rudimentary and there are very few reported state cases dealing with proxy fights.

One significant legal issue relating to proxy fights is the extent to which the corporation may be called upon to pay for its costs. From management's standpoint there appears to be no doubt that the corporation should pay for printing and mailing the notice of meeting, the proxy statement required by Federal law, and the proxy appointments themselves. These are legitimate expenses because without the solicitation of proxy appointments it is unlikely that a quorum of shareholders may be obtained. Most courts have gone further and allowed the corporation to be charged for the reasonable expenses of management of educating shareholders if the controversy involves a "policy" question rather than a mere "personal" struggle for control. Since virtually every proxy fight may be dressed up as a "policy" rather than "personal" dispute, and since what is involved is "education" of the management's side of the controversy, the net effect is to permit the deduction of all reasonable management expenses. While some judges have suggested that a narrower test should be applicable to management expenses, these suggestions have not prevailed.

A somewhat different question is presented if the insurgents are successful and seek to have the corporation also reimburse them for their expenses. If permitted, the net effect is usually to have the corporation pay the expenses of both sides, since management will usually reimburse itself for its expenses from the corporation before leaving office. The additional reimbursement of successful insurgents has been permitted if (a) approved by the shareholders and (b) the dispute involved "policy" rather than "personalities." As a result the corporation ends up paying for the expenses of both sides. Again, there is a strong undercurrent of judicial opinion which would sharply limit or totally preclude insurgents' reimbursement, but this view has not prevailed. Law review writers have sometimes suggested that reimbursement should be permitted for unsuccessful insurgents since they may perform a socially useful function. Most economists and legal writers view proxy fights as basically desirable phenomena that help rid corporations of inefficient or ineffective management.

§ 13.12　Federal Regulations Relating to Proxy Contests

The Securities and Exchange Commission has promulgated special regulations applicable to proxy contests. These regulations require "participants" other than management in a proxy contest to file specified information with the SEC and the securities exchanges at least five days before a solicitation begins. "Participant" is defined to include anyone who contributes more than $500 for the purpose of financing the contest. The information that must be disclosed relates to the identity and background of the participants, their interests in securities of the corporation, when they were acquired, financing arrangements, participation in other proxy contests, and understandings with respect to future employment with the corporation.

The general philosophy of the proxy contest regulations is well expressed by Judge Clark, of the Second Circuit: "Appellants' fundamental complaint appears to be that stockholder disputes should be viewed in the eyes of the law just as are political contests, with each side free to hurl charges with comparative unrestraint, the assumption being that the opposing side is then at liberty to refute and thus effectively deflate the 'campaign oratory' of its adversary. Such, however, was not the policy of Congress as enacted in the Securities Exchange Act." SEC v. May (1956).

§ 13.13　Tender Offers

The growth of cash-oriented takeover techniques has been perhaps the most spectacular development in corporate and securities law since World War II. These techniques became feasible as a result of a major economic development in the 1960s: the growth of very large pools of capital which made purchase-type takeovers of publicly held corporations feasible. The 1980s saw this movement reach new heights, fueled by the availability of huge pools of borrowable capital. This period saw the development of the "leveraged buyout" (LBO), a transaction that involved the purchase of all the outstanding shares of a publicly held corporation for cash raised by the issuance of "junk bonds" and through loans from commercial banks in the hundreds of millions or billions of dollars. The expected source of repayment of these loans was the earnings and cash flow of the target corporation. These transactions involved "bootstrap" acquisitions: the acquired business provided the funds to finance its own purchase. In many instances, incumbent management participated in the buyout, and managed the business after the public shareholders were eliminated. The fear of becoming the target of such a takeover led many publicly held corporations to reduce their attractiveness as an LBO candidate by voluntarily restructuring their capitalization by substituting debt for equity. This might be done by borrowing funds in order to make an extraordinary dividend payment or by distributing debt instruments directly to shareholders. Whether or not all this was desirable from a social or economic perspective is extremely controversial.

An appropriate starting point is a brief description of the classic cash tender as it evolved in the 1960s. A cash tender offer is a public invitation to the shareholders of the "target" corporation to tender their shares to the "aggressor" corporation for purchase at a specified price, usually 25–50 per cent in excess of the then current market price. In the late 1960s, there were numerous cash tender offers, the success of which were largely based on the element of surprise, virtually blitzkrieg tactics. Since then developments in various areas have greatly modified the manner in which takeover bids are pursued, and have largely eliminated the element of surprise. These developments include:

(1) Adoption of the Williams Act, an amendment to the Securities Exchange Act of 1934, which is briefly described below.

(2) Adoption by many states of takeover statutes designed to regulate (and make more difficult) unwanted takeover attempts of businesses active in the state in question.

(3) The increasing sophistication of defensive tactics by potential targets (discussed in § 13.14 of this Nutshell).

As refined in the late 1980s, the success of takeover bids was largely due to the large premiums over market price offered by aggressors, the role of institutional investors (which tended to support the takeover bid), and the activity of market speculators who purchased the target stock on the open market and tendered it to the aggressor. In several spectacular incidents, competing bids from different aggressors were forthcoming. A company that was made the target of a takeover attempt was said to be "in play;" once in play, Wall Street wisdom went, the company was sure to be taken over by somebody, though this was not invariably true. After a company was taken over, portions of the business might be sold off in order to pay down the debt incurred to acquire the business. In many instances, the sum of the value of the parts exceeded the cost of the whole.

If a cash tender offer for all the outstanding shares of a target is successful, there will always remain a handful of shareholders who did not tender. If a partial tender offer is made there will remain a substantial minority interest. In either event, it is generally to the interest of the aggressor to eliminate the minority interest. This may readily be done under present corporation law by a "cash out merger" of the type described in chapter 18 of this Nutshell. If the price of this "mop up" transaction is announced in advance as being significantly lower than the price of the original tender offer (or if subordinated securities rather than cash are offered) the overall transaction is known as a two-tier or "front end loaded" tender offer. The announcement of a lower "mop up" price, of course, tends to encourage all shareholders to tender promptly.

When a cash tender offer is made, the open market price for the shares increases dramatically so that it is close to the tender price. (Whether it equals or exceeds the tender offer price depends on a complex variety of factors, including the probability that a competing offer at a higher price might be made, whether the offer is likely to be over-subscribed, and so forth.) Persons owning shares thus have the choice of selling their shares in the open market or tendering their shares. Most shares sold on the open market are ultimately tendered. A group of speculators, known as arbitragers, purchase shares in the open market at prices below the tender offer price in order to tender them and profit by the difference between the two prices. The volume of transactions effected by arbitragers has been very substantial.

A great deal of attention has been given to the economic effects of these cash-type acquisitions of huge publicly held corporations. There seems to be general agreement that the shareholders of the target corporation benefit; there is less agreement about the effect on the aggressor, whose shares may decline in price if the offer is successful. By adding these two effects together, the economist argues that such transactions have increased value in most cases. The source of this increase in value has been the subject of considerable speculation. The most common suggestions are the elimination of less efficient management, synergy, or the development of monopoly power. It has also been suggested that takeovers have been profitable because the securities markets systematically under-value the break-up value of corporations, or that they are profitable because they involve transfer payments from other constituencies in the corporation, particularly bondholders. Finally, it is also possible that many of these transactions were motivated by a desire for power on aggressors and may have no positive long term effect.

Cash tender offers are subject to regulation by the Securities and Exchange Commission. The Williams Act, technically not a separate statute but a series of amendments to the Securities Exchange Act of 1934, requires disclosure of information in connection with cash tender offers. Any person who makes a cash tender offer for a corporation registered under section 12 must disclose information as to the source of funds used in the offer, the purpose for which the offer is made, plans the aggressor may have if successful, and contracts or understandings with respect to the target corporation. Filing and public disclosure is also required by anyone who acquires more than 5 per cent of the outstanding shares of any class of a section 12 corporation. Similar requirements are also imposed upon (1) issuers making an offer for their own shares, or (2) issuers in which a change of control is proposed to be made by seriatim resignations of directors. The cash tender offer legislation also imposes miscellaneous substantive restrictions on the mechanics of a cash tender offer, as well as a broad prohibition against the use of false, misleading, or incomplete statements in connection with such an offer. In Piper v. Chris–Craft Industries, Inc. (1977), the Court held that a defeated tender offeror did not have standing to sue for damages under this provision of the Williams Act.

In CTS Corporation v. Dynamics Corp. of America (1987), the Supreme Court upheld the Indiana Control Share Acquisitions Act, a statute that was enacted to make unwanted acquisitions of Indiana corporations more difficult. The opinion of Justice Powell for the majority carved out a broad area of state regulation in the takeover area, rejecting the argument that there was a "market for control" that was protected from state interference by the Commerce Clause. The court also rejected the argument that state-created defenses for domestic corporations were preempted by the Williams Act. Since CTS, more than forty states have adopted statutes designed to make more difficult the acquisition of publicly held corporations incorporated in that state. In 1988, Delaware adopted a takeover statute that restricted the power of aggressors to enter into mergers with the target corporation without the consent of the former board of directors for a period of three years after the takeover. These post-CTS Corporation developments may have contributed to the decline of takeover activity in the late 1980s, though undoubtedly economic developments that tended to dry up the pool of capital are a more important explanation.

§ 13.14 Defensive Tactics

With the increasing success of cash tender offers during the 1980s, a great deal of attention has been paid to defensive tactics designed to make takeover bids more difficult. These tactics have clearly increased in sophistication over time. Popular tactics include: finding a more congenial suitor (a "white knight"); buying a business that increases the chances that the threatened takeover will give rise to anti-trust problems; making it difficult for an offeror who acquires a majority of the voting shares to replace the board of directors; instituting suit to enjoin the offer for violations of the Williams Act, the antitrust laws, or on other grounds; issuing or proposing to issue additional shares to friendly persons to make a takeover more difficult (a "lock-up"); increasing the dividend or otherwise driving up the price of shares to make the takeover price unattractive; amending the basic corporate documents to make a takeover by even a majority shareholder more difficult; buying off the aggressor; buying up the corporation's own shares in the market to drive up the price; creating new classes of stock that increase in rights if any person acquires more than a specified percentage of shares ("poison pills"); and imposing restrictions in connection with the creation of debt that thwart attempted takeovers.

Several cases have considered the validity of defensive tactics in different contexts. Of particular importance are several Delaware cases that have largely shaped the permissible area of takeover defenses. Moran v. Household International, Inc. (1985), upheld the adoption of a "poison pill" as a defensive tactic in advance of a specific takeover attempt. In Unocal Corp. v. Mesa Petroleum Co. (1985) the Court set forth the basic test for evaluating defensive tactics: to be protected by the business judgment rule, a defensive tactic must be reasonable in relation to the threat posed to the corporation. In Revlon, Inc. v. MacAndrews & Forbes Holdings, Inc. (1985), the court held that when the board of directors concludes that the sale of the business is inevitable, its role shifts from a participant in the contest to a more neutral stance ensuring that the shareholders get the best possible price for their shares. Subsequent decisions by the Delaware Chancery Court and the Delaware Supreme Court have elaborated upon these basic rules, holding in some cases that the defensive tactic was proper and in others enjoining the use of specific tactics.

[For unfamiliar terms see the Glossary]

CHAPTER FOURTEEN

DUTIES OF DIRECTORS

§ 14.1 "Fiduciary" Duties In General

Because of their broad powers of management, directors occupy a unique position within the corporate structure. They owe a high degree of fidelity and loyalty to the corporation. These duties are often referred to as "fiduciary duties," and directors are sometimes referred to as "fiduciaries" and their duties are analogized to those of a trustee of a trust. References to the "fiduciary duties" of directors often appear in cases involving conflict of interest or self dealing, where the director has entered into transactions of some kind with his or her corporation. However, it is important not to carry this analogy very far: directors of corporations are not strictly trustees, and their duties and liabilities are not identical with those of other fiduciaries. Directors are expected and indeed encouraged to commit the enterprise to risky ventures in order to maximize the return to shareholders; trustees are usually charged with preservation and maintenance of the assets under their control and may be surcharged if they commit the trust assets to speculative ventures. Acts which might be considered breaches of trust by other fiduciaries are therefore often not so regarded in cases of corporate directors. The relationship between director and corporation, in short, is a unique one that cannot be analyzed by reference to other types of fiduciary relationships.

The relationship between corporate officers and agents who are not directors and the corporation depends to some extent on the position occupied by the officer or agent and the type of liabilities that are being imposed. A managing officer may owe substantially the same duties to the corporation as a director. Officers or agents in subordinate or limited positions may owe a correspondingly lesser degree of duty, though even the lowest agent owes the principal certain minimum duties of care, skill, propriety in conduct, and loyalty in all matters connected with his or her agency (see § 11.7 of this Nutshell).

In most instances, directors owe duties to the corporation as a whole rather than to individual shareholders or to individual classes of shareholders. However, if a director deals with a shareholder directly, or acts in a way which injures the economic interest of a shareholder, he or she may become directly liable to that shareholder.

Since shareholders as such have no power to manage the business and affairs of the corporation, it is not surprising that the relationship of a shareholder to the corporation differs from the relationship of a director or officer to the corporation. It is often said that a shareholder owes no fiduciary duty to the corporation or the other shareholders. Such statements, however, are too broad. While shareholders may usually vote as their own self-interest dictates, they may owe a duty to the corporation or their fellow shareholders in some circumstances. Controlling shareholders, for example, owe duties to creditors, holders of senior securities and minority shareholders when they transfer control of the corporation to a third party. Some cases have found fiduciary duties akin to those existing in a partnership in closely held corporations. And, even minority shareholders do not have an open license to abuse or sell their voting power, or exercise it fraudulently.

§ 14.2   Sources of Law Relating to Duties—Common Law, State and Federal Statutes, "Federal Common Law"

The basic relationship between a corporation and its directors traditionally has been established by common law decision rather than statute. Many of the duties hereafter discussed are common law in origin: (1) a duty of exercising care in administering the corporation's business; (2) a duty of loyalty to the corporation; and (3) as a subdivision of the general duty of loyalty, a prohibition against usurping business opportunities belonging to the corporation. These common law duties have given rise to a great deal of litigation; they define fundamental obligations in a complex relationship. State corporation acts address certain aspects of these common law duties, and also supplement them by imposing liability on directors for certain specific acts, such as paying dividends when the corporation may not lawfully do so or making loans to directors in certain circumstances. Indeed, directoral liability to the corporation is the principal or exclusive method by which many statutory prohibitions are enforced.

Federal law is also an important source of legal principles relating to duties and obligations within a corporation. The federal securities acts are the genesis of this development with much of it based on rule 10b–5 promulgated by the Securities and Exchange Commission under the Securities Exchange Act of 1934. Rule 10b–5 is the principal source of law with respect to insider trading and the "fraud on the market" theory by which misleading corporate publicity affecting securities prices is regulated. It is clear that both federal and state law will continue to have their place in the area of duties of directors.

§ 14.3   Duty of Care

A director owes a duty to the corporation to exercise proper care in managing the corporation's affairs. The formal test that is usually quoted is set forth in section 8.30 of the Revised Model Business Corporation Act: duties must be discharged "(1) in good faith; (2) with the care an ordinarily prudent person in a like position would exercise under similar circumstances; and (3) in a manner he reasonably believes to be in the best interests of the corporation." Another test that is often quoted is that degree of diligence, care, and skill "which ordinarily prudent men would exercise under similar circumstances in their personal business affairs." This language is taken from a leading Pennsylvania case, Selheimer v. Manganese Corp. of America (1966). There probably is little practical difference in these two formulations; general language of this sort rarely helps to resolve concrete cases.

The formal standard of section 8.30 of the RMBCA, however, is not the operative test for determining whether directors are liable in damages for failing to exercise reasonable care. Courts feel that they should not second-guess corporate managers with the benefit of hindsight by holding them personally liable for losses incurred by the corporation, particularly on business matters. This feeling finds expression in two important doctrines discussed in the following section: the "business judgment rule" (or "business judgment doctrine") and the recent statutes limiting the liability of directors for monetary damages under broad circumstances. In other words, one may violate the standard of care set forth in section 8.30 and yet not be personally liable for the consequences.

Most cases in which liability for damages has been found involve some element of self-dealing as well as negligence or misjudgment. There are relatively few cases in which liability has been imposed on directors in the absence of self dealing, and these cases involve egregious misconduct. The strongest kind of case for imposing personal liability on a director is where the director knowingly participates in a wrongful act. Thus, personal liability has been imposed on directors where they authorize the improper use of corporate funds, knowing that the use is not in furtherance of corporate affairs, or where they assent to the corporation's use of a financial statement to obtain credit when they know that it is false or fraudulent. Directors have also been held liable for a tortious act of the corporation if they personally participated in the act. On the other hand, in recent years attempts to hold directors or officers personally liable for antitrust fines imposed on the corporation or for bribes or improper payments made by the corporation have generally been unsuccessful, despite evidence in some cases of the directors' or officers' personal involvement in the conduct or payments in question. Of course, the amounts in such situations are usually extremely large when compared to the wealth of even well-to-do individuals, and the directors are in effect being charged with overzealous attempts to maximize the corporation's profitability. Directors also are not automatically liable if they approve an act that turns out to be ultra vires.

In some cases actual knowledge of any wrongful act is lacking but the claim is that the directors should have known of it, and therefore they are liable for failing to direct effectively. These cases are true duty of care cases since they involve basically the question of how much investigation and time the directors should invest in monitoring and overseeing corporate affairs in order to avoid liability. Related cases involve the claim that management was not competent and the board of directors should have realized it and made changes in order to avoid loss. These kinds of cases also may involve claims for damages running into the millions of dollars based on the total loss to all shareholders from the directors' failure to meet their required standard of care. They also usually involve a massive amount of hindsight; information that in retrospect indicates incompetence or improper conduct may have seemed much more innocent, ambiguous, or irrelevant when it was actually received. There is a more basic problem, however. The time that outside directors have available to learn of the affairs of a complex business is necessarily limited and broad areas of business will have to go unexamined by the board of directors as a practical matter. This is obviously true in immense corporations such as General Motors Corporation, and only slightly less true in corporations a fraction of the size of General Motors. The standard of care that is required must be established in the context of the actual business and a realistic assessment of what directors should be expected to do. Most boards of directors can do little more than ensure that apparently competent and honest management is in place and a system of auditing is being followed that minimizes the danger of unlawful conduct.

One case imposing liability because of the failure of a director to direct is Francis v. United Jersey Bank (1981). The sons of the deceased founder of the corporation, an "insurance reinsurance" firm, siphoned large sums of money from the corporation in the form of unsecured loans and other improper payments to family members. Ultimately the corporation became insolvent, and suit was brought by the bankruptcy trustee against the estate of Mrs. Pritchard, the widow of the corporate founder, who was a director during the period the improper payments and family loans were made. Mrs. Pritchard was not active in the affairs of the corporation; she was elderly and alcoholic, and stricken at the loss of her husband. She was also unfamiliar with the insurance reinsurance business generally and the affairs of the corporation in particular. Even though the improper transactions were clearly reflected in the financial statements prepared by the corporation, Mrs. Pritchard was unaware of them since she did not even examine the financial statements. The court upheld a judgment against her estate for more than $10,000,000 since "she never made the slightest effort to discharge any of her responsibilities as a director." The court further concluded that her failure to fill the minimal responsibilities of her office was a proximate cause of the loss, since consultation with an attorney and threat of suit would have deterred the misconduct. A failure to respond to obvious problems, in short, is one way for a director to be held personally liable for losses suffered by the corporation.

What should a director who is aged, ill, resident of a distant state, or merely lazy or unduly trusting, do in order to avoid liability? As an abstract matter the answer is plain: when a person agrees to be a director he or she accepts certain responsibilities and obligations, and if these are too burdensome, the proper course is to resign rather than fail to meet them. In a few cases a director has argued that he or she accepted the position on the understanding that he or she was only to be a "figurehead" and not to have any significant function or role in the corporation. This is certainly an erroneous notion, and a person who accepts a directorship without assuming the responsibilities of a director is courting disaster.

The issue of causation in the failure of the director to direct cases (discussed in Mrs. Pritchett's case) is sometimes a difficult one. Barnes v. Andrews (1924) is the leading case holding that a direct causal relationship must be shown between the director's failure and the specific loss. If this is correct, the burden of proof will often be difficult if not insuperable, since in most cases it may be plausibly argued that the loss would have occurred even if the director had met his or her responsibility.

Also, often helpful to defendants in duty of care cases are the principles (1) that directors, in the absence of other information, may assume that managers and officers are honest, and (2) that directors are not liable if they rely in good faith on information, opinions, reports or statements prepared by responsible corporate officials, counsel, or committees of the board. RMBCA § 8.30(b). However, a director is not considered to be acting in good faith "if he has knowledge concerning the matter in question that would cause such reliance to be unwarranted." In other words, the standard of good faith reliance does not permit a knowledgeable director "to bury his head in the sand" and rely on information or advice he or she should know is erroneous. An attorney who is a director cannot ignore his or her legal background; the same is true of an accountant or banker. On the other hand, a person without specialized knowledge may rely on specialists if acting in good faith, and be immune from liability upon doing so.

All in all, these various defenses, when coupled with the broad immunity from liability discussed in the following section, reduce significantly, but do not eliminate entirely, the risk of liability of directors for breach of the duty of care.

Courts have sometimes buttressed their conclusion that directoral liability does not exist in specific due care cases by arguing that too stringent a test would discourage able and competent persons from agreeing to serve as directors of publicly held corporations.

§ 14.4 The "Business Judgment Rule" and the "Business Judgment Doctrine"

The phrases "the business judgment rule" and "the business judgment doctrine" are helpful shorthand descriptions of two basic principles applicable to business decisions by boards of directors: first, that such decisions made upon reasonable information and with some rationality do not give rise to directoral liability even if they turn out badly or disastrously from the standpoint of the corporation (the "business judgment rule"), and second, such decisions are valid and binding upon the corporation and cannot be enjoined, set aside, or attacked by shareholders (the "business judgment doctrine"). [The "rule" and "doctrine" terminology is useful in pointing out that there are two distinct issues involved in these cases, but has not attained universal usage.]

Most statements of the business judgment rule (or doctrine) add the further qualification that a decision is not protected if the directors making it have "a disabling conflict of interest" or in other words, are involved in self-dealing transactions. The rule and the doctrine thus have their principal application to claims based on alleged mismanagement or misjudgment.

In a broad sense, both the rule and the doctrine reflect the basic principles referred to in the previous section that directors are granted discretion with respect to the management of the corporation, that the exercise of that discretion is generally not subject to judicial review, and that, indeed, most judges are not businessmen capable of second-guessing effectively the exercise of that discretion.

The precise relationship between the duty of care and the business judgment rule (or doctrine) is the subject of some debate. The Revised Model Business Corporation Act sets forth the duty of care in section 8.30 in traditional negligence terms and does not attempt to define the scope of the business judgment rule. The Official Comment, however, recognizes the existence of that rule outside of the statutory language:

Even before statutory formulations of directors' duty of care, courts sometimes invoked the business judgment rule in determining whether to impose liability in a particular case. In doing so, courts have sometimes used language similar to the standards set forth in section 8.30(a). The elements of the business judgment rule and the circumstances for its application are continuing to be developed by the courts. In view of that continuing judicial development, section 8.30 does not try to codify the business judgment rule or to delineate the differences, if any, between that rule and the standards of director conduct set forth in this section. That is a task left to the courts and possibly to later revisions of this Model Act.

The Corporate Governance Project of the American Law Institute did not have the same problem of definition or articulation. Tentative section 4.01(a) sets forth the duty of care in traditional language similar to section 8.30 of the RMBCA, and section 4.01(c) provides that a "director or officer who makes a business judgment in good faith fulfills his or her duty" if (1) he or she is not interested in the transaction, (2) "he is informed with respect to the subject of his business judgment to the extent he reasonably believes to be appropriate under the circumstances," and (3) "he rationally believes that his business judgment is in the best interests of the corporation." This language will probably become the classic definition of the business judgment rule. There have been other attempts at formulation of the business judgment rule that use somewhat different language, but these three basic principles appear essentially in all of them.

The business judgment rule and doctrine protect many types of actions from suit even though they turn out badly from the standpoint of the corporation. Examples include:

(1) A reorganization of a subsidiary company, including a distribution of surplus, reduction of capital, and distribution of a share dividend;

(2) Election of a manager and president;

(3) A sale of part of the assets of a telephone company;

(4) Acceptance of a note for a judgment rather than enforcing it by execution; and

(5) The closing down of an unproductive mine.

The most controversial recent application (or more precisely, recent nonapplication) of the business judgment rule is Smith v. Van Gorkom (1985), a case that led to the enactment of special statutes to protect directors in over 40 states. The court's opinion in Van Gorkom sets forth the facts in great detail, and the correctness or incorrectness of its holding depends in part upon how one categorizes those facts. The majority opinion adopted this categorization: Van Gorkom was the chief executive officer of Trans Union Corporation, a publicly held corporation. The company owned potentially valuable unused investment tax credits. Van Gorkom owned 75,000 shares out of 20,000,000 outstanding. During review of the future of the corporation, the possibility of taking the company private through a leveraged buyout or of selling it outright was discussed. Van Gorkom, who was close to retirement age, stated that he would accept $55 per share for his stock; during this period the stock was trading in the $24–39 range. Studies were run by management to determine whether the cash flow of the corporation at the present level of operations could support the debt needed to support a $55 price in a leveraged buyout. On the basis of projections run by the corporation's financial officer, it appeared that the cash flow might not be adequate for this purpose. Without further investigation into the value of the company, and without seeking other possible buyers, Van Gorkom contacted "a well-known corporate takeover specialist and a social acquaintance" who promptly offered to buy the corporation in a straight purchase at $55 per share. At this point, Van Gorkom resolved to obtain approval of this transaction over some opposition from members of his management team, who felt the price was too low and not supported by adequate appraisals. The board of directors was then presented with the $55 proposal as an emergency matter with a strict three day deadline for approval; Van Gorkom urged approval of the transaction, and the board acquiesced. Van Gorkom thereafter actively worked to obtain shareholder approval of the transaction without considering other possible alternatives, and the transaction was eventually completed at $55 per share. At one stage, a preliminary feeler was received from a third party offering to purchase the company for $60 per share, but was not investigated. Based essentially on these facts, the Delaware Supreme Court by a 3–2 vote concluded that the directors had not adequately informed themselves about the value of the company and the proposed transaction and therefore were not entitled to the protection of the business judgment rule. The basic test of the duty of care, the court stated, was "gross negligence" and the board had failed to meet that standard. The dissenters, and much of the critical commentary about the case, argued that the directors should be able to evaluate a proposed sale of the company on the basis of their own financial experience and background, and in reliance on Van Gorkom's experience and background. Another factor relied upon by the critics of the decision as indicating that the directors had acted properly was the substantial difference between the $55 offering price and the market range in which Trans Union stock had traded in the recent past. The mathematics of the court's holding also received attention: if the measure of damages is $5 per share (not an unreasonable conclusion considering that Trans Union received an apparently serious "feeler" of $60 per share), then the liability of the directors is 5 dollars times approximately 12,700,000 shares, or a cool $63,500,-000. Following the Delaware Supreme Court decision, the case was actually settled for a payment of approximately $22,000,000 from insurance proceeds and funds supplied (apparently voluntarily) by the purchaser in the transaction under attack. The fees payable to the attorneys for the plaintiffs were about $18,000,000.

A person considering this scenario might well raise the question why the outside directors should have been liable when Van Gorkom appears to have been the person primarily responsible. A plausible argument might be made that the outside directors reasonably relied upon Van Gorkom and other members of management. The Supreme Court of Delaware was also aware of possible distinctions among the defendants and at least twice asked the defendants' attorney whether a difference in treatment for the outside directors might be justified. Apparently for strategic reasons, however, the defendants adopted a "one for all and all for one" strategy and refused to address the question whether some defendants might have defenses not available to other defendants.

The immediate consequences of the Van Gorkom decision on the business community were disturbing. Lawyers and law firms sent out memoranda to their clients warning them of the risk of liability in the absence of a careful investigation and recommending that experts be hired and a "paper trail" created to demonstrate compliance with the business judgment rule. Some outside directors began to reassess their decision to be directors, and isolated instances of resignations were reported. The number of lawyers serving on the boards of directors of their clients declined. It became increasingly difficult to persuade desirable persons to serve on boards, despite the level of compensation and the availability of indemnification and insurance.

The response in Delaware to this unexpected decision was prompt. In 1986, section 102(b)(7) of the Delaware General Corporation Law was amended to authorize corporations to amend their certificates of incorporation to eliminate or limit the personal liability of directors for monetary damages, with certain important exceptions. These exceptions are (i) for breach of the director's duty of loyalty to the corporation, (ii) for acts or omissions "not in good faith or which involve intentional misconduct or a knowing violation of law," and (iii) for any transaction from which the director derived an improper personal benefit. Thousands of Delaware corporations promptly amended their articles of incorporation to take advantage of this new statute, which was quickly copied in most other states. Indeed, some states "improved" upon the Delaware statute either by making it automatically applicable to all corporations or by narrowing the exceptions, thereby broadening the protection accorded to directors by the statute.

The effect of closing off suits to recover damages from directors is to encourage suits to enjoin transactions before they are consummated. Such litigation is not affected by section 102(b)(7), since it does not involve the imposition of personal liability.

§ 14.5 The Business Judgment Rule in Takeover Contests

The business judgment rule has been successfully relied upon by directors faced with unwanted takeover attempts who adopt defensive tactics designed to defeat the takeover. See the discussion of defensive tactics in section 13.14 of this Nutshell. In Panter v. Marshall Field & Co. (1981), Marshall Field successfully fended off an unwanted takeover bid by another retail chain primarily by acquiring or opening additional stores that created serious antitrust problems for the aggressor. Following the withdrawal of the offer because of the legal complications created by the expansion policy, the price of Marshall Field shares dropped precipitously, and minority shareholders brought suit against the directors for damages. The court applied the business judgment rule in this situation in a broad and expansive manner over a vigorous and forceful dissent that the majority's opinion permitted incumbent management to entrench themselves in office without limitation at the expense and to the detriment of the public shareholders.

Similarly, Delaware decisions have applied the business judgment rule to protect directors who adopt a "poison pill" preferred stock in advance of any takeover attempt [Moran v. Household International, Inc. (1985)] or a selective stock repurchase plan that is designed to defeat an aggressor who was making an "inadequate and coercive two-tier tender offer." Unocal v. Mesa Petroleum Co. (1985). The Delaware Supreme Court, recognizing that selective stock repurchases (excluding the aggressor but including all other shareholders) had the capacity to defeat every tender offer, adopted a modified business judgment rule. The Court stated:

A further aspect is the element of balance. If a defensive measure is to come within the ambit of the business judgment rule, it must be reasonable in relation to the threat posed. This entails an analysis by the directors of the nature of the takeover bid and its effect on the corporate enterprise.

Shortly following this decision, the Securities and Exchange Commission adopted rule 14d–10 under the Williams Act, generally known as the "all holders rule" that prohibits selective stock repurchases. Nevertheless, the standard of "balance" set forth in *Unocal* has been applied by the Delaware courts to a variety of defensive tactics.

The Delaware Supreme Court adopted yet another twist to the business judgment rule in Revlon, Inc. v. MacAndrews & Forbes Holdings, Inc. (1986). In this case, the directors of Revlon vigorously fought an attempted takeover, but eventually it became clear that the sale of the company to one aggressor or another was inevitable. In this situation, the Supreme Court stated, the directors no longer may exercise business judgment to prefer one bidder over the other, but instead have the duty of obtaining the best possible price for the company. A decision to use a "lock up" to defeat the higher bidder and favor a lower bidder violates this duty and thus is not protected by the business judgment rule. This last holding, in particular, is broadly consistent with the rationale underlying *Van Gorkom* that when the company is being sold, the directors must try to get the best price rather than simply selecting one bidder and dealing exclusively with it. The general principle of Revlon has been considered and applied by the Delaware Supreme Court and Chancery Court in an important series of cases that address a number of subsidiary issues, such as whether this duty requires an auction, and if so, how long it must continue.

These cases involving the application of the business judgment rule in connection with defensive tactics in take-over situations raise a broad question as to whether the directors, or at least some of them, should be viewed as having a "disabling conflict of interest." Incumbent management, of course, has lucrative positions with the target corporation that are likely to disappear if the aggressor is successful and takes over the target. When they propose strategies to defeat the aggressor, is that a conflict of interest? Similarly, outside directors have positions that carry with them considerable prestige as well as financial benefits, all of which would almost certainly disappear if the aggressor is successful. If the outside directors approve of management's proposed defensive tactics, is that a conflict of interest? To disqualify all or part of the incumbent board in this manner may well be counterproductive, since the shareholders may then receive no informed advice as to the desirability of the takeover. In cases where the court has concluded that the board has gone too far in protecting the position of its members, the court is likely to talk about decisions that tend to "entrench management." Such decisions are viewed as involving a conflict of interest and are not entitled to the protection of the business judgment rule. The recent Delaware opinions have indicated that approval by outside directors of defensive tactics will be given greater deference by courts then decisions by a board dominated by inside management who have the greatest conflict of interest and desire to entrench themselves.

§ 14.6 The Business Judgment Rule in Derivative Litigation

Another area in which the application of the business judgment rule has been controversial in recent years is in connection with the dismissal of derivative litigation. Basically the question is whether the business judgment rule should be applied to decisions by an "independent" committee of the board of directors to discontinue derivative litigation (see § 17.1 of this Nutshell) brought by shareholders seeking recovery in favor of the corporation against one or more officers or directors for alleged misconduct or negligence. Typically, the decision whether or not to seek to discontinue such litigation is delegated to a "Litigation Committee" composed of outside directors who are not themselves defendants or involved in the acts complained of. The recommendation to discontinue the litigation is made following an investigation by the committee into the merits of the litigation and the advantages and disadvantages to the corporation of pursuing it. If this is a proper application of the business judgment rule, the decision to discontinue the litigation is binding on the plaintiff shareholder who is foreclosed from litigating the merits of his or her case because of the impartial directors' business judgment; the plaintiff may only litigate issues such as the independence and lack of involvement of the members of the committee recommending discontinuance of the litigation, or of the adequacy of their investigation. At first blush it is somewhat startling to put forward the proposition that a court should dismiss litigation without considering its merits because of the actions of a group of outside directors. However, decisions to discontinue or pursue litigation involve business considerations quite as much as decisions such as to go into a new business or to hire a new executive officer.

A major argument against applying the business judgment rule to decisions to discontinue derivative litigation against other directors is the fear of "structural bias," i.e. the concern that directors "will look out for their own," or take the attitude that "there but for the grace of God go I." It may perhaps be no coincidence that in virtually every instance in which the question was referred to an independent litigation committee, the committee concluded that it was in the best interest of the corporation not to pursue the matter. While early decisions, including decisions by the United States Supreme Court and the Court of Appeals of New York, uncritically applied the business judgment rule to all such decisions, more recent decisions have been more cautious. The decision by the Delaware Supreme Court in Zapata Corp. v. Maldonado (1981) may have marked a turning point in this regard. The court there held that before applying the business judgment rule in a case in which a demand on directors was excused (see § 17.4 of this Nutshell), a court should not only consider the independence and good faith of the "Independent Litigation Committee" but also exercise its own "independent business judgment" as to whether the litigation should be terminated. However, the Delaware Supreme Court subsequently held in Aronson v. Lewis (1984) that this standard only applied in "demand excused" cases and the straight business judgment rule should apply in "demand required" cases. As a result, in Delaware today, the scope of the application of the business judgment rule is determined by whether the case is viewed as a "demand required" or "demand excused" case. This rule has been criticized on the ground that it requires a decision at the pleading stage when there has been no discovery; the Delaware courts require the pleading of "particularized facts" before any discovery has occurred if the demand requirement is to be avoided.

Decisions in other jurisdictions have generally not followed the Delaware approach and have refused to give binding effect to litigation committee decisions based on the demand required/demand excused distinction. In addition, the Revised Model Business Corporation Act was amended in 1989 to provide that demand was required in all cases, but that binding effect should be given to decisions to dismiss such litigation under the business judgment rule only where the directors making the decision are truly independent. The American Law Institute's corporate governance project has also adopted a universal demand requirement, but provides some degree of judicial review and oversight over all decisions to dismiss derivative litigation against officers or directors. As a global observation, it is probably a fair generalization that the decisions since *Zapata* have made it more difficult and expensive to dispose of unwanted derivative litigation by the independent litigation committee route, but that in appropriate cases the business judgment rule may be applied to decisions by such a committee.

§ 14.7 Duty of Loyalty: Self Dealing

The duty of loyalty has produced a steady stream of litigation in which transactions have been set aside or directors and officers have been held liable for breach of duty. These cases may be divided into four general types: (1) cases involving transactions between a director and the corporation; (2) cases involving transactions between corporations with one or more common directors; (3) cases involving a director taking advantage of an opportunity which arguably may belong to the corporation; and (4) cases in which the director competes with the corporation in its business.

The danger of self-dealing transactions between a corporation and a director is the risk that the corporation may be treated unfairly in such a transaction. When such a transaction is questioned, the burden is usually placed on the director as a fiduciary to prove the propriety of the transaction rather than on the person questioning the transaction. The form the transaction takes is not significant. The courts apply essentially the same test to transactions involving the sale of corporate property to a director, the sale of property to a director's spouse, the sale of property by a director to a corporation, a contract between the corporation and a director for the director to perform services such as selling stock or managing the business, or a loan by a director to the corporation.

The early common law took the position that all self-dealing transactions were automatically voidable at the election of the corporation. It was eventually recognized, however, that a black-and-white rule of this type did not fit business needs. Even though self-dealing transactions may be suspect, many of them in fact are entirely fair and reasonable; indeed, in many situations directors may give their corporations benefits that are more favorable than the corporation might obtain elsewhere. For example, loans by directors to the corporation may be made when the corporation could not borrow elsewhere; such transactions should obviously be encouraged.

Since 1975, a number of states have adopted statutes dealing with conflict of interest transactions. The Revised Model Business Corporation Act as adopted in 1984 contained a section based on these state statutes [section 8.31], but in 1988 that section was repealed and a new subchapter F [sections 8.60 through 8.63] was added to deal more precisely with conflict of interest transactions. In the discussion below, the position taken by courts in the absence of statute is first discussed, followed by a brief consideration of statutes similar to old section 8.31, followed by a brief description of the new subchapter F.

While many transactions between directors and their corporation have been held to be valid by courts despite the conflict of interest, in the absence of statute, considerable confusion exists in the case law as to the circumstances which validate such transactions. If one examines the results of the cases (as contrasted with statements in the opinions), the following comments accurately reflect most decisions:

(1) If the court feels the transaction to be fair to the corporation, it will be upheld;

(2) If the court feels that the transaction involves fraud, undue overreaching, or waste of corporate assets (e.g., a director using corporate assets for personal purposes without paying for them), the transaction will be set aside; and

(3) If the court feels that the transaction does not involve fraud, overreaching, or waste of corporate assets, but is not convinced that the transaction is fair, the transaction will be upheld only where the interested director can convincingly show that the transaction was approved (or ratified) by a disinterested majority of the board of directors without participation by the interested director, or by a majority of the shareholders after full disclosure of all relevant facts.

The opinions themselves do not establish a single, neat set of principles from which the foregoing results may be obtained. For example, courts have struggled with the question whether a fair transaction may be avoided if it is not ratified either by disinterested directors or by the shareholders. All the directors may be interested in a fair transaction, and shareholder ratification is not sought. Many cases either state or intimate such a transaction is voidable since it has not been properly approved; other opinions, however, emphasize the fairness of the transaction and have not insisted on formal approval or ratification.

State statutes dealing with conflict of interest transactions are generally similar to old section 8.31 of the Revised

Model Business Corporation Act, which in turn was similar to section 41 of the 1969 Model Act and section 144 of the Delaware General Corporation Law. About 35 states now have such statutes. Section 8.31 provided that a conflict of interest transaction was not voidable "solely" because of the conflict of interest if any one of three requirements were met: (1) the transaction was ratified or approved by the board of directors or a committee of the board after full disclosure and without the participation of interested directors, (2) the transaction was ratified or approved by the shareholders as provided in section 8.31(d) (which required the exclusion of shares owned by or voted under the control of the interested directors), or (3) the transaction was fair to the corporation. There was an unfortunate linguistic trap in this language (which also appears in most similar statutes): the purpose of directoral or shareholder ratification was not intended to be limited only to transactions that cannot meet the test of "fairness," i.e. only to unfair transactions. Rather, they were intended to be alternative ways to establish the enforceability of a conflict of interest transaction without going into the question of fairness at all. In other words, since a judicial inquiry into fairness may involve a complex and expensive hearing and inquiry into difficult business issues, director or shareholder ratification was to be utilized to avoid the need for such a hearing. Ratification was a "safe harbor."

Section 8.31 and similar statutes did not purport to validate all transactions that meet one or more of these requirements. Rather, it simply removed any possible impediment arising from the fact that a director was involved in the transaction. Thus, ratification under section 8.31(a)(1) or (a)(2) did not validate transactions that involved waste, fraud, or actions in excess of authority. This important principle was clearly set forth in the Official Comment and was implicit in the language of the statute itself.

The new subchapter F is a much more ambitious undertaking than § 144 of the Delaware statute or old § 8.31. Its basic structure is similar: a conflict of interest transaction is not voidable by the corporation if (1) it has been appropriately approved by disinterested directors or shareholders, or (2) the interested director establishes the fairness of the transaction. Unlike § 8.31, however, subchapter F creates a series of "bright line" principles that increase predictability and enhance practical administrability of the "safe harbor." Thus it defines with some precision the transactions to which subchapter F is applicable, the types of "interests" that constitute "conflicting interests," the directors that may vote on other directors' conflict of interest transactions, and finally the subchapter gives preclusive effect—there is to be no judicial review—to decisions by such directors that satisfy the requirements of the business judgment rule (established in cases such as *Van Gorkom*).

Let us assume for a moment that a self-dealing transaction is ratified by the board of directors (or a committee of the board) pursuant to subchapter F. The transaction does not involve fraud or waste, but nevertheless is attacked as being unfair to the corporation and unnecessarily favorable to the interested director. Since it was ratified by the directors, a full fairness inquiry is not necessary. Subchapter F provides that if the process followed by the board (or the committee) meets the standards of the business judgment rule, the transaction is binding on the corporation and there is to be no further judicial review of the decision. Is this desirable, or should the court make some kind of residual fairness inquiry before accepting the decision? Or to put the issue in another way, does the act of ratification by disinterested directors "sanitize" the transaction entirely from judicial scrutiny? The American Law Institute's Corporate Governance Project addresses the same issue and permits judicial inquiry into the directors' decision to the extent of determining that "it could reasonably be believed to be fair to the corporation at the time of such authorization." The question of the scope of judicial inquiry into director-approved conflict of interest transactions was immensely controversial within the American Law Institute, and to a lesser extent within the Committee on Corporate Laws of the American Bar Association. The difference in formulations, however, may not be as great as might first appear, because under the RMBCA formulation the court can always inquire into whether the standards of the business judgment rule were met, and it is likely that manifestly unfair transactions may be set aside on the ground that those standards were not met.

The attitude taken by the courts on the question of further judicial scrutiny seems to permit such inquiry, though the cases are not sufficiently clear from doubt as to limit the controversy. The leading case is Fliegler v. Lawrence (1976), which involved ratification by the shareholders rather than the directors. The court stated that section 144 of the Delaware General Corporation Law does not provide a "broad immunity," but "merely removes an 'interested director' cloud when its terms are met and provides against invalidation of an agreement 'solely' because such a director or officer is involved. Nothing in the statute sanctions unfairness to Agau [the complaining shareholder] or removes the transaction from judicial scrutiny." Other recent judicial decisions adopt the position taken in the *Fliegler* case, though a footnote dictum in the decision of Marciano v. Nakash (1987) states that "approval by fully-informed disinterested directors * * * permits invocation of the business judgment rule and limits judicial review to issues of gift or waste with the burden of proof upon the party attacking the transaction."

Two recurring issues relating to authorization or ratification are (1) who may be considered disinterested for purposes of determining who may act on the transaction, and (2) what degree of specific knowledge or notice of the underlying facts (and, indeed, of the existence of the conflict of interest itself) is required to constitute an effective authorization or ratification. These issues are discussed with precision in RMBCA section 8.60. Under more general statutes there is a considerable degree of flexibility on these issues, and there is a tendency in the cases to relax these requirements in situations where the transaction appears to be fair and to stiffen them when the transaction seems questionable.

Suit for rescission is generally the proper remedy to avoid a voidable transaction. In such a suit, the corporation must be prepared to return any consideration received by it in the transaction. It may not simultaneously retain the consideration and attack the validity of the transaction. If modern statutes give conclusive effect to ratifications by directors or shareholders or it is impracticable under the circumstances to rescind the transaction, it may be possible to require the director who benefited from the transaction to account for the benefits, or to surcharge directors or shareholders who voted in favor of the conflict of interest transaction without adequate information.

§ 14.8   Interlocking Directors

Transactions between corporations with common directors may lend themselves to the same evil as self-dealing transactions between a director and the corporation, since the interest of a common director may be small in one corporation and large in the other. The common law standard for setting aside transactions between corporations with common directors is simply one of manifest unfairness to one corporation. The role of the common director in approving the transaction also is inquired into. If the corporation on the losing side of the transaction relied on the views of the common director without a full evaluation of the risks, or without disclosure that the director was interested in the other corporation, the chances that the transaction will be set aside are greatly improved. The stated test, however, is an objective one of fairness, not a procedural test based on the degree of the common director's participation.

Section 8.60(1)(ii) treats as a conflict of interest a transaction between corporations with a common director if "the transaction is brought (or is of such character and significance to the corporation that it would in the normal course be brought) before the board of directors of the corporation for action." This provision recognizes that routine business transactions between large corporations should not be made subject to attack simply because the two corporations happen to have a common director. Even transactions that involve millions of dollars are often routine transactions not considered by the board of directors of large corporations. The quoted language is designed to limit the approval mechanisms of section 8.31 to situations where the transaction is of sufficient importance to the corporation that it is or should be considered by the board of directors.

§ 14.9 Executive Compensation

Directors of a corporation may serve as corporate officers or agents and be compensated for their services. The establishment of the amount of compensation payable to a director involves a specific application of the principles relating to self dealing. Many publicly held corporations have established compensation committees composed of outside directors to monitor compensation levels, though in most corporations the CEO or senior management actually establish the amount of compensation of all officers, either directly or by making recommendations to the board of directors or compensation committee.

In publicly held corporations, outside directors usually receive compensation in the form of directors' fees, and also may be eligible to participate in various deferred compensation plans. Section 8.11 of the Revised Model Business Corporation Act allows the board of directors to establish compensation programs for directors. Presumably, the fairness of these amounts may be inquired into under Subchapter F.

Much modern law relating to executive compensation is directly or indirectly related to the federal income tax. The issues differ in publicly owned corporations and in closely held corporations.

(1) In a closely held corporation, all the shareholders may be employees of the corporation; if so, and the corporation does not elect S corporation tax status, the salaries paid to the shareholders are likely to be set so as to minimize the aggregate tax liabilities imposed on the corporation and the shareholders. A salary payment may be deductible by the corporation while payment of the same sum in the form of a dividend may not.

If some shareholders of a closely held corporation are not employed by the corporation, however, they will be adversely affected by the payment of generous salaries to other shareholders and obviously would much prefer that the same sum be distributed pro rata in the form of a dividend, even though the tax obligations of the corporation may thereby be higher. The adverse effect of generous salaries to some but not all shareholders is independent of the S corporation election. In a closely held C corporation, the Internal Revenue Service routinely reviews the reasonableness of corporate salaries and may disallow deductions for unreasonably large salaries. The total amount paid by the corporation is still taxable to the shareholder-recipient either as a dividend or as compensation; the issue is the deductibility of the payments at the corporate level. If a salary payment is treated as a dividend for tax purposes, it does not necessarily follow that it should also be treated as a dividend under corporation law and distributed pro rata to all shareholders, though the disallowance of a salary deduction may suggest to a minority shareholder that the payment may also have been improper under general corporate fiduciary principles as well.

In an S corporation, all shareholders must pay tax on corporate earnings allocated to them, whether or not actually distributed. Corporations generally distribute at least an amount equal to the increased taxes owed by shareholders; the failure to do so for all shareholders places a considerable burden on individual shareholders not receiving a salary from the corporation and may give rise to claims of breach of fiduciary duty.

(2) In publicly held corporations, executive compensation is not usually considered to be a manner of distributing earnings. The executive is receiving "other people's money," and the effect of his or her compensation on earnings per share is likely to be minimal. However, compensation in public corporations may be very substantial and the question has arisen as to the circumstances under which a court may set aside compensation on the ground that it is excessive and therefore improper. Courts generally are reluctant to conclude that executive compensation is excessive, particularly if procedures are adopted which minimize the appearance of self-dealing. The rationale underlying this reluctance is set forth in an often-quoted statement from the leading New York case of Heller v. Boylan (1941):

Yes, the Court possesses the power to prune these payments, but openness forces the confession that the pruning would be synthetic and artificial rather than analytic or scientific.

If comparisons are to be made, with whose compensation are they to be made—executives? Those connected with the motion picture industry? Radio artists? Justices of the Supreme Court of the United States? The President of the United States? Manifestly, the material at hand is not of adequate plasticity for fashioning into a pattern or standard.

Courts are ill-equipped to solve or even to grapple with these entangled economic problems. Indeed, their solution is not within the juridical province. Courts are concerned that corporations be honestly and fairly operated by its directors, with the observance of the formal requirements of the law, but what is reasonable compensation for its officers is primarily for the stockholders. This does not mean that fiduciaries are to commit waste or misuse or abuse trust property, with impunity. A just cause will find the Courts at guard and implemented to grant redress.

As suggested by the last paragraph of this quotation, the tests applied by the courts to determine whether compensation is excessive in a publicly held corporation is whether the payments constitute spoilation or waste. Total compensation must bear some minimal relation to the services rendered. If it does not, the payment constitutes waste of corporate assets. The leading case of Rogers v. Hill (1933) involved a compensation plan for executives of the American Tobacco Company determined by a formula based on profits which yielded the president of the corporation more than $680,000 of extra compensation in 1929 and more than $1,300,000 in 1930. The United States Supreme Court held that these payments were so excessive as to be subject to examination and revision by the courts. In this case, the court expressly recognized that the formula was reasonable and valid in 1912 when it was approved by the shareholders; subsequent developments, however, resulted in payments so large as to raise the question that they constituted waste.

Relief has also been granted in a few instances in which large, specific payments have raised questions of fairness. Thus, a complaint attacking a very generous pension granted to a CEO shortly before his or her retirement, and funded by a single cash payment of several million dollars, was held to state a cause of action. However, examples of the exercise of this power are rare.

The contrast between the very cautious approach taken on compensation questions in publicly held corporations, and the tax cases dealing with deductibility of compensation in C corporations, is striking. Of course, in the latter there are no restraining influences on compensation levels in most cases, and there is a legislative command to limit deductions only to "reasonable" amounts; in addition, protection of the national fisc may require a more active review and consideration of the reasonableness of compensation. In publicly held corporations on the other hand, there are some outside constraints: information about compensation levels is public, and there is always the possibility of derivative litigation being instituted; the "gold fish" bowl analogy may have some restraining influence.

§ 14.10   Corporate Opportunity; Competition with Corporation

The corporate opportunity doctrine requires a corporate director to render to Caesar at the best possible price that which is Caesar's. As a fiduciary, a director owes a duty to further the interest of the corporation and to give it the benefit of his or her uncorrupted business judgment. He or she may not take a secret profit in connection with corporate transactions, compete unfairly with the corporation, or take personally profitable business opportunities that belong to the corporation.

Very often the application of the doctrine of corporate opportunity to a specific situation comes down to a judicial evaluation of business ethics. Serious problems of definition and evaluation lie close to the surface—when is an opportunity a corporate opportunity? When may a director take advantage of a corporate opportunity on the ground that the corporation is unwilling or unable to take advantage of it? Under what circumstances may a director enter into a business which competes with the corporation? These questions are considered below.

The basic test established by modern cases as to when an opportunity is a corporate opportunity combines a "line of business" test with the pervasive issue whether it is unfair for the director under the circumstances to take advantage personally of the opportunity. Some courts have in effect collapsed the "line of business" requirement into the fairness test and stated that the single test is simply whether it is fair under the circumstances for the director to take advantage of the opportunity. It is probably helpful, however, to recognize that there are two tests: one for determining whether the corporation has an interest in the opportunity at all (the "line of business" test) and, second, if it does, under what circumstances may the director nevertheless take advantage of it (the "fairness" test).

The "line of business" test simply compares the closeness of the opportunity to the types of business in which the corporation is engaged. The closer it is, the more likely it is to be a corporate opportunity. Some courts have articulated narrower tests as to the necessary relation between the opportunity and the corporate business. An earlier test was that the opportunity must involve "property wherein the corporation has an interest already existing or in which it has an expectancy growing out of an existing right." Another test that has been adopted by some courts is that the opportunity must in some sense arise out of the corporation's business as it is then conducted. Both of these tests are somewhat narrower than the "line of business" test, but in the last analysis, the verbal formulation of the test is less important than the court's sensitivity to reasonable business ethics as to what belongs to the corporation and what does not.

Other factors may also be relevant in determining whether an opportunity is a corporate opportunity. For example, weight may be given to factors such as the following: (1) whether there were prior negotiations with the corporation about the opportunity, (2) whether the opportunity was offered to the corporation or to the director as an agent of the corporation, (3) whether the director learned of the opportunity by reason of his or her position with the corporation, (4) whether the director used corporate facilities or property to take advantage of the opportunity, and (5) how substantial was the need of the corporation for the opportunity.

Even if an opportunity is a corporate opportunity, directors are not necessarily precluded from taking advantage of it. The corporation may voluntarily relinquish it, though such a relinquishment will be scrutinized by the courts for fairness and good faith, including full disclosure and free acquiescence in the relinquishment by the disinterested directors. A persuasive policy reason for the relinquishment, e.g., a decision that under the circumstances it would be unwise to expand the corporation's business, helps to make it clear that the corporation voluntarily decided not to pursue the opportunity. Directors may also take advantage of a corporate opportunity if the corporation is incapable of taking advantage of the opportunity, e.g., on the ground the opportunity would be ultra vires, in violation of law, or because the third person refuses to deal with the corporation.

Directors have also sought to justify their utilization of a corporate opportunity on the ground that the corporation is financially unable to capitalize on the opportunity. This defense is often a troublesome one, since directors may be tempted to refrain from exercising their strongest efforts on behalf of the corporation if they can thereafter take advantage personally of a profitable opportunity. There is some support for a "rigid rule" prohibiting directors from taking advantage of a corporate opportunity on this ground; in this view, if the directors do not wish to lend the necessary funds to the corporation, they must forego the opportunity. Such a rule seems unnecessarily strict, however, and most courts have permitted directors to utilize corporate opportunities under such circumstances upon a convincing showing that the corporation indeed lacked the independent assets to take advantage of its opportunity. An important case involving this issue, Klinicki v. Lundgren (1985), relies on a preliminary ALI Corporate Governance Project formulation to conclude that a director may not rely on financial inability of the corporation to justify taking a corporate opportunity unless the opportunity is first presented to the corporation for its consideration. A director who secretly takes advantage of an opportunity obviously has greater difficulty justifying his or her conduct than one who advises the corporation of the existence of the opportunity.

Directors generally may engage in a similar line of business in competition with the corporation's business where it is done in good faith and without injury to the corporation. A number of cases, however, have found a competing director guilty of a breach of fiduciary duty on several possible theories: conflict of interest, corporate opportunity, misappropriation of trade secrets or customer lists, or wrongful interference with contractual relationships. In this area, tort concepts of unfair competition are close to fiduciary duties. Unfair competition with the corporation may involve business activities generally, or may involve specific corporate transactions, such as the director who competes with the corporation in selling shares of stock or who acquires at a discount claims against the corporation when the corporation could have done so. Again, judicial notions of fairness or fair play seem dominant, and a close appraisal of the fiduciary's conduct in light of ethical business practice is necessary.

§ 14.11 Fairness to Minority Shareholders

The preceding sections dealing with various aspects of the director's fiduciary duties to his or her corporation demonstrate that a test of fairness is an important criterion for evaluating the propriety of specific transactions. This test is explicitly a criterion in evaluating transactions between corporations with common directors and in determining whether a director may take advantage of corporate opportunities; it is also the test in evaluating the propriety of self-dealing transactions generally, at least in the absence of approval of the transaction by independent directors under the business judgment rule. The test of fairness serves the interests of the corporation, since well meaning officers and directors should not be discouraged from dealing with the corporation and reasonable transactions should not be set aside merely because of some formal or technical defect in corporate procedure. On the other hand, the fairness test protects shareholders and creditors alike from overreaching or unwise transactions.

The test of fairness is also applicable to a variety of transactions which defy precise categorization, but which may be lumped loosely under the title "fairness to minority shareholders." For example, in closely held corporations, a number of cases have held that shareholders owe one another a fiduciary duty in the operation of the enterprise. The leading case is Donahue v. Rodd Electrotype Co. (1975). This duty could equally be phrased as a duty of fairness owed by directors in such an enterprise to the minority shareholders. A controlling shareholder may not redeem a portion of his holdings at a higher price than offered to minority shareholders. In the absence of preemptive rights, a controlling shareholder may not cause the corporation to issue to himself or herself new or treasury shares to cement control of the corporation, even at a fair price, since to do so would unfairly dilute the voting power of minority shareholders.

A similar principle is applicable to transactions affecting different classes of stock. In Zahn v. Transamerica Corp. (1947), for example, the directors of the Axton–Fisher Tobacco Company knew that the inventory of the corporation had appreciated greatly in value over the value reflected on the books of the corporation. To obtain the greatest portion of this appreciation for itself, the majority shareholder, Transamerica Corporation, caused the corporation to call a senior security (a convertible participating preferred). The corporation did not disclose the inventory appreciation and, as a result, most of the holders of the senior securities permitted their holdings to be redeemed at $80.80 per share rather than converting them into common shares worth considerably more. The court held that the transaction violated a duty owed to the minority shareholders: in effect, the directors are required to treat fairly each class of stock and may not take actions which are designed to enhance the value of one class at the expense of another. It is important, however, that this principle be put into context. Directors elected by the common shareholders may declare extra dividends on common shares so long as the required provision is made for the senior securities; the directors may call a senior security for redemption in order ultimately to improve the position of the common shareholders. These powers are specifically granted to the directors by the articles of incorporation and are part of each shareholder's "contract" with the corporation. The holders of senior securities have no complaint if these powers are exercised ultimately to benefit the common shareholders who have the power to elect the directors. The holders of senior securities, however, may legitimately expect to be given accurate information so that they will not be misled and may make an intelligent selection of the various options available to them. The original opinion in the *Zahn* case contained language which intimated that the mere call for redemption constituted the breach of fiduciary duty, but on a subsequent appeal on the issue of damages, the Third Circuit adopted the theory that the failure to disclose relevant information constituted the breach. Speed v. Transamerica Corp. (1956).

§ 14.12 "Fairness" and the "Business Judgment Rule"

There is some potential overlap between the cases in which the "fairness" test described in the previous sections is applied and the cases described in §§ 14.4 through 14.6 of this Nutshell dealing with the business judgment rule. This is illustrated by two cases involving transactions between parent corporations and their subsidiaries.

In Sinclair Oil Co. v. Levien (1971), a case involving transactions between a parent corporation and its 97 per cent owned subsidiary, the minority shareholders of the subsidiary attacked several transactions, including decisions (1) to pay large dividends by the subsidiary solely in order to ease the cash needs of the parent, (2) to channel oil development in other countries into other subsidiaries of the parent, and (3) to cause the subsidiary not to pursue claims for breach of contract against the parent. The alternative rules potentially applicable, the court noted, are the standards of "intrinsic fairness," on the one hand, or of "business judgment" on the other. Under the latter, actions will be upheld unless there is a showing of "gross or palpable overreaching." The court held that the questions of the excessive dividends and channeling of business opportunities should be evaluated by the "business judgment rule" while the refusal to enforce the contract claim should be judged on the basis of "intrinsic fairness." The basic distinction, the court stated, is whether the transaction involves self-dealing, that is, whether the parent received something from the subsidiary "to the exclusion and detriment of the minority shareholders." Since the dividends were paid proportionally to all shareholders, there was no self-dealing and the business judgment rule should be applied. So far as the business opportunities were concerned, there was no showing that they were ever corporate opportunities of the subsidiary and thus were not taken improperly by the parent. Giving up a contract claim by the subsidiary against the parent, however, constituted self-dealing since the minority shareholders did not participate proportionally, and should be judged by "intrinsic fairness."

The requirement that transactions between parent and subsidiary must be evaluated on the basis of "intrinsic fairness" may sharply limit the power of the parent to utilize the subsidiary's assets most efficiently. For this reason, parent corporations may wish to eliminate the minority shareholders from the subsidiary in a "freeze-out" or "cash-out" merger. As described in section 18.3, modern statutes permit the involuntary elimination of minority shareholders. On the other hand, such a merger is itself a conflict of interest transaction that requires establishment of the intrinsic fairness of the transaction.

In Weinberger v. UOP, Inc. (1983), the court held that a cash-out merger transaction between a parent corporation and its partially owned subsidiary failed to meet the standard of intrinsic fairness. Intrinsic fairness, the court stated, had two basic aspects: fair dealing and fair price. Fair dealing involved fairness in the initiation, structuring, negotiation, and disclosure of the transaction to the minority shareholders of the subsidiary corporation. Fair price, on the other hand, required an examination of the economic and financial considerations underlying the proposed merger: assets, market value, earnings, future prospects and all other elements that affect the intrinsic or inherent value of a company's stock. The burden to establish intrinsic fairness, the court held, was on the parent corporation. In a footnote, however, the court stated that "the result here could have been entirely different" if the subsidiary had appointed an independent negotiating committee of its outside directors to deal with its parent. The court added that "fairness in this context can be equated to conduct by a theoretical, wholly independent, board of directors acting upon the matter before them," and that "particularly in a parent-subsidiary context, a showing that the action taken was as though each of the contending parties had in fact exerted its bargaining power against the other at arm's length is strong evidence that the transaction meets the test of fairness." This statement virtually equates fairness with the exercise of independent business judgment.

Following *Weinberger*, independent directors have been added to the boards of many partially owned subsidiaries to permit arms-length bargaining in the event the parent wishes to enter into a transaction with its subsidiary that implicates the intrinsic fairness standard.

§ 14.13   Shareholder Ratification

Ratification by shareholders of a transaction between a director and his or her corporation will sometimes validate a transaction that otherwise might be voidable. However, not all self-dealing transactions may be ratified by majority vote. Transactions that involve fraud, undue overreaching, or waste of corporate assets (e.g., a director using corporate assets for personal purposes without paying for them) can only be ratified by a unanimous vote, and even then may be attacked by representatives of creditors if the corporation becomes insolvent. The theory is that all the shareholders may dissipate the corporate assets as they wish, so long as creditors are not injured, but that any individual shareholder may object to a clearly improper use of corporate assets even though a majority of the shareholders are in favor of that use.

§ 14.14 Exoneratory Provisions in Articles of Incorporation

Provisions are sometimes placed in the articles of incorporation of a corporation that purport to permit transactions between directors and the corporation which otherwise might be voidable under the principles described elsewhere in this chapter. These clauses are not construed literally to validate fraudulent or manifestly unfair acts. Such clauses may (1) permit an interested director to be counted in determining whether a quorum is present, or (2) exonerate transactions between corporation and director "from adverse inferences which might be drawn against them." Despite such clauses, courts examine with care transactions that may involve conflicting loyalties, and thus the usefulness and effectiveness of such clauses are limited.

§ 14.15 Statutory Duties and Statutory Defenses

State business corporation acts impose liabilities on directors for certain transactions that violate specific statutory provisions. This liability is in addition to other liabilities, and usually is not dependent on bad faith. While provisions vary from state to state, liability for the following actions are typical:

(1) Paying dividends or making distributions in violation of the act or of restrictions in the articles of incorporation. See RMBCA § 8.33. Liability is usually limited to the excess of the amount actually distributed over the amount that could have been distributed without violating the act or restriction.

(2) Purchasing its own shares in violation of the act. The liability again is usually limited to the consideration paid for such shares which is in excess of the maximum amount which could have been paid without violating the statute. The Revised Model Business Corporation Act in effect

combines this prohibition with the previous one since a "distribution" under that Act is defined to include both dividends and repurchases of shares.

(3) Distributing assets to shareholders during the liquidation of the corporation without paying and discharging, or making adequate provision for the payment and discharge of, all known debts, obligations, and liabilities of the corporation. The Revised Model Business Corporation Act does not directly address this kind of misconduct. See RMBCA § 14.05(a)(3).

(4) Permitting the corporation to commence business before it has received the minimum required consideration for its shares. With the elimination of minimum capital requirements in the RMBCA and the statutes of most states, this provision is of less practical importance than it once was. In states that continue to require minimum capital, the liability is limited to the unpaid part of the minimum capital, and the liability terminates when the required minimum capital has actually been received. Earlier statutes in some states extended liability to all debts or liabilities incurred before the required capital has been paid in. Such a provision obviously created a serious trap for the unwary director.

(5) Permitting the corporation to make a prohibited loan to an officer, director, or shareholder of the corporation. The RMBCA has eliminated all restrictions on loans to officers, directors or shareholders; in states where these restrictions continue to exist, liability of directors who approve the loan is usually imposed up to the unpaid amount of the loan.

The Revised Model Business Corporation Act greatly reduces the importance of these statutory liability provisions, in part because it eliminates some of the underlying restrictions on which the liabilities are based and in part because it provides a simpler test for the lawfulness of corporate distributions, the provision most likely to be violated.

Business corporation acts also usually provide for joint and several liability imposed on all directors present at the meeting at which the transaction giving rise to the liability is taken, and a director held liable may be entitled to contribution from other directors who assented to the transaction, and to shareholders who received the unlawful distribution. See RMBCA § 8.33(b). Under the RMBCA, however, only shareholders who accept "knowing the distribution was made in violation of the Act or the articles of incorporation" are liable for contribution. The theory is that shareholders who receive a distribution in ignorance of its illegality are entitled to keep it. In this situation, of course, the possibility of detrimental reliance by such shareholders is quite high.

The directoral liabilities imposed by these statutes may be subject to defenses available to directors generally. For example, in some states it is a defense that the directors met their standard of due care or they relied in good faith upon financial statements or advice given by appropriate corporate officials, attorneys, or others. Not all states recognize such defenses, however, and directors may possibly be liable for violation of these statutory duties even though they acted in good faith and with due care. The Revised Model Business Corporation Act further reduces the significance of these statutory liabilities by making all general statutory defenses applicable to them. It is probable that states will follow the RMBCA in this regard in the future.

There has been virtually no litigation over the scope of these defenses. Indeed, there has also been very little litigation over the statutory liabilities for unlawful distributions or other actions that might give rise to these statutory liabilities.

§ 14.16 Purchase or Sale of Shares or Claims Under State Law

The state law relating to transactions in corporate shares by directors and officers, or by the corporation itself, has been largely overshadowed by the development of federal law, particularly rule 10b–5, discussed in the following section of this Nutshell. As a result, there is relatively little case law on some of the problems discussed in this section.

(1) *Purchase or Sale of Shares by an Officer or Director on the Basis of Undisclosed Information.* An officer or director of the corporation may have knowledge about corporate affairs that is unknown to the general public or to the shareholders. He or she may be tempted either to purchase or to sell shares, depending on the nature of the information, without disclosing the information in order to make a personal profit. An officer or director who capitalizes on inside corporate information for personal gain clearly violates rule 10b–5 and most cases of this type are now brought in federal court under that rule. The common law did not develop a simple test for handling such situations. If an affirmative misrepresentation was made, of course, normal fraud principles dictate that the defrauded person might rescind the transaction. In addition, where the facts were of critical importance and peculiarly within the knowledge of the insider, some courts found a duty to disclose "special facts" without attempting to define which facts are "special." The leading case is Strong v. Repide (1909). Chances of recovery in these early cases appear somewhat greater if the outsider could prove that he or she relied on the insider or if the insider concealed his or her identity from the purchaser (as was the case in Strong v. Repide itself). One can argue, however, that the identity of the purchaser itself may be a "special fact." Kansas early adopted a stricter rule to protect outsiders, though the difference between these cases and the cases applying the "special facts" rule appears to be one of degree.

The broadest state rule was articulated in Diamond v. Oreamuno (1969) where the court permitted the corporation to recover profits made by insiders in securities selling on the basis of advance information that costs would increase materially in the future and the value of the corporation's securities would decline in price. Relying on analogies with the federal securities laws, the court in effect concluded that inside information was corporate property and the insider should not be permitted to profit from the use of that corporate property even though the corporation was not injured thereby. This view has been accepted by some courts and rejected by others.

(2) *Purchase at a Discount of Claims Against the Corporation.* A corporate officer or director may purchase claims against a *solvent* corporation at a discount, and enforce them at face value, though in some circumstances the opportunity to acquire a claim at a discount may itself be a corporate opportunity. It follows that claims validly bought at a discount when a corporation is solvent may share at face value in a subsequent distribution in insolvency or bankruptcy. A different rule, however, is applicable to claims purchased at a discount when the corporation is insolvent, and on the verge of, or in, bankruptcy or liquidation. The theory is that when insolvency, liquidation, or reorganization has occurred or is imminent, corporate directors should attempt to settle or discharge claims against the corporation on the best possible terms from the corporation's standpoint in order to benefit other creditors and the shareholders, rather than seeking to profit personally from the distribution.

(3) *Purchase or Sale of Shares in Competition With the Corporation.* In some circumstances an officer or director may attempt to sell his or her personal stock in competition with the corporation's attempt to raise capital by selling additional stock. Such conduct is actionable if the opportunity to sell shares to a third person is itself a corporate opportunity.

The same principle should be applicable to corporate opportunities to repurchase its own shares as well.

(4) *Purchase or Sale of Shares by a Corporation in a Struggle for Control.* If outsiders are seeking to wrest control of a public corporation away from incumbent management, the incumbents may attempt to use the corporation in order to preserve their position. They may cause the corporation to make open market purchases of its own shares in order to drive up the price. Or they may cause the corporation to buy out the insurgents at a premium price in order to eliminate them. (This strategy is usually described as "green mail.") Or they may issue additional shares to themselves or to friendly persons in order to cement their position. Similarly, in a closely held corporation, the majority may decide to have the corporation purchase at a generous price the shares owned by a particularly obstreperous minority shareholder in order to be rid of him or her. The general test of propriety adopted by the courts to evaluate all such transactions is one of underlying purpose:

> [I]f the actions of the board were motivated by a sincere belief that the buying out of the dissident stockholder was necessary to maintain what the board believed to be proper business practices, the board will not be held liable for such decision, even though hindsight indicates the decision was not the wisest course * * *. On the other hand, if the board has acted solely or primarily because of the desire to perpetuate themselves in office, the use of corporate funds for such purposes is improper.

Cheff v. Mathes (1964). This test may be criticized on the ground that it is possible to dress up virtually every transaction as a "proper business practice." However, a number of cases have invalidated transactions of the type described, so that the test obviously has some teeth. In addition, a special penalty tax has been enacted by Congress to discourage green mail transactions; several states have also enacted statutes attempting to prohibit such transactions.

§ 14.17   Rule 10b–5

Rule 10b–5, promulgated by the Securities and Exchange Commission under section 10(b) of the Securities Exchange Act of 1934, is the source of most current principles relating to transactions in securities by officers, directors, and others. Rule 10b–5 has some of the attributes of a roller coaster: a dizzying growth followed by a sudden decline as the United States Supreme Court sharply limited the growth of the jungle of case law. The deceptively simple language of rule 10b–5 should be quoted—

It shall be unlawful for any person, directly or indirectly, by the use of any means or instrumentality of interstate commerce, or of the mails or of any facility of any national securities exchange,

(1) to employ any device, scheme, or artifice to defraud;

(2) to make any untrue statement of a material fact or to omit to state a material fact necessary in order to make the statements made, in light of the circumstances under which they were made, not misleading, or

(3) to engage in any act, practice, or course of business which operates or would operate as a fraud or deceit upon any person,

in connection with the purchase or sale of any security.

It should be emphasized that rule 10b–5 is a federal regulation and claims arising under it are federal claims. There is no need for diversity of citizenship, suit may be brought only in federal court, and state security-for-expenses statutes (see § 17.4 of this Nutshell) are not applicable. While many rule 10b–5 cases probably could have been brought in state court on state fiduciary or fraud principles, the federal forum is preferred by plaintiffs for several reasons. The procedures may be simpler and discovery procedures broader. There is nationwide service of process and broad venue provisions. The doctrine of pendent jurisdiction permits the joinder of both state and federal claims in a rule 10b–5 suit, but a rule 10b–5 claim cannot be joined with state causes of action in a state court. Further, in the past at least, the principles applicable under rule 10b–5 have been more favorable to plaintiffs than the correlative principles of state law. There are also more rule 10b–5 precedents than state court precedents and hence "more law" on which to build one's case. Finally, there is also the feeling, perhaps unjustified, that federal judges may be more sympathetic to minority shareholder complaints than state court judges. For all these practical reasons, rule 10b–5 has been traditionally preferred over state-based claims, and as a result rule 10b–5 prospered while state law languished. Two Supreme Court opinions, however, have served to restore the balance:

(1) In Ernst & Ernst v. Hochfelder (1976), the United States Supreme Court held that a private plaintiff under rule 10b–5 must allege and prove "scienter," that is, "intentional wrongdoing" or a "mental state embracing intent to deceive, manipulate or defraud." The Court rejected several lower court holdings that mere negligence was sufficient. The Court, however, reserved the issues whether in some circumstances recklessness might satisfy the scienter requirement and whether a lesser standard of conduct might satisfy rule 10b–5 when injunctive relief is being sought by the Securities and Exchange Commission rather than a private plaintiff. All the courts of appeal that have considered the first question have concluded that recklessness may satisfy the scienter requirement, but the United States Supreme Court held that scienter must be established in cases involving injunctive relief as well as in cases seeking damages. [Aaron v. SEC, (1980).]

(2) In Santa Fe Industries, Inc. v. Green (1977), the United States Supreme Court further limited rule 10b–5 to situations involving deception; in other words, a transaction (e.g., a merger) that is adequately disclosed cannot be

attacked under rule 10b–5 no matter how unfair its terms. Roughly contemporaneous with this decision are decisions by the Delaware Supreme Court holding that unfair merger transactions of the type involved in *Santa Fe* could not be validated by literal compliance with the requirements of the state business corporation acts, but that the transaction must meet a test of "entire fairness." See the discussion in § 14.12 of this Nutshell. Other state courts have also adopted a fairness requirement for these merger transactions; these developments obviously have returned some of the prior rule 10b–5 litigation to the state courts.

The following paragraphs summarize the burgeoning law of rule 10b–5:

(1) *Rule 10b–5 as an Antifraud Provision.* It is now firmly established that a private cause of action exists under rule 10b–5 on behalf of a person who bought or sold securities in a transaction involving false or misleading information. Further, the rule is applicable to closely held shares as well as publicly held shares. Federal jurisdiction is triggered by the use of facilities of interstate commerce—e.g. the telephone—or by use of the mails. To use a classroom example, if the president of a small Denver corporation offers over the telephone to purchase the shares owned by a shareholder living in Denver on the basis of a misrepresentation about the corporation, he or she has violated rule 10b–5 without even leaving the Denver office. Rule 10b–5 is obviously a far-reaching antifraud provision.

Rule 10b–5 proscribes not only affirmative misrepresentations and half-truths but also a failure to disclose "material facts"; mere silence may constitute a violation, e.g., by failing to correct a statement that was accurate when made but is now false. The question of what is "material" is necessarily a relative one. The basic test is whether a reasonable person would attach importance to the information in determining his or her course of action—in other words, if the information would, in reasonable and objective contemplation, affect the value of the securities, it should be considered "material." Examples of material information are a significant ore strike, a resale contract for the shares or corporate assets, or a merger opportunity. (See also the discussion of a related issue in § 13.10 of this Nutshell.)

In cases involving publicly held corporations, the issue may arise as to whether the plaintiff, the buyer or seller of shares, must establish that he or she relied on the incorrect information or on the failure to disclose material information. Several courts evolved the rule that reliance may be presumed on the basis of a theory generally known as the "fraud on the market" theory. In Basic, Inc. v. Levinson (1988) the United States Supreme Court, in a sharply divided decision, endorsed the fraud on the market concept as creating a rebuttable presumption of reliance. The fraud on the market theory is an adaptation of the efficient market theory for corporate securities (which states in part that the price of a security at any time reflects all public information about the corporation issuing the security). Since the investor believed he or she was investing in a security at a price properly established in an efficient market, reliance can be presumed since the investor believes generally that the market price is validly set and that no unsuspected fraud has affected the price. In view of the sharp division of the Court in *Basic* and the fact that two justices recused themselves without explanation, it is possible that this issue may be reconsidered at a later date.

(2) *Rule 10b–5 as a Prohibition Against Insider Trading.* The above principles have also been applied in transactions involving securities of the publicly held corporation. Here, however, transactions are usually not with a single known individual, but are effected anonymously over securities exchanges or through brokers. It is usually impractical for the insider to disclose material facts since that is a corporate function. The result is that insiders with material information about corporate matters simply must forego the transac-

tion until after the facts are made public and have been reasonably disseminated by wire services and the like.

The first statement that trading on the basis of inside information in the anonymous securities markets might violate rule 10b–5 appeared in In the Matter of Cady Roberts & Co. (1961), a broker discipline case. Its first widely-publicized application occurred in Securities and Exchange Commission v. Texas Gulf Sulphur Corp. (1968), where the court held unlawful, under rule 10b–5, the purchase of common shares of Texas Gulf, and calls on those shares, by a number of employees, officers, and directors of Texas Gulf based on a preliminary core drilled in an area near Timmons, Ontario, that revealed a major ore discovery. Rule 10b–5 was also held to have been violated by transactions entered into very shortly after the news of the ore strike had been released at a press conference called by the corporation. After this decision, the New York Stock Exchange published guidelines as to when it was appropriate for an insider to purchase shares of the corporation. These guidelines suggest periodic investment purchases (e.g. buying a few shares every month) or limiting transactions to brief periods after public information is released. However, where a development of major importance has occurred, uncertainty may exist as to when an insider may trade even after the information has been released.

The modern law of insider trading has been largely shaped by three decisions of the Supreme Court of the United States: Chiarella v. United States (1980), Dirks v. SEC (1983), and Carpenter v. United States (1987); and by the enactment of two statutes addressing the insider trading problem: the Insider Trading Sanctions Act of 1984 (ITSA) and the Insider Trading and Securities Fraud Enforcement Act of 1988 (ITSFEA). Both of these statutes are amendments to the Securities Exchange Act of 1934; they clearly evince a strong legislative policy against permitting insider trading. These developments are described in the following paragraphs.

(i) In *Chiarella,* the Court set aside a criminal conviction under rule 10b–5 of an employee of a printing plant printing documents for securities transactions who traded on information obtained through his work. The information related to proposed tender offers by aggressor corporations; while the names of both aggressors and targets were left blank (or false names were substituted), Chiarella was able to ascertain the identities of the corporations involved and then use the information to profit on the shares of the target corporations. A majority of the Supreme Court held that Chiarella owed no duty to the general public to disclose the information he obtained since he was not an insider and received no information from the target corporation. There was, furthermore, no general rule that prohibited all persons with inside information from trading.

Shortly after *Chiarella* was decided, the SEC adopted rule 14e–3 which prohibits trading by anyone with undisclosed information about pending tender offers. Thus, even an eavesdropper who overhears discussion of a proposed offer at a restaurant or while walking in the street violates this rule if he or she trades on the basis of the information. On the facts, Chiarella would have violated rule 14e–3 even though he had not violated rule 10b–5. A panel of the Second Circuit has held this rule to be invalid as exceeding the power of the SEC, a conclusion that is still in litigation as this is written.

(ii) In *Chiarella,* the possibility that a criminal conviction under rule 10b–5 might be based on Chiarella's duties to his employer was suggested by a dissent but not squarely addressed by the majority. Following this decision, the Second Circuit on several occasions held that a violation of a duty to persons other than the issuer may be used to ground a rule 10b–5 violation. The leading case involving this theory, usually called the "misappropriation theory," is *Car-*

penter; in this case, Winans, a reporter for the Wall Street Journal and writer of the daily column "Heard on the Street," was tipping associates about the content of the column before it was published. Favorable mention of a stock in this column usually led to a run-up in price of the stock; Winans and his associates purchased the stock in advance of the column and profited from the increase in price. Winans was convicted of a criminal violation of section 10(b) and rule 10b–5, and the Second Circuit affirmed primarily on the misappropriation theory. The Supreme Court divided 4–4 on this branch of the case, so that the status of the misappropriation theory is still in doubt. However, the Supreme Court in Carpenter went on to hold, 8–0, that the misuse of other persons' confidential information may serve as the basis of a criminal prosecution under the mail fraud statute, a criminal statute carrying substantial penalties. This decision has removed much of the urgency in resolving the legal status of the misappropriation doctrine.

(iii) *Dirks* involved a broker who was given information by an insider about a major fraud that was occurring within Equity Funding Corporation, a life insurance and mutual fund corporation. Dirks "blew the whistle" on the fraud only after advising his clients to dispose of their Equity Funding stock. Dirks was a "tippee," that is a person who receives information from a person within the corporation (the "tipper"). Such a person differs from the printer in *Chiarella* in that the tippee is acting on information obtained directly from the corporation. In *Dirks,* the Court held that a tippee was subject to the constraints of rule 10b–5 only if the tipper breached a fiduciary duty in giving the information to the tippee. This question, in turn, is to be resolved on the basis of whether the tipper received a direct or indirect personal benefit from the disclosure, such as a pecuniary gain or a "reputational benefit." In a footnote, the Court also suggested that some nominal "tippees" who receive corporate information in a legitimate manner—such as underwriters, accountants, attorneys, or consultants working for the corporation—should be viewed as temporary insiders so that if they disclose confidential information it is as a tipper and not a tippee.

The requirement of *Dirks* that a tippee is liable under rule 10b–5 only if the tipper obtained an improper benefit from the disclosure, has lead to some unusual allegations. In one case, for example, the former CEO of a major corporation was charged with providing inside information to several friends as well as his mistress; the SEC charged that the former CEO received a direct personal benefit from his "close personal relationship" with his mistress!

(iv) The Insider Trading Sanctions Act (ITSA) constituted the first Congressional recognition of the existence of restrictions on insider trading. That Act authorized the SEC to recover up to three times the amount of trading profit from persons who engage in unlawful insider trading. Under this authority, the SEC has settled a number of insider trading cases, charging the violator with a penalty equal to twice or three times the amount of the trading profit, depending apparently on the degree of culpability. Of course, in addition to this civil penalty, criminal sanctions may be, and often are, imposed.

(v) The Insider Trading and Securities Fraud Enforcement Act (ITSFEA) increased the criminal penalties for securities violations, created a statutory remedy by which contemporaneous traders may bring private actions against persons engaged in unlawful insider trading, added a bounty provision by which informants could receive up to ten per cent of any penalty recovered under ITSA and ITSFEA, and imposed limited civil penalties on persons who directly or indirectly control an inside trader. Probably the most important of these provisions is the one relating to controlling persons: the test for liability is whether such person "knew or recklessly disregarded the fact that such controlled person was likely to engage" in unlawful insider trading or "knowingly or recklessly failed to establish, maintain or enforce" policies or procedures designed to prevent such trading. Under this section, law firms, accounting firms, issuers, financial printers, newspapers and magazines, and others, are required to implement policies designed to prevent insider trading.

Neither ITSA nor ITSFEA contains a definition of insider trading. The test for what triggers the civil penalty and other sanctions under those statutes is based on the Supreme Court cases described above.

There is a possibility that both tipper and tippee may be liable for profits made by the tippee in a transaction that violates rule 10b–5. Indeed, one facet of the *Texas Gulf Sulphur* case involved a holding that a tipper was liable for the profits made by his tippees. While the tippees were not parties to that proceeding, the court noted that their action was at least as reprehensible as that of their tipper; today multiple liability is certainly likely under the tests of the *Dirks* case. If the tipper is liable for the tippee's profits, it is doubtful whether the tipper has an "action over" because of the *in pari delicto* principle. In its administration of ITSFA and ITSFEA, the SEC has accepted settlements based on the tipper paying a civil penalty equal to or in excess of the profits made by his or her tippee.

The case law has also considered the liability of a tipper who gives his tippee knowingly false information. In other words, the tippee lost money trading on false information; however, the tippee thought he or she was violating rule 10b–5 in entering into the transactions in question. An argument may be made that *in pari delicto* should also apply in this type of case to bar recovery by the tippee against the tipper. While some courts accepted this argument, the decision by the United States Supreme Court in Eichler v. Berner (1985) that *in pari delicto* should be applied only where "the plaintiff bears at least substantially equal responsibility for the violations he seeks to redress" probably bars the successful assertion of the *in pari delicto* defense in most cases of this type.

(3) *Rule 10b–5 as a Protection Against Deception of the Corporation.* Rule 10b–5 is potentially applicable when a corporation issues or acquires its own shares. In other words, the phrase "purchase or sale" is literally construed to cover transactions by the corporation in its own shares as well as transactions by third persons. If shares are issued or acquired by a corporation as a result of deception or a failure of some persons to disclose material facts to the corporation, the corporation may have a claim under rule 10b–5, and this claim may be asserted derivatively by a minority shareholder. For example, stock options granted to officers of Texas Gulf Sulphur Corporation who knew of the major ore strike were cancelled since the recipients did not advise the members of the option committee of the material information (the ore strike). Similarly, a rule 10b–5 violation occurs if the corporation is fraudulently induced to issue shares for inadequate consideration even though such conduct also constitutes a violation of state-created fiduciary duties. Of course, in all cases of this type, there must be both deception and scienter in order to meet the fundamental requirements of rule 10b–5.

(4) *Rule 10b–5 as a General Prohibition Against Wrongful Conduct.* At one time courts permitted rule 10b–5 to be cast adrift from its mooring as an antifraud provision, and applied the rule to situations in which bad conduct has occurred and there is some relationship either to the securities market or to trading in securities. The leading case involving this free wheeling approach is Superintendent of Ins. of New York v. Bankers Life & Cas. Co. (1971), where the United States Supreme Court found a rule 10b–5 violation when a corporation sold treasury bonds and the proceeds were fraudulently diverted to third parties. Thus, for a relatively brief period rule 10b–5 appeared to have an

apparently limitless growth potential. However, the United States Supreme Court in Blue Chip Stamps v. Manor Drug Stores (1975) firmly embraced the doctrine that the last clause of rule 10b–5 ("in connection with the purchase or sale of any security") required the plaintiff to be a purchaser or seller of securities in order to state a rule 10b–5 violation. This doctrine, first set forth in the early case of Birnbaum v. Newport Steel Corp. (1952), is generally known as the "Birnbaum doctrine." *Blue Chip* was the first of the famous decisions by the United States Supreme Court limiting the growth of rule 10b–5; some of the language and argument in Justice Rehnquist's opinion appears to show blatant and open hostility to expansive constructions of rule 10b–5 adopted by lower federal courts; indeed this opinion signalled the end of the era of uncontrolled growth of that rule.

(5) *Rule 10b–5 as a Regulator of Corporate Publicity.* The *Birnbaum* rule requires that the plaintiff be a purchaser or seller of shares. There is no similar limitation on defendants; a person may violate rule 10b–5 even though he or she neither purchases nor sells a security. If a person issues a false or misleading statement that might cause reasonable investors to rely and thereby purchase or sell the corporation's securities, that person has violated rule 10b–5. *Texas Gulf Sulphur* applied this principle to a corporate press release, even though in that case it appeared that the misstatements were based on simple negligence. Scienter is now clearly required under *Hochfelder* and *Aaron* (see the beginning of this section).

The Supreme Court considered the problem of the false press release in Basic, Inc. v. Levinson (1988). The corporation was engaged in delicate and long-continuing merger negotiations; during this period it issued three public statements denying that it was engaged in such negotiations. The court adopted the materiality standard of TSC Industries v. Northway (see § 13.10 of this Nutshell) for purposes of rule 10b–5, but noted that the application of this standard to preliminary merger discussions was not "self-evident." Lower courts had established an "agreement in principle" standard that viewed negotiations prior to such an agreement as being immaterial; this view, the lower courts had suggested, produced a simple bright line standard, ensured confidentiality of sensitive preliminary negotiations, and did not overwhelm the investor with excessively detailed and trivial information. The Supreme Court, however, rejected this test in favor of a fact-sensitive consideration of the significance the reasonable investor would place on the withheld or misrepresented information, a test that is consistent with *Northway*, but provides little practical guidance to corporations faced with the decision of what to say about ongoing preliminary negotiations. This issue is one of the more troubling practical problems in this area today.

Under *Texas Gulf* and *Basic,* individual shareholders who relied on the misleading press release may recover damages from the corporation. The potential liability to the corporation as a result of a misleading press release may be very substantial. In the merger negotiation situation involved in *Basic,* for example, all persons who sold shares after the denial and before the formal announcement of the merger are potential plaintiffs. It is in part for this reason that lower courts (prior to *Basic*) were reluctant to brand potentially misleading denials of preliminary merger negotiations as violations of rule 10b–5. Justice White's dissenting opinion in *Basic* questions not only the fraud on the market theory adopted in that case but also the willingness of the court to impose liability under rule 10b–5 on an issuer when it was neither a purchaser nor a seller of securities.

§ 14.18 Section 16(b) of the Securities Exchange Act of 1934

Section 16(b) of the Securities Exchange Act of 1934 is an *in terrorem* provision designed to prevent specified persons from trading in a corporation's securities on an in-and-out basis on the strength of inside information. The following comments outline the scope of this statutory liability:

(1) Unlike rule 10b–5, section 16(b) is only applicable to corporations with a class of securities registered under section 12 of the Securities Exchange Act—that is to corporations (i) with securities traded on a national securities exchange or (ii) with assets of more than $5,000,000 and more than 500 shareholders of record of any class of equity security.

(2) Section 16(b) is only applicable to specified persons, namely officers, directors, and ten per cent shareholders of the issuer. Rule 10b–5 may be applicable to employees of financial printers, geologists, secretaries and others.

(3) Section 16(b) is applicable only if there is an offsetting purchase-and-sale or sale-and-purchase of an equity security of the issuer within any six-month period. For example, if there is a sale on January 1, section 16(b) is applicable if there is an offsetting purchase made at any time from six months before to six months after the sale. The sequence of the transactions or the fact that different certificates are involved, is irrelevant. However, a transaction on July 2, six months and one day after the original transaction on January 1, cannot be matched.

(4) The words "purchase" and "sale" are construed broadly. A gift may be a sale, as may be a redemption, conversion or a simple exchange of shares pursuant to a merger or consolidation. The grant of a warrant may be a purchase, a conversion may also be a purchase of the conversion securities, and so forth. The test is not a dictionary one; rather the definition that is usually stated is that a transaction will be considered a "purchase" or a "sale" for purposes of section 16(b) if it is of a kind that can possibly lend itself to the speculation encompassed by section 16(b). Under this test, commentators and lower courts

have struggled with whether all sorts of transactions, such as recapitalizations, exchanges, conversions, mergers, puts, and calls should be considered "purchases" or "sales."

(5) Actual use of inside information is not a prerequisite for section 16(b) liability. Even a sale for entirely justifiable reasons—e.g. unexpected medical expenses—will trigger section 16(b) if there has been an offsetting transaction within the six-month period.

(6) Profits are payable to the corporation. However, if the corporation fails to take steps to recover the profit, any shareholder may bring suit. It is not necessary that the shareholder have owned shares when either of the transactions took place.

(7) Profits are computed by comparing the highest sale price with the lowest purchase price during any relevant six month period, the next highest sale price with the next lowest purchase price, and so forth. In this computation, all loss transactions are ignored and any individual transaction may be matched only once (though a single large purchase may be broken up and partially matched against two or more sales that occurred at different times). The purpose is to squeeze out all possible profits from the transaction. It is possible to have a substantial loss in a trading account and yet have an equally substantial section 16(b) profit under this method of computation. The United States Supreme Court has never passed on this rather draconian measure of recovery.

(8) All transactions by covered persons must be reported to the SEC and this information is published and is widely available. Certain attorneys regularly review all these filings in order to find section 16(b) violations. They are motivated by the attorneys' fees that may be awarded in a successful section 16(b) suit. Suits brought by these attorneys in the name of nominal shareholder plaintiffs (who need not be shareholders at the time either of the purchase

or of the sale) may be champertous, but are the principal enforcement device of section 16(b). As a result, it is unlikely that a violation of section 16(b) will escape detection.

(9) The Securities and Exchange Commission has authority to exempt classes of transactions from section 16(b). Historically, it has exercised this power sparingly, creating exemptions that tended to be narrowly drawn to cover specific situations. In 1989, however, the SEC published proposed regulations that are of a much broader and more comprehensive nature.

(10) Like rule 10b–5, the jurisdiction of section 16(b) suits is exclusively federal.

The foregoing statement of principles does not explain the substantial volume of section 16(b) litigation that has occurred despite that section's apparent automatic liability. The United States Supreme Court has struggled with the application of section 16(b) to takeover situations where an unsuccessful aggressor acquires over ten per cent of the target's shares and then sells that interest or has it "merged out" within six months thereafter. In Reliance Electric Co. v. Emerson Electric Co. (1972), the Court held that a 13.2 per cent shareholder could dispose of its holding by first selling 3.2 per cent subject to section 16(b) and thereafter dispose of the balance free of section 16(b) since it was then less than a ten per cent shareholder. In Kern County Land Co. v. Occidental Petroleum Corp. (1973), in a complex series of transactions, the Court refused to treat either an "involuntary" merger or an option to sell as "sales" triggering section 16(b). And in Foremost–McKesson, Inc. v. Provident Securities Co. (1976), the Court finally "solved" the application of section 16(b) to the unsuccessful tender offeror by holding that the initial purchase that puts the aggressor over ten per cent was not a section 16(b) purchase. In Blau v. Lehman (1962), the Supreme Court considered the circumstances in which transactions by a partnership not itself a ten per cent holder may violate section 16(b) because one of the partners was a director of the issuer. The test in such a case is whether the partnership "deputized" the partner to represent the partnership on the board.

The purchase and sale matched under section 16(b) must both generally be of the same class of equity security. There is no meaningful basis, for example, for matching a sale of common with a purchase of preferred, though there is at least one judicial opinion in which such a matching was attempted. However, if the preferred is convertible into common and is trading at or close to the conversion price, matching may be permitted since the two securities are then trading as substantial economic equivalents.

People do not knowingly violate section 16(b); most of the violations appear to be a result of ignorance rather than the actual misuse of inside information. Most inadvertent violations probably are a result of the failure to appreciate how broadly the words "purchase" and "sale" may be construed. Corporations subject to this section usually distribute periodic warnings about the responsibility of officers and directors under the securities laws, including section 16(b); despite such warnings, inadvertent violations of this section continue to occur.

Despite its shortcomings and erratic imposition of liability, section 16(b) has been effective in eliminating the in-and-out trading evil that was thought to exist prior to 1934.

§ 14.19 Transfer of Control

For purposes of this section, a "controlling shareholder" is a person who owns either an outright majority of the shares or a minority of the shares but the balance is so fragmented that he or she has working control and can deliver such control to a purchaser of the shares. The simplest method of "delivering" control in this sense is by the seriatim resignation of directors and their successive replacement by nominees of the purchaser.

When a controlling shareholder sells his or her interest to third persons, something more than the property represented by the shares is being sold. The sale also involves transfer of control over a going business in which other persons—minority shareholders, senior security holders, and creditors—may have a substantial interest. Shares owned by a controlling shareholder command a premium over other shares simply because they represent not only a property interest in the shares but also the power to control the business, to designate the corporate officers, and so forth. This premium is usually referred to as the "control premium."

Generally a controlling shareholder may sell his or her shares for whatever price he or she can obtain in the same way as any other property. However, the courts recognize that the seller and buyer are not the only persons interested in this transaction and have imposed duties on the selling shareholder with respect to the purchaser. The "looting" cases are a clear illustration. Several cases have imposed liability on a controlling shareholder when, without investigation, he or she has sold his or her shares to unscrupulous third persons who thereafter "loot" the corporation by stealing corporate assets. The controlling shareholder has a duty to make a reasonable investigation of potential purchasers and not to transfer control to outsiders under circumstances that might awaken suspicion that the outsiders plan to wrongfully convert the assets of the corporation, or to use them to pay the purchase price. Danger signs include, (1) an excessive price for the shares willingly paid, (2) excessive interest in the liquid and readily salable assets owned by the corporation, (3) insistence by the buyers on an immediate transfer of control, (4) insistence by the buyers that the liquid assets be made available to the purchaser immediately, as by the delivery of certificates for negotiable securities endorsed in blank at the closing, (5) little interest being indicated by the purchaser in the operation of the corporation's business, and (6) insistence by the purchaser that the transaction be handled with dispatch. Since the liability is based on negligence, the recovery may be based on the damage suffered, i.e., the amount looted, rather than on the purchase price paid or the amount of the control premium.

Outside of the looting cases, courts have not evolved consistent theories about the propriety of a controlling shareholder receiving a "control premium." Some cases in which the controlling shareholder has been compelled to share the control premium with minority shareholders contain broad statements to the effect that a director owes a fiduciary duty to the corporation and to the minority shareholders. E.g., Perlman v. Feldmann (1955). Such statements are little more than make-weight since they do not explain when the premium may be recovered and when it may not. Law review commentators have put forward theoretical arguments in both directions. Some have suggested that all control premiums in good conscience should be shared with all shareholders. These commentators essentially argue that since shares of stock are fungible, the control premium represents the pure power to control which should, if anything, be a corporate asset available to all shareholders. The cases, however, have not adopted this position. Other commentators, particularly those from the Chicago School of law and economics, have argued that most sale of control transactions are beneficial from the standpoint of the buyer, the seller, the minority interests that remain, and by the economy in general, and that a mandatory sharing requirement would render impractical many desirable transfers of control. Many cases, including virtually all recent ones, have permitted the selling shareholder to keep the premium.

A form of control premium is also involved in cases such as Honigman v. Green Giant Co. (1962), where the holders of a class of voting shares agreed to share the voting power with the holders of a larger class of nonvoting common in exchange for a larger slice of the "equity." Such transactions have been approved where the premium is not excessive, or to put it a different way, where the transaction seems fair. On the other hand, the decision in Jones v. H. F. Ahmanson & Co. (1969), though involving unique facts, contains language that leans toward acceptance of the theory that control premiums are inherently improper, though the case may be viewed as a type of unfair freeze-out or squeeze-out. In this case, the majority shareholders of a savings and loan association created a holding company and exchanged their shares for holding company shares. Minority shareholders in the association were not permitted also to exchange their shares for holding company shares. The holding company then made a public offering and a public market was created for the holding company's shares from which the minority shareholders of the association were precluded while any market for the savings and loan shares dried up. The court held that this conduct violated the majority's fiduciary responsibility to the minority, and that recovery might be based either on the appraised value of the shares when the holding company was created or the value of a "derived block" of the holding company shares on the date litigation was commenced.

Some older cases have permitted the recovery of a control premium on a theory of "corporate action" or usurpation of corporate opportunity. If the purchaser first offers to buy the assets of the corporation at an attractive price, but the controlling shareholder suggests that the transaction be recast in the form of a purchase of the controlling shares, a reasonable argument may be made that the favorable sale opportunity was a corporate opportunity belonging to all the shareholders rather than an opportunity of the majority shareholder to sell controlling shares. The facts of Perlman v. Feldmann arguably present this pattern, though the opinion itself only partially articulates this theory. Other older cases adopt the theory that the control premium is for the sale of a corporate office rather than a sale of stock, and since a sale of office is against public policy, the excess payment may be recovered by the corporation for the benefit of the minority shareholders. The problem with this argument is that it proves too much—all sales of control stock at a premium accompanied by a transfer of control may be analyzed in this fashion. This argument is most likely to be accepted either where an additional payment is conditioned on the immediate transfer of offices or where the selling shareholders own a miniscule proportion of the outstanding shares and the sales agreement carefully provides for a seriatim resignation of directors. Petition of Caplan (1964) is the leading case accepting this argument. In that case the selling shareholders owned only 3 per cent of the outstanding shares.

Liability for a control premium has also sometimes been based on a theory of nondisclosure or misrepresentation. In these cases a controlling shareholder contracts to sell more shares than he or she owns, planning to purchase the additional shares from other shareholders. If the controlling shareholder purchases such shares from other shareholders without disclosing the existence of the resale contract, the controlling shareholder may be liable under state or federal law (though an argument may also be made that the resale opportunity is not material since it was only made to the controlling shareholder). (See §§ 14.16, 14.17 of this Nutshell.) However, frontal attacks on sale of control premiums under rule 10b–5 have been unsuccessful because of the *Birnbaum* principle that the plaintiff must be a purchaser or seller of securities. (See § 14.17 of this Nutshell.)

Where a control premium is recoverable, courts have permitted either the corporation or the minority shareholders to recover, depending on the theory adopted. If the theory of recovery is corporate opportunity, corporate action, or sale of corporate office, logically the corporation should recover. If the theory is misrepresentation or violation of rule 10b–5, the minority shareholders should recover. Since a corporate recovery enriches the purchaser paying the premium, however, the leading case of Perlman v. Feldmann permitted recovery directly by the minority shareholders, even though the theory adopted apparently was corporate opportunity. The court argued that the purchaser who paid the control premium should not be permitted to share indirectly in the recovery, which would be the case if the premium were simply paid over to the corporation. This holding creates some anomalous consequences and appears to be inconsistent with the substantive theory adopted by the court in that case.

§ 14.20 Indemnification by the Corporation

"Indemnification" by the corporation simply means the corporation reimburses a defendant who is a corporate officer or director for (a) expenses incurred in defending against a claim or prosecution, particularly legal fees but including other expenses as well, and (b) amounts paid in settlement of suits or to satisfy a judgment entered against (or fines imposed upon a conviction of) the defendant officer or director.

There are basic policy questions posed by indemnification. Policy justifications for indemnification of officers and directors include: (1) it encourages innocent directors to resist unjust charges, (2) it encourages responsible persons to accept the position of director, and (3) it discourages groundless shareholder litigation. In the modern era, the fear of derivative litigation, and the costs of defending such suits, is so great that most outside directors refuse to serve unless they receive protection from the corporation.

There can be little objection to indemnification of expenses if a director is absolved of liability. However, indemnification against many kinds of wrongful acts clearly violates public policy. Perhaps the clearest example is attempted indemnification against liabilities under section 16(b) of the Securities Exchange Act of 1934. Such indemnification would create complete circularity, and would obviously vitiate the policy underlying that section. Indemnification should not be permitted whenever the defendant is found guilty of some sort of wrongful misconduct and is held liable to a third person in damages for such misconduct. In such situations indemnification of expenses may be as objectionable as indemnification against the judgments themselves. Further, serious doubts may arise as to the propriety of indemnification of substantial amounts paid in settlement (since such settlements may reflect wrongdoing); on the other hand, a small payment to settle a nuisance suit would seem clearly to be appropriate and desirable, and should not bar indemnification either of the amount paid in settlement or the expenses of defending the suit.

State statutes attempt to work out a compromise of these various competing considerations. Modern indemnification provisions developed in the Delaware statute and in Chapter 8 of the Revised Model Business Corporation Act (which itself is a recodification of substantial amendments made in 1980 to earlier indemnification statutes) have been particularly influential. However, a number of states have only very general statutes authorizing indemnification which give little indication of the outer limits.

Under the modern statutes a defendant is entitled to indemnification as a matter of statutory right if he or she "is successful on the merits or otherwise." [RMBCA § 8.52.] Under this provision, a defendant who prevails because of the statute of limitations or because of pleading defects is as entitled to indemnification as the defendant who prevails on the merits. This result has been justified on the theory that otherwise a defendant with a valid procedural defense would have to go to the expense of litigating the merits of the claim in order to establish a right of indemnification; it may also be based on the implicit premise that a defendant with a valid procedural defense has a high probability of winning on the merits as well. In other situations, indemnification is permitted (but as a matter of discretion, not as a matter of right) only if the defendant director "(1) conducted himself in good faith and (2) he reasonably believed: (i) in the case of conduct in his official capacity with the corporation, that his conduct was in its best interests; and (ii) in all other cases, that his conduct was at least not opposed to its best interests." [RMBCA § 8.51(a)(1) and (2).] Further, indemnification may be permitted against criminal fines if the defendant "had no reasonable cause to believe his conduct was unlawful." [RMBCA § 8.51(a)(3)] These broad grants of authority to make discretionary indemnification, however, are limited by RMBCA § 8.52(d), which prohibits indemnification of judgments if (a) the director was adjudged liable *to the corporation*, or (b) the director was adjudged liable "on the basis that personal benefit was improperly received." However, as a further qualification to this qualification, any director denied indemnification at any time may seek a court order that he or she "is fairly and reasonably entitled to indemnification in view of all the relevant circumstances, whether or not" the standards of section 8.51 were met. [RMBCA § 8.54.]

No presumption that a person acted in bad faith is made merely because litigation is settled or plea of *nolo contendere* is entered. Even a judgment or a criminal conviction entered against a director is not conclusive that the defendant is ineligible for permissive indemnification. [RMBCA § 8.51(c).] Of course, a criminal conviction or civil judgment will usually involve a determination of bad faith and prevent indemnification.

Judgments as to entitlement to indemnification under these standards may be made (a) by disinterested directors either as a board or as a committee, (b) by the shareholders, or (c) by independent legal counsel in a written opinion. [RMBCA § 8.55.] Precise rules as to how these decisions are to be made and who may select a committee of the board or the independent legal counsel are set forth.

Section 8.53 of the Revised Model Business Corporation Act, and the statutes of a substantial number of states, permit a corporation to make advances to pay expenses prior to the final termination of the proceeding. The right to make advances is of vital importance as a practical matter, since many directors would find it difficult and unacceptable to advance sizable sums on their own behalf for an extended period. Further, an effective defense may require employment of skilled counsel at the commencement of the proceeding. To deny all advances might therefore create an invidious discrimination against less wealthy directors. If the director is ultimately found not to be entitled to indemnification, of course, a defendant may be compelled to repay such advances, though there does not appear to be a recent litigated example of this occurring.

Section 8.58 of the Revised Model Business Corporation Act makes the provisions described above exclusive as to scope of the right of indemnification. In other words, it is itself defining the scope of public policy. However, section 8.58 does not prohibit corporations from adopting supplementary provisions consistent with the statutory policies, such as a bylaw provision committing the corporation to make indemnification in every situation where it is permitted to make discretionary indemnification. The major purpose of such a supplementary provision is to create a right of indemnification wherever it is permitted, so that defendants who may be indemnified consistently with public policy under the statute are automatically entitled to indemnification even though a change in control may have occurred. On the other hand, the statutory indemnification provisions of Delaware and of many other states expressly do not purport to be exclusive. The trend appears to be in the direction of the Delaware approach and away from the Model Act approach of making the policies embodied in the statute an exclusive statement of public policy. In these states, the draftsmen of corporate bylaws are free to adopt innovative indemnification provisions, subject, of course, to the possibility that courts may later find that they exceed the unwritten public policy considerations that underlie this entire area.

The Revised Model Business Corporation Act also deals with technical questions about the scope of indemnification of officers and agents, and the peculiar problem of the rights of a director who is also an officer or agent. [RMBCA § 8.56.] It also recognizes a distinction between decisions *determining* that a director has met the standards for discretionary indemnification (a quasi-judicial determination of good faith, etc.) and decisions *authorizing* such indemnification (a business determination that limited corporate resources should be expended for indemnification rather than for other purposes). [RMBCA § 8.55.]

Section 16.22(b) requires that discretionary indemnification or decisions to grant advances for expenses be reported to shareholders.

§ 14.21 Liability Insurance

Insurance against directors' and officers' liabilities (usually called "D & O" insurance) is of increasing importance in providing meaningful protection to corporate directors. It provides useful but limited protection against costs and liabilities for negligence, for misconduct not involving dishonesty or knowing bad faith, and for false or misleading statements in disclosure documents. Increasingly, however, it has become important because it also covers amounts that the corporation may be obligated to pay to directors under the indemnification statutes and provisions in articles of incorporation or bylaws, and therefore provides assurance that funds for indemnification will be available even if the corporation is in financial difficulty or in reorganization.

Companies writing D & O liability insurance are not eleemosynary institutions; they establish premiums in light of the magnitude of the contemplated risks. During the middle 1980s as perceived risks grew, the cost of D & O insurance escalated rapidly; there was a "D & O insurance crisis." Premiums were increased, often several fold while maximum limits of coverage were simultaneously being reduced. This "crisis" has passed, and such insurance is generally available in the 1990s, though at costs that reflect the increased risks of the modern litigious climate. During this "crisis" several states enacted legislation to enable corporations to provide protection to outside directors independently of the traditional D & O insurance policy—"captive" insurance companies, for example, that insure only a single company, or escrow or trust arrangements for the benefit of officers and directors. During the same period, the indemnification provisions of many statutes were also broadened to increase the protection available to officers and directors.

Insurance companies write policies that cover only insurable risks; in modern policies there are numerous express exceptions and exclusions. Thus wrongful misconduct, dishonest acts, acts in bad faith with knowledge thereof, or violations of statutes such as section 16(b) are specifically excluded, and in any event are not insurable events. Also excluded are actions entered into for personal profit or gain or suits based on claims of libel or slander. There is also an exclusion for failing to disclose contingent liabilities in the application for insurance. Most policies also contain a co-insurance feature that requires the insureds to share a portion of the risk; a typical co-insurance clause states that the insurer agrees to pay 95 per cent of any loss that is incurred and the insured warrants that the additional 5 per cent will not be covered by alternative insurance. During the insurance "crisis" described above, a number of these provisions were tightened to narrow the risks faced by insurers.

D & O insurance is purchased by the corporation to cover all its officers and directors. The cost of the premium is shared: a typical pattern is for the corporation to pay 90 per cent and the covered persons 10 per cent. This division in cost reflects the fact that D & O insurance protects the corporation's obligation to indemnify officers and directors under statute or bylaw provisions, as well as providing protection to the officers and directors themselves.

Many state statutes specifically permit corporations to purchase D & O insurance. [RMBCA § 8.57.] Where there is no statutory authorization, the power to purchase such insurance is probably implicit in the corporate power to provide executive compensation. Corporate bylaws also specifically authorize the purchase of such insurance.

§ 14.22   Liability to Creditors

Generally, the liabilities of officers and directors discussed in this chapter run to the corporation rather than to creditors. Certainly, in the absence of insolvency, a corporate creditor has an adequate remedy against the corporation itself, and there is no reason to permit a creditor to proceed also against an officer or director who has acted wrongfully. Where the corporation is insolvent, the usual recourse of a corporate creditor is through a receiver or bankruptcy trustee; to permit a direct suit by a creditor against a director or officer in effect would permit the creditor to obtain a priority or other advantage over other creditors. Of course, bankruptcy trustees, receivers, and assignees for the benefit of creditors are charged with collecting the assets of the corporation and distributing them equitably among the creditors; among the assets may be claims against directors or officers. Basically, however, the representative of creditors is suing on behalf of the corporation, and the corporation or specific shareholders are the persons in whose favor the duties set forth in this chapter run.

[For unfamiliar terms see the Glossary]

CHAPTER FIFTEEN

INSPECTION OF BOOKS AND RECORDS

§ 15.1 Inspection by Directors and Shareholders Compared

Both shareholders and directors have the right to inspect corporate books and records in certain circumstances. However, the inspection right of a director is considerably broader than the right of a shareholder and rests on an entirely different theoretical base. A director is a manager of the corporation and owes certain duties to it and to all the shareholders. Indeed, a director may be liable for negligent mismanagement if he or she does not adequately acquaint himself or herself with the business and affairs of the corporation. For this reason, some cases state that the directors' right to inspect books and records is absolute and unqualified. However, as with many supposedly absolute principles, there are exceptions. Courts have sometimes denied inspection rights to directors where it was clear that the director was acting with manifestly improper motives and adequate information prepared by unbiased persons was otherwise available to the director. Such cases, however, are exceptional and unusual. The Corporate Governance Project recognizes that the directors' right of inspection is qualified; it states that a court may refuse to enforce that right if it is established "that the information is not reasonably related to the performance of directoral functions and duties" or that the director is likely to misuse the information and that misuse cannot be prevented by a protective order.

The right of a shareholder to inspect books and records, on the other hand, is considerably narrower. A shareholder of course has a financial interest in the corporation, and the common law recognizes a right to inspect books and records to protect this interest. However, because the shareholder is not charged with management responsibility and is not subject to broad duties, the right to inspect is available only for a "proper purpose," and is otherwise hedged with restrictions. The balance of this chapter deals exclusively with the more limited inspection rights of shareholders.

§ 15.2   Common Law and Statutory Rights of Inspection by Shareholders

A right of shareholders to inspect books and records of the corporation may arise from several different sources. Corporation statutes grant a right of inspection in some circumstances and these statutes form the bulk of the discussion in the balance of this chapter. In addition, a shareholder who is in litigation against the corporation may have the same rights of discovery as any other litigant. Some state statutes require corporations to make reports or submit tax statements that are then available for inspection by shareholders. And, of course, if information must be made publicly available, any shareholder may examine it. Finally, in some states there may exist a residual common law right of inspection that has not been superseded by the statutory right of inspection.

From the standpoint of the corporation, a shareholder's demand to inspect books and records is almost always viewed as a hostile and threatening act. Before the statutory right of inspection was created, the practice developed of denying all inspection requests out-of-hand and compelling the shareholder to litigate, relying on whatever pretext may be available for the denial. The first statutes defining a statutory right of inspection were enacted in an effort to combat this attitude. The most notable feature of these statutes was that they combined a restatement of the common law right of inspection with penalties imposed on corporate officers with custody of the books and records who arbitrarily refuse to permit proper examination of books and records. Nevertheless, because of the possibility that inspection rights may be abused, these statutes retain the "proper purpose" standard of the common law.

The statutory right of inspection in many states is available to persons whose shareholdings meet certain objective criteria; section 52 of the 1969 Model Act provision, for example, extends the statutory right to persons (1) who have been shareholders of record for at least six months prior to the demand or (2) who own at least five per cent of the outstanding shares of the corporation. Some states use different numbers but the principle is the same. As indicated above, a person who meets these objective criteria must also state a "proper purpose" for the inspection in his or her written demand. However, under many statutes, the burden of proof as to proper purpose shifts if the shareholder meets the objective criteria and alleges a proper purpose, so that the corporation then has the burden of showing the plaintiff did not in fact have a proper purpose; shareholders who do not meet these objective criteria continue to have the common law burden of establishing that their purpose is a proper one.

Under the old Model Act, a corporate officer who improperly refused to grant a statutory right of inspection was liable for a penalty equal to ten per cent of the value of the shares owned by the shareholder. Many state statutes used a similar *in terrorem* approach: several states made the penalty one or two per cent of the value of the plaintiff's shares, others imposed a maximum penalty of $500; still others imposed a per diem penalty of $25 or some other amount. Some states required the officer to pay the litigation expenses, including attorneys' fees, of the shareholder who was forced to sue in order to vindicate his or her right to inspect. As a practical matter, these provisions were not widely invoked, though there are a handful of instances in which penalties of fairly substantial amounts were actually imposed on recalcitrant officers. Of course, the number of litigated cases may not describe the informal impact that these penal provisions had, since the potential of a substantial penalty may have caused some corporate officers to grant inspection rights they might otherwise have resisted for fear of the consequences.

The Revised Model Business Corporation Act rejects the penalty approach, though it does contain provisions designed to assure that the right to inspect is made available on a timely basis. First, like the statutes of several states, section 16.02(a) requires a shareholder desiring to inspect books and records to give five days written demand in advance. Second, section 16.02(b) describes in considerable detail the types of records a shareholder may examine. Third, in an effort to reduce "fishing expeditions," section 16.02(c) requires the demand to be in "good faith" and for a "proper purpose" and that the shareholder define with reasonable particularity his or her purpose and establish that the records sought are "directly connected" with that purpose. Section 16.04(b) provides for direct judicial action to enforce a right of inspection under section 16.02; the court is directed to dispose of such a case on an "expedited basis." Further, if the court orders inspection, under section 6.04(c), it must order the corporation to pay the shareholders' costs of the proceeding, including reasonable attorney's fees unless the corporation can prove "that it refused inspection in good faith because it had a reasonable basis for doubt about the right of the shareholder to inspect the records demanded." This is a corporate obligation, not an obligation of the officer with custody of the books and records, as was the case under older inspection statutes.

§ 15.3 Corporate Records: What May Be Examined?

Business corporation acts require each corporation to keep minutes of meetings, books and records of account, and information about record shareholders so that an appropriate voting list of shareholders may be created. The language of these statutes varies widely from state to state. Section 16.01 of the Revised Model Business Corporation Act is a carefully drafted provision that is designed not to impose unreasonable record-keeping requirements on corporations. In addition to a record of shareholders [section 16.01(c)], it generally requires keeping of "records" of actions taken at meetings rather than "minutes" of meetings; it also requires only "appropriate accounting records" to be maintained rather than the older language of "books and records of account." RMBCA §§ 16.01(a), (b). Of course, many corporations may find it necessary to keep much more detailed and elaborate records: section 16.01 sets forth the irreducible minimum. In a bow to the computer age, section 16.01(d) of the Revised Model Business Corporation Act, and the statutes of many states, permit these records to be kept on tape or in machine-readable form capable of being converted into written form in a reasonable time.

Under most state statutes, the right to inspect extends not only to enumerated records but to corporate records in general. Case law has tended to be expansive in this regard. One case authorized the examination of "records, books of account, receipts, vouchers, bills and all other documents evidencing the financial condition of the corporation." Another case authorized the examination of the books of a subsidiary controlled by the corporation. Corporate contracts and even the correspondence of the chief executive officer have been held to be subject to inspection in appropriate cases. The right generally extends to all relevant records necessary to inform the shareholder about corporate matters in which he or she has a legitimate interest. The corporation cannot defeat this right by offering summaries, substitute papers, or financial statements prepared by the corporation's auditors.

Section 16.02(b) of the Revised Model Business Corporation Act is considerably more restrictive than most statutes, since it contains an exclusive enumeration of what records may be examined. Shareholders may inspect only excerpts of minutes, the accounting records, and the record of shareholders under this section. This does not mean, however, that all records not described in that section are immune from inspection. Rather the shareholder seeking such information must persuade the court that he or she has a nonstatutory right to the documents under section 16.-02(c)(2) of the Revised Model Business Corporation Act.

§ 15.4   What Is a "Proper Purpose"?

The basic test of inspection by shareholders is a "proper purpose." A "proper purpose" means a purpose that is reasonably relevant to the shareholder's interest as a shareholder. A purpose is proper under this definition if it is directed toward obtaining information bearing upon or seeking to protect the shareholder's interest and that of other shareholders of the corporation. A purpose to determine the worth of the shareholder's holdings is a proper purpose. So is a purpose of seeking reasons for a decline in profits. So is a purpose of ascertaining whether there has been mismanagement or alarming transactions.

A corporation cannot deny the right to inspect by arguing that the shareholder has an improper purpose simply because he or she is unfriendly to management. An improper purpose is one with ulterior or vindictive motives. Obvious examples are general harassment of management or a desire to obtain trade secrets for a competitor. Probably mere idle curiosity is not a proper purpose, though it is a rare shareholder who cannot allege a more specific purpose.

Some courts appear to be more willing than others to countenance "fishing expeditions."

Obviously, substantial and difficult factual issues arise as to the shareholder's true purpose. The issue may come down to predominant motive and intent. The burden of proof, discussed earlier, may be significant. It is probably fair to conclude that it is always easy to couch an inspection demand in the form of a purpose that is proper, and that careful coaching of testimony may lead to the conclusion that the purpose for inspection is proper, while an outspoken or unusually forthright witness may run into difficulty. The mere fact that a shareholder making a demand to inspect books or records is a competitor of the corporation does not necessarily make the demand improper, though it may raise suspicions. In this type of situation, some courts have imposed restrictions on the use or distribution of the information being produced, apparently without express statutory authority to do so. Section 16.04(d) of the Revised Model Business Corporation expressly endorses this practice.

§ 15.5   Who Is Entitled to Inspect?

A person who is a beneficial owner of shares but is not the record owner has a common law right of inspection, and depending on the wording of the specific statute, may have a statutory right as well. See RMBCA § 16.02(f). Pledgees, judgment creditors, and holders of voting trust certificates also have a statutory right to inspect under the statutes of many states.

Section 16.03 of the Revised Model Act makes clear that an inspecting shareholder may be accompanied by an attorney or agent. Further, the right to inspect entails, if reasonable, the right to obtain copies of the inspected documents; the corporation may impose a reasonable charge for providing those copies. While many courts doubtless would require corporations to provide copies as a matter of common sense, express provisions covering these commonly recurring issues seem desirable.

§ 15.6 Inspection of Shareholders Lists

Every corporation must maintain "a record of its shareholders, in a form that permits preparation of a list of the names and addresses of all shareholders in alphabetical order by class of shares showing the number and class of shares held by each." [RMBCA § 16.01(c).] This record is subject to the statutory or common law right of inspection possessed by every shareholder. In contrast, the voting list compiled immediately before the meeting (see § 9.3 of this Nutshell) is automatically open to inspection by any shareholder without any proof of proper purpose before and during the shareholders meeting. There has been a substantial volume of litigation over shareholders' lists in publicly held corporations since such lists are, to quote a colorful phrase, "the line of scrimmage for contests involving incumbent management, dissident shareholders, acquisition-minded corporations, and those who have been described in current fiction as 'corporate raiders'." Also, a list of names and addresses of numerous well-to-do persons (as shareholders are likely to be) is itself valuable, and at least theoretically may be sought in order to sell it to mail solicitation firms. Indeed, some state statutes, including New York's, specifically provide that a shareholders' list need not be produced if the applicant has offered to sell or assisted another person in the sale or offering for sale of a shareholders' list within the preceding five years. This provision has been included in some statutes even though there appears to have been no recent reported incident of improper trafficking in such lists. Of course, the widespread use of nominees, street names, and book entry systems for recording ownership (see § 13.5 of this Nutshell) all greatly reduce the value of such a list from a commercial standpoint. On the other hand, many institutional investors regularly disclose their entire portfolios, so that considerable information about holdings of securities in specific companies by specific institutional investors is publicly available.

Much of the litigation dealing with shareholders' lists also involves the "proper purpose" test. Generally it has been held that it is a proper purpose to desire to communicate with other shareholders about matters of corporate concern: to solicit proxies, to initiate a proxy contest, to publicize mismanagement, to discuss a derivative suit, to discuss proposals of management, to form a protective committee, and the like. It has also been held to be a proper purpose to communicate to other shareholders an offer to purchase the shares of the corporation. Courts probably tend to be more lenient in granting access to shareholders' lists than to other books and records. However, it has been held that it is not a proper purpose to seek the list in order to sell to the shareholders securities of unrelated corporations. Similarly, in a Viet Nam war era case, it was held that a purpose to seek the list in order to communicate one's own social or political views to shareholders was not a proper purpose.

Where a corporation is large enough to be registered under section 12 of the Securities Exchange Act of 1934 (500 shareholders of record of any class and $5,000,000 of assets), the federal proxy regulations provide an alternative basis for an inspection of the shareholders' list. Rule 14a–7 requires a corporation either to supply a shareholders' list or to mail solicitations to shareholders on behalf of a shareholder upon payment of the postage by that shareholder. The corporation will usually elect the latter alternative so that an insurgent faction may have to seek to obtain the production of the shareholders' list under the applicable state law. The insurgent faction needs the list (rather than merely communicating with shareholders) in order to identify the large shareholders and make personal contact with them. However, a solicitation of shareholders asking them to join in a request for a shareholders' list (in order to meet the 5 per cent requirement of state law) is itself a solicitation under the proxy rules, and requires filing with the Securities and Exchange Commission if more than ten such solicitations are made. Studebaker Corp. v. Gittlin (1966).

§ 15.7 Financial Reports for Shareholders

Corporations that have a class of securities registered under section 12 of the Securities Exchange Act of 1934 must provide shareholders with annual reports that contain audited financial statements. Such corporations also must provide data on a quarterly basis.

In most states, there is no requirement that other corporations provide any financial information to shareholders, though some states provide that tax returns or annual reports filed with state officials may be inspected by shareholders.

Section 16.20 of the Revised Model Business Corporation Act requires all corporations to provide at least some financial data to shareholders. Because many small corporations do not have auditors or accountants, the requirement is carefully phrased so as not to impose unreasonable burdens on small corporations. However, section 16.20(a) requires a corporation that prepares financial statements on the basis of generally accepted accounting principles to prepare annual financial reports to shareholders on the same basis.

[For unfamiliar terms see the Glossary]

CHAPTER SIXTEEN

DIVIDENDS, DISTRIBUTIONS, AND REDEMPTIONS

§ 16.1 Cash or Property Dividends and Distributions

The profits of a business corporation—the purpose or goal of such a corporation—may be accumulated by the corporation or paid out, in whole or in part, in the form of dividends. The decision whether or not to pay dividends rests in the hands of the board of directors of the corporation.

The dividend policy of a corporation depends in part on whether the corporation is publicly held or a close corporation. In the large publicly held corporation, dividends are usually paid on a periodic basis, in amounts that remain stable from period to period. Stability of dividend policy is maintained by such corporations because frequent changes— and any downward change—is interpreted by investors as indicating that the corporation has financial difficulties. Unpleasant surprises should be avoided. Many corporations will maintain a stable dividend even though current earnings are not sufficient to support the dividend in the hope that operations will improve in the future. Public shareholders, without effective voice in the management of the business, may look in part to the history of dividends by the corporation to determine whether to purchase shares of the corporation. Probably greater attention, however, is paid to the prospects of dividends in the future and to the hope that the market price of the shares will rise (which itself may be a function of the business prospects of the corporation).

In a closely held corporation that is taxed as a C corporation, on the other hand, the principal owners of the business usually prefer, for tax reasons, to distribute earnings in the form of salaries, interest, or rent to the principal shareholders rather than distribute them as dividends. See § 2.3 of this Nutshell.

The term "dividend" refers to distributions of earnings; where a distribution of capital (which may be in partial liquidation of the business of the corporation or simply a distribution of excess capital not needed in current operations) is made, the term "distribution" is more accurate than "dividend," though this usage is not uniform—e.g. it is not uncommon to refer to a "liquidating dividend" rather than a "liquidating distribution." The Revised Model Business Corporation Act does not generally use the word "dividend"; section 1.40(6) defines the term "distribution" to include all distributions of assets or debt by corporations to their shareholders on account of their shares without regard to their source, and, as described below (see § 16.6 of this Nutshell), provides a simple test for the validity of all distributions. Statutes of many states, however, do establish different legal tests for distributions of current or retained earnings on the one hand, and distributions of capital on the other.

Most discussions of dividends classify them into three categories: cash dividends, dividends-in-kind or property dividends, and share dividends (discussed in the following section). Cash and property dividends are true distributions by the corporation of assets or property whereas a share dividend is not. A cash dividend—the most common—as the name implies, divides cash (from legally available funds) among the shareholders. The amount may be expressed either as so many cents or dollars per share or as a percentage of the par or stated value of the shares. A property dividend is a division of assets other than cash of the declaring corporation among the shareholders. For obvious reasons, the property so divided is usually fungible; it may consist, for example, of shares of a subsidiary corporation or of a corporation in which the declaring corporation has an investment, or undivided fractional interests in an asset or a fund.

Most corporations that pay cash dividends do so on a quarterly or semi-annual basis. Such dividends are usually referred to as "regular" dividends. A special dividend is a one-shot, non-recurring payment that cannot be counted on to be paid again in a following year. Most property dividends are special dividends. A special dividend that accompanies the payment of a regular dividend is sometimes referred to as an "extra."

An informal or irregular payment may be a "dividend" for some purposes. For example, excessive payments in the form of salary, rent, or interest may be treated as a dividend for tax purposes. Such payments, of course, usually will not be proportional to share holdings.

§ 16.2 Share Dividends

A share dividend or stock dividend distributes additional shares of the declaring corporation among the shareholders. A share dividend is not a true dividend since no cash or property leaves the corporation; a distribution of additional shares does not reduce the real worth of the corporation or increase the real worth of the shareholder. Rather, a share dividend increases the number of ownership units outstanding without decreasing the corporation's assets. Share dividends, however, may adversely affect the rights of other classes of shares. A distribution of common shares to common shareholders does not affect the interest of any senior class of shares: the residual ownership is simply divided up into a larger number of units. The same may not be true of distributions of senior securities, since the increased number of shares may lead to a larger preferential right to cash or property dividends or a larger preference on liquidation, thereby adversely affecting the interests of holders of more junior securities.

Share dividends are usually declared on the same class of shares: additional common shares may be distributed to the common shareholders and, less commonly, additional preferred shares may be distributed to the preferred shareholders. However, this is not necessarily so; a holder of common shares may receive a dividend in the form of preferred shares, or vice versa. Such interclass distributions will almost always affect the interests of holders of both classes of shares.

Consider the practice of many publicly held corporations of declaring annual share dividends rather than cash dividends. As described above, such dividends do not reduce the aggregate assets of the corporation. If a shareholder receiving such a dividend sells the additional shares, he or she may view the transaction as involving essentially the same thing as a cash dividend, since the same number of shares are owned as before and the shareholder has, in addition, the cash received from the sale of the dividend shares. However, the shareholder who sells the dividend shares thereafter owns a slightly smaller percentage of the enterprise than he or she owned before the dividend. The dilution in such situations may be so slight as to be unimportant. But it is nevertheless a dilution. It is surprising that many people apparently are unaware that a share dividend is unlike property or cash dividends in this regard.

Where shares are publicly traded, a share dividend, other things being equal, will reduce the market price for each share proportionately; however, other things usually are not equal, and other factors may cause a price change which masks the decline attributable to the dividend. If no decline occurs, a small shareholder may sell his or her dividend shares for cash and yet have a diluted investment with undiminished market value.

A share dividend is often expressed as a ratio. Thus, a 20 percent distribution means that a shareholder receives a 20 percent increase—one additional share for each five shares held; a shareholder who owns less than five shares or a number of shares not divisible by five, will receive either a fractional share or "scrip," or at the election of the directors the fair value of the fractional share in cash. See RMBCA § 6.04. "Scrip" differs from fractional shares in that it grants no voting or dividend rights; it represents merely the right to a fraction of a full share and may be bought or sold so that a full share may be assembled from the rights to fractional shares. Fractional shares may also be created in other ways as well.

A share "dividend" and a share "split" are closely related. Indeed, a dividend can be readily envisioned as a small split. In states with par value statutes, however, such transactions are accounted for differently in the capital accounts of the corporation. A share dividend results in the transfer of an amount equal to the par value of the dividend shares being transferred from earned surplus (or some other surplus) to stated capital and increases that account by the par value of the new shares, while a "split" simply divides the shares into a greater number of shares and reduces proportionally the par value of those shares so that there is no change in the aggregate stated capital of the corporation. A share split, like a share dividend, does not decrease the real worth of the corporation. The Revised Model Business Corporation Act and the states that have eliminated the concept of par value generally do not distinguish between share dividends and splits. However, this distinction is recognized by the New York Stock Exchange in its *Listed Company Manual* which requires more realistic accounting treatment than provided in the corporation statutes. The *Manual* defines a "stock dividend" as the distribution of less than 25 per cent of the outstanding shares (calculated before the distribution) while a "stock split" is a distribution of 100 per cent or more of the outstanding shares. Distributions of between 25 per cent and 100 per cent are called "partial stock splits." The *Manual* also requires the capitalization of the full market value of share dividends (rather than merely the par value) but no capitalization of stock splits and warns against the use of the word "dividend" in connection with splits or partial stock splits.

A practical difference between stock dividends and stock splits may also exist in connection with the adjustment of dividend rates on shares on which a dividend or split has been announced. Since cash dividend rates are usually not adjusted for a share dividend, such a dividend may increase slightly the effective rate of dividend pay-outs. In other words, the dividend rate remains the same but the total number of shares against which that rate is applied has been increased. The dividend rate is usually adjusted in a stock split; for example, if a share of a corporation which regularly pays dividends of $1.00 per share is split two-for-one (i.e. each holder of 100 shares receives a certificate for another 100 shares and now owns 200 shares in all), the dividend on the split shares may be set at $0.55 cents per share, or an effective rate on the old shares of $1.10.

Stock may be split by publicly held corporations in order to keep the trading price within its historical range, or to broaden the market for the shares by decreasing the cost of a round lot for trading purposes. The New York Stock Exchange *Listed Company Manual* lists these as among the justifiable reasons for a corporation to split its stock.

§ 16.3   Distributions of Rights or Warrants

"Rights" or "warrants" are simply options to purchase additional shares at a price usually (through not invariably) below the current market price of the shares. Most rights are short lived (usually a period of weeks at the most); where they remain in effect for longer periods they are usually called warrants. Rights or warrants when distributed to shareholders are also not true dividends, though they may be so regarded by recipients. The effect of a distribution of rights or warrants in proportion to existing shareholdings is that a shareholder must add new capital to the enterprise in order to retain his or her relative ownership interest in the corporation. Rights or warrants issued by publicly held corporations are themselves traded and often listed on securities exchanges, the price fluctuating with the price of the underlying shares. A shareholder who sells rights or warrants distributed as a "dividend" thereby dilutes his or her proportionate interest in the corporation.

The price at which rights or warrants may be exercised is sometimes called the strike price. The value of rights or warrants that are issued with a strike price below the current market price is based on two variables: the inherent value reflected by the difference between the market and strike price and the time value that reflects the possibility that the market price of the underlying stock will rise during the life of the right or warrant. Rights or warrants that are issued with a strike price above current market price may have a time value even though they have no inherent value.

§ 16.4 Share Reacquisitions as Distributions

The acquisition by a corporation of its own shares decreases the real worth of the corporation by the amount of the consideration paid for the shares. The shares so acquired are not assets of the issuing corporation any more than authorized but unissued shares. As a result, a reacquisition of shares is a type of distribution, and is included within the Revised Model Business Corporation Act definition of that term. If the corporation reacquires a proportional part of the shares owned by each shareholder, the result is the equivalent of a dividend. If the reacquisition is not proportional (the normal case), the interest represented by each share in the corporation which is not reacquired is increased proportionally to the shares reacquired.

Only reacquisitions of a corporation's own shares constitute distributions. If a corporation purchases shares of another corporation, that is an investment. The difference can be readily envisioned by considering how the transactions are reflected on a balance sheet. A purchase of shares of another corporation affects only the asset side of the balance sheet; a corporation that purchases its own shares, however, must account for the transaction by reducing both the "asset" and "equity" sides of the balance sheet.

Under most state statutes, shares issued by a corporation that are reacquired by that corporation are called "treasury shares"; such shares are viewed as having an intermediate status. They are not issued shares for purposes of quorum or voting purposes, or for the payment of dividends. On the other hand, they are also not viewed as having been cancelled: they have an intermediate status of being held for resale, and may be resold without regard to the restrictions on original issue of shares described in an earlier Chapter (see § 7.8 of this Nutshell).

Obviously if treasury shares are thereafter issued as a stock dividend, the assets and relative positions of the common shareholders are unchanged; if they are resold to third persons, the assets of the corporation will be increased by the resale price and the relative voting interests of the other shareholders will be diluted. If the treasury shares are resold at a bargain price, the financial interest of the remaining shareholders will also be diluted.

The Revised Model Business Corporation Act does not recognize the concept of treasury shares. Section 6.31(a) provides simply that reacquired shares have the status of authorized but unissued shares. This simplification was a byproduct of the elimination of the concepts of par value and stated capital in the Revised Act.

§ 16.5   Shareholders' Rights to a Dividend

A dividend is distributable to shareholders of record on a specific date. Record dates may be determined in the same ways as record dates are established to make determinations of eligibility to vote at meetings. (See § 9.2 of this Nutshell.) If no record date for a distribution is fixed, the record date is the date the directors authorize the distribution. RMBCA § 6.40(b). Generally, when a dividend has been declared it becomes a debt of the corporation and cannot be rescinded or repealed by the directors.

Where shares are transferred shortly before or shortly after the record date but before the dividend is actually paid, the purchaser and seller may agree between themselves as to who is entitled to the dividend. Such agreement, of course, is binding between the purchaser and seller but generally not binding on the corporation, which will simply pay the dividend to whoever is the record owner on the record date. The date on which payment is actually made is usually referred to as the "payable date," which in the case of a publicly held corporation may be set three weeks or so after the record date. Securities exchanges have promulgated conventions or rules dealing with whether the buyer or seller of publicly held shares is entitled to dividends. The "ex dividend" date is the first date the seller becomes entitled to keep the dividend, i.e. the date that a purchaser of the shares buys the shares without the dividend. Under the New York Stock Exchange rules, shares normally are traded ex dividend on and after the fourth business day before the record date for the dividend. For example, a dividend may be made payable on March 28 to shareholders of record on March 14. The stock goes ex dividend on March 10 according to the conventions of the New York Stock Exchange. A purchaser of the stock on March 9 is entitled to the dividend; a purchaser on March 10 is not. In either event the dividend will be paid on March 28 to whoever was the record owner on March 14.

In contracts for the purchase and sale of shares after the ex dividend date, the seller retains the right to the dividend, and the amount of the dividend is not included in the contract price. Since most transactions in publicly held shares involve brokers, the purchaser or seller is not directly involved in the mechanics of transferring the amount of the dividend if it is received by a selling party to a transaction occurring before the ex dividend date.

The price of a stock usually declines when it goes ex dividend. It may or may not decline from the previous closing price by exactly the amount of the dividend; other factors may also affect the market price simultaneously and bring about a greater or lesser change than the adjustment due to the shares going ex dividend. Where the corporation issues rights, shares go "ex rights" on the same basis as they go ex dividend.

§ 16.6 Statutory Restrictions on the Declaration of Dividends

Statutory restrictions on the distribution of dividends are basically designed to assure that such payments are made out of current or past earnings and not out of capital. The Revised Model Business Corporation Act has developed a simpler set of rules that are discussed below after the discussion of statutory restrictions appearing in traditional par value statutes.

(1) *Traditional Statutes.* In these statutes restrictions are phrased in accounting terms applicable to the right hand side of the traditional balance sheet. (If this reference is unclear read § 7.4 of this Nutshell.) Unfortunately the language of traditional state statutes varies widely, and an examination of the specific statute is necessary to ascertain whether specific payments are prohibited. The principal state statutory provisions are as follows:

(a) *Solvency.* All states provide that the payment of a dividend is prohibited if the corporation is "insolvent" or the payment of the dividend will render the corporation insolvent. "Insolvency" is usually defined in the equity sense of being unable to meet corporate obligations as they mature, though a few states define insolvency in the bankruptcy sense of the corporate liabilities exceeding the corporate assets. A payment in violation of the bankruptcy test may also constitute an act of bankruptcy under the Federal Bankruptcy Act.

(b) *Surplus Test.* A number of states permit dividends to be paid from "surplus" as contrasted with "capital." Under statutes of this type, dividends usually may be paid from earned surplus or capital surplus, or both, without special designation of the source. The statutes of this type may be phrased in terms of prohibitions against impairment of "capital" or "capital stock," but the net effect is that the available assets may be reduced to the minimum core of "capital" that the corporation must maintain. California has a surplus test, but it is unusual in that it is not based on an irreducible minimum of capital; rather it requires assets to be maintained at least equal to one and one fourth times specified liabilities.

(c) *Earned Surplus Test.* This test was established in pre–1980 versions of the Model Business Corporation Act and is followed by many states. It permits dividends to be paid only from "earned surplus." (As described in the following section, however, these statutes also usually permit distributions from capital accounts such as capital surplus but they are not "dividends" in the strict sense.) In these statutes earned surplus is defined to be a composite income item determined by adding together all net profits, income, gain and losses during each accounting period going back to the original creation of the corporation with reductions for prior dividends or transfers to other accounts.

Randall v. Bailey (1940) raised the question whether it was permissible for directors to write up the value of appreciated assets on the books of the corporation in order to increase the amount available for distribution as dividends. In holding that it was permissible to use such writeups, the court relied in part on the language of the New York statute that only prohibited dividends that "impaired capital stock." It is questionable whether similar writeups are permissible to increase earned surplus available for dividends in Model Act states, and if written up, it is also questionable whether they may thereafter have to be written down.

(d) *Distributions From Capital.* State statutes based on the older versions of the Model Business Corporation Act often permit distributions to be made from capital accounts when there is no earned surplus. The 1969 Model Act, for example, permitted distributions of capital surplus to common shareholders if the articles of incorporation so provided or with the approval of the holders of a majority of the shares. (MBCA § 46.) Distributions of capital surplus to holders of cumulative preferred shares in discharge of cumulative dividend rights were also permitted in any event. The justification for permitting preferential dividends to be paid from capital surplus was that it permitted a corporation to avoid building up preferred arrearages during the early years of operation when there may be no earned surplus. It also permitted dividends to be paid to common shareholders at an earlier time and in a greater amount. While not all Model Act states are this liberal, some distributions from capital surplus are permitted in most states following this statutory approach.

Distributions from capital surplus, however, could not be made if the corporation was insolvent or the distribution rendered the corporation insolvent. Further, a distribution to common shareholders was permitted only if all preferential cumulative dividends had been paid, and the capital remaining in the corporation was sufficient to cover all preferential rights on liquidation.

The 1969 Model Act and the statutes of most states following this approach required that payments made from capital surplus be identified as such when made to shareholders.

(e) *Net Profits Test.* A number of states permit distributions from current profits even if there is an earnings deficit from operations for prior periods. These dividends are sometimes called "nimble dividends." The leading case holding that current earnings may be distributed without being used to eliminate prior deficits is Goodnow v. American Writing Paper Co. (1908). Some states with traditional statutes do not permit nimble dividends.

(f) *Restrictions on Surplus.* The 1969 Model Business Corporation Act generally permitted dividends to be paid only from "unrestricted" earned surplus and distributions of various kinds only from "unrestricted" capital surplus. Restrictions on surplus arose from the acquisition of treasury shares by the corporation. When treasury shares were acquired, the earned or capital surplus used for their acquisition was restricted so that the same surplus could not be used again for distributions or dividends. Restrictions on surplus rather than reductions of surplus were used in this situation because the treasury shares might later be reissued, in which event the restrictions were removed *pro tanto* to the extent of the consideration received for the treasury shares. If the treasury shares were instead cancelled, the restrictions were changed to permanent reductions in the appropriate surplus accounts.

(g) *Reduction of Stated Capital.* The 1969 Model Business Corporation Act permitted the reduction of stated capital by the simple expedient of amending the articles of incorporation to reduce the par value of outstanding shares. (MBCA § 60(b).) Stated capital represented by no par shares or by amounts previously transferred from other accounts to stated capital could be reduced by a simple procedure involving approval by the shareholders and directors. (MBCA § 69.) In some states the surplus created by the reduction of stated capital is called "reduction surplus." Under the 1969 Model Act, however, it was considered simply capital surplus.

These provisions relating to the reduction of stated capital made it clear that the older par value capital structure provided no protection to creditors if the shareholders desired to distribute capital to themselves, since it was possible for the shareholders to eliminate the "cushion" reflected by stated capital by amendment to the articles of incorporation without the approval of creditors.

(h) *Restrictions on Distributions by Repurchase or Redemption of Shares.* Statutory restrictions in traditional statutes on the power of a corporation to repurchase its own shares are analogous to statutory restrictions on the payment of dividends. For example, they are also phrased in accounting terms applicable to the right hand side of the traditional balance sheet and are subject to insolvency prohibitions, or, in some states, the requirement that after such purchase, the fair value of the corporation's total assets will be less than the total amount of its debts.

Section 6 of the 1969 Model Business Corporation Act dealing with share repurchases permitted such repurchases out of earned surplus, or out of capital surplus if authorized by the articles of incorporation or a vote of shareholders. It also permitted shares to be purchased out of stated capital (or any other capital account) for certain limited purposes, namely:

(1) To eliminate fractional shares;

(2) To collect or compromise indebtedness owed by or to the corporation;

(3) To pay dissenting shareholders entitled to payment for their shares under the act; and

(4) To effect the purchase or redemption of its redeemable shares in accordance with the provisions of the act.

(2) *The Revised Model Business Corporation Act.* In 1980 amendments were adopted to the Model Business Corporation Act that drastically revised its financial provisions. The provisions relating to distributions now appear in section 6.40 of the Revised Model Business Corporation Act. This section applies the same tests to all types of distributions: distributions of cash or property, corporate reacquisitions of shares, and less common types of distributions, such as a corporation creating evidences of indebtedness and distributing them to its shareholders. No distinction is made between distributions of capital or of earnings; all distributions are subject to the same tests. Section 6.40 also provides firm answers for a number of technical questions about the lawfulness of distributions that are not covered in most statutes, such as the date on which the determinations of lawfulness are to be made.

Section 6.40(c) sets forth a dual test for the legality of distributions of all types: after giving effect to the distribution, (a) the corporation must be "able to pay its debts as they become due in the usual course of business," and (b) the corporation's assets must exceed its total liabilities after making provision for the liquidation preferences of senior securities. The first test is usually referred to as the "insolvency" test (since it in effect defines equity insolvency) and the second "the balance sheet" test. Both must be satisfied if the distribution is to be lawful.

The balance sheet test presupposes the use of some kind of accounting conventions to determine "assets" and "liabilities." Section 6.40(d) permits the board of directors to base a determination either on "accounting practices and principles that are reasonable in the circumstances" or on a "fair valuation or other method that is reasonable in the circumstances." Because section 6.40 is applicable to all corporations, large and small, it was not thought appropriate to require all corporations to use generally accepted accounting principles that might require the employment of an accountant. The Official Comment describes in some detail what the determination of solvency requires and also points out that in making all decisions under this section, the directors are liable for an unlawful distribution (see RMBCA § 8.33) only if the directors fail to meet their duty of care under section 8.30.

Section 6.40(e) also describes at what time the insolvency and balance sheet tests are to be applied. To some extent, the time is determined by the nature of the distribution, and to a lesser extent, the time of declaration in relation to the time of payment.

§ 16.7 Contractual Provisions Relating to Declarations of Dividends

Because of the great liberality of many modern business corporation statutes in permitting distributions to shareholders of earnings and capital, much of the modern law of dividends is contractual in nature. Creditors of a corporation are naturally anxious that the assets of the corporation not be dissipated through unwise distributions. Provisions are therefore routinely inserted in loan agreements to prohibit or restrict the power of the corporation to make distributions to stockholders. The nature of such restrictions varies widely. If the debtor is a publicly held corporation with an established history of regular dividend payments, the loan agreement may permit dividends of specified amounts provided that certain ratios are maintained between assets and liabilities, or between current assets and current liabilities. Other restrictions may permit any distribution so long as a minimum net worth and minimum cash balance are maintained.   Loan agreements with closely held corporations may prohibit all dividends, and may even impose restrictions on salary payments, bonuses, and other distributions having the effect of a dividend.

Contractual provisions relating to dividends also may appear in articles of incorporation. Where preferred as well as common shares are authorized, provisions relating to dividends are apt to be complex. Not only must the preference rights of the senior security be defined (e.g., cumulative, noncumulative, or cumulative to the extent earned), but provisions may be inserted as part of the preferred shareholders' rights requiring a portion of earnings to be set aside in a sinking fund or to be used to retire a portion of the preferred each year, limiting senior indebtedness that may be created, and so forth. The preferred shareholder otherwise receives scant protection under most business corporation acts since his or her claim to preferential dividends, even if cumulative, is not a corporate debt but a mere priority to possible future distributions.

§ 16.8 Liability of Directors and Shareholders for Illegal Dividends

Directors who vote for or assent to a declaration of dividends or the distribution of assets to shareholders which is wholly or partially in violation of statutory limitations or a provision in the corporation's articles of incorporation, are jointly and severally liable to the corporation for the illegal portion of the dividend or distribution. This statutory liability is ameliorated in many states by possible defenses discussed earlier. See § 14.15 of this Nutshell. The risk of liability for an illegal distribution under the Revised Model Business Corporation Act is reduced even further.

Shareholders "who accepted [a distribution] knowing the distribution was made in violation of this Act or the articles of incorporation" also are liable to return or restore the unlawful payment received. This provision, discussed in § 14.15 of this Nutshell, thus protects the probable reliance of the innocent shareholder upon receipt of a distribution; in this event the directors are solely responsible to restore the unlawful payment. If the shareholder knows the payment was unlawful, he or she may be required to restore it to the corporation, and the liability of the directors will be reduced accordingly. Not all states extend similar protection to innocent shareholders.

§ 16.9 Shareholders' Right to Compel a Dividend

Minority shareholders in closely held corporations are likely to be unhappy about the dividend policy established by the corporation. In a C corporation, for tax reasons, the shareholders in control of the corporation usually prefer to pay salaries to themselves or make other tax-deductible payments rather than pay the same funds in the form of dividends. In an S corporation, shareholders must include their pro rata share of corporate earnings in their own tax returns whether or not anything is distributed to them. A no-dividend policy in such a corporation may cause serious cash flow problems to minority shareholders who may lack the funds to pay the additional tax due as a result of the S corporation election. Distributions in the form of salaries to controlling shareholders in an S corporation also have the effect of diverting corporate income to the controlling shareholders at the expense of the minority. What, if anything, can the minority shareholder do to secure a more favorable dividend policy? The two most likely approaches involve suits either (1) to compel the controlling shareholders to return part of the amounts distributed to them as being irregular dividends or amounts paid in violation of fiduciary duties, or (2) to compel the declaration of a dividend to all shareholders.

In light of the business judgment rule and the principle of fairness applicable to self dealing transactions, attempts to pare back salaries face formidable hurdles though some cases have been successful. This approach is often less attractive than suits to compel a dividend, since success does not necessarily lead to a greater distribution to the plaintiff.

Historically, suits to compel the declaration of a dividend also faced serious obstacles. The discretion of the board of directors with respect to business decisions was so broad that a strong showing of fraud, bad faith, or abuse of discretion was necessary. In short, an abuse of power or a clear failure to exercise it honestly for the corporation and all its shareholders must be shown. Dodge v. Ford Motor Co. (1919) was one of the first cases in which minority shareholders were successful in compelling the declaration of a dividend, though the court there appeared to rely heavily on the unusual frankness of the majority shareholder and the court's own view of social policy. Other cases have also compelled the declaration of a dividend particularly where the defendant was outspoken as to his or her strategy of freezing out the minority, though in a "head count" of such cases, plaintiffs come off as net losers. A major concern of courts in ordering a dividend to be paid is that there appears to be no standard to guide the court as to how much may safely be paid out and how much should be retained by the corporation for contingencies and future growth. Judges are usually not businessmen and in any event have little knowledge or familiarity with the specific business before them. Hence even where a finding of bad faith may be made in connection with refusing to declare a dividend, a court is likely to be extremely cautious in establishing the amount of any judicially-declared dividend.

§ 16.10 Tax Consequences of Failure to Pay Dividends in Closely Held Corporations

Section 531 of the Internal Revenue Code imposes a special penalty tax on C corporations "formed or availed of for the purpose of avoiding the income tax with respect to its shareholders" by the expedient of permitting earnings and profits to accumulate rather than distributing them in the form of taxable dividends. A tax is imposed on that portion of current earnings which is retained in excess of the "reasonably anticipated" needs of the business. The tax is at a rate of 27½ per cent on the first $100,000 and 38½ per cent on the balance, and is in addition to the regular federal income taxes applicable to corporations. However, a deduction may be taken for dividends paid shortly after the close of the taxable year, and an aggregate of $150,000 may be accumulated without any justification. A test based on the "reasonably anticipated" needs of a business is obviously very imprecise, and in fact has given rise to a substantial amount of litigation. Guidelines for the proper application of this test appear in IRS regulations.

Section 531 is often administered informally. An internal revenue agent auditing a closely held corporation may raise an issue about paying a dividend without actually seeking the imposition of a section 531 penalty tax. The corporation may take the hint and declare a dividend in the immediate future.

Because of changes in the tax laws under the Reagan administration, the tax incentive to permit earnings to accumulate in C corporations has been virtually eliminated. It is almost always advantageous to distribute earnings rather than to accumulate them, despite the double tax problem. As a result the practical importance of section 531 has declined.

§ 16.11 Corporate Repurchase of Its Own Shares

The distributional aspect of repurchases by corporations of their own shares has previously been commented upon (see § 16.4 of this Nutshell). Such transactions create several additional problems that are not present in the dividend area that deserve additional consideration.

Since redemptions are almost never proportional to shareholdings, the shareholders' relative positions among themselves are affected by the corporate repurchase, and it is often possible for managing shareholders in a closely held corporation to utilize a share repurchase for personal reasons. For example, a Massachusetts case has held that it is a breach of fiduciary duty for the majority shareholder to cause the corporation to purchase a portion of a family member's shares at inflated prices while offering to purchase the shares owned by a nonfamily member at significantly lower prices. Donahue v. Rodd Electrotype Co. of New England, Inc. (1975). In this case, the family member whose shares were redeemed was elderly and the effect of the redemption was to further the goals of an estate plan set up some time earlier. The court articulated the view that shareholders in a closely held corporation have fiduciary duties to each other that rival those that exist in a partnership; at a narrower level this case in effect recognized a reverse preemptive right on the purchase of shares in some situations. While later Massachusetts cases have retreated to some extent from the broad fiduciary duty language in the opinion and not all cases from other jurisdictions involving disproportionate redemptions have followed this decision, it nevertheless is an important case describing duties that exist among shareholders in closely held corporations in connection with transactions that favor some shareholders but not others without any apparent business justification.

In a closely held corporation, the usual reason to reacquire shares is to eliminate the interest of one or more shareholders in the enterprise. The reason for the elimination may be a death or desired retirement, or a negotiated withdrawal following disagreements as to business policies. Often, the remaining shareholders may not wish to increase their investment in the business by purchasing the shares personally, or they may lack the liquid assets to do so. Hence acquisition by the corporation may be the logical choice. If the corporation has not been in existence for a long time or has suffered losses in the past, the legal restrictions on repurchase of shares discussed in a preceding section are apt to create serious problems in effectuating the corporate repurchase.

The corporation may deliver promissory notes to the selling shareholder representing the future payments of principal. Usually, an installment sale occurs because the corporation lacks the assets to buy the shares outright and it is contemplated that future payments will be made in whole or in part out of (hoped for) future earnings. Where an installment sale is made the question arises whether the insolvency and availability of surplus requirements should be applied only when shares are reacquired and the notes issued, or whether those requirements should be repetitively applied to determine the validity of each payment when it is made. The limited case law tends to apply the tests to each payment but section 6.40(e)(1) of the Revised Model Business Corporation Act provides that the test should be applied only when the shares are acquired and the notes issued. The argument for this position is that the transaction should be treated no differently than if the corporation borrowed the purchase price from a bank in order to acquire the shares for cash. The alternative view would require at least the insolvency test to be applied at the time of each payment. A further question may arise as to whether the promissory notes issued by the corporation for the balance of the purchase price should be viewed as on a parity with general trade creditors or subordinate to them. Section 6.40(f) provides that such notes should be on a parity with general unsecured creditors if the notes were validly issued to begin with; the theory is that the corporation could have used cash to buy the shares, borrowing if necessary from a third party, and there is no reason to treat the shareholder who accepts promissory notes from the corporation any differently from a third party lender.

In a public corporation, on the other hand, a corporation may reacquire its own shares in order to have them available for stock options or other compensation plans, or for acquisitions of other corporations. Many corporations purchase large amounts of their own shares for these purposes. Publicly held corporations may purchase their own shares for financial reasons, planning to retire them. In these situations the corporation has made the judgment that the market has in some way underpriced the corporation's securities. Retirement of shares may have the effect of increasing the price and earnings per share of the remaining outstanding shares; this assumes, of course, that the corporation has idle cash that is surplus to its reasonably anticipated business needs and its use to retire shares will not significantly reduce earnings.

A corporation may desire to purchase its own shares for improper considerations as well as proper ones. Corporate management faced with the threat of a takeover by an outside corporation may cause the corporation to purchase its own shares as a defensive measure to entrench incumbent management. Purchases on the open market may drive up the price of the shares, thereby tending to defeat a cash tender offer or public exchange offer. A filing under the Williams Act may be required before such transactions are undertaken. Or the insurgent group may be willing to accept "green mail," i.e. to sell its block of shares (at a premium over what it paid for them) back to the corporation, thereby eliminating a threat to control. The appropriate test in such a case, according to the Delaware Supreme Court, is whether the directors were "motivated by a sincere belief that the buying out of the dissident stockholder was necessary to maintain what the board believed to be proper business practices" or whether the board "sanctioned the use of corporate funds to advance the selfish desires of directors to perpetuate themselves in office." Cheff v.

Mathes, (1964). Since most transactions involve elements of both factors, the usefulness of this test is debatable.

§ 16.12 Redeemable Securities

Corporations may, when permitted by their articles of incorporation, issue shares that are redeemable at the option of the corporation. See RMBCA § 6.01(c)(2). Earlier versions of the Model Act and the statutes of many states permit redeemable preferred shares but not redeemable common shares, but the RMBCA does not contain such a limitation. The concern with redeemable common shares is that management may use the redemption device to discipline or eliminate antagonistic shareholders. One commentator has stated that even the suggestion of redeemable common shares is "corporate heresy." Such concerns, however, do not appear to be borne out in practice.

In modern financing practice within publicly held corporations, preferred shares are usually cumulative and redeemable, and often convertible into publicly traded common shares (the "conversion shares") as well on a predetermined ratio. Typically, the conversion ratio is established when the preferred shares are issued at a level that requires a significant increase in price of the conversion shares before conversion becomes economic. Thereafter, if the market price of the conversion shares does in fact rise to the point that the conversion shares are worth more than the preferred shares priced without the conversion feature, the preferred will fluctuate in price with the common. If such securities are thereafter called for redemption, preferred shareholders should rationally elect to convert rather than permit the shares to be redeemed. Such conversions are described as "forced." The economic justification for a forced conversion is that usually the dividend payable on the conversion security is significantly lower than the preferred dividend rate applicable to the convertible security.

In modern financing practice, shares may also be made redeemable at the option of the holder or upon the occurrence of some event (such as an increase in interest rates). Earlier statutes contemplated redemption only at the option of the corporation, but section 6.01(c)(2) of the RMBCA authorizes redemptions to be triggered by other events as well. Shares redeemable at the option of the holder have some of the same characteristics of a demand note.

See generally §§ 7.10–7.12 of this Nutshell.

[For unfamiliar terms see the Glossary]

CHAPTER SEVENTEEN

SHAREHOLDER'S SUITS

§ 17.1 Direct and Derivative Suits in General

Litigation brought by shareholders against the corporation may be divided into two basic categories: direct and derivative. A *direct* suit involves the enforcement by a shareholder of a claim belonging to the shareholder on the basis of being an owner of shares. Examples are suits to recover dividends, to examine corporate books and records, and to compel the registration of a securities transfer. These are suits involving the shareholder, the shares themselves, or rights relating to the ownership of shares. A *derivative* suit is an action brought by one or more shareholders to remedy or prevent a wrong to the corporation as such. In a derivative suit, the plaintiff shareholders do not sue on a cause of action belonging to themselves as individuals. They sue in a representative capacity on a cause of action that belongs to the corporation; the real party in interest is the corporation though it may be formally aligned as a defendant for procedural purposes. In effect, the shareholder is suing as a champion of his or her corporation. The derivative suit raises a number of procedural and substantive questions and is the principal topic of this chapter.

A class suit is a direct suit in which one or more shareholder plaintiffs purport to act as a representative of a class or classes of shareholders for injuries to the interests of the class as such. It differs from a derivative suit in that the claim being sued upon is direct—all shareholders of a particular class (or all shareholders) are claiming they were injured as shareholders by an act which was not an injury to the corporation as such. A derivative action, it should be added, usually has a class aspect: the shareholder is suing to protect the interest of all other shareholders when righting a wrong done to the corporation.

§ 17.2   The Distinction Between Derivative and Direct Claims

Since different procedural and substantive rules are applicable to direct and derivative claims, it is important to distinguish between them. Unfortunately, however, the line between the two classes is sometimes hazy. Anything that harms the corporation also harms the shareholder by reducing the value of his or her shares. However, it is clear that a shareholder may not transmute a derivative claim into a direct one merely by alleging a direct reduction in value of his or her shares because of injury to the property of a corporation, or the impairment or destruction of its business. Generally, the individual shareholders have no separate and independent right of action for injuries suffered by the corporation which merely result in the depreciation of the value of their stock. Where such an injury occurs each shareholder suffers relatively in proportion to the total number of shares owned, and each is made whole if the corporation recovers damages from the wrongdoer. Such an action brought by the corporation obviously avoids a multiplicity of suits by the various shareholders; also, the damages so recovered by the corporation are then available for the payment of the corporation's creditors, and ultimately for proportional distribution to the shareholders as dividends.

Many cases have considered whether a claim is derivative or direct. A suit charging officers and directors with misapplication of corporate assets or other breaches of duty is derivative in character. Suits to recover improper dividends or to require a controlling shareholder to account for a premium on the sale of his or her shares have also been held to be derivative since the benefit inures to the corporation. However, a suit charging that it was improper for a majority shareholder to vote on a resolution authorizing the corporation to repurchase the shares owned by the majority shareholder is direct: to prevent the dilution of the voting power of the complaining shareholder's shares. Cases also have held that a conspiracy of the directors to use their powers to depress the market price of the shares so that they can be bought at less than fair value states a direct rather than a derivative claim. A suit claiming a denial of preemptive rights seems direct; however, it may also be considered derivative if it is alleged that the corporation was induced to issue the shares for inadequate consideration through fraud or a violation of federal securities law.

As these examples indicate, not only is the line sometimes hazy, but careful pleading may affect the categorization. In some situations a single claim may give rise to both a direct and a derivative claim. The American Law Institute's Corporate Governance Project includes a sensible provision that authorizes courts to treat derivative claims as direct claims in cases involving closely held corporations if it determines that to do so would not unfairly expose the defendants to multiple actions, prejudice the interests of creditors, or interfere with the fair distribution of the recovery among all interested persons.

§ 17.3 Jurisdiction of Federal Courts

In recent years, the bulk of shareholder class and derivative litigation has been brought in the federal courts, usually under the federal securities laws, but sometimes on the basis of diversity of citizenship. For purposes of diversity in derivative suits, if it appears on the face of the pleadings and by the nature of the controversy that the corporation is antagonistic to the enforcement of the claim, the corporation should be aligned as a defendant for purposes of determining diversity.

As federal corporation law developed, plaintiffs increasingly became able to state a cause of action under both federal and state law. Suits involving such situations are usually brought in the federal courts since the concept of "pendent jurisdiction" permits the federal courts to determine both the federal and state claim in a single proceeding even in the absence of diversity of citizenship. In contrast, state courts do not have jurisdiction over claims arising under the federal securities acts, and thus cannot adjudicate all claims for relief in a single proceeding. The preference for the federal forum also may be based on generous discovery rights, nationwide service of process under the federal securities acts, and the avoidance of state security-for-expense statutes. Substantive advantages that are sometimes cited—a belief that federal courts are more sympathetic to minority plaintiffs than state courts and the greater liberality of federal securities law—are more doubtful. (See Chapter 14, particularly § 14.17 of this Nutshell.)

The Federal Rules of Civil Procedure contain carefully drawn and elaborate procedural requirements for maintaining class (rule 23) and derivative (rule 23.1) suits in the federal courts. Many states have adopted similar rules in whole or in part. These requirements are discussed briefly in the following sections.

§ 17.4   Prerequisites for Derivative Suit

In evaluating the procedural requirements discussed in this section, it should be recognized that most derivative litigation is brought by attorneys operating on a contingent fee basis; they discover the claim and then locate a plaintiff that qualifies to bring the suit. Further, most such litigation is settled rather than going to a final judgment. Whether or not most of such litigation is without substantive merits is an issue on which the plaintiff's bar and corporation attorneys vigorously debate. There is, however, a widespread feeling that most derivative litigation is brought on a speculative basis by attorneys who invest their own resources in the litigation and control all aspects of it. As a result, much derivative litigation is in fact champertous. Many of the procedural requirements discussed below reflect this concern.

(1) *Demand on the Corporation and the Directors.* Generally, in a derivative suit, the burden rests upon the plaintiff to allege and prove that he or she first made a good faith effort to obtain action by the corporation on the claim. Thus a good faith demand on the directors is usually a prerequisite to such a suit. Most state statutes are similar to rule 23.1 of the Federal Rules of Civil Procedure which states "the complaint shall also allege with particularity the efforts, if any, made by the plaintiff to obtain the action he or she desires from the directors or comparable authority and the reasons for his or her failure to obtain the action or for not making the effort." Under these statutes a demand is not required in all cases; in the alternative, the plaintiff may allege and prove a state of facts that makes it clear that an appeal to the directors would have been useless. One such example might be where "the wrongdoers are in complete control and management of the corporation." To phrase the applicable legal principle somewhat differently, the plaintiff must allege and prove that he or she exhausted all remedies within the corporate structure unless it is clear that such attempts would be futile.

For many years, the requirement of a demand on directors was viewed as a minor procedural obstacle. Many suits were brought directly, based on the allegation that demand would have been futile; if the court disagreed, a formal demand could then usually be made. This rather simple view of the demand requirement disappeared when the Supreme Court of Delaware in two important decisions held that an independent litigation committee (see § 14.6 of this Nutshell) could dispose of litigation under the business judgment rule in "demand necessary" cases but that courts should utilize their own "independent business judgment" in reviewing dismissal recommendations in "demand excused" cases. These holdings greatly increased the importance of the question whether demand on directors was excused, and has led to increased litigation on the question. Much of this litigation has tended in the direction of requiring such a demand in close cases.

The independent litigation committee issue has caused a rethinking of the desirability of the "demand excused" exception. Why not require a demand in every case? It is relatively simple to make a demand. Why should not the board in every case have the option to consider whether to respond to the claim before suit is filed? In 1989 the Revised Model Business Corporation Act was amended to make a demand a universal prerequisite for instituting a derivative suit (RMBCA § 7.42); the American Law Institute's Corporate Governance Project has also taken essentially the same position. In both of these codifications, the intent is to divorce the issue of the standard of review of dismissal recommendations from the demand requirement.

(2) *Demand Upon Shareholders.* In many states and under the Revised Model Business Corporation Act no demand on shareholders is required.

The Federal Rules of Civil Procedure (as well as the rules of several states) require either a demand on shareholders or the showing of an adequate reason for not making the effort. Adequate reasons for omitting a demand on shareholders have been held to include the following: (1) the wrongdoers own a majority of the shares and hence favorable shareholder action is impossible, (2) the number of shareholders is so large that it is unreasonable to require the plaintiff to incur the expense of what is essentially a proxy solicitation when there is little chance of success, or (3) the acts complained of cannot be ratified by the shareholders, so that action by the shareholders is useless. While some cases have required a demand on shareholders even when the cost would be substantial, many cases have held that such an act may be omitted on this ground. Massachusetts appears to have adopted the most stringent rule, requiring a demand in every case where a majority of shareholders are not wrong-doers. Other state courts that require a demand on share-holders unless excused have proceeded on a case-by-case basis, not requiring a demand when there are thousands of shareholders, and apparently taking into account the motives of the plaintiff, the number of shareholders joining in the action, and the proximity to the next shareholders meeting.

(3) *Contemporary Ownership.* Section 7.41(1) of the RMBCA and most state statutes dealing with derivative litigation require the plaintiff to have been a shareholder when the cause of action arose and continuously since that time. A handful of states, most notably California, permits a shareholder to serve as a plaintiff even though not a shareholder when the cause of action arose if the sharehold-er acquired the shares in ignorance of the existence of the claim.

The Federal Rules of Civil Procedure contain a contem-porary ownership requirement primarily to prevent the col-lusive establishment of diversity citizenship. The state stat-utes described in the previous paragraph appear to be based primarily on notions of preventing "the buying of a law-suit." Of course, if "buying a lawsuit" were the only concern, the contemporaneous ownership requirement might be safely liberalized, as in California, to allow suit by plaintiffs who discover the facts giving rise to the lawsuit only after becoming a shareholder. In fact this requirement appears to be largely grounded on antipathy to derivative litigation.

(4) *Security for Expenses.*   Security-for-expenses statutes require certain plaintiff shareholders in derivative suits to give to the corporation "security for the reasonable expenses, including attorneys' fees" which the corporation or other defendants may incur in connection with a derivative suit. Many states have such statutes, though as described below, such a provision was not included in the Revised Model Business Corporation Act even though it appeared in the 1969 Model Act. The shareholders required to post security for expenses are usually defined in terms of the size of their holdings: the 1969 Model Act provision, for example, required security from plaintiffs whose ownership was less than one per cent of the outstanding shares or the value of the shares was less than $25,000. Other states had similar provisions though the dollar and percentage limits varied from state to state.

In a few more modern statutes, security-for-expenses is required only upon a court finding that the suit was apparently brought without reasonable cause or seems patently without merit.

Where security has to be posted, it is usually in the form of a bond with sureties, though it also may be in the form of cash or marketable securities. The expenses for which security may be required include not only the direct expenses of the corporation, but also the expenses of other defendants for which the corporation may become liable by indemnification or otherwise. Such expenses may be substantial, running into the hundreds of thousands of dollars. The requirement of posting security of this magnitude obviously creates a major obstacle to the successful prosecution of a derivative suit, and a decision that the securities-for-expenses statute is applicable may well be the substantive decision that ultimately results in the litigation being terminated.

Security-for-expenses statutes usually do not define when the corporation may actually look to the security for reimbursement; rather they usually state in effect that "[t]he corporation shall have recourse to such security in such amount as the court having jurisdiction shall determine upon the termination of such action." (This quotation is taken from the 1969 Model Act, § 49, last par.) In the absence of such a provision, the corporation normally has no right at all to be reimbursed for any of its expenses; thus security-for-expenses statutes have the secondary effect of creating a right of reimbursement where none existed before as well as providing that security may have to be posted in the first place. As a further consequence, an unsuccessful shareholder-plaintiff posting security-for-expenses may well end up paying the expenses of both sides of the litigation.

The numerical limits on the security-for-expenses requirement gave rise to a considerable amount of litigation. In most states with such statutes it was held that intervening shareholder plaintiffs may have their shares counted toward meeting the statutory minimum, though a solicitation of shareholders for this purpose may be deemed a proxy solicitation subject to the proxy solicitation rules adopted by the Securities Exchange Commission. Another case held that if the value of the holdings of a plaintiff declined during the litigation to below the statutory minimum, the plaintiff could not then be required to post security.

Security-for-expenses statutes are applicable under the Erie principle to suits in federal court based on state-created causes of action. In other words, if a state has a security-for-expenses statute, the federal courts in that state must require security in cases arising under state law. Federal jurisdiction over such cases may be based on diversity of citizenship or on the doctrine of pendent jurisdiction. However, such statutes are not applicable to suits in federal court based on the federal securities laws. Nor are they applicable to direct class actions brought either in the federal or state courts since such statutes are only applicable to derivative suits.

One purpose of security-for-expenses statutes is to deter "strike" suits, that is, suits brought not to redress an injury to the corporation but in the hope of securing a settlement profitable to the plaintiff shareholders and their attorneys. However, the older statutes do not distinguish between "strike" suits and bona fide shareholder suits. Rather, they are applicable to all shareholder suits, and thus have the effect of making all such suits more difficult. They were upheld against constitutional challenge, despite the arbitrary numerical limit, in Cohen v. Beneficial Industrial Loan Corp. (1949). Such statutes also probably have the incidental effect of encouraging suits to be brought under the federal securities acts rather than under state law.

The Revised Model Business Corporation Act repealed the security for expenses provision that appeared in the 1969 version of that Act, citing the arbitrary nature of the provision. Instead, it substituted a simple provision authorizing the court to assess costs, including attorneys' fees, against a plaintiff or defendant if the court determined that the suit was brought without just cause. See RMBCA § 7.46.

(5) *Verification of Complaint.* Many state statutes, as well as rule 23.1 of the Federal Rules of Civil Procedure, require that complaints in derivative suits be verified, i.e., sworn to. The purpose of this requirement is to provide some protection against groundless litigation without deterring suits brought in good faith. The leading case involving this requirement is Surowitz v. Hilton Hotels Corp. (1966), where the court held that a complaint in a derivative suit verified by the plaintiff should not be dismissed because the plaintiff did not understand the specific allegations in the complaint.

A verification requirement appeared in the 1984 RMBCA but was eliminated by the 1990 amendments to that Act.

(6) *Dismissal as an Exercise of Business Judgment.* The use of litigation committees to determine whether the maintenance of a derivative suit is in the best interest of a corporation is discussed in § 14.6 of this Nutshell.

§ 17.5   Defenses in a Derivative Suit

Defenses in derivative suits may be grouped into three broad categories. One category involves alleged failure to comply with requirements peculiar to such suits. A failure to make a demand on the directors, or a failure to post security when required to do so under the applicable security-for-expenses statute, for example, will result in the dismissal of the suit. A second category of defenses are those that would be available to the third party defendants if the corporation had sued directly on the claim that is the underlying basis of the derivative suit. If the action is barred by the statute of limitations or statute of frauds, for example, the derivative suit based on the same claim is also barred. Presumably, such defenses may only be raised by the third party defendants, not the corporate defendant. Somewhat similarly, a defense based on ratification of the transaction by directors or shareholders may be available if the transaction is voidable rather than void, or if it arguably falls within the ordinary business judgment of the directors. Such defenses may arise from director or shareholder action after the claim is presented by the plaintiff shareholder, and presumably may be raised by the corporate defendant. A third category of defenses are those available against the specific plaintiff shareholder but not against other shareholders.

Derivative suits basically involve two separate claims: the substantive claim by the corporation against a third person and the claim by the shareholder that he or she should be permitted to represent or champion the corporation. The particular category of defense may go to one claim or the other with quite different consequences. Laches, for example, may bar some shareholders but not others from acting as plaintiff. If the plaintiff shareholder actually participated in the wrongful transaction, or assented to it, he or she may be estopped from questioning the transaction. Shares owned by such a person may be considered "tainted shares" or "dirty stock" and even innocent transferees of such shares may be estopped from questioning the transaction. Such a transferee may also be barred if there is a contemporaneous ownership requirement.

§ 17.6 Procedural Problems in Derivative Suits

In derivative suits, the shareholder is aligned as a nominal plaintiff and the corporation is aligned as a nominal defendant even though recovery usually runs exclusively in favor of the corporation. The corporation is a necessary party in a derivative suit; without it, the action cannot proceed. The unique roles of the plaintiff shareholder and defendant corporation have other procedural consequences as well. It has been held for example, that the plaintiff shareholder may not combine individual or direct actions with a derivative action in the same suit, though many cases are more liberal. Similarly, the traditional view is that the plaintiff shareholder may not be subject to personal counterclaims.

Since a derivative suit has class as well as derivative aspects, multiple derivative suits may be filed by several different shareholders; in the absence of other considerations, the suit first filed is generally permitted to proceed while later actions may be stayed or dismissed, or consolidated with the initial suit. Intervention by other shareholders is permitted and indeed may be encouraged. Presumably, holdings of intervening shareholders may be counted toward meeting the security for expenses requirement, but intervention may also be encouraged because for some reason the representation of the original plaintiff shareholder may be considered inadequate. Perhaps the original plaintiff may be subject to a personal defense, or a collusive settlement is feared.

Counsel for the shareholder first bringing suit is usually permitted to control the litigation from the plaintiffs' standpoint, though the court undoubtedly has discretion to designate an attorney for another shareholder as the principal counsel for plaintiffs. This decision may be of importance in determining fees at a later date. In all such matters, the trial court has "great discretion."

Even though the corporation is technically a defendant, its interest in the litigation is usually adverse to the interest of the other defendants. Therefore, generally, common counsel will not be permitted to represent the defendant corporation as well as other defendants; problems arising from common representation may be complicated because some defenses may be available to some defendants but not to others.

Derivative suits are equitable in nature, a categorization which may be significant in resolving procedural questions. In Ross v. Bernhard (1970), the United States Supreme Court held that a right to jury trial may exist in derivative suits brought in federal courts where the issue is of a "legal" (as contrasted with an "equitable") nature.

§ 17.7 Private Settlement of Derivative Suits

Historically, the secret settlement of shareholders' suits was a serious evil. "Strike" suits were thereby encouraged, and the settling shareholder received substantial sums which in fact was a payment to ignore a corporate wrong. This evil has now been largely resolved by bringing the process of settlement of derivative or class suits under judicial control. The Federal Rules of Civil Procedure provide that derivative actions may "not be dismissed or compromised without the approval of the court, and notice of the proposed dismissal or compromise shall be given to shareholders or members in such manner as the court directs." A similar provision is applicable to class suits. Many state statutes (as well as section 7.45 of the Revised Model Business Corporation Act) contain similar requirements.

In exercising discretion to review proposed settlements, courts consider several factors, including:

(1) The size of the potential recovery and the size of the suggested settlement;

(2) The probability of ultimate success; and

(3) The financial position of the defendants.

Shareholders may appear at the hearing on a proposed settlement and object to its terms.

Courts have held that where a secret settlement has led to a payment to the shareholder plaintiff, other shareholders may bring a derivative suit in the name of the corporation against the settling shareholder to recover the amount of the secret settlement.

§ 17.8　To Whom Recovery Is Paid in a Derivative Suit

A recovery in a derivative suit is usually payable to the corporation rather than to individual shareholders on a pro rata basis. This principle normally protects fully the interests of shareholders and creditors alike, and does not involve the court in making a business judgment as to whether corporate funds should be distributed to some or all of the shareholders, or reserved for creditors.

If an individual wrongdoer is also a shareholder, a corporate recovery permits that wrongdoer to share indirectly in the recovery. In a few instances, courts have been persuaded to grant shareholders a pro rata recovery in order to limit the recovery to "innocent" shareholders. For example, in Perlman v. Feldmann (1955) a control premium paid to a former controlling shareholder was held to be recoverable and payable to the nonselling shareholders pro rata on the theory that it was improper for the persons presently in control (who had paid the control premium to the defendants) to share in the recovery. Similarly, if the corporation is controlled by the wrongdoers, the court may order a pro rata recovery by the innocent shareholders on the theory that it is improper to permit the funds recovered to revert immediately to the control of the wrongdoers. Such situations, however, are uncommon, and a pro rata recovery is therefore the exception rather than the rule. Such a recovery may give rise to serious logical and practical problems. In the Perlman case, for example, the pro rata recovery by nonselling shareholders creates the possibility that the persons presently in control may themselves resell at a premium and then argue that the remaining shareholders have already been compensated for the loss of the control premium and should not be permitted to question the propriety of the second sale.

§ 17.9 Res Judicata Effect of Derivative Suits

A final judgment on the merits in a derivative suit is *res judicata,* binding on all other shareholders, including any who were original parties to the suit but thereafter withdrew. This assumes that the plaintiff shareholder was an adequate representative of the class of shareholders. A court-approved settlement ordinarily has the same effect as a final judgment on the merits, though problems may arise as to whether shareholders are bound if they were not notified of the proposed settlement.

The *res judicata* effect of a dismissal of a derivative suit depends on the reason for the dismissal. A voluntary dismissal, or a dismissal because the plaintiff shareholder is not a proper plaintiff (e.g. for not being a contemporaneous owner or for not posting security-for-expenses), is "without prejudice" and does not bind the remaining shareholders. On the other hand, a dismissal on the merits may be binding upon the remaining shareholders. In some situations, the court may order that notice be given to all other shareholders before a derivative action is dismissed voluntarily. Such action may then be continued by intervening shareholders, or if none appear, the action may be dismissed "with prejudice."

§ 17.10   Reimbursement of Plaintiff's Expenses

If the plaintiff is successful, he or she may be awarded expenses, including attorneys' fees. Since most such cases are taken on a contingent fee basis, the attorney will receive compensation either on the basis of the successful prosecution of the suit or by its settlement. Such a recovery is justified in equity as encouraging meritorious shareholder suits. Usually the recovery will be paid out of the funds obtained by the corporation as a result of the suit; however, expenses may be awarded even where the corporation receives no money so long as the result of the suit "was of some benefit to the corporation." Thus, expenses and fees may be awarded in a suit which results only in an injunction against the officers and directors of a corporation engaging in improper conduct. A settlement under which the corporation agrees to amend bylaws or make some procedural changes also may justify a payment of a fee to the attorney. It should be noted that these rules may well encourage the filing of marginal suits on a contingent fee basis, since the attorney representing the plaintiff is the person with the principal financial interest and is apt to accept a nonmonetary settlement so long as an attorney's fee is provided for.

Theoretically, a payment of the plaintiffs' expenses by the corporation does not compel the "losing party" to pay the other's expenses since both the corporation and the plaintiff are winning parties.

The size of the attorneys' fee to be awarded depends on a variety of factors—the nature and character of the litigation, the skill required, the amount of work actually performed, the size of the recovery, the nature of the harm prevented, and other factors. The size of the fee is a question of fact. To choose one example more or less at random, a fee of $200,000 in a suit leading to a $1,025,000 settlement was upheld. Of course, in cases that are settled, the fee is a matter of direct negotiation between the attorney and the corporation.

[For unfamiliar terms see the Glossary]

CHAPTER EIGHTEEN

ORGANIC CHANGES: AMENDMENTS, MERGERS, AND DISSOLUTION

§ 18.1 Amendments to Articles of Incorporation

Under modern statutes, articles of incorporation may be freely amended subject only to the broad requirement that the amended articles of incorporation may contain only provisions that may be lawfully contained in original articles of incorporation at the time of the amendment. RMBCA § 10.01(a). Also, if a change in shares or rights of shareholders, or an exchange, reclassification or cancellation of shares or rights is to be made in connection with the amendment, either the articles of amendment, or the amendments themselves, must set forth the provisions necessary to effectuate the change, exchange, reclassification, or cancellation. RMBCA § 10.06(3).

Under modern statutes no shareholder has a vested right in any specific provision in articles of incorporation. RMBCA § 10.01(b). It is possible for the majority of the shareholders to adopt amendments that dramatically change or eliminate the rights of minority shareholders or the rights of holders of classes of nonvoting or senior securities. As a result, attention must be given to the procedural protections provided in the corporation statutes; while it is possible that a court might give shareholders protection not found in the statute, on the basis of self dealing or fiduciary principles in connection with an amendment, one can hardly count on it. In the Revised Model Business Corporation Act and the statutes of most states there are two basic protections against abuse of the power of amendment: first, the right to vote by classes on specified kinds of amendments (in the RMBCA this right is described as the right to vote by "voting groups," but the concept is the same) discussed immediately below; and second, the statutory right of dissent and appraisal described in § 18.6 of this Nutshell. Outside of class voting and statutory appraisal rights, some states also require amendments to be approved by a greater than majority vote, two-thirds being the most common number. Most states today, however, require amendments only to be approved by an absolute majority of the shares entitled to vote, and the Revised Model Business Corporation Act even reduces this requirement in certain situations. See RMBCA § 10.03(e).

Outside of these protections, it is probable that minority holders have no basis for objecting to amendments validly approved which they consider adverse to their interest. Some early judicial decisions evolved the theory that certain rights, such as accrued cumulative dividend rights of preferred shares, are "contractual" or "vested" rights and cannot be eliminated over the objection of the owner by an amendment to the articles of incorporation. In order to reverse such decisions, decisively and unambiguously, the statutes of many states contain a "laundry list" of permissible amendments which itself is not exclusive. In the Revised Model Business Corporation Act this "laundry list" appears in the Official Comment rather than in the statute itself. Among the powers referred to in this list are the following:

Amendments increasing or decreasing the number of shares a corporation is authorized to issue;

Amendments exchanging, classifying, reclassifying, or cancelling any part of a corporation's shares, whether or not previously issued;

Amendments limiting or cancelling the right of holders of a class of shares to receive dividends, whether or not the dividends or rights to receive the dividends had accumulated in the past;

Amendments creating new classes of shares whether superior or inferior to shares already outstanding, or changing the designations of shares or the preferences, limitations, or rights of classes of shares, whether or not previously issued; and

Amendments changing the voting rights of outstanding shares, including elimination of the power to vote cumulatively or assigning multiple or fractional votes per share, or denying the power to vote entirely to classes of shares, whether or not previously issued.

It should be added parenthetically that not all statutes contain all of these broad provisions; in some states there may be limitations on the power of amendment, though there is not in most states.

Under the Revised Model Business Corporation Act and most state statutes, the board of directors must first recommend that an amendment be adopted before it can be considered by the shareholders. The board has a "gate keeper" function in this regard; its favorable recommendation is necessary before the shareholders may even consider a proposed amendment. The board of directors has a similar function in connection with mergers, sales of assets requiring approval of the shareholders, and other organic changes discussed in this chapter.

In the absence of specially tailored voting provisions in the articles of incorporation, the major protection of shareholders against unacceptable amendments imposed by other classes of shares is the right to vote by class (or "by voting groups") on specific amendments. The scope of this right depends on the specific statute, but generally, the objective is to require class voting on all amendments that are burdensome to the class as such and beneficial to other classes. See RMBCA § 10.04. In most states such amendments must be approved by the required percentage (usually an absolute majority, but two-thirds in a significant number of states) of each class voting as a separate class, and in addition, by the required percentage of all voting shares in the aggregate. Shares that are otherwise nonvoting are entitled to vote as a class if they are affected in one of the ways specified in the statute. See RMBCA § 10.04(d). The basic idea is that if the specified percentage of a class of shares is willing to accept a burdensome amendment, the balance must accept it as well.

The concept of "voting groups" in the Revised Model Business Corporation Act is identical to class voting. Because the RMBCA permits some series of shares to vote as separate classes in some circumstances [see RMBCA §§ 10.-04(b) and (c)], and requires combinations of two or more series in some situations to vote together, a new linguistic convention was necessary to distinguish between voting units and classes as set forth in the articles of incorporation. See also RMBCA §§ 1.40(26), 7.25, 7.26.

Despite the apparently unlimited statutory power, there is also a broad equitable principle that majority shareholders and directors must act in a fair way toward the corporation and minority shareholders. This principle may provide entry into the courtroom for minority shareholders who claim that an amendment serves no purpose other than injuring minority shareholders. In other words, vindictive amendments that seem to serve no purpose other than to enrich the majority at the expense of the minority may be subject to attack on fiduciary principles. The test may be phrased as "good faith" or "reasonableness" or "conflict of interest." (See §§ 14.7, 14.12 of this Nutshell.) Also, if there is a failure to provide accurate and complete information about the effect of a proposed amendment, the amendment may be attacked under federal or state law discussed earlier. (See §§ 14.16, 14.17 of this Nutshell.)

§ 18.2 Mergers and Consolidations

Business corporation acts specifically authorize certain kinds of corporate amalgamations:

(1) The merger of one domestic corporation into another domestic corporation;

(2) The consolidation of two domestic corporations into a new domestic corporation;

(3) The merger or consolidation of a domestic corporation and a foreign corporation, with the surviving or new corporation being either a domestic or a foreign corporation.

(4) In about a dozen states, the mandatory exchange of shares of one corporation for shares, cash, or other consideration provided by another corporation.

Technically a "merger" of corporation A into corporation B means that corporation B survives and corporation A disappears, while in a "consolidation" of corporation A and corporation B, both corporation A and corporation B disappear and a new corporation C is created. The Revised Model Business Corporation Act does not recognize the consolidation as a separate amalgamation device; the Official Comment states that such a device is obsolete since it almost always is advantageous for one entity or the other to survive, and if it is not, it is always possible to create a new entity and merge the other corporations into it.

These statutory methods of amalgamations are often simply described as "statutory mergers" to distinguish them from the asset-purchase and stock-purchase transactions described immediately below. Upon a statutory merger, the surviving or new corporation automatically has title to all assets of the disappearing corporations, and assumes all the liabilities of those corporations. Shareholders in all the corporations involved are entitled to receive whatever consideration is specified in the plan of merger.

A statutory merger or consolidation is only one of several possible ways of effecting a corporate acquisition or creating an amalgamated corporation out of formerly independent operations. The Internal Revenue Code has its own set of definitions that provide a useful summary of nonstatutory amalgamation techniques. It describes a statutory merger or consolidation as a class "A" reorganization.

A class "B" reorganization occurs when one corporation exchanges its voting shares for all or most of the outstanding shares of the other corporation, if the acquiring corporation has control of the other corporation immediately after the transaction. The distinguishing feature of a class B reorganization is that it involves an acquisition of stock. Two possible disadvantages of a stock acquisition are that the acquiring corporation may have to deal with a fairly large number of sellers, and the acquired business remains liable for all undisclosed or unknown liabilities, such as income tax deficiencies of prior years. This transaction often is referred to as a "stock purchase" or "stock acquisition" transaction.

A class "C" reorganization occurs when one corporation exchanges its voting shares for the assets of another corporation. The purchase may include all or most of the assets of the acquired corporation, or may include only the assets used in one line of business. After the transaction is completed, the acquired corporation remains in existence with assets consisting primarily of the proceeds of the sale. It also remains liable for liabilities not expressly assumed by the purchaser. Usually such a corporation will thereafter liquidate after making provision for liabilities not assumed by the purchaser, distributing the remaining proceeds to its shareholders. However, such a corporation may continue in existence operating as a holding or investment corporation. This transaction is often referred to as an "asset purchase" or "asset acquisition" transaction.

Clearly, the same basic economic result can be reached by casting a transaction in the form of a statutory merger, a stock purchase, or an asset purchase. The question as to which form a particular transaction should take is a complex one, involving a variety of tax and nontax considerations, on which an attorney may provide useful assistance. Often the parties to a specific transaction may have different views on this question, one preferring an asset purchase, the other a stock purchase or statutory merger.

Because of the similar economic effect no matter which form is followed, there is a possibility that the selection of a particular form to achieve some goal, such as not assuming certain types of liabilities, will not be successful. A court may reject form, "look at substance," and recast the transaction into a different form. This is the "de facto merger" notion, adopted in Farris v. Glen Alden Corp. (1958). The court held in that case that dissenting shareholders had the appraisal rights of a statutory merger despite the fact that the transaction was cast as an asset transaction. In this transaction the "selling" corporation sold assets for shares of the acquiring corporation and was required to dissolve and distribute the shares to its shareholders after the completion of the transaction. Because the "selling" corporation was much larger than the "acquiring" corporation, the latter dominated the former after the transaction in all material respects. The court referred to this transaction as a "hybrid form of corporate amalgamation" and said:

[I]t is no longer helpful to consider an individual transaction in the abstract and solely by reference to the various elements there in determining whether it is a "merger" or a "sale." Instead, to determine properly the nature of a corporate transaction, we must refer not only to all the provisions of the agreement, but also to the consequences of the transaction and to the purposes of the provisions of the corporation law said to be applicable.

Several cases are contra to *Farris,* and most academic writing has been critical of the de facto merger doctrine, since it makes rational corporate planning difficult if not impossible in many situations.

§ 18.3 Triangular Mergers, Cash Mergers, Short Form Mergers, and Related Developments

Until about 1960, statutory mergers and consolidations contemplated that mergers involved the amalgamation of two independent businesses into a single business, and that all shareholders in a disappearing corporation would receive shares in the surviving corporation in exchange for their shares in the disappearing corporation. These notions are now obsolete; today the consideration in a statutory merger may consist in whole or in part of cash or property other than shares, and most mergers do not involve the amalgamation of corporations of approximately the same size with both sets of shareholders being involved in the combined enterprise. Rather, they usually involve acquisition-type transactions, the elimination of minority interests in corporations for cash, the change in the state of incorporation of a corporation, or some other unexpected kind of transaction that at first blush has nothing to do with the traditional concept of a merger.

Many mergers today are triangular or reverse-triangular mergers. In a triangular merger the acquiring corporation forms a wholly owned subsidiary, "drops" cash or its own shares into that subsidiary, and then merges a corporation being acquired into the subsidiary. The shareholders of the acquired corporation may receive the cash or shares of the acquiring corporation (not, it should be noted, shares of the subsidiary into which the acquired corporation is merged). In this way, the shareholders of the acquired corporation receive cash or marketable shares of the acquiring corporation, but that corporation does not become responsible for liabilities of the acquired corporation. A reverse-triangular merger is a more complex transaction in which the wholly-owned subsidiary is merged into the acquired corporation (which itself ends up being a wholly-owned subsidiary of the acquiring corporation); the shares of the subsidiary held by the acquiring corporation are exchanged for newly issued shares of the acquired corporation and the shareholders of the acquired corporation receive cash or shares of the acquiring corporation in exchange for their shares of the acquired corporation. As a result, the acquired corporation becomes a wholly-owned subsidiary of the acquiring corporation and unassignable government contracts or untransferable tax characteristics will be (hopefully) unaffected. The critical point here is not the detail of the transactions: indeed, one commentator has stated that the "procedure is a magical one" and those who claim to understand it fully "are under an illusion." Rather, the critical point is that in both instances a three-way merger is used as an acquisition device and the acquired corporation's shareholders receive cash or shares of the parent corporation even though the merger is with a subsidiary of the parent corporation. (In these situations, the parent corporation is usually a publicly held corporation and a market exists for its shares; the subsidiary is created solely for the purpose of the particular transaction and obviously there is no market for its shares.)

Section 11.02 of the Revised Model Business Corporation Act creates a mandatory "share exchange" procedure as a substitute for a reverse triangular merger. This transaction is misnamed; it is not so much an exchange of shares as it is a device to compel a mandatory sale of shares. Under this procedure, a corporation may adopt a plan by which all the shares of a class are sold upon approval by a majority of the shares of that class. Shareholders who object to the sale are bound by it but have a statutory right of dissent and appraisal.

In order to clearly validate all triangular mergers, the merger statutes of most states now provide expressly that some parties to the merger might have their shares converted into "shares, obligations or other securities of the surviving corporation or any other corporation, or into cash or other property in whole or part." [RMBCA § 11.01(a)(3)] Such amendments permit another type of transaction, the "cash merger" (or "freeze out" or "squeeze out" merger, as they sometimes are called) in which certain shareholders are compelled to accept cash or property for their shares. For example, a corporation might merge into its own subsidiary with the majority shareholders receiving stock in the subsidiary and other shareholders being compelled to accept a specified amount of cash for their shares. Such a merger is in effect a device to force out or chase out unwanted shareholders. This procedure has been used to force out an unwanted minority shareholder, to eliminate all public shareholders in a "going private" transaction, to "mop up" the nonselling shareholders following a successful tender offer, and to eliminate unwanted minority shareholders in a subsidiary. It also has been used as an affirmative weapon to encourage shareholders of an unwilling target corporation to tender their shares. At the time of the initial tender offer, the second step is announced—the merger of the target into the aggressor on terms which are considerably less attractive than the terms of the initial offer. This type of transaction is sometimes called a "two tier" or "front-end loaded" tender offer, and is designed to panic shareholders into tendering their shares immediately in order to avoid the less attractive second step.

Transactions of this nature raise two basic questions to be addressed in section 18.4 of this Nutshell: (1) may such transactions be attacked on the ground that they lack any business purpose other than freezing or squeezing out a minority, or are unfair to the minority, and (2) are statutory appraisal rights an adequate protection for the frozen- or squeezed-out shareholder?

A somewhat parallel development to cash mergers has occurred in a related area: mergers between parent corporations and their subsidiaries. Such a merger is referred to as an "up stream" merger if the surviving corporation is the parent corporation and a "down stream" merger if the surviving corporation is the subsidiary. A publicly held corporation that wishes to change its state of incorporation, for example, may create a wholly-owned subsidiary in the new state, and then merge itself into its subsidiary in a down stream merger with all share and financial interests of the parent being mirrored in the subsidiary. Many states have adopted statutes that provide a special summary merger procedure for up stream mergers by which a parent corporation owning a large majority but less than all (e.g., 90 or 95 per cent) of the subsidiary shares may merge the subsidiary into the parent without a shareholders' vote of either corporation. (RMBCA § 11.04) This procedure is usually called a "short form merger." The theoretical basis of omitting both votes is that (1) a vote of the subsidiary's shareholders is unnecessary because the minority shareholders are, in any event, unable to block the merger, and (2) a vote of the parent's shareholders is unnecessary because the merger will not materially affect their rights which already include a 90 or 95 per cent interest in the subsidiary. The latter conclusion is based on the relatively slight increase in the parent's interest in the subsidiary resulting from the merger. The major practical justification for the short form merger statute is to effectuate a saving of the cost of proxy solicitations and meetings where the parent corporation is publicly held. The short form merger procedure creates no appraisal rights on the part of dissenting shareholders of the parent though it does for minority shareholders of the subsidiary who are "cashed out."

Short form merger statutes are applicable only to up stream mergers; they are not applicable to down stream mergers of the type used, for example, in changing the state of incorporation.

The most difficult theoretical problem with the short form merger statute lies in its treatment of the minority shareholders of the subsidiary. In a merger between independent corporations, it is unlikely that the shareholders of a corporation will approve a merger that is unfair to them. However, in the merger of a subsidiary into its parent, no such automatic protection exists against terms unfair to the subsidiary's minority shareholders; indeed, terms which are unfair to the minority shareholders are advantageous from the standpoint of the majority shareholder who is the parent. The short form merger statute attempts to avoid this problem by creating appraisal rights. (See § 18.6 of this Nutshell.)

§ 18.4 Fiduciary Duties in Mergers

Modern developments—cash mergers, going private transactions, short form mergers, and related practices— raise the question whether courts should have any role in judging or evaluating such transactions so long as the formal statutory procedural requirements are complied with. Despite some academic argument that courts should not judge motive or subjective fairness, and judicial review should be limited to assuring that the minority protection devices granted by statute are made available, the case law has developed in the opposite direction.

Cases have recognized that cash mergers and related practices should be judged by fiduciary principles applicable to self-dealing transactions since the price being offered the minority shareholders is in effect being set by the majority. The first case clearly accepting this principle was Singer v. Magnavox Co. (1977) which established a dual test: the transaction must have a "business purpose" and the transaction must meet a standard of "intrinsic" or "entire" fairness. Other states quickly followed the lead of Delaware in this regard. However, in Delaware the court, after struggling in several cases with the meaning of "business purpose," concluded in Weinberger v. UOP, Inc. (1983) that the "business purpose" test provided little protection to shareholders and eliminated it; the court continued to apply a strict "intrinsic fairness" test that included a requirement of full and meaningful disclosure. See § 14.12 of this Nutshell. The court also concluded that in the future the remedy in the event of a claim of inadequate price should be limited to a more generous appraisal remedy (see § 18.6 of this Nutshell) than was available in Delaware previously.

Not all courts, however, have followed the lead of Delaware in eliminating the business purpose test in evaluating such transactions. Both New York and Massachusetts, for example, apparently still impose the dual test derived from *Singer.*

These fiduciary duty tests for cash merger and similar transactions were developed by state courts as a matter of state law. An attempt to find a "fairness" standard in rule 10b–5 to evaluate such transactions was rejected by the United States Supreme Court in Santa Fe Industries, Inc. v. Green (1977), holding that the essence of a rule 10b–5 violation was nondisclosure or misrepresentation of material facts. As a result of this holding, judicial controls over the transactions described in this section are solely within the province of state courts.

§ 18.5 Sales of All or Substantially All the Assets of a Corporation

A sale, lease, exchange, or other disposition of all, or substantially all, the property and assets of a corporation, not in the usual and regular course of business, must, under the statutes of most states, be approved by the shareholders as an organic change in the corporation. RMBCA § 12.02. If the transaction is in the ordinary course of business, shareholder approval is not usually required. RMBCA § 12.01. Most states specifically consider a pledge, mortgage, or deed of trust covering all the assets of the corporation to be within the ordinary course of business and therefore shareholder approval is not required. Section 12.01 also includes deployment of assets through a wholly-owned subsidiary as a transaction not requiring shareholder approval.

The phrase "all or substantially all" has received varied judicial treatment. Most courts have construed this language flexibly, and required shareholder approval when significant components of a corporation are sold even though other significant components are retained. The Official Comment to section 12.01 of the Revised Model Business Corporation Act suggests that this phrase is synonymous with "all or nearly all" and "was added merely to make clear that the statutory requirements could not be avoided by retention of some minimal or nominal residue of the original assets." Most decisions have not adopted this stricter approach.

In most states, shareholders have a statutory right of dissent and appraisal in connection with transactions involving the disposition of substantially all the assets of the corporation not in the ordinary course of business. RMBCA § 13.02(a)(3).

When a corporation sells substantially all its assets, the business is normally continued by the purchaser of the assets, though it may be broadened or narrowed in scope. In such a transaction, the purchaser may assume specified liabilities arising in the ordinary course of business, but typically will not assume any other liabilities of the enterprise. Following the sale, the selling corporation usually dissolves and distributes the remaining assets to its shareholders without making any provision for unknown liabilities that may arise in the future. A major problem is thereafter created if persons are injured by products manufactured by the selling corporation, which injuries may occur many years after the transaction in question and many years after the dissolution of the selling corporation. The purchaser of the assets (that is continuing the business) is invariably sued in this situation, and will typically argue that it is not liable because it did not expressly or impliedly assume products liabilities in connection with the asset purchase. In recent years, many courts have evolved theories of de facto merger, continuity of business, or product line liability by which the purchaser may be held liable for such claims despite the absence of an express assumption of liability (or, indeed, despite an express negation of any such assumption). A number of courts, however, have also declined to impose liability on the purchaser in this situation, either because of the specific facts of the transaction or by rejecting broad theories by which liability might be imposed.

§ 18.6   Appraisal Remedies

State statutes give shareholders the right to dissent from certain types of transactions and to obtain the appraised value of their shares through a judicial proceeding. RMBCA ch. 13. Since the right is entirely the creature of statute, it is generally thought to be available only when the statute so provides. In a handful of cases, however, innovative courts have created appraisal-type remedies in nonstatutory situations.

The statutory appraisal remedy may be lost if the elaborate statutory procedures are not precisely followed. If the right is lost, the dissenting shareholder must go along with the objectionable transaction.

Under section 13.02 of the Revised Model Business Corporation Act the appraisal right is extended only to regular mergers, short form mergers (shareholders of the subsidiary only), compulsory share exchanges, sales of substantially all corporate assets not in the ordinary course of business, and specific types of adverse amendments to articles of incorporation. The standards for determining when the right of dissent and appraisal exists in section 13.02 differ to some extent from the standards for determining when shares are entitled to vote by classes (or by voting groups) in section 10.04. The RMBCA further limits the right of dissent and appraisal basically to shares that are entitled to vote on the transaction, but many states do not impose this limitation and may permit nonvoting shares to elect to dissent from specific transactions.

The statutes of many states purport to make the statutory appraisal remedy exclusive in the absence of fraud, though some states purport to make it exclusive without exception, and some make it nonexclusive in all cases. Section 13.-02(b) of the Revised Model Business Corporation Act follows the New York statute and makes that remedy exclusive "unless the action is unlawful or fraudulent with respect to the shareholder or the corporation."

The Delaware Supreme Court in Weinberger v. UOP, Inc. (1983) indicated that in the future, shareholders objecting to cash mergers on the basis of inadequate price should rely on the appraisal remedy rather than seek recissory damages or an order setting aside the transaction. (See § 18.4 of this Nutshell.) The court also relaxed the principles previously applicable in Delaware to determine the value of shares in appraisal proceedings, which should also make that remedy more attractive. Cede & Co. v. Technicolor, Inc. (1988) permits the plaintiff in an appraisal proceeding to maintain simultaneously a suit for recissory damages based on a breach of fiduciary duty discovered after the appraisal proceeding was commenced.

The statutory dissent procedure usually requires that a written notice of dissent be filed by the dissenting shareholder before the vote of shareholders on the proposed action. Because appraisal claims may constitute serious cash drains, it is not uncommon in merger and other agreements to provide an "out" for the parties if an excessive number of dissents are filed. Following the affirmative vote on the proposal, the dissenting shareholder automatically has the status of creditor rather than shareholder. The RMBCA sets forth an elaborate procedure by which the shareholder must designate in writing a price at which he or she is willing to sell, the corporation must respond by setting a written price at which it is willing to buy; if negotiation fails, a court proceeding to establish the appraised price follows. This appraised price is to be fixed as of a time immediately before the transaction in question is to occur, but no account is to be taken of the potential impact of the transaction on the value of the shares.

Under traditional statutes, the corporation must pay the price in cash only after the appraised price is finally determined.

The traditional appraisal remedy has a superficial appeal and plausibility. However, from the dissenting shareholder's point of view it is not an attractive remedy, and there has been considerable litigation seeking to avoid appraisal proceedings. Not only does the process involve potentially long delays while the price is established, but litigation over the value of shares is likely to be viewed as expensive and unrewarding. Since the corporation is an active participant in the judicial proceeding seeking to establish the lowest possible valuation, the cards are to some extent stacked against the dissenting shareholders. They must accept the judicially determined price which may be based primarily on the evidence and materials presented by the corporation with its extensive knowledge about its own affairs and virtually unlimited resources. Finally, the corporation need pay nothing until the proceeding is completed years later, and many corporations have apparently decided to litigate at leisure in an effort to wear down the dissenting shareholders.

Chapter 13 of the Revised Model Business Corporation Act was designed to make the appraisal remedy more attractive and useful. On the one hand, provisions were included requiring potential dissenters to identify themselves as early as possible so that corporations would know the extent of the potential liability. Further, when the corporation estimates the value of the dissenters' shares, it must pay that amount immediately without waiting for a final disposition of the appraisal. Procedures were also established that were designed to encourage a negotiated price rather than a litigated price; if a judicial appraisal is necessary, the court has authority to award costs, including attorneys' fees, either for or against the corporation depending on the court's estimate as to whether valuations were made in good faith.

The statutes of many states contain a "market exception" to the appraisal remedy. Under these statutes, the right to dissent does not exist if there is a market for the shares in question. Earlier versions of the Model Business Corporation Act contained such a provision, but it was not included in the Revised Model Business Corporation Act. The theory behind the market exception is that the dissent remedy is appropriate only for minority shareholders locked into the corporation, and that there is no need for a statutory appraisal if an established market exists for the dissenters' shares. The argument against such a restriction basically is that the appraisal remedy protects minority shareholders against transactions not related to the liquidity of their investment.

§ 18.7 Voluntary Dissolution

Most state statutes contain a variety of dissolution provisions. These include streamlined provisions for dissolution before commencement of business by the incorporators or initial directors and dissolution at any time with the unanimous consent of the shareholders. The latter is widely used in closely held corporations, though the same result can usually be reached under unanimous shareholder consent statutes. The regular dissolution process involves adoption of a resolution to dissolve by the board of directors and approval of it by a majority or some other specified percentage of the shareholders. In this regard, dissolution is similar to other organic changes by the corporation in which the board of directors serves a gate keeping function.

Some states require the filing of a notice of intent to dissolve, followed by a period in which the business and affairs of the corporation are wound up, followed by the filing of final articles of dissolution. In other states, only articles of dissolution are filed when the corporate affairs are wound up. Irrespective of the type of statute involved, notice to creditors must be given, and final dissolution is permitted only after all franchise and other tax obligations have been fully satisfied. Directors are under a fiduciary duty to pay, discharge, or make provision for all known liabilities of the corporation before making final liquidating distributions to shareholders.

State statutes provide that the existence of a corporation continues after dissolution for a stated period so that the corporation may be sued on pre-dissolution claims. A major problem in post-dissolution litigation is the status of tort claimants who are injured by products manufactured by the corporation years after the corporation has dissolved. The stated period in which suit must be brought may have expired long before the injury occurred. If the corporation sold its operating assets before dissolving, suits by such claimants may be brought against the purchaser of the assets on theories of de facto merger, continuity of enterprise, or similar theories.

For obvious reasons, there is no statutory right of appraisal in connection with a voluntary dissolution. There may be, however, some equitable limitations on the power to dissolve. These involve situations where a voluntary liquidation is arguably unfair to minority shareholders or which may constitute a "freeze out" of such shareholders. Standards, however, are elusive. Cases have arisen where the objective of dissolution was apparently to eliminate some shareholders from sharing in the profits of a good business, or where the proposal was not to discontinue the business, but to turn it over to a new corporation owned by some but not all of the original owners. Were such behavior sanctioned, a minority could be ejected from a successful venture through the process of dissolution as readily as through a cash merger. If so, the test of "entire fairness" developed in the merger cases should logically apply to at least some statutory dissolutions as well.

[For unfamiliar terms see the Glossary]

GLOSSARY

ACCOUNTS PAYABLE are amounts owed by a business on open account to creditors for goods and services. Analysts look at the relationship between accounts payable and total purchases as an indication of sound day-to-day financial management.

ACCOUNTS RECEIVABLE are amounts owing to a business for merchandise or services sold on open account.

ADOPTION is a contract principle by which a person agrees to assume a contract previously made for his or her benefit. An adoption speaks only from the time such person agrees, in contrast to a "ratification" which relates back to the time the original contract was made. In corporation law, the concept is applied when a newly formed corporation accepts a preincorporation contract made for its benefit by a promoter.

AFFILIATE is a corporation that is related to another corporation by shareholdings or other means of control. It includes not only a parent or a subsidiary but also corporations that are under common control.

AGGRESSOR CORPORATION is a corporation that attempts to obtain control of a publicly held corporation, often by a direct cash tender or public exchange offer to shareholders, but also possibly by way of merger, which requires agreement or assent of the target's management.

ALL HOLDERS' RULE is a rule adopted by SEC that prohibits a public offer by the issuer of shares to all but certain designated shareholders.

AMORTIZATION is an accounting procedure that gradually reduces the cost or value of a limited life or

447

intangible asset through periodic charges against income. For fixed assets amortization is called "depreciation," and for wasting assets (natural resources) it is "depletion." The periodic charges are usually treated as current expenses for purposes of determining income.

AMOTION is the common law procedure by which a director may be removed for cause by the shareholders.

ANTIDILUTION PROVISIONS appear in convertible securities to guarantee that the conversion privilege is not affected by share reclassifications, share splits, share dividends, or similar transactions that may increase the number of outstanding shares without increasing the corporate capital.

APPRAISAL is a limited statutory right granted to minority shareholders who object to specified fundamental transactions, e.g. mergers. In an appraisal proceeding a court determines the value of their shares and the corporation pays such appraised value to the dissenting shareholders in cash. The Revised Model Business Corporation Act uses the term "dissenters' rights to obtain payment for their shares" to describe this right. The appraisal right exists only to the extent specifically provided by statute.

ARBITRAGERS are market investors who take off-setting positions in the same or similar securities in order to profit from small price variations. An arbitrager, for example, may buy shares on the Pacific Coast Exchange and simultaneously sell the same shares on the New York Stock Exchange if any price discrepancy occurs between the quotations in the two markets. By taking advantage of momentary disparities in prices between markets, arbitragers perform the economic function of making those markets more efficient.

ARBS is a slang term for arbitragers.

ARTICLES OF INCORPORATION is the name customarily given to the document that is filed in order to form a corporation. Under various state statutes, this document may be called the "certificate of incorporation," "charter," "articles of association," or other similar name.

AUTHORIZED SHARES are the shares described in the articles of incorporation which a corporation may issue. Modern corporate practice recommends authorization of more shares than it is currently planned to issue.

BEAR is a slang term for a speculator who believes securities prices are going to decline. A pessimist is "bearish." Contrast: bull.

BENEFICIAL HOLDERS OF SECURITIES are persons who own shares but who have not registered the shares in their names on the records of the corporation. See also: record owner.

BID AND ASKED are terms that deal with price quotations for securities or commodities. "Bid" is the highest price a prospective buyer is prepared to pay at a particular time for a trading unit; "asked" is the lowest price a prospective seller of the same unit is prepared to accept. Together, the two prices constitute a quotation by a market maker in the security or commodity; the difference between the two prices is the "spread." Although bid and asked prices are common to all securities trading, "bid and asked" usually refers to securities traded "over the counter" and to commodities and commodities futures trading.

BLOCK is a large quantity of securities involved in a single trade. As a general guide, block trades involve 10,000 or more shares or bonds with a total face amount in excess of $200,000.

BLOCKAGE is a price phenomenon: a large block of shares may be more difficult to market than a smaller block, particularly if the market is thin. The discount at which a large block sells below the price of a smaller block is blockage. Blockage is generally a phenomenon of shares which do not represent the controlling interest in a corporation. Compare: control premium.

BLUE CHIP shares are common shares of nationally known companies that have a long record of profit growth and dividend payment and reputations for quality management, products, and services. Blue chip shares typically are relatively high priced and low yielding, and are viewed as conservative investments.

BLUE SKY LAWS are state statutes that regulate the sale of securities to the public within the state. Most blue sky laws require the registration of new issues of securities with a state agency that reviews selling documents for accuracy and completeness. Blue sky laws also often regulate securities brokers and salesmen.

BONDS are long term debt instruments secured by a lien on some or all the corporate property. Historically, a bond was payable to bearer and interest coupons representing annual or semi-annual payments of interest were attached (to be "clipped" periodically and submitted for payment). Today, most bonds are issued in registered or book entry form. Bondholders in effect have an IOU from the issuer; they are creditors and not owners of the enterprise. The word bond is sometimes used more broadly to refer also to unsecured debt instruments, i.e., debentures. Income bonds are hybrid instruments that take the form of a bond, but the interest obligation is limited or tied to the corporate earnings for the year. Participating bonds take the form of a typical debt instrument but the interest obligation is not fixed so that holders are entitled to receive additional amounts from excess earnings or from excess distributions, depending on the terms of the participating bond.

BONUS SHARES are par value shares issued without consideration, usually in connection with the issuance of preferred or senior securities, or debt instruments. Bonus shares are considered a species of watered shares and may impose a liability on the recipient equal to the amount of par value.

BOOK ENTRY describes the method of reflecting ownership of publicly traded securities in which customers of brokerage firms receive confirmations of transactions and monthly statements but not certificates. Brokerage firms also may reflect their customers' ownership of securities by book entry in the records of a central clearing corporation, principally Depository Trust Company (DTC). DTC reflects transactions between brokerage firms primarily by book entry in its records rather than by the physical movement of securities. Shares held by DTC are recorded in the name of its nominee, Cede and Company.

BOOK VALUE is the value of shares determined on the basis of the books of the corporation. Using the corporation's latest balance sheet, the liabilities are subtracted from assets, an appropriate amount is deducted to reflect the interest of senior securities (preferred shares), and what remains is divided by the number of outstanding common shares to obtain the book value of a share. Book value is widely used as an estimate of value, particularly of closely held shares, but has certain limitations: it is based on accounting conventions, may not reflect unrealized appreciation or depreciation of assets, and does not take into account future prospects of the business.

BROKER in a securities transaction, means a person who acts as an agent for a buyer or seller, or an intermediary between a buyer and seller, usually charging a commission. A broker who specializes in shares, bonds, commodities, or options must be registered with the exchange where the specific securities are traded. A broker should be distinguished from a dealer who, unlike a broker, buys or sells for his own account. Securities firms typically act as dealers and brokers, depending on the security involved.

BULL is a slang term for a speculator who believes securities prices are going to increase. An optimist is "bullish." Contrast: bear.

BUYOUT is the purchase of a controlling percentage of a company's shares. A buyout often involves all of the company's outstanding shares. A buyout can be accomplished through negotiation, through a tender offer, or through a merger.

BYLAWS are the formal rules of internal governance adopted by a corporation. Bylaws define the rights and obligations of various officers, persons, or groups within the corporate structure and provide rules for routine matters such as calling meetings and the like. Most state corporation statutes contemplate that every corporation will adopt bylaws, though special close corporation statutes may make bylaws optional for qualifying close corporations.

CALL FOR REDEMPTION. See: redemption.

CALLS are options to buy securities at a stated price for a stated period. Many calls (or call options) to purchase shares of companies listed on the New York Stock Exchange are themselves publicly traded. Calls also are written on a variety of indexes, foreign currencies, and other securities. The person who commits himself or herself to sell the security upon the request of the call holder is referred to as the call writer; the act of making the purchase of the securities pursuant to the call option is referred to as exercise of the option. The price at which the call is excercisable is the strike price. See also: puts.

CAPITAL STOCK is another phrase for common shares, often used when the corporation has only one class of shares outstanding.

CAPITAL SURPLUS, in the old Model Business Corporation Act nomenclature, is an equity or capital account which reflects the capital contributed for shares not allocated to stated capital: the excess of issuance price over the par value of issued shares or the consideration paid for no par shares allocated specifically to capital surplus. Capital surplus may be distributed to shareholders under certain circumstances or used for purchase or redemption of shares more readily than stated capital.

CAPITALIZATION is an imprecise term that usually refers to the amounts received by a corporation for the issuance of its shares. However, it may also be used to refer to the proceeds of loans to a corporation made by its shareholders (which may be in lieu of capital contributions) or even to capital raised by the issuance of long term bonds or debentures to third persons. Depending on the context, it may also refer to accumulated earnings not withdrawn from the corporation.

CASH FLOW refers to an analysis of the movement of cash through a venture as contrasted with the earnings of the venture. For example, a mandatory debt repayment is taken into account in a cash flow analysis even though such a repayment does not reduce earnings. See: negative cash flow.

CASH MERGER is a merger transaction in which certain shareholders or interests in a corporation are required to accept cash for their shares while other shareholders receive shares in the continuing enterprise. Modern statutes generally authorize cash mergers, though courts test such mergers on the basis of fairness and, in some states, business purpose.

CASH TENDER OFFER is a technique by which an aggressor corporation seeks to obtain control of a target corporation by making a public offer to purchase a specified fraction (usually a majority) of the target corporation's shares from persons who tender their shares.

C CORPORATION is a corporation that has not elected (or is disqualified from electing) S corporation tax status.

The taxable income of a C corporation is subject to tax at the corporate level while dividends continue to be taxed at the shareholder level. See Double Taxation. Compare S Corporation.

CEDE & COMPANY is the nominee for Depository Trust Company, the principal central clearing corporation. See: book entry.

CEO stands for "chief executive officer" of a publicly held corporation. *CEO* is a preferred and useful designation because official titles of such persons vary widely from corporation to corporation.

CERTIFICATE OF INCORPORATION in most states is the document prepared by the Secretary of State that evidences the acceptance of articles of incorporation and the commencement of the corporate existence. In some states the certificate of incorporation is the name given to the document filed with the Secretary of State, i.e., the articles of incorporation. The Revised Model Business Corporation Act has eliminated certificates of incorporation, requiring only a fee receipt.

CHARTER may mean (i) the document filed with the Secretary of State, i.e., the articles of incorporation, or (ii) the grant by the State of the privilege of conducting business with limited liability. Charter is often used in a colloquial sense to refer to the basic constitutive documents of the corporation.

CLASS VOTING. See: voting group.

CLOSE CORPORATION or **CLOSELY HELD CORPORATION** is a corporation with relatively few shareholders and no regular markets for its shares. There is no litmus test for when a corporation should be considered closely held and the definition may in part depend on the substantive context in which it arises. In addition to the small number of shareholders and lack of public market, close corporations usually have made no public offering of shares and the shares themselves are usually subject to restrictions on transfer. Close and closely held are synonymous in this context.

CLOSELY HELD. See: close corporation.

COMMERCIAL PAPER is a generic term for short-term obligations usually with maturities ranging from 2 to 270 days, issued by banks, corporations, and other borrowers. Such instruments are unsecured and usually sold at a discount from face value, although some are interest-bearing.

COMMON SHAREHOLDERS are holders of common shares, the ultimate owners of the residual interest of a corporation. See: common shares.

COMMON SHARES represent the residual ownership interests in the corporation. Holders of common shares select directors to manage the enterprise, are entitled to dividends out of the earnings of the enterprise declared by the directors, and are entitled to a per share distribution of whatever assets remain upon dissolution after satisfying or making provisions for creditors and holders of senior securities.

CONSOLIDATION is an amalgamation of two corporations pursuant to statutory provision in which both of the corporations disappear and a new corporation is formed. The Revised Model Business Corporation Act eliminates the consolidation as a distinct type of corporate amalgamation.

CONTROL OF A CORPORATION BY A PERSON normally means that the person has power to vote a majority of the outstanding shares. However, control may be reflected in a significantly smaller block if the remaining shares are scattered in small, disorganized holdings.

CONTROL PERSON in securities law is a person who is deemed to be in a control relationship with the issuer.

Sales of securities by control persons are subject to many of the requirements applicable to the sale of securities directly by the issuer. In addition, controlling persons have a duty under ITSFEA to prevent insider trading by persons under their control. See ITSFEA.

CONTROL PREMIUM refers to the pricing phenomenon by which shares that carry the power to control a corporation are more valuable per share than the shares that do not carry a power of control. The control premium is often computed not on a per share basis but on the aggregate increase in value of the "control block" over the going market or other price of shares which are not part of the "control block."

CONVERSION SECURITIES are the securities into which convertible securities may be converted. See: convertible securities.

CONVERTIBLE SECURITIES are securities that include the right of exchanging the convertible securities, usually preferred shares or debentures, at the option of their holder, for a designated number of shares of another class, usually common shares, called the conversion securities. The ratio between the convertible and conversion securities is fixed at the time the convertible securities are issued, and is usually protected against dilution.

CO–PROMOTERS. See: promoters.

CORPORATE OPPORTUNITY is a fiduciary concept that limits the power of officers, directors, and employees to take personal advantage of opportunities that belong to the corporation.

CORPORATION BY ESTOPPEL is a doctrine which prevents a third person from holding an "officer," "director," or "shareholder" of a nonexistent corporation personally liable on an obligation entered into in the name of the nonexistent corporation on the theory that the third person relied on the existence of the corporation and is now "estopped" from denying that the corporation existed.

CUMULATIVE DIVIDENDS on preferred shares carry over from one year to the next if a preference dividend is omitted. An omitted cumulative dividend must be made up in a later year before any dividend may be paid on the common shares in that later year. However, cumulative dividends are not debts of the corporation but merely a right to priority in future discretionary distributions.

CUMULATIVE TO THE EXTENT EARNED DIVIDENDS on preferred shares are cumulative dividends that are limited in any one year to the available earnings of the corporation in that year.

CUMULATIVE VOTING is a method of voting that allows substantial minority shareholders to obtain representation on the board of directors. When voting cumulatively, a shareholder may cast all of his or her available votes in an election in favor of a single candidate.

CURRENT YIELD See: nominal yield.

D & O INSURANCE refers to directors' and officers' liability insurance. Such insurance, which is widely available commercially, insures such persons against claims based on negligence, failure to disclose, and to a limited extent, other defalcations. Such insurance provides coverage against expenses and to a limited extent fines, judgments, and amounts paid in settlement.

DEADLOCK in a closely held corporation arises when a control structure permits one or more factions of shareholders to block corporate action if they disagree with some aspect of corporate policy. A deadlock often arises with respect to the election of directors, e.g., by an equal division of shares between two factions, but may also arise at the level of the board of directors itself.

DEBENTURES are long term unsecured debt instruments. Historically, a debenture was payable to bearer and interest coupons representing annual or semiannual payments of interest were attached. See: bonds.

DEEP ROCK DOCTRINE is a principle in bankruptcy law by which unfair or inequitable claims presented by controlling shareholders of bankrupt corporations may be subordinated to claims of general or trade creditors. The doctrine received its name from the corporate name of the subsidiary involved in the leading case articulating the doctrine.

DE FACTO CORPORATION at common law is a partially formed corporation that provides a shield against personal liability of shareholders for corporate obligations; such a corporation may be attacked only by the state.

DE FACTO MERGER is a transaction that has the economic effect of a statutory merger but is cast in the form of an acquisition of assets or an acquisition of voting stock and is treated by a court as if it were a statutory merger.

DE JURE CORPORATION at common law is a corporation that is sufficiently formed to be recognized as a corporation for all purposes. A de jure corporation may exist even though some minor statutory requirements have not been fully complied with.

DELECTUS PERSONAE is a Latin phrase used in partnership law to describe the power each partner possesses to accept or reject proposed new members of the firm.

DEPOSITORY TRUST CORPORATION is the principal central clearing agency for securities trades. See: book entry.

DEREGISTRATION of an issuer occurs when the number of securities holders of an issuer registered under section 12 of the Securities Exchange Act of 1934 has declined to the point where registration is no longer required. See: registered corporation.

DERIVATIVE SUIT is a suit brought by a shareholder in the name of a corporation to correct a wrong done to the corporation.

DILUTION of outstanding shares results from the issuance of additional shares. The dilution may be of voting power if shares are not issued proportionately to the holdings of existing shareholders, or it may be financial, if shares are issued disproportionately and the price at which the new shares are issued is less than the market or book value of the outstanding shares prior to the issuance of the new shares.

DIRECTORY REQUIREMENTS are minor statutory requirements. At common law, a de jure corporation may be created despite the failure to comply with directory requirements relating to its formation. Important statutory requirements are called mandatory requirements.

DISCOUNT SHARES are par value shares issued for cash less than par value. Discount shares are considered a species of watered shares and may impose a liability on the recipient equal to the difference between the par value and the cash for which such shares were issued.

DISSENSION in a closely held corporation refers to personal quarrels or disputes between shareholders that may make business relations unpleasant and interfere with the successful operation of the business. Dissension may occur without constituting oppression or causing a deadlock or adversely affecting the corporation's business.

DISSENTERS' RIGHT. See: appraisal.

DISTRIBUTION is a payment to shareholders by a corporation. If out of present or past earnings it is a dividend. The word distribution is sometimes accompanied by a word describing the source or purpose of the payment, e.g., Distribution of Capital Surplus, or Liquidating Distribution.

DIVIDEND is a payment to shareholders from or out of current or past earnings. The word dividend is sometimes used more broadly to refer to any payment to shareholders though a more appropriate term for payments out of capital is distribution.

DOUBLE TAXATION refers to the structure of taxation under the Internal Revenue Code of 1954 which subjects income earned by a C corporation to an income tax at the corporate level and a second tax at the shareholder level if the previously taxed income is distributed to shareholders in the form of dividends.

DOWN STREAM MERGER is the merger of a parent corporation into its subsidiary.

EARNINGS PER SHARE equals a firm's net income divided by the number of shares held by shareholders. Earnings per share is a key statistic in evaluating a share's outlook.

EQUITY or **EQUITY INTEREST** are financial terms that refer in general to the extent of an ownership interest in a venture. In this context, equity refers not to a legal concept but to the financial definition that an owner's equity in a business is equal to the business's assets minus its liabilities.

EQUITY FINANCING is raising money by the sale of common shares or preferred shares. Equity financing is most popular when securities prices are high so that the most capital can be raised with the issuance of the smallest number of shares.

EQUITY SECURITY is a security that represents an interest in the equity of a business. See: equity. Equity securities are usually considered to be common and preferred shares.

EX DIVIDEND refers to the date on which a purchaser of publicly traded shares is not entitled to receive a dividend that has been declared and the seller of such shares is entitled to retain the dividend. The ex dividend date is a matter of agreement or of convention to be established by the securities exchange. On the first day shares are traded without the right to receive a dividend, the price will decline by approximately the amount of the dividend; such shares are referred to as "trading ex dividend."

EX RIGHTS refers to the date on which a purchaser of publicly traded shares is not entitled to receive rights that have been declared on the shares.

FACE VALUE is the value of a bond, note, mortgage, or other security, as given on the certificate or instrument, payable upon maturity of the instrument. The face value is also the amount on which interest or coupon payments are calculated. Thus, a 10% bond with a face value of $1000 pays bondholders $100 per year. Face value is also often referred to as the par value or nominal value of the instrument.

FORCED CONVERSION refers to a conversion of a convertible security that follows a call for redemption at a time when the value of the conversion security is greater than the amount that will be received if the holder permits the security to be redeemed. Normally, a holder of a convertible redeemable security has a period of time after the call for redemption to determine whether or not to exercise the conversion privilege.

FREEZE–OUT refers to a process, usually in a closely held corporation, by which minority shareholders are prevented from receiving any direct or indirect financial return from the corporation in an effort to persuade them to liquidate their investment in the corporation on terms favorable to the controlling shareholders. See: squeeze out.

FREEZE–OUT MERGER. See: cash merger.

GENERAL PARTNERS are unlimitedly liable for the debts of the partnership. General partner is usually used in contrast with limited partner in a limited partnership, but general partner is also sometimes used to refer to any partner in a general partnership.

GOING PRIVATE refers to a transaction in which public shareholders of a publicly held corporation are compelled to accept cash for their shares while the business continues to be owned by officers, directors, or large shareholders. A going private transaction may involve a merger of the publicly held corporation into a subsidiary in a cash merger.

GOING PUBLIC refers to the first public distribution of securities by an issuer pursuant to registration under the securities acts. If a corporation has been in business for several years, the initial registration by which the corporation goes public is apt to be difficult and expensive.

GOLDEN PARACHUTE is a slang term for a lucrative contract given to a top executive of a company. The contract usually provides additional benefits in case the company is taken over and the executive is either forced to leave the target company or voluntarily leaves it. A golden parachute might include generous severance pay, stock options, or a bonus payable when the executive's employment at the company ends.

GREENMAIL is a slang term that refers to a payment by the target to a potential aggressor to purchase at a premium over market shares that have been acquired by the aggressor. The acquirer in exchange agrees not to pursue its takeover bid.

HOLDING COMPANY is a corporation that owns a majority of the shares of one or more other corporations. Usually a holding company is not engaged in any business other than the ownership of such majority shares. See: investment companies.

HYBRID SECURITIES are securities that have some of the attributes of both debt securities and equity securities.

INCORPORATORS are the person or persons who execute the articles of incorporation. In modern statutes only a single incorporator is required and the role of the incorporator is largely limited to the act of execution of the articles of incorporation. Restrictions on who may serve as incorporators have largely been eliminated.

INDEMNIFICATION refers to the practice by which corporations pay expenses of officers or directors who are named as defendants in litigation relating to corporate affairs. In some instances corporations may indemnify officers and directors for fines, judgments, or amounts paid in settlement as well as expenses. Broad indemnification rights may raise issues of public policy; on the other hand, it may be difficult or impossible to persuade persons to serve as directors in the absence of indemnification.

INDENTURE is the contract which defines the rights of holders of bonds or debentures as against the corporation. Typically, the contract is entered into between the corporation and an indenture trustee whose responsibility is to protect the bondholders. The indenture often constitutes a mortgage on specified corporate property to secure the bonds.

IN PARI DELICTO is a common law principle also known as the "unclean hands" doctrine. The principle limits a person intending to engage in wrongful conduct from suing another wrongdoer when things do not work out as expected.

INSIDE DIRECTORS are directors of a publicly held corporation who hold executive positions with management.

INSIDER is a term of uncertain scope that refers to persons having some relationship to an issuer, and whose securities trading on the basis of nonpublic information may be a violation of law. Insider is broader than inside director.

INSIDER TRADING refers to transactions in shares of publicly held corporations by persons with inside or advance information on which the trading is based. Usually the trader himself is an insider with an employment or other relationship of trust and confidence with the corporation. See: tip.

INSOLVENCY may refer to either equity insolvency or insolvency in the bankruptcy sense. Equity insolvency means that the business is unable to pay its debts as they mature while bankruptcy insolvency means that the aggregate liabilities of the business exceeds its assets. Since it is not uncommon for a business to be unable to meet its debts as they mature yet have assets that exceed in value its liabilities, or vice versa, it is often important to specify in which sense the term insolvency is being used.

INSTITUTIONAL INVESTORS are large investors, such as mutual funds, pension funds, insurance companies, and others who largely invest other people's money. Since World War II, institutional investors have accounted for an increasing portion of all public securities trading.

INTERLOCKING DIRECTORS are persons who serve simultaneously on the boards of directors of two or more corporations that have dealings with each other. Federal antitrust law prohibits interlocking directors of competing businesses; such directors may also create problems involving fiduciary duties.

INTRA VIRES means acts within the powers or stated purposes of a corporation. Intra vires is the opposite of ultra vires.

INVESTMENT BANKERS are commercial organizations involved in the business of handling the distribution of new issues of securities. See: underwriters. An investment banker may also provide other investment and advisory services to corporations.

INVESTMENT COMPANIES are corporations that are engaged in the business of investing in securities of other businesses. The most common kind of investment company is the mutual fund. An investment company differs from a holding company in that the latter seeks control of the ventures in which it invests while an investment company seeks the investment for its own sake and normally diversifies its investments. Investment companies are subdivided into "open end" and "closed end" companies. An "open end" company stands ready at all times to redeem its securities at net asset value and to issue new shares to investors on demand; such an investment company is usually known as a mutual fund. An investment company that has a fixed capitalization and neither issues new shares or redeems outstanding shares on request is called a "closed end" company.

ISSUED SHARES are shares a corporation has actually issued and has not cancelled. Issued shares should be contrasted with authorized shares. Issued shares that have been reacquired by the corporation are called treasury shares. The Revised Model Business Corporation Act and the statutes of several states have eliminated the concept of treasury shares.

ITSA is the acronym for the Insider Trading Sanctions Act of 1984.

ITSFEA is the acronym for the Insider Trading and Securities Fraud Enforcement Act of 1988.

JOINT VENTURE is a limited purpose partnership largely governed by the rules applicable to partnerships. In an earlier day, many states permitted corporations to participate in joint ventures but treated as ultra vires an attempt by a corporation to become a partner in a general partnership.

JUNIOR SECURITIES are issues of debt or equity that are subordinate to other issues in terms of dividends, interest, principal, security, or payments upon dissolution. See: preferred share; senior security.

LEVERAGE refers to the advantages that may accrue to a business through the use of debt obtained from third persons in lieu of contributed capital. Such debt improves the earnings allocable to contributed capital if the business earns more on each dollar invested than the interest cost of borrowing funds.

LEVERAGED BUYOUT (or "LBO") is a transaction by which an outside entity purchases all the shares of a public corporation primarily with borrowed funds. Ultimately the debt incurred to finance the takeover is assumed by the acquired business. If incumbent management has a financial and participatory interest in the outside entity, the transaction may be referred to as a management buyout or MBO.

LEVERAGED RECAPITALIZATION is a transaction by which a corporation substitutes debt for equity in its capital structure. A leveraged recapitalization may involve borrowing of substantial sums and distributing them as an extraordinary dividend to existing shareholders, or by the direct distribution to shareholders of a dividend consisting of debt securities.

LIMITED PARTNER. See: limited partnership and general partner.

LIMITED PARTNERSHIP is a partnership consisting of one or more limited partners (whose liability for partnership debts is limited to the amount originally invested) and one or more general partners (whose liability for partnership debts is unlimited). To create a limited partnership a certificate must be filed with a state official.

LIQUIDATING DIVIDEND is a distribution of assets in the form of a dividend from a corporation that is reducing capital or going out of business. Such a payment may arise, for example, when management decides to sell off certain company assets and distribute the proceeds to the shareholders. Such a distribution may not be from current or retained earnings.

LIQUIDITY refers to the market characteristic of a security or commodity with enough units outstanding and traded to allow large transactions to occur without a substantial variation in price. Most shares traded at the New York Stock Exchange have liquidity. Institutional investors usually prefer liquid investments since their trading activity have less influence on the market price than if they traded in less liquid securities.

LISTED SECURITY is a security that is publicly traded on a securities exchange. For a security to be listed the issuing corporation must meet the requirements established by the exchange and, in most exchanges, sign a listing agreement with the exchange.

LOCKUP is a slang term that refers to a transaction that is designed to defeat one party in a contested takeover. A lockup usually involves the setting aside of securities for purchase by friendly interests in order to defeat or make more difficult the competitive takeover.

MANDATORY REQUIREMENTS are substantive statutory requirements that must be substantially complied with if a de jure corporation is to be formed.

MARGIN is the amount a purchaser of a security must deposit with a broker if the purchaser wishes to borrow from the broker part of the purchase price on the collateral of the shares. If the margin requirement is fifty per cent, for example, a speculator purchasing $10,000 of securities would have to deposit $5,000 in cash and could thereafter borrow the remaining $5,000 from the broker at the market rate of interest for such transactions. A margin transaction increases the leverage of the transaction. See: margin call and margin requirement.

MARGIN ACCOUNT is a brokerage account that permits customers to buy securities on margin.

MARGIN CALL occurs when the market price of securities purchased on margin declines to the point that the investor must increase the amount deposited with the broker to maintain the minimum required margin. The minimum required margin is 125 per cent of the amount of the loan (though some brokerage firms require a higher minimum required margin). For example, if one bought 200 shares of a $100 stock on margin, putting up $10,000 in cash and borrowing the remaining $10,000, a margin call would be made when the stock declined to a value of $12,500, or a price of $62.25 per share. At that point the amount of the loan is $10,000 and a 25 per cent margin ($2,500) must be maintained above that amount.

MARGIN REQUIREMENT is the percentage of the original purchase price that must be deposited with a broker to purchase a security on margin. The margin requirement is set or adjusted by the Federal Reserve Board.

MATURITY DATE is the date on which the principal amount of a note, draft, acceptance, bond, or other debt instrument becomes due and payable.

MERGER is an amalgamation of two corporations pursuant to statutory provision in which one of the corporations survives and the other disappears.

MUTUAL FUND is a publicly held open end investment company that usually invests only in readily marketable securities. See: investment company. An "open end" investment company stands ready at all times to redeem its shares at net asset value. A mutual fund thus provides the advantages of complete liquidity, diversification of investment, and skilled investment advice for the small investor. A mutual fund that sells its shares for a premium over net asset value charges a front end load; a mutual fund that does not charge such a premium is called a no-load fund.

NASDAQ is an acronym for "National Association of Securities Dealers Automated Quotations" and is the principal recording device for transactions on the over-the-counter market.

NEGATIVE CASH FLOW refers to a situation where the cash needs of a business exceed its cash intake. Short periods of negative cash flow create no problem for most businesses; longer periods of negative cash flow may require additional capital investment if the business is to avoid insolvency in the equity sense. See: insolvency.

NET WORTH is the amount by which assets exceed liabilities.

NET YIELD is the rate of return on a security net of out-of-pocket costs associated with its purchase, such as commissions or markups.

NEW ISSUE is a security being offered to the public for the first time. The distribution of new issues is usually subject to SEC rules. New issues may be initial public offerings by previously private companies or additional securities offered by public companies.

NIMBLE DIVIDENDS are dividends paid out of current earnings at a time when there is a deficit in earned surplus (or other financial account from which dividends may be paid). Some state statutes do not permit nimble dividends; these statutes require current earnings to be applied against prior deficits rather than being used to pay a current dividend. The concept of nimble dividends has application only under traditional legal capital statutes.

NO–LOAD FUND is a mutual fund that imposes no sales charges (load) on purchases of its shares. See: mutual fund.

NOMINAL YIELD is the annual income received from a fixed-income security divided by the par or face value of the security. It is stated as a percentage figure and is sometimes called current yield.

NOMINEE registration is a form of securities registration widely used by institutional investors to avoid onerous requirements of establishing the right of registration by a fiduciary.

NONCALLABLE preferred shares or bonds are securities that cannot be redeemed at the option of the issuer.

NONCUMULATIVE VOTING or STRAIGHT VOTING limits a shareholder to voting no more than the number of shares he or she owns for a single candidate. Compare: cumulative voting. In noncumulative voting, a majority shareholder elects the entire board of directors.

NONVOTING COMMON SHARES are shares that expressly have no power to vote. Such shares may be created in most states; nonvoting shares may also be entitled to vote as a class on certain proposed changes adversely affecting that class as such. See: voting groups.

NO PAR SHARES are shares issued under a traditional par value statute that are stated to have no par value. Such shares are issued for the consideration designated by the board of directors; such consideration is allocated to stated capital unless the directors or shareholders determine to allocate a portion to capital surplus. As a result, in many respects no par shares do not differ significantly from par value shares. In states that have abolished par value, the concept of no par shares is obsolete.

NOVATION is a contract principle by which a third person takes over the rights and duties of a party to a contract, such party thereby being released from obligations under the contract. In the law of corporations, the concept may be applied to the release of a promoter who is personally liable on a preincorporation contract when the corporation is formed and adopts the contract. A novation requires the consent of the other party to the contract, but that consent may be implied from the circumstances.

ODD LOTS are units of securities less than the standard trading unit or round lot. In market trading, a purchase or sale of less than 100 shares is considered an odd lot transaction, although inactive shares often are traded in round lots of 10 shares. See also: round lot.

OPPRESSION in a close corporation involves conduct by the controlling shareholder that deprives a minority shareholder of his or her legitimate expectations concerning roles in the corporation, including management and earnings.

ORGANIZATIONAL EXPENSES are the costs of organizing a corporation, including filing fees, attorneys' fees, and related expenses. Organizational expenses may also include the cost of raising the initial capital through the distribution of securities. Under the Internal Revenue Code of 1954, organizational expenses may be capitalized and written off against income over a five-year period.

OUTSIDE DIRECTORS are directors of publicly held corporations who do not hold executive positions with management. Outside directors, however, may include investment bankers, attorneys, or others who provide advice or services to incumbent management and thus have financial ties with management.

OVER–THE–COUNTER refers to the securities market consisting of brokers who purchase or sell securities by computer hook-up or telephone rather than through the facilities of a securities exchange. At one time completely unorganized, the over-the-counter market is now relatively organized with computerized quotation and transaction reporting services.

PAR VALUE or STATED VALUE of shares is an arbitrary or nominal value assigned to each such share. At one time par value represented the selling or issuance price of shares, but in modern corporate practice, par value has little significance and serves only a limited role. Shares issued for less than par value are usually referred to as watered shares. The Revised Model Business Corporation Act and the statutes of about 15 states have eliminated the concept of par value.

PARTICIPATING BONDS. See: bonds.

PARTICIPATING PREFERRED SHARES are preferred shares that, in addition to paying a stipulated dividend, give the holder the right to participate with the common shareholder in additional distributions of earnings, if declared, under specified conditions. Participatory preferred shares may be called class A common or given a similar designation to reflect their open-ended rights.

PAYABLE DATE is the date on which a dividend or distribution is actually paid to a shareholder.

PENDENT JURISDICTION is a principle applied in federal courts that allows state-created causes of action arising out of the same transaction to be joined with a federal cause of action even if diversity of citizenship is not present.

PHANTOM STOCK PLAN is an employee benefit plan in which benefits are determined by reference to the performance of the corporation's common shares. For example, a person receiving benefits based on 1,000 "phantom shares" will have credited to his account each year an amount equal to the dividends declared on 1,000 shares; the number of "phantom shares" will be increased by share dividends or splits actually declared on real shares; on his or her death or retirement the person will receive a credit equal to the difference between the market price of the "phantom shares" on the date of death or retirement (or a related date) and the market price of the "phantom shares" on the date he or she was awarded the rights.

PLOW BACK is the reinvestment of a company's earnings in the business rather than paying those profits to shareholders as dividends.

POISON PILL is an issue of shares by a corporation as a protection against an unwanted takeover. A poison pill creates rights in existing shareholders to acquire debt or stock of the target (or of the aggressor upon a subsequent merger) upon the occurrence of specified events, such as the announcement of a cash tender offer or the acquisition by an outsider of a specified percentage of the shares of the target. A poison pill raises the potential cost of an acquisition, and either deters a takeover bid or compels the aggressor to negotiate with the target in order to persuade it to withdraw the pill.

POOLING AGREEMENT is a contractual arrangement among shareholders relating to the voting of their shares. So long as such agreement is limited to voting as shareholders, it is enforceable.

PORCUPINE PROVISIONS are defensive provisions in articles of incorporation or bylaws designed to make unwanted takeover attempts impossible or impractical without the consent of the target's management.

PREEMPTIVE RIGHTS give an existing shareholder the opportunity to purchase or subscribe for a proportionate part of a new issue of shares before it is offered to other persons. Its purpose is to protect shareholders from dilution of value and control when new shares are issued. In modern statutes, preemptive rights may be limited or denied.

PREFERRED SHARES are shares that have preferential rights to dividends or to amounts distributable on liquidation, or to both, ahead of common shareholders. Preferred shares are usually entitled only to receive specified limited amounts as dividends or on liquidation. If preferred shares are entitled to share in excess distributions with common shareholders on some defined basis, they are participating preferred shares.

PREFERRED SHAREHOLDERS' CONTRACT refers to the provisions of the articles of incorporation, the bylaws, or the resolution of the board of directors, creating and defining the rights of holders of the preferred shares in question. Preferred shareholders have only very limited statutory or common law rights outside of the preferred shareholders' contract. However, even provisions creating and defining the rights of holders of preferred shares may usually be amended without the consent of each individual holder of preferred shares. The major protection provided by statute against onerous amendments is the right of preferred shareholders to vote as a separate voting group on such changes.

PREINCORPORATION SUBSCRIPTION. See: subscription.

PRICE–EARNINGS RATIO is the ratio of earnings per share to current stock price.

PRIVATE PLACEMENT of securities is the sale of securities to sophisticated investors without registration under federal or state securities acts under the private offering exemption or under Regulation D.

PROMOTERS are persons who develop or take the initiative in founding or organizing a business venture. Where more than one promoter is involved in a venture, they are usually described as co-promoters.

PROSPECTUS is a document furnished to a prospective purchaser of a security that describes the security being purchased, the issuer, and the investment or risk characteristics of the security. SEC regulations require a prospectus meeting specified requirements to be provided to each prospective purchaser of registered public offerings of securities.

PROXY is a person authorized to vote someone else's shares. Depending on the context, proxy may also refer to the grant of authority itself [the appointment], or the document granting the authority [the appointment form].

PROXY SOLICITATION MACHINERY is a phrase commonly used to describe the phenomenon that incumbent management of a publicly held corporation may usually produce large majorities of shareholder votes on any issue it desires. This power is based in part on the ability of incumbent management to use corporate funds to communicate at will with the shareholders and partially on the ability to represent their views as the views of "management."

PROXY STATEMENT is the document that must accompany a solicitation of proxy appointment under SEC regulations. The purpose of the proxy statement is to provide shareholders with the appropriate information to permit an intelligent decision.

PUBLIC OFFERING involves the sale of securities by an issuer or a person controlling the issuer to members of the public. Generally, any offering that is not exempt under Regulation D or the private offering exemption of the Securities Act of 1933 and/or similar exemptions under state blue sky laws is considered a public offering. Normally registration of a public offering under those statutes is required though in some instances other exemptions from registration may be available.

PUBLICLY HELD CORPORATION is a corporation with shares held by numerous persons. Typically, a publicly held corporation has shares registered under section 12 of the Securities Exchange Act of 1934, though such registration is not an essential attribute of being publicly held. Shares of publicly held corporations are usually traded either on a securities exchange or over-the-counter.

PUTS are options to sell securities at a stated price for a stated period. If the price declines, a holder of a put may purchase the shares at the lower market price and "put" the shares to the put writer at the contract price. Puts on some New York Stock Exchange securities are publicly traded. See: calls.

QUALIFIED STOCK OPTION is an option to purchase shares awarded to an employee of the corporation under terms that qualify the option for special tax treatment under the Internal Revenue Code.

QUALIFYING SHARE is a share of common stock owned by a person in order to qualify as a director of the issuing corporation in a corporation that requires directors to be shareholders.

QUO WARRANTO is a common law writ designed to test whether a person exercising power is legally entitled to do so. In the law of corporations, quo warranto may be used to test whether a corporation was validly organized or whether it has power to engage in the business in which it is involved.

RAIDER is a slang term for an aggressor, an individual or corporation who attempts to take control of a target corporation by buying a controlling interest in its stock.

RECAPITALIZATION is a restructuring of the capital of the corporation through amendment of the articles of incorporation or a merger with a subsidiary or parent corporation. Recapitalizations may involve the elimination of unpaid cumulated preferred dividends, the reduction or elimination of par value, the creation of new classes of senior securities, or similar transactions. A leveraged recapitalization involves the substitution of debt for equity in the capital structure.

RECORD DATE is the date on which the identity of shareholders entitled to vote, to receive dividends, or to receive notice is ascertained.

RECORD OWNER of shares is the person in whose name shares are registered on the records of the corporation. A record owner is treated as the owner of the shares by the corporation whether or not the beneficial owner of the shares.

REDEMPTION means the reacquisition of a security by the issuer pursuant to a provision in the security that specifies the terms on which the reacquisition may take place. A security is called for redemption when the issuer notifies the holder that the redemption privilege has been exercised. Typically, a holder of a security that has been called for redemption will have a limited period thereafter to decide whether or not to exercise a conversion right, if one exists.

REDUCTION SURPLUS is a term used in a few states with par value statutes to refer to the surplus created by a reduction of stated capital. In many states, such surplus is treated simply as capital surplus.

REGISTERED CORPORATION is a publicly held corporation which has registered a publicly held class of securities under section 12 of the Securities Exchange Act of 1934. Section 12 may apply to issuers other than corporations. The registration of an outstanding issue under this section of the 1934 Act should be contrasted with the registration of a public distribution under the Securities Act of 1933.

REGISTRATION of an issue of securities under the Securities Act of 1933 permits the public sale of those securities in interstate commerce or with the use of the mails. That registration should be distinguished from the registration of already publicly held classes of securities under the Securities Exchange Act of 1934.

REGISTRATION STATEMENT is the document that must be filed to permit registration of an issue of securities under the Securities Act of 1933. A major component of the registration statement is the prospectus that is to be supplied prospective purchasers of the securities.

REORGANIZATION is a general term describing corporate amalgamations or readjustments. The classification of the Internal Revenue Code is widely used in general corporate literature. A Class A reorganization is a statutory merger or consolidation (i.e., pursuant to the business corporation act of a specific state). A Class B reorganization is a transaction by which one corporation exchanges its voting shares for the voting shares of another corporation. A Class C reorganization is a transaction in which one corporation exchanges its voting shares for the property and assets of another corporation. A Class D reorganization is a "spin off" of assets by one corporation to a new corporation. A Class E reorganization is a recapitalization. A Class F reorganization is a "mere change of identity, form, or place of organization, however effected." A Class G reorganization is a "transfer by a corporation of all or part of its assets to another corporation in a title 11 or similar case."

RETAINED EARNINGS are net profits accumulated by a corporation after payment of dividends. Retained earnings are also called "undistributed profits" or "earned surplus."

RETURN ON EQUITY is calculated by dividing common stock equity (net worth as shown on the books of the corporation) at the beginning of an accounting period into net income for the period after payment of preferred stock dividends but before payment of common stock dividends. Return on equity indicates the amount earned on each dollar of invested capital: it is expressed as a percentage and is a guide to common shareholders as to how effectively their money is being employed.

REVERSE STOCK SPLIT is an amendment to the articles of incorporation that reduce the number of shares outstanding. The amendment must specify the basis on which existing shareholdings will be adjusted to reflect the smaller number of shares outstanding. Reverse stock splits may create fractional shares and may be used as a device to go private by reducing the number of shares to the point that no public shareholder owns a full share of stock, and then providing that all fractional shares are to be redeemed for cash.

REVERSE TRIANGULAR MERGER. See triangular merger.

RIGHTS are short term options to purchase shares from an issuer at a fixed price. Rights may be issued as a substitute for a dividend or as a "sweetener" in connection with the issuance of senior or debt securities. Rights are often publicly traded.

ROUND LOT is the standard trading unit of securities. On most securities exchanges a round lot is 100 shares.

S CORPORATION is a corporation that has elected to be taxed under Subchapter S. The taxable income of an S corporation is not subject to tax at the corporate level, but is allocated to the shareholders to be taxed at that level. S corporation taxation is similar but not identical to partnership taxation.

SCRIP is issued in lieu of fractional shares in connection with a stock dividend. Scrip merely represents the right to receive a portion of a share; scrip is readily transferable so that it is possible to acquire scrip from several sources and assemble the right to obtain the issuance of a full additional share.

SATURDAY NIGHT SPECIAL is a surprise tender offer which expires in one week. Designed to capitalize on panic and haste, such an offer may be made Friday afternoon to take advantage of the fact that markets and most offices are closed on Saturday and Sunday. Saturday night specials have been effectively prohibited by the Williams Act.

SECONDARY MARKET consists of the securities exchanges and over-the-counter markets where securities are bought and sold after their original issue (which took place in the primary market). Proceeds of secondary market sales accrue to selling investors, not to the company that originally issued the securities.

SECURITIES is a general term that covers not only traditional securities such as shares of stock, bonds, and debentures, but also a variety of interests that have the characteristics of securities, i.e., that involve an investment with the return primarily or exclusively dependent on the efforts of a person other than the investor.

SECURITIES EXCHANGES are markets for the purchase and sale of traditional securities at which brokers for purchasers and sellers may effect transactions. The best known and largest securities exchange is the New York Stock Exchange.

SECURITY–FOR–EXPENSES statutes require certain plaintiffs in a derivative suit to post a bond with sureties from which the corporation and the other defendants may be reimbursed for their expenses if they prevail. Designed as a protection against strike suits, security-for-expenses statutes have been criticized as being illogical and unnecessary. The Revised Model Business Corporation Act does not impose a security-for-expenses requirement.

SENIOR SECURITY is a debt security or preferred share that has a claim prior to that of junior obligations or common shares on a corporation's assets and earnings. See: junior security.

SERIES OF PREFERRED SHARES are subclasses of preferred shares with differing dividend rates, redemption prices, rights on dissolution, conversion rights, and the like. The term of a series of preferred shares may be established by the directors so that a corporation periodically engaged in preferred shares financing may readily shape its preferred shares offering to market conditions through the use of series of preferred shares. Under the Revised Model Business Corporation Act, the board of directors may establish the terms of either a "class" or a "series."

SHARE REPURCHASE PLAN is a program by which a corporation buys back its own shares in the open market. It is usually done when the corporation believes its shares are undervalued by the market.

SHAREHOLDERS or **STOCKHOLDERS** are the persons who own shares of stock of the corporation. Such shares may be either common shares or preferred shares. The Revised Model Business Corporation Act and modern usage generally tends to prefer "shareholder" to "stockholder" but the latter word is deeply ingrained in common usage.

SHORT FORM MERGER is a merger of a largely or wholly owned subsidiary into a parent through a streamlined procedure permitted under the Revised Model Business Corporation Act and statutes of many states.

SHORT SALE is a sale of a security or commodity futures contract not owned by the seller. The security to be sold is borrowed from a broker and the short seller anticipates replacing the borrowed security at a lower price at a later time. A short sale permits an investor: (1) to take advantage of an anticipated decline in the price, or (2) to protect a profit in a long position against an anticipated price decline.

SHORT SALE AGAINST THE BOX is a short sale where the speculator owns enough shares of the security involved to cover the borrowed securities, if necessary. The "box" referred to is the hypothetical safe deposit box in which the certificates are kept. A short sale against the box is not as risky as a short sale.

SINKING FUND refers to an obligation sometimes imposed pursuant to the issuance of debt securities or preferred shares by which the issuer is required each year to devote a certain amount to the retirement of the securities when they mature. A sinking fund may be used each year either to redeem a portion of the outstanding securities or to purchase the securities on the open market and retire them.

SPIN–OFF is a form of corporate divestiture that results in a subsidiary or division of a corporation becoming an independent company.

SPREAD. See: bid and asked.

SQUEEZE–OUTS are techniques by which a minority interest in a corporation is eliminated or reduced. Squeeze-outs may occur in a variety of contexts, e.g., in a "going private" transaction in which minority shareholders are compelled to accept cash for their shares, or the issuance of new shares to existing shareholders in which minority shareholders are given the unpleasant choice of having their proportionate interest in the corporation reduced significantly or of investing a large amount of additional or new capital over which they have no control and for which they receive little or no return. Many squeeze-outs involve the use of cash mergers. Squeeze-out is often used synonymously with freeze-out.

STAGGERED BOARD is a classified board of directors in which a fraction of the board is elected each year. In staggered boards, members serve two or three years, depending on whether the board is classified into two or three groups.

STATED CAPITAL in the old Model Business Corporation Act nomenclature represented the basic capital of the corporation. Technically, it consisted of the sum of the par values of all issued shares plus the consideration for no par shares to the extent not transferred to capital surplus plus other amounts that may be transferred from other accounts. Distributions generally may not be made from stated capital.

STATED VALUE. See: par value.

STOCK DIVIDEND is a proportional distribution of shares without payment of consideration to existing shareholders. A stock dividend is often viewed as a substitute for a cash dividend, and shareholders may sell a stock dividend without realizing that they are diluting their ownership interest in the corporation.

STOCK SPLIT is a proportional change in the number of shares owned by every shareholder. It differs from a stock dividend in degree; however, typically in a stock dividend no adjustment is made in the dividend rate per share while such an adjustment is usually made in a stock split. There are other technical differences in the handling of stock splits and stock dividends under the statutes of most states. Stock splits usually result in an increase in the number of outstanding shares.

STOCKHOLDERS. See: shareholders.

STRAIGHT VOTING. See: noncumulative voting.

STREET NAME refers to the practice of registering publicly traded securities in the name of one or more brokerage firms with offices on Wall Street. Such certificates are endorsed in blank and are essentially bearer certificates transferred between brokerage firms. The use of street name shares has declined with the creation of a central clearing corporation and book entry registration of ownership.

STRIKE SUITS is a slang term for derivative litigation instituted for its nuisance value or to obtain a favorable settlement.

SUBCHAPTER S refers to the subchapter of the Internal Revenue Code of 1954 that regulates the S corporation. See S Corporation.

SUBORDINATED. See: junior security.

SUBSCRIBERS are persons who agree to invest in the corporation by purchasing shares of stock. Subscribers usually commit themselves to invest by entering into contracts defining the extent and terms of their commitment; at common law subscribers usually executed "subscriptions" or "subscription agreements." Modern contracts for the purchase of corporate shares from the issuer usually use the phrase "agree to purchase and subscribe for * * * ."

SUBSCRIPTION is an offer to buy a specified number of theretofore unissued shares of a corporation. If the corporation is not yet in existence, a subscription is known as a preincorporation subscription, which is enforceable by the corporation after it has been formed and is irrevocable despite the absence of consideration or the usual elements of a contract.

SUBSIDIARY is a corporation that is at least majority owned, and may be wholly owned, by another corporation.

SURPLUS is a general term in corporate accounting that usually refers to either the excess of assets over liabilities or that amount further reduced by the stated capital represented by issued shares. Surplus has a more definite meaning when combined with a descriptive adjective from par value statutes, e.g., earned surplus, capital surplus, or reduction surplus.

TAINTED SHARES are shares owned by a person who is disqualified for some reason from serving as a plaintiff in a derivative action. The shares are "tainted" since for policy reasons a good faith transferee of such shares will also be disqualified from serving as a plaintiff.

TAKEOVER ATTEMPT or **TAKEOVER BID** are generic terms to describe an attempt by an outside corporation or group, usually called the aggressor or "insurgent," to wrest control away from incumbent management. A takeover attempt may involve purchase of shares, a tender offer, a sale of assets, or a proposal that the target merge voluntarily into the aggressor.

TARGET CORPORATION is a corporation the control of which is sought by an aggressor corporation.

TENDER OFFER is a public invitation by an aggressor to shareholders of a target corporation to tender their shares for purchase by the aggressor at a stated price. Tender offers are regulated by the Williams Act. A creeping tender offer is a series of private acquisitions in the market place and may or may not be classed as a tender offer for regulatory purposes.

THIN CORPORATION is a corporation with an excessive amount of debt in its capitalization. A thin corporation is primarily a tax concept.

THIN MARKET is a market in which there are relatively few and infrequent transactions.

TIP is information passed by one person (a "tipper") to another (a "tippee") as a basis for a decision to buy or sell a security. Such information is presumed to be of material value and not available to the general public. Trading by tippees in some circumstances may violate federal law.

TRANSFER AGENT is an organization, usually a bank, that handles transfers of shares for a publicly held corporation. Generally, a transfer agent assures that certificates submitted for transfer are properly endorsed and that there is appropriate documentation of the right to transfer. The transfer agent issues new certificates and oversees the cancellation of the old ones. Transfer agents also usually maintain the record of shareholders for the corporation and arrange for the distribution of dividends.

TREASURY SHARES are shares that were once issued and outstanding but which have been reacquired by the corporation and "held in its treasury." Treasury shares are economically indistinguishable from authorized but unissued shares but historically have been treated as having an intermediate status. Many of the complexities created by treasury shares revolve around accounting concepts. The Revised Model Business Corporation Act and the statutes of several states have eliminated the concept of treasury shares, reacquired shares automatically having the status of authorized but unissued shares.

TRIANGULAR MERGER is a method of amalgamation of two corporations by which the disappearing corporation is merged into a subsidiary of the surviving corporation and the shareholders of the disappearing corporation receive shares of the surviving corporation. In a reverse triangular merger the subsidiary is merged into the disappearing corporation so that the corporation being acquired becomes a wholly owned subsidiary of the surviving corporation.

ULTRA VIRES is the common law doctrine relating to the effect of corporate acts that exceed the powers or the stated purposes of a corporation. The modern view generally validates all corporate acts even though they may be ultra vires.

UNDERWRITERS are persons who buy shares with a view toward their further distribution. Used almost exclusively in connection with the public distribution of securities, an underwriter may be either a commercial enterprise engaged in the distribution of securities (an investment banker), or a person who simply buys securities without an investment intent and with a "view" toward further distribution.

UP STREAM MERGER is a merger of a subsidiary corporation into its parent.

VOTING GROUP is a term defined in the Revised Model Business Corporation Act to describe the right of shares of different classes or series to vote separately on fundamental corporate changes that adversely affect the rights or privileges of that class or series. The scope of the right to vote by voting groups is defined by statute. The right is of particular value to classes or series of shares with limited or no voting rights under the articles of incorporation. Most older state statutes use the terms "class voting" or "voting by class" to refer to essentially the same concept.

VOTING TRUST is a formal arrangement by which record title to shares is transferred to trustees who are entitled to exercise the power to vote the shares. Usually, all other incidents of ownership, such as the right to receive dividends, are retained by the beneficial owners of the shares.

VOTING TRUST CERTIFICATES are certificates issued by voting trustees to the beneficial holders of shares held by the voting trust. Such certificates may be as readily transferable as the underlying shares, carrying with them all the incidents of ownership of the underlying shares except the power to vote.

WARRANTS are a type of option to purchase shares issued by a corporation. Warrants are typically long period options, are freely transferable, and if the underlying shares are listed on a securities exchange, are also publicly traded. The price of warrants of publicly held corporations will obviously be a function of the market price of the shares and the option price specified in the warrants.

WATERED SHARES are par value shares issued for property which has been overvalued and is not worth the aggregate par value of the issued shares. Watered shares is often used as a generic term to describe all shares issued for less than par value—including discount and bonus shares. The issuance of watered shares may impose a liability on the recipient equal to the amount of the shortfall from par value.

WHITE KNIGHT is a friendly suitor: a potential acquirer usually sought out by the target of an unfriendly takeover to rescue it from the unwanted bidder's takeover.

WORKING CAPITAL is a measure of a corporation's liquidity and ability to discharge its liabilities as they arise. Working capital is the difference between current assets and current liabilities as shown on the corporation's balance sheet.

INDEX

References are to Pages

FACE VALUE
Defined in Glossary

FEDERAL CORPORATION LAW
Discussed, 11, 305

FEDERAL INCOME TAXATION
Discussed, 17–18, 21–24

FEDERAL INCORPORATION
Discussed, 11

FICTITIOUS ENTITY
Corporation as, 1–3

FIDUCIARY DUTIES
Generally, 303–305
Care, 306–321
Close Corporations, 256–257
Common directors, 327–328
Compensation, 328–332
Competition with corporation, 335
Corporate opportunities, 332–335
Defenses,
    Business judgment rule, 310–321, 338–340
    Exoneratory provisions, 341
    Indemnification, 367–371
    Insurance, 371–373
    Ratification, 340
Insider trading, 347–362
Issuance of shares, 152–154
Minority interests, 336–340
Promoters, 71–73
Purchase of shares or claims, 344–362
Rule 10b–5, pp. 347–358
Section 16(b), pp. 358–362
Self dealing, 321–327
Shareholders, 256–257
Statutory duties, 341–344
Transfers of control, 362–367

FINANCIAL REPORTS
To shareholders, 383

FLOAT
Defined in Glossary

FORCED CONVERSION
Defined in Glossary
Described, 130

†